Praise for *Tell Them I Didn't Cry*

"Spinner's fresh eyes, unlike those of more war-weathered correspondents, provide an honest look at what it means to cover a country that often appears to be coming apart at the seams. It is a tale she weaves well, bolstered by the moral, spiritual, and literary support she gets from her twin sister. Spinner's willingness to lay bare her posting's side effects, from the droll to the devastating, sets her book apart."

—*The Washington Post*

"Jackie Spinner's book is not only a war memoir full of precisely detailed encounters with fear and death, it is also an odyssey of closely observed and beautifully sequenced stages of an emotional and professional life as reporter for *The Washington Post* in Iraq. She pulls no punches; truth prevails over cant, over precooked templates of patriotism and its opposite, irony and sarcasm."

—Ellen Mickiewicz, director,
DeWitt Wallace Center for Media
and Democracy, Duke University

"[Spinner's] harrowing but funny new memoir [is] the most honest war story you'll ever read. This woman is bravery personified."

—*Glamour*

"*Washington Post* reporter Jackie Spinner is the very picture of a journalist: curious, dedicated, and methodically objective. *Tell Them I Didn't Cry*, her poignant memoir of nine months as a foreign correspondent for the *Post*'s Baghdad bureau in 2004 and 2005, gives a vivid picture of the sacrifices journalists make in war zones."

—*Chicago Tribune*

"Not just a reporter's dispatch on the Iraq war, Jackie Spinner's book is a journalistic original and a rare insight into both a reporter's mind and the heart of a people at war. Unlike any other chronicle of the war, this book draws the reader into the lives of the subjects of journalism, the real people of a country in chaos, and makes us care about them. As a journalist, I saw a side of the story I had not yet seen. As a Marine who has spent time in Iraq, I came away from this book caring more about the outcome of our nation's effort."

—Andrew B. Davis,
president and executive director,
American Press Institute

"The Iraq story has long needed a woman's touch, and Jackie Spinner tells this war tale better than any account I've seen: how and why American journalists risk everything to report the most dangerous story on earth. She takes a welcome departure from our male-slanted view of Iraq, putting a human face on the soldiers, truck drivers, translators, American and Iraqi families, and, yes, journalists as they cope with the overwhelming anxieties of life in the crosshairs."

—Tod Robberson, correspondent,
The Dallas Morning News

"This is a moving, personal account of a young woman's head-first immersion into a war where she finds unexpected beauty and love, and unimagined horrors and loss. In Iraq, Jackie Spinner loses a friend and some of her own innocence. But she also gains—and now offers readers of her fine, tender book—important insight into a country that will for generations be intricately tied to the lives of all Americans."

—Matthew McAllester, *Newsday* correspondent
and author of *Blinded by the Sunlight:*
Surviving Abu Ghraib and Saddam's Iraq
and *Beyond the Mountains of the Damned:*
The War Inside Kosovo

"[Spinner] writes in simple yet descriptive language about the daily challenges and rewards of life in a war zone. She objectively reports on the struggles and aspirations of everyday Iraqis, the triumphs and failures of the military, and the violence that traps her indoors most of the time—but the heart of this book is in her personal involvement in the bureau's Iraqi staff. Affable and earnest, Spinner made herself at home in war . . . and hers is a unique perspective on living and reporting in Iraq."

—*Publishers Weekly*

"In this intensely personal account, Spinner recalls how being a woman simultaneously freed and constrained her efforts—giving her closer access to Iraqi families but keeping her at a distance from Iraqi men and U.S. soldiers. The stark contrast between Jackie's recollections and [twin sister] Jenny's horrified perspective from home adds to the intensity of this very human look at war in a nation that Jackie Spinner openly declares she loves and admires."

—*Booklist*

TELL THEM I DIDN'T CRY

◆ ◆ ◆

A Young Journalist's Story of Joy, Loss,
and Survival in Iraq

JACKIE SPINNER

With Jenny Spinner

SCRIBNER
New York   London   Toronto   Sydney

SCRIBNER
A Division of Simon & Schuster, Inc.
1230 Avenue of the Americas
New York, NY 10020

First Scribner trade paperback edition August 2007

SCRIBNER and design are trademarks of Macmillan Library Reference USA, Inc.,
used under license by Simon & Schuster, the publisher of this work.

For information about special discounts for bulk purchases,
please contact Simon & Schuster Special Sales:
1-800-456-6798 or business@simonandschuster.com

DESIGNED BY ERICH HOBBING

Text set in Janson

Manufactured in the United States of America

1   3   5   7   9   10   8   6   4   2

Library of Congress Control Number: 2005057530

ISBN-13: 978-0-7432-8853-8

ISBN-13: 978-0-7432-8855-2 (pbk)

In my head, I swim, slow laps in the chilly waters of a long rec-tangular pool that exists only in my imagination. My arms, pale and thin, dip in and out of the water in methodical strokes. I am alone, and the sun is shining. It seems the sun is always shining in Baghdad. I swim whenever I start to panic: when my breath comes in short gasps and I feel like I will float away, a drifting, tattered kite that disappears into the endless red glow of a desert sunset. If I don't keep moving, I won't survive.

FOREWORD

by David Ignatius

I first met Jackie Spinner in 1994 while I was on a recruiting trip interviewing potential summer interns for *The Washington Post*. I had stopped at Berkeley and was talking to several dozen eager, talented candidates. One of them was fifteen minutes late for the interview. She said she was sorry but she had been doing something more important—working on a story. That was Jackie.

Sometimes you get a feeling about someone—the spark of talent and desire is so powerful that you just have to throw out the normal rulebook. Reading Jackie's clips and listening to her talk about journalism, I had the feeling she might be one of those people. It was obvious, even from her student writing, that she connected with stories at a visceral level. She described to me a series of articles she had done the previous summer about youth gangs in San Diego, and she explained that she had lived in the streets for several weeks to get the facts right. That sounded like someone we wanted at the *Post*. When I got back to Washington, I urged my colleagues to give her one of our coveted internships; when the initial decision was no, I wheedled and whined until they said yes and gave Jackie a slot.

Jackie's early years at the *Post* weren't always happy. It's an unfortunate fact that *The Washington Post*, like many great newspapers, can be an overwhelming place for a young reporter. There are so many tickets to punch and editors to please that it's easy to lose the fire that made you want to be a journalist in the first place. Jackie held on to the raw hunger for a story that had been so obvious that day at Berkeley. Maybe she was waiting for a story that was as passionate as her talent.

Jackie found that story in Iraq. She initially went to Iraq almost by accident, but she distinguished herself with her courage, her hustle, and the sense of humanity and decency that drove her coverage. She stayed and stayed in Iraq. On the day she was almost kidnapped outside Abu Ghraib prison, she pleaded with her editors not to force her to come home. The war and its intense emotions had gotten into her bloodstream. I know that feeling because the war got under my skin, too, and I kept going back again and again to write columns about it. Iraq is an inspiring, heartbreaking story. I don't know anyone who has felt it more deeply than Jackie, or expressed the hope and anguish better than she has here.

As readers of this book will see, Jackie has written a love story. It records her passionate commitment to the people caught up in this war—Iraqi civilians and American soldiers, alike. It expresses her love for her colleagues—especially the courageous Iraqis who work in *The Washington Post* bureau in Baghdad and have kept us alive and functioning. Jackie baked them cookies, read them poetry, suffered and rejoiced with them. When she became bureau chief, her first order was that everyone take a ride on the backyard swing to relax. In these pages, you'll come to know our cooks, bodyguards, drivers, and translators—and understand why, for those of us who have spent time in Baghdad, they feel like part of our family. I hope that Omar, Abu Saif, Falah, Little Naseer, and the rest of our wonderful Baghdad bureau will come to feel like part of your family, too.

Above all, this is a love story about journalism. Anyone who feels cynical about the state of the American press or the commitment of its journalists to their mission should read Jackie's tale. This is the work she was put on earth to do. She is a blue-collar girl from the Midwest who writes from the heart. Whatever you think you know about Iraq, I suspect it will be changed once you have seen that tormented country through Jackie Spinner's eyes.

A NOTE FROM THE AUTHOR

This book is a personal account of the more than nine months I spent in Iraq as a reporter for *The Washington Post*. After a brief visit to Iraq in January 2004, while embedded with the U.S. Army Corps of Engineers, I returned in May—arriving eight days after U.S. soldiers on a routine patrol found the decapitated body of American businessman Nick Berg on a highway overpass west of the Iraqi capital. His gruesome video-taped execution at the hands of insurgents—coupled with the deaths of four U.S. contractors whose mutilated bodies were strung from a bridge in the city of Fallujah the month before—marked what we only now realize was a free fall into a dark cavern of blood and violence. It will be a difficult climb out.

During the time I was in Iraq, the deteriorating security situation changed the way we covered the news, challenging every convention for how to report on and in a conflict in which we, the press, had no immunity, no white flag to save us from the car bombs, the mortars, the gunfire, and the kidnappers. The bad guys were aiming for us, too. By the fall of 2004, stuck in our fortified bunkers in Baghdad, we were largely cut off from the rest of the country, unable to travel to many parts of Iraq without the U.S. military because of the threat of attacks on foreign reporters. And yet our mandate never changed: Iraq was a story that had to be told.

I reported on car bombs and power plant reconstruction, wrote stories about soldiers in battle, soldiers waiting for battle, soldiers dying in battle. I interviewed hundreds of Iraqis, sometimes without ever leaving my hotel. I met them instead through the scribbled notes of our Iraqi translators. When they came back from an assignment too dangerous for me as a Westerner to cover, we sat together in front of my computer while I grilled them about what they saw. *What color were his eyes? Did he really say that? How did he say that? What do you mean he looked anxious? Tell me how he looked. Was he sweating? What were his hands doing while he talked?*

I asked each member of our Iraqi staff individually how they wanted to be identified in this book because they remain at risk as long as they work for an American company. Although the full names of our translators are published in *The Washington Post* in story credits and bylines, connecting their names to additional information about their families might put them at greater risk. For the book, most asked to be referred to by their first names only or by a common Arabic title for mothers and fathers: if a son is Ali, his father is Abu Ali, his mother Um Ali. Our conversations, as detailed in the book, are precisely as I remember them. All of the people are real, not characters. They exist in flesh and blood and blood and flesh, the living story of Iraq. To them, I owe everything.

I never really swam in Baghdad, although the pool at the Ishtar Sheraton Hotel taunted me on impossibly hot days when it seemed Mother Nature had turned a hundred hair dryers on an already brittle split-end. I went to the Sheraton pool once, long after dark. My *Post* colleague, Robin Shulman, and I had just sat down at the edge of the pool when six or seven members of the hotel staff, wearing sweat-stained white shirts and dark trousers, came out to watch us from the shadows of the pool deck. They dragged on cigarettes, the fiery glow lighting up the night like fireflies suspended in flight. Robin and I tried to ignore them, but eventually, we got up and left, unwilling to give them the satisfaction of a cheap peep show of our bony knees and bare shoulders. We walked by their disappointed faces and disappeared back into the grungy hotel, back into our uniform of long sleeves and long skirts.

From then on, the only swimming I ever did was in my imaginary pool. I called up the image to keep from under the pressure and fright of being in a war zone. A journalist who claims that being in Iraq is not scary is probably lying. I went to my pool during mortar attacks, as I hovered in a stairwell while

the hotel shook from repeated blasts. I went during a gun battle in Fallujah. I went whenever I got into a car and pushed out
into traffic, weaving between potential car bombers, outrunning
the insurgents who chased down foreigners to kidnap for ransom, or worse. I went every time the lights went out, when my
military convoy stopped suddenly in the middle of the night,
when the rocket landed inside the Internet café at the Marine
camp minutes after I walked out. I went when I saw soldiers
wounded or dead, when I saw Iraqi people wounded or dead,
when I wore their blood home on my shoes.

Iraq is not frightening all of the time. I did not feel in imminent danger every minute of the day or even every day. It felt
like a manageable risk. I told myself when that changed I would
go home, fully aware that the longer I stayed, the more Iraq felt
like my home, the more difficult that would be. I fell in love with
Iraq, this horrible, awful, violent, beautiful, hopeful place,
where many Iraqis, in spite of the horrors of the insurgency, felt
better off without Saddam in power, felt better off with American troops on their soil. I fell in love with the story of Iraq and
with the purpose I felt delivering it. I found meaning in the people I met, whose lives unfolded at my fingertips. My life didn't
feel on hold when I was in Iraq. It was my life.

I made cookies in the hotel late at night to stay awake while
waiting for foreign contractors to be beheaded: literally killing
time waiting for someone else to die. I was convinced that if I
sent the fledgling Iraqi police guarding the hotel baked goods
on a regular basis, then when the insurgents came, they'd line
us up and I'd hear them say, "Let the little one go. She made us
cookies."

Between stories, I played soccer barefoot on the filthy, musty
carpeted hallways of the Sheraton. I cooked dinner on Friday
nights and invited Western and Iraqi journalists to eat whatever
themed concoction I could deliver with the limited ingredients
available in Iraqi supermarkets. We dined on Italian, Cuban,
Mexican, and even Thai. After dinner, I washed the dishes in a
bathroom sink. I chased these moments, my oasis of joy, string-
ing together a life among the long hours of reporting and

writing, day after day, week after week, month after month. In some ways, I never felt more alive than while simultaneously trying to defeat death and find the truth.

That is the dichotomy of daily life in Baghdad, where survival is about staying sane and staying normal just as much as it is about staying alive. We ordered pizza from the rip-off "Pizza Hot"—always carry-out because it was too dangerous by late summer of 2004 for foreign reporters to venture out to restaurants, too dangerous for our Iraqi staff to be seen with us. I spent countless hours in the markets searching for the perfect substitute for ricotta cheese to perfect my lasagna recipe. I memorized the inside of my favorite grocery shops so when it became too risky to go myself, I could map out the store to show our driver exactly where he'd find the vegetarian refried beans. (Just before Aisle No. 2, the display on the right with the dusty cans. Evidently, vegetarian refried beans aren't a big seller in Baghdad.)

Meanwhile, back home in Washington, my twin sister, Jenny, was settling into a new job and a new house fifteen minutes away from my empty apartment. In our thirty-four years, Jenny and I had never been apart for more than a few months at a time. My sister always was my identity, the other half of the Spinner Twins. We grew closer in college, realizing for the first time what absence meant as we set off to opposite ends of Illinois to pursue similar degrees in writing. We called each other when we got lonely and looked at the moon from our dorm room windows, our own hokey moment stolen from a Disney movie.

Being a twin, I never felt loneliness. To this day, I have no idea what that feels like. I have always had a soul mate, someone whose thoughts echo within me before they ever are birthed into words. I know instinctively how she feels, and she knows me better than anyone.

When we were about eight years old, late at night, alone in our togetherness, we imagined our worst-case scenario. A man with a gun was going to shoot us both. We wondered who should die first and what would be worse: being the last one standing, grieving, or leaving the last one standing, grieving. We simply could not imagine life without each other. We debated this scenario into young adulthood without finding an answer. We debated it until speaking the unthinkable became too morbid. We replaced it with more realistic fears of cancer and car accidents—but never war.

Before I left for Iraq, Jenny told me that if anything happened to me, she would never feel joy again. I tucked her voice, those words, deep within me, and off I went, on a journey of a lifetime, on a journey into life.

I went alone.

TELL THEM
I DIDN'T CRY

◆ ◆ ◆

A SHORT GUIDE TO HOW NOT TO BE AN AMERICAN WOMAN IN IRAQ

1. Wear lots of lipstick. Modern Iraqi women love flashy lips painted in bright reds and oranges.
2. Trade in all silver jewelry for gold. Iraqis wear gold.
3. Don't look happy. Iraqis are suffering.
4. Never drink directly out of a water bottle even if it is 120 degrees outside and you're about to pass out. Wait until you get home and pour the water into a glass like a proper Iraqi.
5. When walking down the street, never look a man directly in the eyes. He will think you are a whore.
6. Wear shirts long enough to cover your behind. The goal is to act like a lady without really looking like one.
7. Buy a purse your grandmother would love and hang it on the crook of your arm just like she would.
8. You're a vegetarian? Well, that's just silly. Eat a kabob.
9. If you're invited to tea, drink it even if you are not thirsty or question the water source. Only rude Americans would not accept an invitation to tea. In fact, if someone offers you anything at all, take it.
10. If you are going to attempt to hide underneath a scarf, make sure you tuck the hair completely under the fabric.

CHAPTER 1

The hot cement burned the rubber soles of my sandals as I ran through the barricaded maze of blast walls, sandbags, and barbed wire sealing off the compound of the U.S. occupation authority in Baghdad. Behind me, an angry mob of young and graying men chanted in uniform protest and pumped long, black rifles toward the sky. Some of them held signs with American flags crossed out in thick black lines. I could not have looked more American at that moment, wearing black REI sandals, khaki pants, and a white linen button-down shirt. Although my brown, sun-streaked hair was pulled back in a tight bun, I was not wearing a traditional Muslim headscarf that would have better disguised me. I knew it would only be a matter of time before someone spotted me in the unforgiving blaze of the bright May sunshine.

I sprinted toward the guarded entrance of the Green Zone, where American and Iraqi civil authorities had encamped in Saddam Hussein's ornate former presidential palaces since the March 2003 invasion, fourteen months earlier. The four-square-mile zone in the heart of the Iraqi capital was a city within a city. It had brown cement apartment buildings and lush single-family homes, where palace servants and key employees of Saddam's regime lived. Most of those people fled at the start of the war as U.S. forces dropped bombs on the government buildings and palaces and later when the U.S. Army's 3rd Infantry Division marched into the government compound. The Green Zone earned its name as a security designation. *Green* was safe. *Red* was not. The Red Zone was all of Iraq out-

1

side the protected Green Zone. There is a great myth that journalists in Baghdad stay in the Green Zone, sharing it with U.S. officials and contractors who live in white single-wide trailers and work in the palace and other government buildings. In fact, almost all of the foreign journalists in Iraq live in hotels and heavily guarded residences in the Red Zone, using private or Iraqi security forces for protection and making the harrowing ride to the Green Zone for press conferences and meetings with government officials who rarely leave it.

The Green Zone—or "the Bubble," as officials who work inside refer to it—is one of the safest places in Iraq, in large part because it is so sealed off from the rest of the capital and country. The only way for journalists or Iraqi civilians to get into the Green Zone is to pass through a single military checkpoint open to the general public, who must produce at least two pieces of identification and a written invitation or a darn good reason to come in, which, of course, is subject to the review of the soldiers guarding the gate. Once inside, you have to pass through three more security checkpoints, two of which require a complete pat down that most Americans would find utterly objectionable if performed by a U.S. airport screener.

As a member of the press, I could get into the Green Zone more easily than an Iraqi citizen as long as I had a proper credential issued by the U.S.-led coalition government. That was the reason I had come to the Green Zone the day of the protest. I was merely trying to get my press badge. But the U.S. soldiers guarding the checkpoint had padlocked the gate, wrapping a thick steel cord around the chain-link fence. These soldiers were the front line of the war in Iraq. If a suicide bomber tried to enter the Green Zone, for example, theirs would be the first lives lost. Guarding a checkpoint is one of the most dangerous jobs in the military.

I fumbled in my computer bag for my passport.

"I'm an American citizen," I yelled, flashing my distinguishable blue passport. "Please let me in."

"The checkpoint is closed," one of the soldiers shouted. I wasn't close enough to see his face, which was mostly hidden anyway behind large dark glasses and a camouflage-covered helmet. A green strap encircled his chin.

"But I'm a *Washington Post* reporter, and things are really heating up out here."

"You better leave then," another soldier called to me. "It's dangerous for you."

Well, that was kind of obvious, I thought to myself, as I turned around and stood for a moment, no clue what to do. I had only been in Iraq for about twenty-four hours.

People spend a lifetime obsessing over time, what they did with it, whether there was enough of it, wasted, earned. I used to spend hours plotting what steps to take, the next career move. But when my father died suddenly from cancer something told me to run, and I have been running ever since, running all the way to Baghdad, away from the image of a man too-young taking his last gasps of life before my shocked eyes. I needed a purpose. Most of my family and friends could not understand why anyone would volunteer to go to a place where every day would be a test of survival. I went to Iraq because I am a journalist: we drive into hurricanes, not away from them. We chase the very elements of life that most people try to avoid.

When I left for Iraq, I had no idea what danger really was; I knew only that I had a deep sense of responsibility for the story, and I was bored. I had been sitting in Washington writing about accounting policy and Iraq reconstruction contracts the year before I went to Iraq. I was dying a slow professional death. After a decade at the *Post*, the only writing that mattered to me anymore was my travel stories, which took me away to Finland, Spain, the Galápagos Islands. Like the places I uncovered on those journeys, I wanted to see Iraq for myself, see the country and the people behind the contract stories I wrote from the comfort of the newsroom in Washington. I wanted to prove there was more to the stories—and to me.

I had been trying for a year to convince my editors to let me go to Iraq. I was frustrated sitting on the sidelines of the Iraq reconstruction story. It was a hugely important story, with more than $20 billion of taxpayer money funding the largest nation-rebuilding effort since the Marshall Plan of 1947, which aided repair of infrastructure damaged in World War II.

From the get-go, the Iraq reconstruction project was ripe with allegations of abuse, in large part because most of the rebuilding contracts were awarded without competition, as allowed by law in emergency situations. The agencies awarding the contracts cited the speed with which they needed to get the money flowing into Iraq as the prime reason not to take them out into the marketplace for bidding. Much of the attention centered on Houston-based KBR, a subsidiary of Halliburton that Vice President Dick Cheney led as chief executive from 1995 to 2000. The connection itself was enough to raise suspicions about Halliburton's multibillion Iraq contracts, even though set profit margins make it difficult for companies to reap huge benefits from the spoils of war. My editors had instructed me to dig in and find out what I could about contract abuse. I struggled for more than a year to do so, following a loose paper trail in Washington when most of the decisions were being made on the ground in Baghdad. I was constantly frustrated by the geographical limitations that prevented me from seeing the potential abuse for myself. Occasionally, we'd get lucky: some whistleblower from Iraq would come back with stories of overpriced gasoline and gym towels. These accounts were difficult to verify independently, and mostly we had to rely on audit reports and independent investigations by members of Congress, which, while often useful as starting points, were almost always politically motivated.

One allegation against KBR involved its potential overcharging on meals served at military dining facilities in Kuwait and Iraq. A routine Defense Department audit in January 2004 found that the company had not properly estimated the numbers of meals served to soldiers and contractors. Lawmakers critical of the company and suspicious of the more than $3 billion in contracts awarded to it for Iraq-related work seized on the finding as a prime example of KBR's alleged war profiteering. KBR responded that it was difficult to determine how many people would be at dinner in the middle of a war zone.

But it pledged to do better. I wrote multiple stories about the allegations without ever having eaten in a military dining facility in Iraq. It was a context that would have been helpful. When I did get to Iraq, I found that the military units with which I was embedded often would not know from hour to hour where they would be or if they'd be back at a base in time for dinner. During the battle of Fallujah in November 2004, the dining facility unexpectedly shut down for several days. This did not excuse KBR, but it helped better explain how the company could have miscounted the meals.

From Washington, my stories were neither dazzling nor spectacular, making it difficult for me to convince my editors that I had to go to Iraq, that I had to follow the story from there. I was desperately waiting for a break. In journalism, you're only as good as your stories, and it helps if you can deliver the stories your editors want. The subtle mandate I sensed from my editors: Find the dirt on Halliburton. I wasn't doing that. In my attempts not to get caught up in the politics of the story, I was coming across as soft, and I knew it. Plenty of people in newsrooms worry endlessly about getting on the front page. Perhaps to the detriment of my career, I never really sweated it. I wrote good stories, fair stories, and I charged hard when I needed to. But I didn't—and I don't—try to make dirty stories look dirtier just for the sake of getting on the front page. I love scoops as much as any journalist, but I love being right more; the struggle in journalism, of course, is being first and being right, which is not always the way it turns out. I have always felt more responsible to my sources and to our readers than I have to my editors. Journalists who go for the one big hit and get it wrong have short-changed every future exchange with the people who follow their work expertly. But there is a price, too. Sometimes journalists get lost in their own newsroom. When the war broke out in Iraq, I had already felt lost for some time.

In May 2004, Jill Dutt, the assistant managing editor for the Financial section, wanted someone to go to a KBR job fair to write a story about the kind of people who would risk everything for a chance to work in Iraq. I assumed I would be put on the story because I had been writing about contracting and KBR for more than a year. But my assignment editor told me that Dutt was reluctant to send me because I was not enough of a feature writer. I was furious, depressed and frustrated. I knew I was a good reporter, but I struggled with my writing on the Financial desk. I had a hard time finding a voice like the one that came so easily to me when I wrote for the Travel section. Writing is a personal endeavor for me, every sentence a painstaking creation. It was a huge blow, personally and professionally, to be told that I wasn't good enough to tackle a story that would require narrative writing. If my editors had really lost that much faith in me, I didn't know how I was going to scrape myself from the bottom, because this definitely felt like the bottom. Nonetheless I convinced my assignment editor, Chuck Babcock, to get me to Texas, no matter what he had to do. Fortunately, it worked.

A few days later, at the KBR job fair in Houston, I met Allen Petty, a thirty-one-year-old father of six girls who was leaving the next day for Iraq. I spent an hour with him at the job fair, carefully watched over by a small crew from KBR's public relations department. With the blessing of the PR folks, because even chance encounters of these sorts were carefully monitored, I then drove north of Austin to meet Allen's wife, Sylvia, and their daughters.

Sylvia invited me into their modest ranch home on Main Street in Burnet, Texas, which the couple rented from her parents. We spent hours talking about why she and Allen decided he should go to Iraq. The family had no insurance, no credit, bills they couldn't pay. They were scraping by on Allen's $30,000 annual salary—he drove a big rig for a private company in a neighboring quarry town. They felt stuck.

Sylvia is a gracious woman, deeply rooted in her Christian faith. She invited me to go to church with her family at the Grace Christian Center in Killeen, a large, charismatic congregation, where a live band belts out contemporary gospel tunes while the worshipers clap and sway.

I grew up in the more buttoned-down Lutheran church but had gone to my share of Christian youth camps as a child. I understood Sylvia's need to reach into this part of her life as she was sending her husband off to war, even if it was voluntarily, even if it was for the money. At one point during the service, the pastor asked the congregation to pray for all of the soldiers who were serving in Iraq. No one offered up prayers for the truck drivers. This was the story I had to tell. Allen Petty was a hardworking, honest American, desperate to make a better life for his family. The soldiers in Iraq needed him. Truck drivers like Allen carry food, medical supplies, and vehicle parts through Iraq. Sure, they make a ton more money than the soldiers—some of them get more than $100,000 in pay for the most dangerous assignments—but these contractors also were risking their lives to do it. And yet they were completely marginalized by the public and, admittedly, by us in the media.

My story about Allen Petty ran on the front page of the *Post*, opening with the scene of Allen and Sylvia on their front porch, enjoying a quiet "date" while the kids were in bed. "Baby, you've got to go," Sylvia remembered telling her husband after their hours of discussion about whether he should risk everything so the family had a chance, a tiny little chance at a tiny bigger bite of the American dream. When I found out I was going to Iraq, Sylvia was one of the first people I called. She wrote me the entire time I was in Iraq.

Before I left Texas to return to Washington, I got word from Chuck Babcock that the wire services were reporting that CBS's *Sixty Minutes II* news program planned to break a huge story on television. The story was about a big abuse scandal at the notorious Abu Ghraib prison in Iraq, a torture chamber for common criminals as well as political enemies of Saddam, which was emptied right before the invasion. After rolling into Iraq, the U.S. military took over the prison and used it to house security detainees. The CBS segment showed the first images of American soldiers humiliating Iraqi prisoners. I had already started reporting on an element of the scandal, which is why my editor had called. A mutual acquaintance had put me in connection with Sabrina Harmon, one of seven members of the Army military police unit initially charged with abuse. Babcock wanted to know how long it would take for me to get the story completed. Sabrina and I had been instant-messaging for weeks but our conversations had all been on background, kept private between us. Sabrina was not sure she wanted to go public while she was in the middle of legal proceedings. I frantically emailed her in Iraq and encouraged her to talk to her lawyer, Frank Spinner (no relation to me). They decided to go public with her story. At that point, pictures of Sabrina giving a thumbs-up in front of an Iraqi corpse were already being circulated. Back in Washington, I raced to write her account of how her unit was ordered to break down detainees. As a military police soldier, her job was to "keep them awake, make it hell so they would talk," Sabrina told me.

The story sailed into the paper a few days later, landing the *Post* a major exclusive in what quickly had become an international scandal that further inflamed the Arab world after the U.S. invasion. The American military announced that it would start legal proceedings against the soldiers almost immediately. I knew this was my chance to get to Iraq. In 1996 I spent eight months helping cover another Army scandal—this one involving male drill sergeants accused of rape and inappropriate sexual relations with female recruits. I used this experience as my pitch to Phil Bennett, then the Foreign assistant managing editor and now the managing editor of the paper. The *Post's* Baghdad bureau chief, Rajiv Chandrasekaran, had been trying to figure out a way to get me to Iraq, too. We had grown up at the *Post* together, part of a Brat Pack of young twentysomethings who got their start as summer interns. Rajiv had ridden his star from a suburban Virginia Metro beat, to a spectacular run covering the Microsoft antitrust trial for the Financial desk, and then on to the Foreign staff. He appreciated that I needed a chance to prove myself, and he knew the commitment I felt to understanding the Iraq story. We had been exchanging emails and telephone calls about it for months. We pressed Bennett to let me come cover the courts-martial.

He agreed, and with about seven days' notice before the first legal proceeding was scheduled to begin, I had my ticket to Baghdad.

And that is how I found myself outside the military checkpoint, twenty-four hours after arriving in Baghdad, standing in the Red Zone, so close to the Bubble, yet unable to penetrate its sanctuary of safety.

I crept around the sandbags that divided the two zones of Iraq and headed back to the protest. I couldn't really cover it because I had no translator with me. I could only watch and wait to see if they would start shooting or try to charge the Green Zone. Just that morning one of our translators had shown me a blurry photo of our young Iraqi officer manager, Omar, whom I had not yet met. In the photo, taken in the summer of 2003, Omar watches in horror as a crowd of demonstrators turned on him and my colleague from Washington, Theola Labbé. They roughed up Omar and tried to take Theola's notebook. She held tight, refusing to give it up. The photo was a source of pride for our Iraqi translators. They were in the struggle with us.

I had forgotten the mobile telephone the bureau had issued to me the day before, which I discovered with a gulp after ransacking the computer bag for it. Instead, my hand brushed over something soft. It was the cheese sandwich I had packed before setting out earlier that morning. I walked toward a rusted metal guard shack the color of a roasted red pepper with the words "Parking Guard" painted in English in large, white block letters below an Arabic inscription. I had to step gingerly around a tangle of barbed wire and over the trash piles that had blown up against it. I stole a wary look at the crowd of protestors and then picked a cool spot in the shade on the other side of the shack so I could peek around to watch. As I chewed the sweet, nutmeg-infused Iraqi bread, called *samoon*, I heard a soft voice call out, "Taxi, madam?" Startled, I whipped around and saw a clean-shaven, brown-skinned man in neat trousers and a blue short-sleeve checked shirt approaching me. He had rolled up in a ramshackle car, crudely painted in orange and white. During Saddam Hussein's rule, drivers often painted their cars in the signature taxicab colors to get around restrictions and taxes on private vehicle use, making it difficult to tell the difference between the real and fake taxis.

"No, no, thanks," I replied, immediately suspicious and reluctant to jump in a car with a man who might be an insurgent or potential kidnapper. "You need ride," the driver insisted gently in broken English. "No, I'm just having lunch," I told him before realizing that this not only sounded absolutely ridiculous but that this taxi might be my only chance to get back to the Sheraton Hotel, where the *Post* bureau was located. I had no idea when the soldiers might let me in or if things would suddenly become violent.

"Well, okay, I need to go to the Sheraton. Do you know where that is?"

"Of course, madam," he said, opening the door of the car to reveal filthy, torn seats covered in dust and what appeared to be grease stains from lunches gobbled in a hurry. He jumped in the other side of the car and, to my relief, sped off in what appeared to be the direction of the hotel. I knew only a few Arabic words, and he knew very little English, but we exchanged short sentences while he raced his clunker past government buildings bombed by U.S. fighter jets a year earlier. Their crumbled shells were singed with soot; their interiors completely gutted by looters, who even carried off nails if they could find them intact.

The taxi driver asked me if I were married. "Oh yes," I lied, thinking that might be more honorable than being single. He asked if I had children, and I lied again, adopting my two-year-old nephew as my own. "Good, good," he responded after each lie. Better, I thought, in this country where family mattered more than anything, to be a mother who left her child behind than not to be a mother at all.

The hot, stale air blew through the open window as we passed street vendors selling cheap plastic bowls and kitchen utensils imported from China. It was late afternoon, and most of the shops in the Karrada commercial district where the Sheraton was located were closed because of the afternoon heat. The streets were practically deserted, and the vendors sat idly, with few customers.

We pulled up to the checkpoint outside the towering, brown brick Sheraton, which was guarded by private contractors, and I handed the driver a $5 bill before hopping out. I waved as I ducked through another trail of barbed wire.

The *Washington Post* driver who had dropped me off at the Green Zone entrance an hour earlier was surprised to see me walk into our bureau office. We had an elaborate system for ferrying reporters around—chase cars and armed guards and detailed travel plans. A reporter didn't simply show up after an afternoon out. I explained what had happened, only to be chastised by our security director, Muhanned, a former Iraqi army officer who had betrayed Saddam by fighting with the U.S. Army's 82nd Airborne during the 2003 invasion. He was a trusted man, whose knowledge of Iraq and loyalty to *The Washington Post* kept us safe.

"You could have been kidnapped!" Muhanned admonished. We went back and forth, as I explained to him that I had two choices: taxi or the mob, neither of which seemed better than the other to him. I showed him the digital picture I had taken of the guard shack before I got into the taxi. I figured I could always throw the camera out the window—a clue, perhaps, in case I needed to leave a trace. Muhanned looked at me like I had been watching too many U.S. detective television series, fiction. This was real, his look said.

When I arrived the day before, I had literally fallen into Muhanned's arms. He had been sent to help retrieve me after my commercial flight into Iraq, a harrowing, spiral descent to avoid antiaircraft fire. As I stepped off the crowded bus that transported me from the dirty Baghdad International Airport to a parking lot near yet another military checkpoint, the weight of my purple and black backpack carried me forward in a stumble. Looking back, it was a fitting entry for the junior-most member of the *Post*'s Baghdad bureau. I had only been to the Middle East once, earlier that year, during a brief ten-day trip with the U.S. Army Corps of Engineers to Iraq and then to Afghanistan.

I was just aware enough when I left for Iraq the first time to be scared, to write letters to my family, sealed, stamped, and given to friends to mail—just in case. During my time in Iraq, soldiers would often puzzle over why I had offered to step into a war zone. They were perplexed why I did not carry a gun. "You don't carry a weapon?" they would ask quizzically, clutching their own rifles a bit closer to their bulletproof vests. I would always bring out my pen, tucked somewhere on my body, and hold it up. "This is my weapon."

I am the first journalist in my family. My father was a pipe fitter who died in 2001 of pancreatic cancer. He never went to college and struggled most of my childhood to provide for us. My mother is a retired elementary school teacher who left the classroom for almost two decades to raise her three children in a split-level house in Decatur, Illinois, a mostly blue-collar city of factories that spews stinky white steam and smoke into the skies above the soybean and cornfields of the surrounding prairie.

My parents met on a school bus when they were sixteen-year-old students at Stephen Decatur High School. I got my start in the newspaper business at the same school after a chance encounter between two Little League moms. My brother, Tim, played baseball with the son of the newspaper adviser at the high school where my twin sister, Jenny, and I were going to be freshmen in that fall of 1984. The adviser, Barbara Fuson, convinced my mother that my sister and I should join the newspaper staff, and so my fate was sealed one steamy summer night on the grassy sidelines of a ball field behind Stevenson Elementary School.

My sister remembers far more of our childhood than I do. Perhaps, as the family essayist, she somehow knew she was destined to be our storyteller, and so she unwittingly memorized scenes and moments and details that I had no use for. But amid the gray of my own memory, that night at the ball field emerges in full color. I can hear the cheers of the parents, the sound of plastic cleats sprinting through the fine dust, the smell of fresh-cut grass. I can see the purple sky of the setting sun. We were the home team. I was thirteen.

Twenty years later I delivered the commencement address to my alma mater, Southern Illinois University in Carbondale, where I had earned a journalism degree in 1992. I had come back after my assignment in Iraq to accept an alumni achievement award. During the commencement address, I tried to explain how a kid from Illinois with humble Midwestern roots had ended up in Iraq on one of the most significant stories of my generation. I ended my speech with this advice: *There is only one way to get where you want to go, and it really is quite simple. Start walking.* On that balmy summer night, while my brother took his turn at bat, I did just that.

My sister and I were together when the war began in March 2003. On a hotel room television screen in Manhattan, we watched news footage of the black Iraqi night lit by American fire. Standing shoulder to shoulder at the end of the bed, we couldn't take our eyes from the screen. It was hard to shake the significance of what we were watching from our vantage point near the empty sockets of the Twin Towers. Something dark hung in the room that day that I only recognized when, nine months later, Jackie first uttered, "I'm going to Iraq." It was the black color of fear.

I was furious at my sister not just for agreeing to go to Iraq, but for wanting to. When people enlist in the military, they understand the risk that one day they may engage in battle. But my sister? She was a journalist, a business reporter no less, where she daily battled numbers, not bullets, not bombs. What was she thinking? What career move could possibly be worth death? I argued with her for days, furious arguments in which I said terrible things. I reminded her that Dad had been in his grave just three years; our family, still scrambling from its loss. Cancer, I said, is something you can't avoid. But war? And in a country so far from here, from what I knew, that I could barely place it on a map? "You are the most selfish person I know!" I screamed. "Why are you doing this to me? Don't go.

Please, don't do this." But she didn't answer back—because I never said these things to her directly. I said them to the wall. I said them to the sky. I said them to her face, looking back at me in the mirror. There's a certain responsibility in being a twin that I've come to accept over the years: your love must be unconditional and selfless. When everyone else fails your twin, you must be there. So I swallowed my dread and sang into the mouthpiece of the telephone, "I'm so happy for you! What an honor!"

It would take months before I would understand why she wanted to go, why she needed to go, and why, eventually, I wanted her to be there, too.

CHAPTER 2

The sun rose each morning over the Tigris River, illuminating my hotel balcony with bright splashes of orange and offering postcard views of the black smoke plumes rising from rocket attacks on the Green Zone. I often awoke to the gigantic booms of American artillery firing on Haifa Street, a dirty two-mile stretch of tower blocks controlled by insurgent gangs. In the street below the balcony, Iraqis who worked at the Sheraton and neighboring Palestine hotels hurried along the broken cement sidewalks, past the barbed wire and the cement walls that tried to shield us all from danger.

Like many other large foreign news organizations, the *Post* had rented a house shortly after the fall of Baghdad when it became clear that we would need a more permanent base for an indefinite period of time. The house in the Jadriya neighborhood was a lovely residence with a large pool and garden, protected by walls of sandbags, reinforced windows, and armed guards. In early February 2004, a car bomb exploded outside the home of one of the *Post*'s translators. The same day, a car drove by the *Post* house while someone snapped pictures. Within hours, Rajiv relocated the entire bureau to the Sheraton Hotel in the Karrada neighborhood of Baghdad, a middle-class commercial district. The new Sheraton had long lost its official corporate affiliation, even though it held on to its original name. This was more of a Sher, although at one time it was one of the nicest hotels in Baghdad. At nineteen stories high, it was also the tallest, making it a perfect insurgent target.

The *Post* had part of a floor with individual rooms for correspondents, an office for the translators, a converted kitchen, a room for our drivers to hang out in between assignments, and a dining room/lounge for the correspondents that we referred to by its room number: 107. The rooms were crummy, the out-dated, mismatched furniture faded and filthy, but I didn't mind. I had one of the smallest rooms when I first arrived. It had a flea-infested bed and lacked air conditioning.

Over the blood-splattered wall, its origins unknown, I hung an Iraqi flag to remind myself that I was a visitor in this occu-pied country. There were enough signs of American dominance elsewhere. Private contractors, particularly security contractors, seemed to be the least sensitive about this matter. That is not meant to be a blanket indictment, but it always infuriated me to see foreigners being disrespectful to Iraqis, barreling around a country as if it belonged to them. Even my Iraqi colleagues and friends who were grateful that the Americans invaded bristled when a clomping foreigner clomped a little too hard.

The Sheraton and the Palestine were both prime clomping grounds. The hotels, which were filled with foreigners, share real estate on Abu Nawas Street, one of the most enviable and famous addresses in Baghdad. During its heyday in the 1960s and 1970s, the wide boulevard along the Tigris River was lined with nightclubs, fish restaurants, and a lush carpet of grass. Families gathered for picnics on the lawn, and children scam-pered up and down slides in a special playground.

But the grounds closed to the public in the late 1980s as Sad-dam Hussein became increasingly more paranoid about threats on his life and on his government. Abu Nawas, and the Shera-ton and Palestine hotels, sit directly across from the former presidential compound, now the Green Zone.

The U.S. military closed the street to protect foreign journal-ists and contractors housed in the hotels after car bombers began targeting "soft"—nonmilitary—targets. In one of the deadliest incidents, a truck bomb detonated on August 19, 2003, at the Canal Hotel in Baghdad, which housed the United Nations. The UN top envoy, Sergio Vieira, was killed in the blast. At the Sheraton-Palestine compound, Iraqi police and burly, private security contractors manned checkpoints at the closed portion of the road, allowing through only drivers with homemade badges created by their employers. The vehicles were then steered into a dusty parking lot, a quarter mile from the hotels to keep potential car bombers from driving up to the entrances. Once on foot, you passed through an additional security checkpoint, one line for women and the other for men. After a good pat down, a staple of postwar Iraq, you walked the rest of the way through a column of large concrete barriers erected on the street.

The Palestine had a livelier social scene than the Sheraton, with CNN and the Associated Press camped there until both organizations moved out in the fall of 2004. We shared the Sheraton space with Fox News, foreign contractors, and a revolving contingent of U.S. soldiers who guarded us from posts on the rooftop. When journalists were still able to travel after dark for social calls—a practice that ended around the beginning of October as the threat of kidnapping intensified— the AP could get a crowd of several hundred reporters from across the city to show up for cans of Carlsberg beer and dated 1980s music in a patio garden lined with palm trees. During one of those parties, you almost forgot you were in Iraq. American soldiers there often told me about the mindless boredom of guard duty, the long hours spent repeating drills, cleaning weapons, waiting. Soldiers wait a lot. They have duty hours and off-duty hours. We simply had hours. If you weren't writing, you were chasing a story to write. That didn't leave a whole lot of downtime.

Both hotels operated restaurants but the larger news organizations had their own cooking operations. In the *Post* bureau, we survived, sometimes begrudgingly, on the greasy food prepared by the two Iraqi women who took turns making lunch and the rotating cast of male chefs who put dinner on our table every night. Lunch was typically a meaty stew, rice, and salad. Dinner was a more elaborate culinary affair, with curried cauliflower, baked chicken, pickles, hummus, and bread. We paid two Sheraton cleaners, Mushtaq and Waad, $100 a month under the ruse that they would give our rooms a little extra attention, which meant they'd actually clean them. We were really paying them not to steal from us, and even when they did come in to swipe at the dust, a *Post*-employed armed guard or driver came with them to watch. Foreign news organizations were prime targets for petty theft. From the thieves' perspective, we were from supersized America. We had fat to spare—cases of soda, bottles of wine, food—all loot that disappeared over time.

My first few weeks in Iraq were a whirlwind of adjustment. Everything was foreign to me: the language, the customs, the life of a foreign correspondent. Only the job felt familiar. A story is a story, no matter where you report it. Before I left Washington, David Hoffman, the *Post*'s Foreign editor, who has since been promoted to assistant managing editor of the section, called me in to his office. I was terrified of David at that time. He could be brusque, a seasoned correspondent who had covered the Reagan and senior Bush presidencies, and then went overseas to Jerusalem and Moscow. He seemed skeptical of my abilities. My previous work at the *Post* had largely gone unnoticed. I was too far down the food chain for a foreign editor used to managing some of the best and most experienced reporters at the paper. I knew I had a lot to prove in Iraq and to no one more than David. I was determined to earn his respect and took notes as he sternly offered a crash course in foreign reporting, which included one of the best pieces of advice I could have carried throughout my assignment in Iraq: "Keep your notebook open." A foreign correspondent sees parts of the world that are completely unimaginable and unattainable for most people. *Keep your notebook open* meant it was my job to be the window for our readers who could not be there to experience the story. Later, I would have to concede that job to our Iraqi translators, a frustrating necessity forced upon us by the dangerous environment. "Keep your notebook open—for me."

Unlike other foreign assignments, this one had few perks. I wasn't paid extra to go to Iraq, not that anyone gets into journalism for the money. When people are posted overseas for permanent assignments (for the *Post*, that usually means three to four years in one place), they bring parts of their life with them, including families, pets, and furniture. In Iraq, you go in alone, and the bureau becomes your life, even your prison, as we used to call it after being cooped up for days at a time, unable to leave because of security threats.

Most of my colleagues who shipped off to Iraq from Washington went through survival training offered by the U.S. military or a private security firm. In boot camp–like environments, journalists learn how to handle themselves in a hostage crisis and how to tell the difference between different military firepower. I never had the training because I was sent on both trips with too little notice. Instead, I went to Tom Ricks, the *Post's* senior Pentagon reporter, a broad-shouldered man with a shock of white hair. Tom's reputation among the younger set was such that if you didn't know what you were doing and you didn't want your editor to know, you could go to him first. He dispensed advice without judgment and freely opened his huge database of sources. Tom, who had made several trips to Iraq since the invasion, directed me to an office in the *Post* where I could pick up my battle gear: a black helmet and flak jacket. He handed me a packing list he had come up with for reporters embedded during the war, and he advised me to buy a pair of ski goggles to protect my eyes from the blowing sand.

On the way to the elevator, with my battle gear tucked in a large black nylon bag that Tom assured me would get confiscated in Amman, Jordan, as terrorist equipment, I ran into Don Graham, former publisher of *The Washington Post* and now the *Post* company board chairman. Don had heard that I was headed to Iraq. He put his arm around me and guided me to a small set of chairs and table near the elevator bank of the fifth floor newsroom. He talked to me as a parent, not as the heir of a newspaper fortune, not as the Godfather of the *Post*. He was kind and assuring, and he was clear: "No story is worth your life." He admonished me gently to stay safe and come back in one piece. As we got up, he grabbed my hand, bent down, and kissed it. "Be careful," he said, before walking off.

I had no idea how long I would be in Iraq. I expected that it would be a couple of weeks and then I would head home to see if the editors wanted to keep me on the story or pass it off to someone more experienced. I warned my family that I could be gone for a couple of months, but realistically I thought it would be far shorter. I was clinging to the story, hanging by a tiny thread of responsibility to cover the court-martial of former Army Spc. Jeremy C. Sivits, the first soldier to stand trial for mistreatment of detainees at Abu Ghraib. Hoffman had instructed me to stay focused on Abu Ghraib and not get involved in other stories in Iraq unless Rajiv specifically requested or needed my help. Hoffman had expressed reservations about sending an inexperienced reporter to Iraq. He did not want me tromping into the bureau, grabbing stories and causing troubles with the other reporters. The best way for me to get along, he advised, would be to mind my own story. So sure that my trip would be a quick in and out, I left food in my refrigerator that I figured would not spoil in my short absence. I bid my elderly grandmothers farewell by telephone and promised to visit as soon as I came home. Had I known I would be gone for months, I would have thrown out that brick of cheddar cheese. Had I known that one of my grandmothers would die six weeks after I left, I would have said good-bye in person.

I knew how scared Jenny was. At Newark International Airport the night I left for Amman, en route to Baghdad, I looked back at her as long as I could, before disappearing into the terminal. I could see it on her face, her mouth stretched into a tight smile that said *I am trying to be happy for you, see?* I knew she was memorizing the moment, memorizing me. Once inside the secure terminal, I didn't look back.

Iraq shares its borders with six countries: Kuwait and Saudia Arabia to the south, Jordan and Syria to the west, Turkey to the north and Iran to the east. Iraq is like the Kansas of the Middle East. You have to fly or drive over seemingly endless terrain to get to it.

After Baghdad fell to U.S. and coalition forces on April 9, 2003, journalists rushed into the country, most of them coming from Jordan or Kuwait. In the months that followed, we could still drive into Iraq, and many of my colleagues did just that, making the dusty 600-mile journey by car from Jordan. By May, when I returned without the military, it was no longer deemed safe to drive. The highway from the Jordanian border to Baghdad went past Fallujah and the village of Abu Ghraib—two places where you did not want to get a flat tire. In fact, looters and insurgent fighters patrolled the highways, sometimes setting up illegal roadblocks, looking for people to rob or foreigners to grab. I had a flight from Amman to Baghdad on Royal Jordanian, Jordan's national airline and the only commercial carrier in May 2004 that offered service between the two capital cities. The Queen Alia International Airport just outside of Amman is dark and shabby—not a pleasant place to ponder whether this was the last bit of earth my feet would touch before getting shot out of the sky. Passengers traveling to Baghdad are herded into a small, glass-encased waiting area, where the mood feels more resolved than doomed. There was no turning back. This was it. What the hell were we doing? The waiting area was a good place to size up what other idiots had volunteered for Iraq duty. The contractors were easy to spot. They were usually bearded, dressed in jeans and boots, and they carried Eddie Bauer duffle bags. The crowd included Iraqi businessmen in dark suits and beefy civilian security contractors, their bulging muscles distinguishing them from the contractors who came to drive trucks and oversee the repair of the infrastructure. After a half dozen trips in and out, I learned how to pick out the journalists: we had iPods.

When I had landed in Amman the day before, I spotted the sleek, newly painted Royal Jordanian jets parked at the terminal. I was relieved. I had pictured myself flying into Baghdad on an African crop duster. About five minutes before our flight was scheduled to depart, the passengers coming from Baghdad walked by the glass and we sized one another up. Occasionally you spotted someone you knew, some lucky bastard who made it out, and you could wave and offer a thumbs-up that was really meant for yourself, as if to say, "I'll be okay. I'll make it out, too." After a few minutes an airport employee opened a door that led to an escalator. He said nothing. We said nothing and followed him to a waiting bus. The bus drove past the sleek, newly painted Royal Jordanian jets, past the Iraqi Airways plane that had been grounded for more than a decade during the UN sanctions. It rolled up to a dingy one-hundred-seat Fokker F-28. I gulped.

The South African crew, which came with the plane that Royal Jordanian leased from the charter service AirQuarius Aviation, welcomed us aboard in cheery, starched blue uniforms. The plane was half empty when we took off for the hour-and-twenty-minute flight into Baghdad. The flight itself was uneventful . . . the landing was harrowing.

At about 4,500 feet, the pilot began a slow, stomach-churning spiral descent, a tactical maneuver to avoid missiles, gunfire, or whatever the insurgents might be shooting that day. On November 22, 2003, a DHL cargo plane was hit by a surface-to-air missile as it was taking off from the Baghdad International Airport. The pilot safely landed the damaged plane. On December 10, another surface-to-air missile hit a U.S. Air Force C-17 transport plane. Again, the pilot safely landed. The corkscrew maneuver was supposed to increase the odds that we would not be hit. I gripped the seat tightly and looked over at the other passengers. Everyone was gripping. My ears popped and my stomach flipped as we made our wide circular sweeps to the ground.

During my first trip to Baghdad, I flew in from Kuwait on a C-130 military plane. I traveled with Lt. Gen. Robert Flowers, commander of the Army Corps, who has since retired, trading the Army for a private sector job. Flowers invited me onto the flight deck with him. I was anxious to see the landscape unfolding under the belly of the huge cargo plane. I had been sitting inside the cavernous hulk, strapped into a red, mesh seat in the back of the plane with the general's staff. My "minder" for the trip was Scott Saunders, a civilian public affairs officer who suggested to Flowers that I be the sole reporter allowed to go along. Saunders and I had worked together for months on the Iraq reconstruction story, and I had grown to trust his no-bullshit style. He appreciated my attempt to be fair. He grinned when a National Guard crew member came back to tell me that the general wanted me up front for the flight into Iraq. It was a smile that said, you lucky dog, good for you. I gave him a wave and hopped up the stairs to the flight deck. Flowers patted the seat next to him, and I strapped myself in.

Baghdad came to me for the first time through the cockpit window in a slide show of visual vignettes, unfolding beneath me as I strained to see. It was too noisy for conversation so I scribbled a question on a pad of paper, "Do the insurgents ever take a crack at these big planes?" I handed it to Flowers. He stared at the paper, then turned to me and bobbed his head up and down. "Yes," he mouthed. I looked back out the window, at the brown scoops of sand the January wind had resettled into a desert glacier, a timeless geographical requiem that has played out over the centuries.

I recognized the same landscape from my seat on the Royal Jordanian plane. I sucked in my breath as we headed down, on our own, landing without incident. I wondered if my face had the same look as the other passengers': *I wasn't scared. See, that was easy. Piece of cake. Of course, we made it.*

Before the Americans handed civilian authority of the country back to Iraq in June 2004, U.S. officials largely controlled immigration at the airport. I flashed a letter from the U.S. Embassy in Jordan, paused to have my passport marked with the Baghdad airport stamp, which bore the letters CPA, for Coalition Provisional Authority, the U.S. occupation government. I collected my luggage and headed out to the curb. The airport was completely secured. No taxis were allowed. No private vehicles except for those with special Department of Defense permits. I joined the other non-DOD people on a hot bus that carried us to Checkpoint 1, a dirt parking lot where I met Muhanned and one of our drivers, Omar 2. Our Omars and Naseers were given numbers based on when they had joined the bureau. Omar 2 came after Omar, who was technically Omar 1, though we simply referred to him as Omar.

Once I arrived in Iraq, I had only a few days to sign up for a seat at the first court-martial and to get the press credential allowing me access into the Green Zone. The U.S. military did not have a courtroom in Iraq big enough to accommodate the hundred-plus swarm of journalists who showed up to cover the court-martial of Jeremy Sivits. The proceeding was held instead in a drab, brown-carpeted conference room in the equally drab, brown Convention Center in the Green Zone.

Saddam had used the Convention Center as a stage to declare himself the winner in Iraq's uncontested elections. In October 2002, Saddam held a referendum with a single question regarding keeping their leader in power. Voters would respond "yes" or "no." Every single one of Iraq's 11.4 million eligible voters cast a ballot to "reelect" Saddam for another seven years.

The Convention Center is the only place in the Green Zone that journalists are allowed without an escort. As members of the press, we could not visit the U.S. Embassy in the Green Zone without special permission. We could not hang out with the contractors at the Lone Star restaurant (not the American chain). We could not go to the U.S. military hospital unless we came during business hours, were cleared in advance for treatment, or had a life-threatening injury.

The biggest fear of Westerners working in the Green Zone was infiltration by insurgents. And it was a real fear. In October 2004, two suicide bombers detonated themselves in the popular Green Zone Café and adjacent bazaar, killing five people—three of them Americans working for the defense contractor DynCorp. A homemade explosive device was found about nine days earlier outside the same café but was discovered before it exploded.

By then, journalists had fewer reasons to go to the Green Zone. The nightly press conferences given by Army Brig. Gen. Mark Kimmit and Dan Senor, a senior adviser to the Coalition Provisional Authority, stopped after the CPA disbanded on June 30, 2004, and U.S. officials turned control of the country over to an interim Iraqi government. Journalists jokingly referred to the press conferences as the "Five O'Clock Follies." The press conferences provided a rat-a-tat-tat of statistics, mostly aimed at showing the world that Iraq was getting safer and getting better. Kimmit and Senor presented a version of reality in conference room number 3 that did not fit what we were seeing outside of the Bubble.

The Convention Center was one of the few places where American and Iraqi journalists mingled, though, in some ways, we remained segregated like students in a high school cafeteria. Much of it could be chalked up to language barriers. But the foreign press did not always treat the Iraqi journalists like colleagues. The Iraqi press was not polished, and they did not know the rules of engagement. Instead of questions, they offered up statements, long opinionated criticisms. But in a sense, we were watching the birth of a free press, and I was captivated by it. I sought out the Iraqi journalists and peppered them with questions about their craft—what they did before the war and what they did after. I invited them to dinner at our bureau. I felt an ambassador-like sense of responsibility to the Iraqi journalists. The U.S. military always seemed a tad suspicious of them, and for some good reason. In Iraq, it is impossible to tell who your enemies are. Anybody could declare himself a journalist, it seems.

When I was in line to get my press credential, a man who identified himself as a columnist was also trying to get one. He was, in fact, a lawyer who wanted to write about legal issues but did not work for a specific publication. More than two hundred newspapers sprang up in Baghdad after the fall of Saddam. The deposed leader had tightly controlled the press, and reporters who fell out of line were often beaten.

The war in Iraq and the new press freedoms that came as a result had created an instant pack of new Iraqi journalists. For many, Sivits's court-martial was their first opportunity to cover an open court proceeding, albeit one which the general public was not allowed to attend. Only thirty journalists received a coveted spot in the back two rows of the converted courtroom. The rest were steered begrudgingly to an overflow room to observe the proceedings on a giant TV screen.

We had to turn in all electronic equipment before entering the courtroom, including mobile telephones and recorders.

To call in an update during the trial, we dashed out with our numbered tickets while a soldier poked through a stack of plastic bags with electronic contraband, and then if time permitted, we could find a place to press up against a window to call in a report. Soldiers escorted us to the bathrooms for breaks and searched us with electronic wands before we returned to the courtroom. K-9 dogs also searched our bags of pens, notebooks, and energy bars. This happened every time the court recessed during the four-hour proceeding, and every time we walked in or out of the room.

Sivits's court-martial was important because it was our first chance to hear detailed accounts of what happened at Abu Ghraib from someone who was directly involved. Some of the statements Sivits made to Army investigators had been made public. But we only knew pieces of the whole story.

Sivits was charged with mistreating the detainees but it was not clear exactly what his role had been in the scandal that resulted in charges against seven members of the 372nd Military Police Company from Maryland. Sivits, twenty-four at the time, was a mechanic, not a military police soldier responsible for guarding the detainees. According to his testimony, he was hanging out in a break room at the prison on November 8, 2003, when Staff Sgt. Ivan L. Frederick, another soldier charged, asked him to follow him to the cellblock where guards were processing detainees involved in a riot in another part of the prison. Frederick asked Sivits if he wanted to escort a detainee to another tier, and Sivits said yes. As he led the hooded but still clothed detainee by the arm, Sivits said, he rounded a corner and saw a pile of prisoners on the floor.

He saw the naked prisoners put into a pyramid—an image widely publicized from photographs taken that night. He saw military police officers from the unit stomp on the toes and fingers of a pile of detainees, strip them of their blue and orange jumpsuits and civilian clothes, and force them to simulate and perform sexual acts with one another. The soldiers also hit two prisoners—one so hard that he blacked out. Sivits said he left when the prisoners were forced to masturbate. He broke down on the stand repeatedly. "I'd like to apologize to the Iraqi people and to those detainees," he said. "I let everybody down. I should have protected those detainees that night. You have to stand up for what's right. You can't let people abuse people like that. It was wrong. It shouldn't have happened." The military judge, Col. James Pohl, sentenced Sivits to a year in prison and discharged him from the Army under a deal he made with prosecutors to avoid serving more time. In exchange, he agreed to testify against the other soldiers.

After the court-martial was over, I called our drivers, who were waiting down the street to avoid the threat of car bombs right at the Green Zone checkpoint. Once the two cars (one for me and one for an armed guard) got within a few minutes of the Green Zone, I made the half-mile walk to the fifteen-foot blast walls and barbed-wire barrier between Green and Red. I positioned myself behind a concrete blast wall until I saw the car and then dashed out as fast as I could.

The Green Zone had a far less menacing feel to it during my first trip to Iraq in January 2003—four months before Sivits went on trial. In January, I embedded with the Army Corps of Engineers, which was responsible for part of the massive reconstruction effort to restore public services after the war and repair Iraq's crippled infrastructure. The Corps' operational headquarters was in the Green Zone, where I stayed exclusively during the four-day trip. I ate meals with soldiers and contractors in the dining facility at the Republican Palace, the nucleus of the U.S. occupation government. Saddam had passed judgment on his enemies in one of the rooms in the palace, sitting on a throne under a large mural of a rocket. In January 2004, the throne had been removed and the room converted to a massive dormitory, with cots for sleeping soldiers. I ran in the mornings along the streets of the Green Zone and took pictures of the setting sun from the balcony of a smaller palace where I slept. At night I brushed my teeth in a gold and marble bathroom that I shared with six other women.

The Army Corps was responsible for administering the contract to rebuild Iraq's oil infrastructure and provide emergency fuel. The Corps had awarded KBR the contract in March 2003 without putting it out for bid. Government auditors and members of Congress subsequently accused KBR of paying too much for the fuel it was importing into Iraq from Kuwait. Although the Army Corps had directed KBR to buy the fuel from Kuwait, the company took the brunt of the criticism. Flowers, a graduate of Virginia Military Institute who wore both Airborne and elite Ranger patches, was unapologetic in the face of the criticism. Of course KBR had paid a lot for the fuel, Flowers told me, responding to allegations that the company overcharged the government $61 million for buying fuel from Kuwait instead of from other countries. Flowers said Kuwait was the only place KBR could buy the fuel, sweeping aside what he deemed to be sophomoric comparisons to fuel prices in Turkey and Syria. The State Department had forbidden the Army from buying the fuel from Syria, and it would have been too expensive to truck the fuel in from Turkey in the north, he said.

As chief of engineers for the Army, Flowers took seriously his mandate to make sure the Iraqi people had the fuel they needed. It was a tactical strategy to avert a riot, chaos in the streets. If it cost a little extra, so be it, he reasoned—and reasoned openly with me. For an Army general, Flowers was accessible to the press, perhaps more so because of his work in reconstruction, not street fighting, although his engineers were certainly under the same threat as any soldier in the Army.

I had it good back then. We all did, I realize now. During that first trip, I paraded around Iraq with the word "PRESS" written in masking tape on my Army-issued flak jacket. There is another picture of me a public affairs officer snapped during that short visit: I have my father's blue hanky tied around my neck. The chinstrap of my camouflage-covered helmet is crooked. So are my Jackie O sunglasses, the cheap plastic kind purchased off a street vendor in New York City. In the photo, I'm smiling. I'm playing a war correspondent, and I do not have the sense to be scared because no one around me is all that concerned.

We're still at war, but man, we're making progress. That was the message the Army was delivering. That also was the reality I saw and was eager to report. I saw Army Corps engineers making repairs to power substations in Iraq, and I reported that repairs were being made. I described in detail why there was less electricity in Baghdad after the war than before it: the Americans had started redistributing it more fairly. That meant more power to southern Iraq at the expense of the centrally located capital. At the same time, I wrote about the dangers facing the people rebuilding the power plants. Many could no longer safely travel between the capital and their projects, so they built miniature camps on the work sites. This was one example of a worsening security situation that the Army and the press was only beginning to process. People assume that journalists are only interested in negative news, in death and destruction, and frankly, there is some truth to that. We do gravitate toward the ugly more than the pretty because the impact of the ugly side of human nature seems more significant in some sense. More is at stake when people are dying instead of living.

As the months passed, the pace of reconstruction slowed so much that when I returned, just four months later in May, it was hard to measure progress. Because of the insurgency and repeated attacks on infrastructure, Iraq looked under siege, with Iraqi and U.S. soldiers manning checkpoints throughout the country, now a puzzle of barriers, barbed wire, bombed-out buildings, and watch towers.

One of the consistent complaints I heard from Iraqis when I returned in May 2004 was that they had not expected their lives to be suspended in violence and uncertainty for so long after the war. The Americans had promised them a better life, but as the months passed since the invasion, Iraqis complained that it was hard to appreciate this theoretical notion being offered, this democracy, when the trash was piled up and stinking outside their door, when they were afraid of car bombs and mortar attacks. The struggle did not erase the hope that the ouster of Saddam brought for so many. It just made it harder to hold on to.

A week after I arrived the ceiling above the tub in my hotel bathroom collapsed and water poured in. A maintenance man in filthy blue overalls fixed the leak but left greasy, black boot marks and ceiling chips in the tub. As I scrubbed the tub on my knees later that night, I wondered what he did before the war. I wondered if his family were alive to greet him when he went home that night. I wondered how many checkpoints he'd have to pass through. I wondered if he felt free yet. I spent the rest of my time in Iraq trying to find out, trying to get a feel for how Iraqis really felt, how their lives had been changed— made better or worse. Sometimes they would ask me if I were for or against the war. It didn't matter, I told them. I am here because there was a war. I was not in Iraq to take sides. I was there to listen.

✦ ✦ ✦

In three days she'd be gone, and I was on a plane from Connecticut to Baltimore because I needed to see her before she went. Besides, I could water the plants and take out the trash while she worried about visas and plane tickets.

In the last weeks of my father's life, my mother kept to her teaching schedule, to a facade of normalcy, with a rigor that bewildered me. I couldn't understand why she didn't just quit her job and go home to her dying husband. I didn't expect my sister to die, but I dropped everything to spend the last few days with her—not so much to bring her comfort but to give myself something to remember, a slide of memory to hold up to the light of an uncertain future that I could not imagine without her.

Jackie and I spent the first eighteen years of our life about four feet from each other, our twin beds lining opposite walls of a very small, and very pink, room. In kindergarten we concocted an elaborate nighttime ritual that carried us into our teenage years. Just before falling asleep, one of us would say, "I love you," and the other was to respond in kind. "Too" was not allowed, for "I love you, too" hinted of an afterthought, of love out-of-sync. As we grew older, the ritual became a game. In the dark I would whisper "t," my tongue a nearly silent pop against the roof of my mouth, and Jackie would shout, "I heard that! Start over!" In college, away from each other for the first time and protective of our love affair—for it often felt like that—we turned the game into code. "Me, too" meant "I love you, you are my world, never leave me." You could say it in your dorm room, at the student newspaper office, in a crowd of friends at a party, and nobody would know who you were talking to or what you were saying.

I'd been away from my sister for long stretches before—the summer I lived in England, the graduate school years we lived on opposite coasts. In fact, since graduating from high school, we had always been a plane ride away, and we rode often. But this assignment to Iraq was different. We weren't sure how we were going to communicate, or how often. My husband wondered what I would do without my morning "Jackie fix." "I can survive," I retorted, while he kindly reminded me that during our honeymoon Jackie and I had talked every day—"every other day," I insisted.

We weren't even sure how long she would be gone, and not having an ending date to live toward was maddening. Jackie was convinced, however, that she would be home by the end of the summer, so on the plane to Baltimore, I wrote her fifteen letters, one to open each Sunday for the next three months, plus three extra for desperately homesick moments.

I gave her the letters the last night we were together. She had picked up her protective gear that morning—goggles, mask, helmet, and a flak jacket marked "PRESS." She made me try everything on, too, and I stumbled around her air-conditioned apartment, struggling to breathe—and walk—under the hot, heavy weight of the equipment and what it meant. I handed it back to her. "How will you do this in the desert?" I asked. "Or running from someone?"

She shrugged, donning the goggles and mask again. I tried to look bland, as if I recognized this war correspondent before me, as if I weren't afraid.

"Me, too," came a muffled voice from behind the mask. It sounded like a cry muted by fog, like someone calling to me from far, far away.

CHAPTER 3

Big Mohammed ran down the hall of the Sheraton, his leather shoes hitting the wet, moldy carpet in loud smacks. He shouted in Arabic and then motioned with his hand. "Come, Jackie, come. Run!" I had just fallen asleep on the floor of my room when the building shook with a thunderous blast. I bolted upright, still in my clothes—which I slept in for just this reason, the unexpected nighttime wake-up call. *Boom! Boom!* I ran to the door and peered out into the dark hallway. "Mortars," Big Mohammed explained as he reached my door. He led me to the staircase nearest my room, where the cold cement floor offered a welcome relief from the summer heat. Big Mohammed, thick as a linebacker, stood watch over me while I flattened my body against the wall to wait out the attack. Another guard brought a can of 7-Up. I closed my eyes and wondered if I could fall asleep counting my heartbeats.

In the United States, I have one brother; in Iraq, I have thirty-seven. The Iraqi men on our staff took special care of their female charges, whom they considered to be the more vulnerable sex of the correspondents who passed through the bureau. When I arrived in Iraq in May, Omar 2, the driver who collected me from the airport, speculated that I wouldn't last more than a month. I looked too delicate to be in Iraq, he later told me. It was hard for the staff to reconcile their traditional images of women with what stood before them. They were delighted when I baked them sweet breads and brownies. They watched me pamper my colleagues, making them meals when the cook had a day off and taking them plates of food when they failed to show up for dinner. But I could also throw a base-

33

ball better than all of them, could outshoot them at hoops. I could hold my own in pickup soccer games, and I could definitely outrun them. Once during an evacuation drill, I scolded the bald bodyguard who ran up the stairs to "lead" me to a safe place. I beat him there by a good five minutes. "Baldy," I asked, using his nickname, "how are you going to save me if you can't even make it up these stairs without losing your breath?" The next day, I looked out the window to see Baldy doing slow laps around the garden in his street clothes, his pistol still strapped to the holster at his side.

The Baghdad bureau was a large, blended brood, with all the quirks and personalities of two dozen Iraqis and a rotation of American correspondents forced together by the marriage of events. One afternoon I traveled back from a press conference at a military base with Muhanned and Falah, a former Iraqi air force lieutenant colonel who was now a *Post* driver. Falah, who was in his early forties, loved American rock and folk music. I had given him a tape cassette I made in college, and every time he drove me, he stuck it in the deck and blared the speakers. Music is a great weapon against fear—it allows you to disappear from reality—so I was grateful to be rolling along the Baghdad streets to the tunes of Peter Paul & Mary. During this particular drive, Falah's cheap sports watch kept beeping, causing Muhanned to curse at a sound too similar to the beep of a time bomb. We made a quick stop on the way back to the bureau so Falah could dash in to my favorite falafel shop in the Karrada neighborhood. The spicy smell of fried chickpeas drifted up from the bag at my feet as we passed donkey carts filled with vegetables headed to the market, shrouded women carrying sacks of rice on their heads, and barefooted children playing soccer among the sewage in the streets. Outside the car, it was 2004. Inside, it was 1972, and we were on a grassy lawn in upstate New York, singing, "If I had a hammer, I'd hammer in the morning. I'd hammer in the evening, all over this laaand." Our voices loud with song, we forgot all about Falah's bomb-beeping watch, the mortars, the kidnappers, and the suicide bombers lurking outside the car.

The Iraq bureau is the largest foreign operation at *The Washington Post*, which has twenty foreign bureaus around the world. More than forty people make up the staff, including bodyguards, maids, cooks, drivers, translators, and stringers who bring us the news from all parts of Iraq. In no other part of the world do any news organizations staff bureaus of this size cover just one single country. One correspondent, with a local staff of two to three people, typically can be responsible for an entire continent. The size of our Baghdad bureau indicates just how important, how big the Iraq story is to *The Washington Post*.

Because we have to trust the people we hire not to rat us out to the insurgents, the staff members are all connected in some manner— family members, neighbors, or former colleagues. Most of them are significantly overqualified for their new jobs in the new Iraq. Before the war, Abu Saif, now a translator, was a former Iraqi Airways engineer and pilot who ran a travel and tourism business on the side. In his former life, Ghazwan, one of our drivers, had ferried college and high school students in his taxi. Our laundress Um Hussein was a cook in one of Saddam's palaces. One of the lunch cooks, Wijdan, was a kindergarten teacher. Most of our staff members either lost their jobs because of the war or did not want to return to work that paid far less than the *Post*.

Rajiv built the bureau from scratch when he arrived in April 2003, and he built it into a mini empire. By the time I arrived, everything was already in place. I merely rented a room in the Rajiv Palace, as Tom Ricks called the bureau, a kingdom presided over by a man the staff referred to as "Little Saddam." Rajiv ruled with a dictator's style, and when he barked a command or shouted his displeasure the staff often grumbled and complained behind his back. But they loved him and protected him and, in the end, that was what mattered and what ultimately made the bureau function. We were asking our Iraqi employees to risk their lives and the lives of their families to work for us. In exchange, they got a job, a decent paycheck, and a marketable skill. We did not ask them to pledge allegiance to a nation, theirs or ours. We were a newspaper. We could only hope that if the insurgents came for us, our staff would love us enough not to open the door. Through this complexion of authority, Rajiv had to run a bureau. His successor, Karl Vick, would have to navigate it, too. And so, ultimately, would I.

It took weeks for me to figure out my extended family, to learn names that sounded impossibly foreign on my English-speaking tongue, to learn the social politics of our Iraqi staff. In that complex social hierarchy, age mattered; religion did not. Education mattered; how one felt about Saddam did not. Translators were one step up on the rung from drivers, who were one step above the guards, who were above the house staff. When I first arrived, Rajiv warned me about the intricacies of the Iraqi social caste system with a story of a young *Post* colleague who had asked a driver to fix his bathroom, a mistake that seemed to seal his fate. He might have asked one of the house staff but never a driver. Our staff seemed to need this system to negotiate postwar Iraq when power shifted so completely. One day you were *the man* in your neighborhood because you were an officer in the elite Republican Guard, someone to be feared. The next day, you were, like the rest of your neighbors, out of work. Unemployment was an effective equalizer. After the U.S. invasion, it became the country's school uniform, hiding former titles, income levels, tribal affiliations, and religion. A poor Shiite Muslim living in a slum was no better off than a Sunni Muslim soldier who had no money to feed his kids. By the same token, that poor Shiite's religion did not matter to the well-paying foreign companies that flooded into Iraq after the war. It had mattered under Saddam, a Sunni, who oppressed the country's majority Shiite populace. No matter what their loyalties before the war, our staff reflected a rather optimistic view of the American occupation and of Iraq without Saddam. They had jobs. *The Washington Post* was the American Dream.

Little Naseer, a spindly man barely five feet tall, was the smallest fish in our social pond, both in size, age, and stature. At twenty-four, Little Naseer was the errand boy, the chore boy, the kitchen help who arrived nightly at the door of each correspondent to sputter shyly after a quick knock, "The dinner ready." After we acknowledged him, he responded with a quick, "Hello, thanks," before rushing off in embarrassment. It was an endearing ritual. A few months after I settled into the bureau, I taught Little Naseer how to tell us in proper English that dinner was ready. I coached him for a week before sending him to Rajiv's room. From a short distance down the hallway, I watched him knock on Rajiv's door. "The dinner is ready," he said, carefully, followed by, "You are welcome." There was silence, then Rajiv screamed, "Spin!"—his nickname for me. I had ruined the ritual. Little Naseer and I bolted off together, Naseer grinning widely.

Little Naseer left school in the sixth grade because he could not afford the bribes the teachers demanded, still a widespread practice in Iraqi schools that reaches up to the university level, where students can buy better grades and second chances to pass their examinations. Teachers demanded the bribes to supplement their meager salaries. Although the new Iraqi government pays better, teachers still accept bribes. So does the trash collector. People who do not pay up don't get their garbage picked up, or worse, they get trash dumped in their neighborhood from someone who has paid. Every facet of Iraqi society can be maneuvered easily with a bribe, a practice Saddam openly endorsed during the 1990s. In TV spots, he encouraged his citizens to give a "gift" to a government employee who helped process paperwork. He acknowledged that these employees were struggling to make it on the pittance the government paid them. According to Saddam, the gifts were a way for Iraqis to help one another during the UN-enforced sanctions.

After he left school, Little Naseer spent three years in the Iraqi army, mandatory service that he could not escape unless he had enough money to cover the bribe, which, of course, he did not. He starved on meager military rations and spent most of his time at a base isolated and crying. When he got out, he worked in a laundry shop, sweating the long hours and dirty, suffocating work for $20 to $25 a month. After the war, his uncle Karim told him that a newspaper needed a handyman.

Karim was already working for *The Washington Post* as a driver. Rajiv hired Little Naseer the next day for about $100 a month.

Little Naseer started at the *Post* as a kitchen assistant to Muhnthir, a man whose ego surpassed his cooking skills, even though he was widely considered one of the best chefs in Baghdad. Naseer was Muhnthir's lackey. While Muhnthir smoked cigarettes and hung out with the drivers, Naseer chopped the vegetables and stirred the sauce over the hot stove in a kitchen where the temperature climbed past 100 degrees in the summer. Little Naseer washed the pots and pans and, after dinner, cleared the table and did the dishes. He never complained. A guard once ordered Little Naseer off the bare, twin mattress where he slept, threatening to sodomize him if he did not comply. It was an empty threat, but Little Naseer moved anyway to allow the guard a place to sleep. The next day Little Naseer demanded an apology, but it did not get him far. The guard denied the incident, although everyone knew that Little Naseer would not lie. A man who showed up for work four hours early every day to help out, a man who did more than he was asked, a man who studied English late into the night so that he could do his job better was someone who could be trusted. The guard, on the other hand, had been caught stealing alcohol a few times.

Naseer said his life changed after the U.S. invasion. "I have a free life now," he told me. "If the *Post* closes its office here, I can buy a taxi and work. Under Saddam, I could not do this because in any moment, he would call us in to go fight someone." He spoke with the same commitment that I heard constantly from the other members of our staff, a loyalty to defend the newspaper and its reporters, and really, to defend their piece of the American Dream as they saw it. "I am ready to sacrifice myself for this office," Naseer said. "If the insurgents attacked the office, I would go with the guards and defend it." I have no doubt that he would.

Most of our staff told no one except their closest relatives where they worked. It is just too dangerous. Iraqis who work for Americans are at the top of the insurgents' long list of infidels. U.S. soldiers are definitely infidels. Same goes for U.S. reporters, citizens, and contractors. Iraqis engaged in the political process or postwar government are infidels. Iraqi police and soldiers are infidels for defending it. Law-abiding citizens are infidels because whose laws are they obeying? If someone blames the insurgents for the violence in Iraq, he is an honest infidel but he is still an infidel. That is the minefield in which our staff travels daily from work to home and home to work. In this respect, life is not so different without Saddam. Iraqis still fear their friends and neighbors. Even a family member cannot always be trusted because the thing they fear now is not one man but any man.

When our driver Falah first began working for the *Post*, he told his neighbors about his job. After all, they saw him coming and going at relatively the same time every day after the war, even though there was not an Iraqi air force to which Falah had to report. Falah is a sincere man and a devout Muslim. He used to run an auto shop on the side to supplement his military salary. Colleagues urged him to accept the bribes that came with servicing military vehicles, but he refused. It would be *haram*, he told me, the Arabic word for an unforgivable sin. No good would come to a man who accepted a bribe. He approached his job at the *Post* with the same integrity. It bothers him that he has to lie to people now about where he works. I know it without even asking him. Falah is not a man who lies. But he has no choice. Insurgents live in his Baghdad neighborhood—bad guys with ties to more bad guys in Fallujah. He told his neighbors that he quit his job. They didn't believe him so he started to hang around his house in the morning like a man who had no particular place to go. He hated that, too—the ruse that kept him from his job. Only his wife, three children, and mother know he still has his job for the *Post*. Every morning when he heads off to work, Falah's family is never sure if he will come back.

Falah is proud of his job at the *Post* but, more important, he is proud of his ability to provide for his family. The $1,450 monthly salary he receives from the *Post* far exceeds the $13 a month he earned as a lieutenant colonel in the air force after receiving a bachelor's degree in military science. In June 2003, Abu Saif had told him that the *Post* needed a driver for a day to go with a reporter to Karbala. The two men are related by marriage. Abu Saif's wife is an aunt of Falah's wife, though the two women are not even a decade apart in age. Falah accepted the trip to Karbala, happy for the $50 day rate he would be paid. Rajiv liked him so much that he hired him full-time. Falah had the two necessary stamps of approval for any new hire at the *Post* Baghdad bureau: one from Rajiv and one from Abu Saif, Rajiv's chief fixer and adviser for the eighteen months he ran the bureau.

It took me months to figure out the confusing connections that brought each member of our staff to the office, the tangle of relations between this one and that one. Abu Saif, a former Iraqi Airways pilot, knew Naseer 1, a former minder for Saddam who worked as a translator for the *Post* after the war. Naseer 1 recommended Abu Saif for a job as a fixer. This word *fixer* is a designation that foreign correspondents give to people who fix appointments and fix problems. They are the essential part of any reporting assignment. Without fixers, it would be difficult, if not impossible, to navigate a foreign country. They are like Moroccan guides in Tangier who follow strangers off the boat and pester them until they give up and agree to be led around the port city for a sum. The guides know where to get the best kabob, the cheapest place to buy leather, and the history behind the cityscape. You could wander around yourself for free, but you'd be doing it blindly. If you got into a tangle, who would get you out? The fixer, of course. This is what fixers do, and Abu Saif was the ultimate fixer, a self-professed scoundrel who thought all of life's problems could be solved with a simple bribe. In fact, Abu Saif was his own best salesman, but he always came through. "I know my people," Abu Saif loved to say when explaining why his advice was worth taking, why we were wrong and he was right.

Abu Saif's vision of America was frozen in the year 1975 when, at eighteen, he arrived for aviation school in Tulsa,

Oklahoma. From Abu Saif's tale of life in America, sometimes stretched just a little bit to solicit backslaps, a picture of the protagonist emerges: Abu Saif was a full-fledged, smooth-talking gigolo. His favorite expression was, "If you're going to get raped, you might as well enjoy it." This became his mantra for postwar Iraq under the American occupation.

Iraqi Airways stopped flying for a year and a half after the war. When they resumed, however, the pay was dismal compared to the nearly $2,000 monthly salary Abu Saif made at the *Post*, which also employed his son as a driver. And while Abu Saif could have gone back to the skies, he would have gone back to an airline that was bankrupt and still unable to fly internationally.

When first offered a job at the *Post*, Abu Saif worried that he wasn't suited for life as a journalist, but on the streets of Baghdad, dodging bullets and car bombs in pursuit of a story, Abu Saif remembered how Iraqi Airways had trained him to talk and deal with hijackers. He was soon attracted to the most dangerous assignments. "I became the best one in this," he bragged. "I can go out to these areas and return back alive."

One of the most remarkable things about our staff in Baghdad was their fierce loyalty—not only to the *Post* but to the story of Iraq. They adopted our "mission" to find the truth. In April 2003, Abu Saif's first reporting assignment was to the Baghdad Fair where Saddam hid rice, sugar, tea, and cooking oil. The looters had discovered the hidden bounty, and hundreds of them entered the grounds and started taking everything. It was a dangerous mission for Abu Saif and Rajiv, and because there were no police, no law, just a crowd of looters, Abu Saif simultaneously had to translate for and protect Rajiv. From that moment, Abu Saif felt an unflinching responsibility. "It was an honor to share these moments with great reporters writing our history," he later reflected. "I also had to stick with them to be sure that I will have my eyes on them to protect them from anything that could harm them."

All of our staff put themselves at such risks. They are baptized quickly into our head-toward-the-hurricane profession;

only the hurricane is war, making landfall in their country among their friends and their family. The drivers idle at the entrances of targeted buildings, waiting for correspondents to come running out. They drive us into chaos, to scenes of car bombings where subsequent bombs are sometimes detonated after the blast. They are our protectors and our heroes.

Falah was the one who drove Rajiv to the Baghdad Hotel on October 12, 2003, so Rajiv could interview one of the members of Iraq's Governing Council, the transitional body established under the CPA. The council had set up its headquarters in Baghdad. U.S.-hired security contractors from DynCorp had put protective covering on the windows a few days earlier to protect the building from bomb blasts, a standard precaution taken after the bombing of the UN headquarters. Falah was about 100 meters from the hotel when a car bomb exploded. Falah reached up. His head was bleeding from a piece of metal shrapnel that rocketed from the blast—tiny shots of deadly splinters showering anyone in their path. Falah ran toward the building, pushing past people to find Rajiv. He begged a security guard to help. The man ordered Falah away from the carnage and debris. Meanwhile, inside the building, Rajiv was in a panic. His back had been to a window when the bomb went off, sending him and the man he was interviewing to the floor. Blown by the blast, the window broke in large pieces but did not shatter, saving Rajiv's life. After the explosion, security guards raced into the room and pounced on Rajiv and the council member to protect them if another bomb went off. When it was clear, they got up and made their way to a hallway. Rajiv shouted for Falah through his two-way radio. Unable to reach him, Rajiv switched frequencies and began alerting other reporters who used the radio network to look for Falah. Against the advice of the security guards, Rajiv raced down the stairs to the lobby where the wounded were being treated. Eight people died in the blast. Rajiv picked his way through body parts and twisted metal. He could hear gunfire outside the hotel. He saw another reporter he knew across the barricaded entrance and shouted to find out if Falah was okay. Rajiv was relieved to learn that Falah only had a cut on his forehead, but it would be another twenty-five minutes before the two were able to reunite, to clasp hands in shared survival.

Each day with our staff felt like shared survival. I worried about their safety when they went home at night, imagining the cat-and-mouse games they played with the insurgents to avoid being killed. I worried about the double lives they had to lead, the secrets they kept from their closest friends. It is one thing to face death openly. It is another altogether to face it alone. I became the sister in whom they could confide. I became the daughter they could protect. I became the friend they could trust. And they became my family, too, instant and immediate, able to understand what daily existence in a war zone meant.

Huda was the lone female translator in our office when I came to Iraq in May. She is a year older than me, wise, strong, and nothing that I foolishly and ignorantly imagined a devout Muslim woman would be. At the time, she wore her hair tightly concealed behind beautiful silk scarves, accenting a silk-skinned cherub face. Huda and I became fast friends. Her presence helped soften the office and keep the machismo in check. Huda also had access to parts of Iraqi society that were more difficult for a male translator to reach. The women of a house were more likely to invite me in and talk openly about their lives without the presence of a male. And tucked into our scarves, Huda and I—at least in the beginning—could wander the streets together, shopping while whispering our English to each other. Our hushed conversation in the presence of male shopkeepers seemed perfectly respectable and natural.

At the same time, few men would turn the bullish Huda down when she demanded an answer to her question. She had sharp elbows and could push herself into any situation. She was my closest friend, a sister to me and to Jenny because with twins, you marry in. I needed Jenny to know my new Iraqi family as well as I did. I needed them to know her. It helped to bridge the two halves of my life. One by one, I brought our Iraqi staff into my room in Baghdad to see my wall of photos, a bulletin board tacked with pictures of my family and friends back home. "These are my grandmothers," I told Omar, our office manager, the day he came to see the wall. "I miss them so much." Omar, who was twenty-six at the time, looked at me kindly and declared, "I'll be your grandmother in Iraq."

I was devastated when Huda left the *Post* in July to work for Knight Ridder, another American news organization in Iraq, but I supported her move to a better position. She would be working for one of my favorite correspondents in Iraq, Knight Ridder's bureau chief, Hannah Allam. Hannah and I bumped into each other for the first time in June at Abu Ghraib prison. She was a former *Washington Post* intern who had been a roommate of one of my closest friends at the *Post*, Jamie Stockwell. I had not been around the globe, reporting from the world's critical places, as so many of the foreign correspondents in Iraq had. These reporters knew one another from Afghanistan, Africa, Russia, the Balkans. Hannah was my lone connection to a familiar place and to shared acquaintances. Even after Huda left for Knight Ridder, the three of us continued to hang out, and I relied on their companionship even when we went weeks without seeing one another. I made certain not to talk too much to Huda about her replacement, Luma, who swore off scarves and wrote love poems to the American soldiers she met. To Luma, I was more of a surrogate older sister, a sister she never had. Though her English was terrible, Luma was a bouquet of daisies, a beautiful, vivacious, soulful woman who breathed life into the office. She fought with her fellow twentysomething translators, Omar and Bassam. We often had to drag her out of her musical daze—headphones tuned to the latest American hit CD single—to translate a breaking news report. But she was a quick study, ambitious and fearless. She loved being around U.S. soldiers. She saw them as her ticket to a better life—a ticket to America with her young daughter, whom she was raising with her mother after catching the girl's father cheating. Luma left her husband on the spot, even though she was pregnant, even though being a divorced woman in Baghdad made her a social misfit, an outcast. Luma lived by her own code.

Omar told Luma she had to be at work by 9 every morning and could not be late. Her first day of work, the streets of Baghdad were clogged with some of the worst traffic congestion the Iraqi capital had experienced. Omar was stuck in that traffic when he looked over and spotted Luma driving her flashy BMW. It was 8:45 A.M., and the cars were not budging. The next time he looked over, he saw that Luma had driven her car up on the sidewalk. She got to the end, where there was a bit of a drop-off. Seeing this damsel in distress, a half dozen men jumped out of their cars, grabbed some bricks, and built a ramp so that she could drive her car back into traffic. When Omar finally got to the office, Luma was already there. He asked why she had driven on the sidewalk. She said, "Well, you told me I couldn't be late."

Our staff, their stories of suffering and survival, the hopeful ways they simply carried on, inspired me. They were Iraq—not just representations of it, but the real thing, the people whose fractured lives, stitched together, were the battleground of their country. As I write, it is easier to describe a place, a rock, a mountain, an ocean. People are far more complex. How do you capture the essence of a person, a being, in a single word? You can humanize a landscape but how do you make a human being human? As journalists, we have the luxury of looking at people as they are, in front of us, scarred, broken, whole, good, bad. I felt like I knew Iraq through our staff. They offered me a glass box in which I could observe the country, its traditions, its religion, its sins of the past, and its hopes for the future. The U.S. soldiers generally did not have the same opportunity to interact with ordinary Iraqis, people who were not trying to kill them. They mostly communicated through the fence with a rifle. I often wondered what a difference it would have made in the relationship between the U.S. military and Iraqi civilians if the soldiers had known the Iraq I knew—through our staff, through the people I met on the streets. The soldiers and the civilians truly do not trust one another. In war, I understand the need to disconnect from the human face of the enemy. But what happens when you disconnect from the human face of the person you are trying to protect? Everyone becomes the enemy, and winning peace becomes impossible.

Two weeks after I got to Baghdad, Omar 2 was behind the wheel of the armored car, weaving in and out of Baghdad traffic. We were racing to get to Camp Victory, the Army base near Baghdad International Airport, so I could interview an Army general about detainees. We flew down the road at nearly 100 miles per hour. This stretch of pavement from Baghdad to the airport was the most dangerous in Iraq. Insurgents fired on it frequently. Omar weaved between the potholes of previous bomb blasts. Suddenly, a U.S. military convoy roared past, a column of Humvees with gunners positioned in their turrets, 50-caliber weapons sweeping across the roadway. Omar braked and pulled to the right of the convoy. He cut our speed to 30 miles per hour and flipped on the hazards. Behind the wheel of the car, Omar was just another Iraqi face, a potential suicide bomber, the enemy. In the split second it would take to spook one of the gunners, Omar would have no chance to explain that he supported the U.S. occupation, that he wanted the soldiers to stay to keep peace and prevent civil war.

Omar 2 was a lieutenant colonel in the Iraqi air force. He flew fighter jets until the government forced him to retire in 2000, at age thirty-two, because he had too many relatives living outside of Iraq. This made him a security risk, according to the government. After his mandatory retirement from the air force, Omar 2 opened a shop in Baghdad selling purses and women's shoes. He also began to plot an escape from Iraq. Then came September 11, 2001. After the terrorist attacks on America, "the Iraqis and Arabs in general weren't welcomed anywhere in foreign countries," Omar 2 discovered. He had no choice but to stay in Iraq. After the U.S.-led war in 2003, Omar 2 showed up at the Hamra Hotel in Baghdad, which was filled with foreign journalists, many of them freelancers or reporters from smaller news organizations. Rajiv, who had set up the *Post* bureau in the Hamra when he arrived in Baghdad a few weeks after the start of the invasion, asked the receptionist for a driver, and Omar 2 found himself an employee of *The Washington Post*. More than two years later, Omar 2's parents and siblings still think he is a driver for freelance journalists, picking up work when he can. His wife is the only one who knows he works for the *Post*.

Before the war, none of the Iraqis on our staff had much experience with journalists, certainly not foreign journalists. Under Saddam, Iraqis would be punished for talking to foreigners, and the foreign press was carefully monitored. Journalists allowed into the country were assigned minders who controlled who they could interview. The fall of Baghdad brought most average Iraqis in contact with outsiders for the first time in their lives. Omar the office manager was twenty-five when Baghdad fell. Although he had a degree in English literature from a private college in Baghdad, after graduating in 2002 he had no opportunity to speak the language that he studied. He applied to graduate school, hoping to earn a master's degree in English, but he was rejected. His family name was blacklisted under Saddam, who refused even to allow the surname to be printed on their passports. Instead, they were forced to use their tribal affiliation, an insult to a family of intellectual elite: Omar's father is a well-known writer in Iraq, and his uncle was an exiled politician who fled the country in 1979. Omar's father was also in exile for several decades, returning eventually to marry a woman of Kurdish descent, who gave Omar his long, black eyelashes, sharp nose, and pale skin. Under Saddam, the telephones of his family clan were bugged and their houses under constant surveillance. A few months before the war in 2003, Omar's father asked him to take a pile of prohibited newspapers from the house and burn or dump them. The family had been tipped off that some of Saddam's intelligence officers were coming to raid the house.

Unable to attend graduate school, Omar had to wait for his mandatory eighteen-month military service to begin on January 2, 2003. He paid $1,000 to avoid having to go to camp to train, a legal way for Iraq's economic elite to avoid military service. Young men who paid the fee were only obligated to serve for three months, a duty called "flag service" to pay respect to the flag. Omar paid even more in bribes, but his paperwork was delayed for three months. In the interim, he was stationed in three different places, leaving his house in Baghdad at 2:30 every morning to arrive in time for roll call and returning at 8 P.M. In March 2003, as war with the United States became more certain, Omar was sent north to a camp in a Kurdish village the Iraqi Army seized in 1982. The village of Qara-Hnjeer, which the military renamed Rabie, was seven miles from Kirkuk in northern Iraq. In the days leading up to the war, Iraqi soldiers who tried to surrender to the Kurdish civilian population were shot by their Iraqi comrades. Omar did not have to report every day; he went once a week to pay the bribe. According to Iraqi law, once war started, Omar could no longer bribe his way out of military service. Instead, he would have to stay and fight. His family refused to allow him to serve in the military. He and his two brothers were taught that it was a shame to fight or struggle for Saddam. His father told him, "We are writers, artists, doctors, engineers, and politicians. But never hypocrites."

On March 14, 2003, Omar reported to the Iraqi military base in the north. He took $1,500 with him and paid $1,000 to a bank in Kirkuk. He had done his three months, and now he wanted out. He took the paperwork to the base and asked a commander to hasten the process so he could go back to Baghdad the same day. At this point, Omar knew his American "brothers" were coming any minute. The commander ordered him to stay until the next morning. He spent the night wide awake. The next morning he again asked the commander to approve his papers. The commander told him that he did not have the proper stamp. The commander forced Omar to spend another night in the base. Again, he did not sleep. On the morning of March 16, the commander told Omar that all soldiers would have to stay in the bases to prepare to fight. He would not be allowed to leave. Omar offered to give the commander his remaining $500. The commander laughed: "What should I do with your $500? We are going to die anyway."

Omar decided to end what he called "this stupid play." He ate and drank nothing in the three nights and four days he spent at the base. He had not gone to the bathroom or slept.

The next morning he left the base at 6:30 A.M. and headed to Baghdad, somehow managing to pass undetected through the checkpoints that had been set up to arrest soldiers who were deserting. He made it back to Baghdad safely, and on March 19, President Bush declared that the war in Iraq had started. U.S. fighter planes began dropping bombs on the capital city.

Omar spent the days during the war in his house. He could not even stand at the door for fear that Saddam's informers would hand him over to police. The sentence for desertion was execution in front of a soldier's house. At night, he drove through the streets of Baghdad to see where the bombs landed and to see the destruction. He returned home and stayed on the roof to watch the exchange of fire between the Iraqis and the U.S. forces.

After Baghdad fell, Omar heard rumors that journalists in the Palestine and Sheraton hotels were allowing Iraqis to use their satellite telephones to make contact with the outside world, something most citizens had been unable to do for more than a decade; under Saddam, satellite telephones were banned. On one of his first assignments as a translator for the *Post*, Abu Saif accompanied reporter Peter Finn to Abu Ghraib prison, where a mass grave had been unearthed: the victims had been killed for using satellite telephones during the war.

On April 17, 2003, Omar went to the Palestine to try to call his relatives in London to tell them his family had survived the war, but he could not find a phone. As he was leaving, he saw a reporter trying to interview Iraqi citizens. She didn't speak Arabic, and the citizens didn't speak English well enough to communicate. Omar volunteered to translate. He was thrilled to be speaking to a foreigner and practicing the language he had studied. He translated for more than an hour and a half. The sun was going down, and Omar did not want to be caught out past the curfew imposed by the U.S. military. He told the reporter he needed to leave. She told him to hang on for a minute and dashed off to find a colleague. She came back a few minutes later with Rajiv. He asked Omar if he was interested in working for *The Washington Post*.

"No, thanks. I just came here to make a phone call."

"If you change your mind, come to the Hamra Hotel tomorrow at 9 A.M. I am Rajiv Chandrasekaran, the bureau chief."

Omar went back home to talk about the offer with his two brothers and his father, who was thrilled. He always wanted his middle son to be a journalist. The next day Omar showed up at the Hamra and was off to Saddam's hometown of Tikrit with Rajiv. Two years later, Omar made another journey, this one on a tourist ferry boat that churned past Ellis Island on its way to the Statue of Liberty. Omar stood riveted at the boat's edge, ignoring the splashes of water from the Hudson River. He had dreamed of this moment his whole life. He wanted to touch her. He had to touch her. As young American teenagers wrestled on the boat deck, and a group of school kids dug into their lunches, Omar did not move. The day before his brother had telephoned from Baghdad. The insurgents in their neighborhood were talking, speculating that Omar was in the United States. Only traitors, spies, and infidels who worked for Americans went to the United States. The insurgents' threat was unspoken but Omar and his family knew what would happen if they found out he was working with Americans—Americans who had brought him to the United States for a visit. He and his family were in grave danger. But Omar resisted their requests that he try to stay in the United States or that he quit his job. "If I stop working, I'll die," he told me repeatedly. "If I continue, I might be killed, but there is a chance I'll live. I would like to die and leave something behind me for people to remember me by. I don't want to be someone who came to this life and left and no one noticed."

✦ ✦ ✦

"Please, Brother," I type to Omar. "Your wife is stranded. Where is the driver?"

After my sister had been in Iraq for several months, such moments no longer seemed surreal: my sister—somewhere in Iraq, cell phone service cut off and unable to reach her driver—

calls me in the United States on a satellite phone and tells me to email Omar to send a driver. I email Omar, but hear nothing. Jackie calls again. "Please get hold of him," she pleads. "I'm a sitting duck out here." I can tell she is nervous, and now I'm edgy, too. Again and again I email Omar, the translator who has, in jest, taken my sister as his fourth wife. That makes me his sister-in-law, an increasingly angry sister-in law. In my last email, I get right to the point: "Send someone to get her now BEFORE SHE IS KILLED." Finally, he responds, "Don't worry, Sister. Driver on the way."

My sister and I have always shared our closest friends. Even my husband knew when he married me that he was, in some way, marrying my sister, too. I loved him for being the kind of man who respected and understood the nature of twins. "A backup," he told me, "just in case something happens to you." The closer my sister grew to her new family in Iraq, the women and men who worked with her and protected her, the more she drew me in, too.

Each night my two-year-old son ended his prayers with blessings for the staff: "Keep Abu Saif, Omar, and Bassam safe in Iraq," he said solemnly. The names of these men were his first Arab words. When we hooked up a web camera, he was able to talk to them, waving hello, showing them his toys. In return, they walked their computer around the rooms in their Baghdad office, the house where my sister lived and worked, to show him their space. My son thought they lived in my computer. When asked where Iraq was, he pointed to my iBook.

On Christmas, Jackie sent us a video of their celebration in Baghdad—a silent video taken on her digital camera. She was the star of the movie, surrounded by Iraqi men, her gold Christmas jewels hanging from her ears and neck, the staff dancing around her. I thought of the wedding celebration for our friends Sofia and Frank. Sofia's family is from Iran, and their reception was attended by scores of young Iranian cousins who filled the dance floor, their bodies waving in beat to the Persian music. My husband and I felt like the proverbial bulls in the china shop, so we sat and watched, seduced by the beauty of their motion, their long brown arms reaching into the air, their fingers tickling the air like harp strings.

I watched my sister circle the room with Omar, Bassam, and the others, the mortars and bullets forgotten. She had never looked so full of life. I couldn't hear the music, but I felt it, watching from the sidelines, yearning to join the dance.

CHAPTER 4

Abu Ghraib was Saddam's house of torture, a horrific place that swallowed people into the dark belly of a whale, gone without a trace. Those fortunate enough to leave during his three decades of reign were often spit out with missing tongues and ears. Saddam's henchmen reportedly executed thousands of people at the 280-acre prison. After the U.S. invasion, former prisoners told stories of the horrors inflicted on them at Abu Ghraib, which had held common criminals, political dissidents, foreign fighters, and people simply swept up in the fury of the regime's paranoia. Prisoners, whose numbers topped 10,000 at its peak, described seeing guards beat inmates to death with sticks and cables and then leave the rotting bodies for dogs to eat. Others were executed by hanging, electrocution, or a giant paperlike shredder that ripped its victims' bodies apart.

The prison was empty by the time the U.S. military rolled through in spring 2003. Saddam had released the prisoners who were still alive right before the invasion in a goodwill gesture supposed to galvanize support in the country. Prisoners set fires as they left, and looters hauled off furniture and supplies. After Saddam was deposed, the U.S. military used the prison to hold security detainees whom the Americans accused of taking part in insurgent attacks, hiding weapons, running insurgent cells, or funding the insurgency. Soldiers who guarded the prison during the fall of 2003 said it was a lousy assignment. The prison was constantly being mortared, and the soldiers lived in stark conditions in the dirty cells. They had no hot showers or hot meals. The detainees, we later learned, had it much worse.

The world turned its attention on Abu Ghraib in April 2003

when CBS broke the story that U.S. soldiers had abused and sexually humiliated detainees in their custody. By the time the public and the media became aware of the abuse, the U.S. military already had begun implementing new operating procedures in response to the scandal, which prison commanders in Iraq knew about months earlier. In response to the public outcry, the military opened the prison to the media, offering tours of the tented camps it was building to house the detainees.

The Army units that had been at the prison when the abuse occurred in October and November 2003 had already left Iraq by the time I got there in May, six months later. There wasn't really much to dig up at the prison at that point, but I was interested in seeing the complex for myself, at the very least to provide context for the stories I would write about new prison conditions and the pending legal proceedings.

I made my first trip to Abu Ghraib a few days after Jeremy Sivits's court-martial. The Army made special bus runs between the Green Zone and the prison, about 20 miles west of Baghdad, to handle all of the journalists who wanted a tour, including hundreds of Iraqi journalists, who remembered Abu Ghraib as one of the darkest symbols of terror under Saddam. As our converted tourist bus rolled down the highway, flanked by military vehicles, the mood reminded me of the first time I rode a Metro train in Washington a few days after the September 11 terrorist attack on the Pentagon. As the train passed the Pentagon, passengers silently strained to see the blackened, crushed wall of the building. No one spoke. As we rolled up to the cement wall of the prison, built by Western contractors in the 1960s, the Iraqi journalists sat similarly quiet. From the outside, Abu Ghraib looked like a regular maximum penitentiary, isolated by dusty fields and groves of palm trees.

Army Lt. Col. Barry Johnson, a slim, athletic man, was the spokesman for Maj. Gen. Geoffrey D. Miller, commander of detention operations in Iraq from March 2003 to February 2004. Miller had asked Johnson to accompany him to Iraq. The two had worked together at the U.S. intelligence-gathering prison camp in Guantanamo Bay, Cuba, a post Miller commanded from fall 2002 until the Pentagon sent him to Iraq to run the prison operations there.

I liked Johnson immediately. He didn't try to spin me, a journalist term for a public relations professional who tries to steer a reporter in a particular direction. Nor did he offer up a party line. He was frank about the abuses that had taken place at Abu Ghraib and about the challenges that remained. He was a diplomat for Miller, careful not to criticize his demanding boss, who did not like the media and seemed uncomfortable in their presence. In May 2004, Abu Ghraib was a prison under siege by the media, and Miller was the levee holding back the storm of reporters searching for accountability and the big scoop.

In May, during my first trip to Abu Ghraib, most of the detainees were housed in large tents encircled with barbed wire. They wore civilian clothes or towels wrapped around their waists. The camps smelled like a giant outdoor toilet, and trash piled against some of the fences. The ground was thick with mud from leaking shower stalls. As our press pack followed Miller through the camp, detainees made hand signals and called out in Arabic to the Iraqi press, proclaiming their innocence and asking when they were getting out.

We wore our flak jackets and helmets throughout the tour because insurgents frequently pounded the prison with mortars. In one attack in April 2004, twenty-two Iraqi detainees died as a barrage of rockets rained down on the open-air prison. By that time, all of the detainees had been moved from the prison's hard site, the cellblocks where the prison abuse had occurred. More than ninety detainees were injured in the attack, prompting the Army to place concrete bunkers throughout the camp for detainees to take cover in case of future attacks.

Miller dropped one tidbit of news in a press conference that followed the tour, telling us that the Army planned to close Abu Ghraib and relocate detainees to another detention facility in southern Iraq called Camp Bucca. (That plan was scrapped in 2005, as the detention population soared to nearly 10,000, requiring the military to keep Abu Ghraib open to hold the large number of suspected insurgents.) I was the only American journalist at the press conference—Hannah Allam had gone off to interview family members visiting detainees, and the Iraqi journalists seemed interested in other facets of the story, including prisoner allegations they heard while walking through the camps that the prisoners were forced to drink dirty water. Miller told them that the detainees and their military guards drank from the same water source, which was purified. The Iraqi press seemed skeptical. If Abu Ghraib was really going to be shut down, I needed to write a story about Camp Bucca. So before I left, I made arrangements with Johnson to take a trip down there the next time Gen. Miller planned a visit.

A week later, I hopped on a C-130 and flew with Miller and Johnson to the airport in Basra, which was controlled by British troops. We transferred to a Chinook transport helicopter for the hot, dusty ride over the port of Um Qasr to Bucca. I baked in the back of the helicopter, sweat wetting my linen shirt under my flak jacket, even though the crew left the back end of the helicopter open to let in a breeze. I willed myself not to throw up in front of Miller and his beefy gun-toting personnel protection detail. (All of the generals in Iraq had personal bodyguards, even if they did not want them. Losing a general to insurgents would be a huge moral victory for the bad guys.) It was already more than 120 degrees outside the helicopter, and we were flying into the middle of the desert, where miles of sand isolated Camp Bucca, built to house Iraqi prisoners of war following the U.S. invasion. The camp was named for Ron Bucca, a New York City firefighter who died in the September 11 terrorist attacks.

Camp Bucca looked a lot like Abu Ghraib, with white tents pitched for the detainees, who lived within circles of barbed wire. Miller let me tag along as he inspected the camp, but he made sure to lower his voice when he wanted to talk privately with the commanders of the facility. Miller was in cheerleader mode. He wanted to put an honorable stamp on military operations, even though, back in Washington, he was smack in the middle of implementing interrogation techniques at Guantanamo and in Iraq. The Pentagon had dispatched Miller to Iraq in September 2003 to assess the military's detention and interrogation operations there. Based on his visit, he made a number of recommendations, most rooted in practices at Guantanamo, including the idea that military police and interrogators should work closely together. The soldiers charged in the abuse scandal at Abu Ghraib said they were acting on orders from military interrogators to toughen up prisoners, which put Miller in the middle of the muck. Miller was not eager to talk to me about his role in setting conditions at Abu Ghraib, and I did not push him on that initial visit to Bucca. He was not going to blab anything to a reporter he did not know or trust. The key to good beat reporting—and I considered the Abu Ghraib story my beat—is to cull sources. I would write a few softball stories, colorful features on the soldiers who guarded the prisoners, and hopefully Miller would start to open up to me, leading to better access and more hard-charging stories. And really these features were important stories, too. Despite the scandal, a lot of soldiers in Iraq *were* trying to do the right thing. Those guarding the detainees by the summer of 2004 were being maligned along with the seven soldiers charged with abuse. It was only fair to write about their struggle to maintain order in the camps under the stain of the abuse scandal, which, without question, had been a giant can of lighter fluid dumped on the hot coals of an angry insurgency.

At Bucca, I tried mostly to stay out of Miller's way and instead hung out with Johnson. If I wasn't in with the general's press guy, I reasoned, I wasn't going to be in with the general. Between interviews with guards and other commanders at Bucca, I eagerly anticipated mealtime at the mess hall: the soldiers called it the "DIFAC," short for dining facility. Almost all of the DIFACs in Iraq have salad bars, with honest-to-goodness American iceberg lettuce, a rare treat for a vegetarian journalist forced to dine on heavy, local Iraqi fare in the Red Zone. I told Johnson that I would cover any story he wanted me to in exchange for iceberg salad. At night, when Miller went back to tour the detention camp without me, I didn't argue. I retreated to my empty tent on the far side of the camp to jot some notes. Johnson was in an empty tent next to mine. Before crawling onto my cot, I hung my shoes by their laces from a rope so the desert spiders would not crawl in while I slept. I spent a restless night in the heat, waiting for the sun to come up and replace the red desert moon. When we left the next day to return to Baghdad, I had a decent story about the camp but no breaking news. After the Bucca piece appeared in the paper, Johnson called to tell me that Gen. Miller was pleased with my reporting. My good behavior had paid off. Now it was time to make my move. I asked Johnson if I could spend the night at Abu Ghraib later that week. The military had been releasing hundreds of detainees several times a week for the past month. I had already covered one of these events from outside the prison. Typically, the military announced a release, and the press corps would drive from Baghdad to the gates of the prison to interview family members who waited for the buses carrying their loved ones and recovering insurgents back to their hometowns. It was hard for the family members to fathom that anyone actually got out of Abu Ghraib, which had been rare under Saddam. Because we could not talk to the detainees on organized prison tours, this was our chance to ask them about alleged abuses. Over time, I realized that some of the detainees were simply making up fantastical stories that did not pan out. I hardly ever found a detainee who ever admitted to being guilty. But these interviews provided the only outlet we really had to talk to accused insurgents and their families and balance those stories with what the military was telling us about life in the detention camps.

After Nick Berg was kidnapped and killed in May, journalists were more careful about covering the detention releases, which occurred outside the wire, on an open stretch of highway between Baghdad and volatile Fallujah. In fact, we were more careful about everything, wary of going places where we would be identified easily as foreigners, wary of lingering too long in interviews on the street, wary of being caught by insurgents on highways. We were easy targets, all congregating in a single spot on this spurt of dangerous roadway. We could easily be followed back to Baghdad, shot at or kidnapped. Dan Williams, the *Post*'s Rome correspondent who was doing a rotation in Iraq when I arrived in May, had a terrifying encounter on this highway in early June. He and our driver Faiah were coming back to Baghdad from a reporting trip to Fallujah when they were ambushed by gunmen. Falah's steady hand at the wheel of the armored SUV kept them alive, as the gunmen raked the car with bullets, blew out the tires, and left Falah and Dan for dead after the car spun out near a patch of tall reeds. The gunmen sped off, seemingly satisfied that they got their targets. Falah drove the crippled car with Dan in it to Abu Ghraib prison, where the Army doctors bandaged their cuts and gave them a cot to sleep off their brush with death.

The incident had spooked everyone in the bureau, so when I set off with one of our translators, Bassam, and our driver, Ghazwan, to cover my first detainee release, Muhanned warned me not to get out of the car and wander around. *Of course I'm getting out of the car*, I thought to myself. I did not want to be so cautious that it prevented me from doing what I had been sent to Iraq to do—report. But when we arrived at the release, demonstrators had convened to protest the United States's presence in Iraq. I tucked my headscarf tighter and popped open the door to get out. "Don't worry," I told Bassam. "I won't speak English." Ghazwan jumped out from the driver's seat and hurried over.

"Get back in," he hissed. Bassam and Ghazwan had a bad feeling about the crowd. Although I was wearing a scarf, I was not wearing the *abaya*, the long black cloak that would have better shielded my Western identity. Our female translator Huda was there with Andrea Woodall, the *Post* photographer. Both of them were dressed in *abayas*. Andrea offered to lend me her cloak when she was done, but Huda didn't think it would be a good idea for us to be seen changing in and out of them in public. I sulked in the backseat, drinking a cold soda that Ghazwan had pulled from a cooler. "Don't worry," Huda whispered. "I will take you to the market tomorrow to buy an *abaya*." So I remained in the back of the car, writing down the scene, everything I saw, as Bassam interviewed the demonstrators.

Bassam was still unsteady on his feet, unsure of himself in this situation. He was our youngest translator, just twenty-four in the summer of 2004 and a recent college graduate who had been at the top of his class. He was more sheltered than Omar, whose family was openly persecuted by Saddam. Bassam grew up with a younger sister and doting mother. His family was more traditional than Omar's. Bassam was a dutiful son who did not dream of speaking out against his parents, though, like Omar, he would later end up fighting with his parents about why he felt so committed to his job as a translator, why he would not quit. Omar and Bassam went to college together, and Omar brought Bassam to the *Post*'s Baghdad bureau shortly after the Americans seized Baghdad. At first Rajiv was unsure of Bassam's English skills and was concerned about how timid Bassam seemed, how easily he could be pushed around. He was, in fact, the perfect silent child-citizen of Saddam Hussein's Iraq. Under Saddam, he had no passionate ambitions. His only dream was to establish a translation office in Baghdad near a university or a school. Because neither he nor his parents were members of the Baath Party, Bassam had no chance to work for the Foreign Ministry or any ministry that could capitalize on his English skills. Huda had been locked out of the Foreign Ministry for the same reason, although she had left Iraq for eight years to work as a translator for various private companies in Libya, Tunisia, and the United Arab Emirates. Bassam had no such chance, so working for the *Post* gave him a chance to use his undeveloped English skills.

In the field across from the prison where the demonstrators gathered, Bassam wandered through the crowd, asking the questions I had given him. He came back every fifteen minutes or so to pass on his reports. I followed up with more questions and sent him back out again. It was not an ideal way to cover the story, but it was the best we could do. I would not have imagined that a few months later it would be too dangerous for me to come to this place without a military escort. By August, we would not dream of driving the road to Fallujah. It would have been suicide.

Because of my frustration with this awkward interview system, I cooked up a new plan—to cover the release from inside the prison. No other reporter had done this. It would be a good exclusive. When Johnson called to tell me that the general liked my stories, I knew this was my chance. "So look," I told Johnson, starting my pitch. "I need you to get the general to let me spend the night at Abu Ghraib. I'll be good as gold. I think it's a great story, a great way for the general to show off the prison." Johnson knew there was more in it for me than the general but he went along. "I can ask," he said. He rang back the next day. The general had agreed. Johnson told me to come to Abu Ghraib the next night.

I consulted with Rajiv and Abu Saif about the best way to get there. We decided it would be safer if a driver dropped me off with Andrea, the *Post* photographer. Huda had made good on her promise, and I had an *abaya* for disguise. We determined the best time to go, when no one was likely to be hanging around outside the prison. Dusk was perfect, but if we went any later, the driver who left us there would be caught driving after dark on the highway, dangerous for him. Not wanting to take chances in case we were ambushed, Muhanned decided he would come, too, with an AK-47. We opted against taking one of our armored vehicles because it might attract too much attention. Every detail had to be planned carefully, from the route we took from the Sheraton Hotel to the kind of bag Andrea and I would carry into the prison. We settled on our dirty hotel pillowcases because they looked like flour sacks Iraqi women might have on hand. Abu Saif made sure I knew a few words in Arabic. "Say it like this," he instructed. *Ani Sahafiya.* I repeated after him. *Ani Sahafiya.* I am a journalist.

On Sunday, June 13, 2004, Andrea and I slipped out of the car and walked into Abu Ghraib under a pink sky. Johnson met us at the gate with an amused look at our get-up. We toured the grounds of the prison, brightly illuminated by large spotlights. The detainees who would be released in the morning were separated from the rest of the camp. Relatives and friends shouted at one another through the barbed wire, and soldiers allowed a departing son to say good-bye to his father who would have to remain. The men were handcuffed and led to a small pavilion, where they held hands and talked quietly.

Andrea and I were assigned to share a small, white washed cell in a large warehouse, where hundreds of soldiers stretched on cots for the night, waiting to take detainees back to the various parts of Iraq where they had been arrested. The soldiers played cards and video games and read magazines, while Andrea and I plotted how we would cover the story the next day. The Army had painted over the walls of our cell, but it did not completely hide the stains, blood, sweat, dirt, mud. Saddam crammed as many as sixty-four prisoners into the same space where Andrea and I had two single cots, separated by only an arm's length.

Jenny. Her name often came out of nowhere when I found myself in a nearly unimaginable place. I needed to describe this to her. I needed her to see the colorful murals of Saddam still painted above the cellblocks: Saddam in a white military uniform surrounded by white doves, with the snowcapped mountains of the Kurdish north over his left shoulder; Saddam in dark shades and a white fedora painted on a splashy black and orange background; Saddam in a dark suit, his eyes scratched by vandals.

I took my satellite phone outside and pointed it in a southeastern direction where I could get a signal. I didn't have a compass, so I just kept spinning around, waiting to see a line of bars across the digital display. Bats fluttered in the artificial lights as I talked to Jenny a half-world away. "You'll never guess where I am. Abu Ghraib! The prison. Yes, I'm inside. It's so creepy, Jenny. I have to sleep in a cell. And I'm looking up right now, and there are all these bats, which makes it even more creepy. But I had salad for dinner."

With Jenny, I could be wide-eyed, excited to be in Iraq—sad, scared, elated, real. In the bureau and with my editors, I had an expectation to live up to. The other correspondents were so hardened. They had seen war before. They had seen it many times. They had faced down dictators, guerrilla leaders, and warlords in exotic, far-off places. This—Iraq— was all I had. I could not pretend to be more experienced than I was. But I could at least hide how green I was from them. I didn't need to act like a clown who just joined the circus. No, I saved that for Jenny.

My words gushed out, as they usually did when I talked to her from Iraq. I tried to call her at least once a day when I could get a signal on my cell phone or sat phone. We never talked very long, especially on the sat phone, which cost several dollars a minute. I called to check in, to bring her with me, when I just needed to hear her voice, when I was full of new sights and sounds, so full that I had to empty some of it. I could tell Jenny what it felt like to be at Abu Ghraib. I could tell her the part of the story that could not go in the news articles. I could tell her my story.

Back in my cot in the cell, I could not sleep. I kept imagining the ghosts of the detainees who had died in that room, kept hearing their screams, their voices finally growing hoarse, then fading into the nothingness that had already consumed them.

Andrea and I got up early the next morning to watch the release of about 500 detainees. The prisoners lined up according to the direction they were headed: Tikrit here, Baghdad there. They clutched juice boxes and homemade bags sewn from brown plastic MRE packages. Most professed their innocence when I asked what they had done to be locked up, some of them for more than six months.

Johnson offered to let us watch the buses leave from a guard tower where bored Marine infantrymen complained that they were not seeing any action, not getting to shoot and fight as they had been trained. Instead, they were here for eight-hour stretches watching the horizon, scanning for trouble. They pointed to the spot where Falah and Dan Williams's battered, bullet-ridden *Post* car had sat for a few days until someone from the bureau was able to come get it. We stayed up there for hours, watching the buses roll out, the crowd of nearly 600 waiting family members slowly thinning as the morning went on. Ghazwan and Bassam were outside the prison watching for Andrea and me to come out. I wanted to wait until most of the onlookers had left so we would not attract as much attention.

Andrea decided to follow a bus of released detainees and jumped into a car with an Associated Press photographer and reporter. I called Bassam to let him know I was on my way and asked the Marines in the tower to make sure I made it to my car. I said it with such breeze, as if I were leaving a movie theater in the United States and getting ready to walk across a dark parking lot.

I followed a narrow patch through barbed wire that led from the prison to a small parking lot near the front. Several cars idled in the noon heat. No one seemed to pay much attention to me. I walked along the perimeter of the parking lot and headed to the highway. I could not see Bassam or Ghazwan, but based on our telephone contact, I knew they were waiting in Ghazwan's yellow sedan.

Suddenly, a man ran toward me, grabbed me by the wrist, and began pulling me toward an orange and white car. At first I said in Arabic, "*La. La. Rajan.*" No, no, please. I pointed to the highway, where Bassam and Ghazwan were hidden from view. But he kept pulling me by the wrist. Another man came up behind me and grabbed me around the waist. Someone else grabbed the pillowcase that held my belongings and threw it aside. At first I couldn't fathom what was going on. What was happening to me? Were they trying to kidnap me? They were trying to kidnap me! My heart pounded.

I had avoided watching the video footage of Berg's beheading that played repeatedly on Arab satellite television. I imagined it now anyway. I could not let these men put me in that vehicle.

I was trying to remember how to say "I am press" in Arabic as Abu Saif had instructed. I couldn't find the words. Instead, in a panic, I told them that I was a vegetarian. *Ani Nabatiya! Ani Nabatiya!* I fell to the ground and started kicking them. It did not stop them. They just dragged me on the ground, still trying to pull me by my hand. Someone yanked me up, and the man who first grabbed me ripped off my *abaya*. They saw the blue bullet-proof flak jacket foreigners wore in Iraq. He said, "No Iraqi, no Iraqi." Shit, now they think I'm CIA. So I screamed back, *Washington Post! Washington Post!* Until then, I had tried not to raise my voice. I did not want to attract the crowd of relatives still waiting for the detainees, but our tussle finally drew their attention, and a crowd formed around me. Where was Bassam? Where were the Marines I told to watch me make it to my car? I looked over at the faces in the crowd, and I didn't see a single person who saw me as a human. I tried to plead with a woman standing there, plead with my eyes, and she looked like she wanted to spit on me. I was an American woman, no better than the American soldier in the photographs of the abused detainees who dragged one of their bloodied sons or husbands naked on a leash.

Bombs were going off almost daily. Iraqis were dying. They blamed the Americans. This is not what they had imagined when they imagined democracy. There was no distinction made between the American press and U.S. soldiers and contractors who had promised electricity and had not delivered it. They felt occupied, and I was part of that occupation.

I saw the helicopters blaze in the sky, coming out of the prison, while the Marines followed on foot, pointing their weapons and shouting at the crowd. I didn't hear anything at first but the sound of my own voice, which had grown hoarse from my mantra: *Washington Post! Washington Post!*

Once the men who grabbed me saw the Marines, they let go, and everyone scattered. Bassam came running as the crowd parted. He had been trying to get a better look at what had drawn the people. But he had not seen me. Please, my bag, I mimed to Bassam, as the Marines led us back inside Abu Ghraib.

I balled up my headscarf and threw it on the dirt. "It didn't even work!" I yelled. I was furious that something about me—my walk, my body, the way I carried myself—had tipped them off that I was a foreigner. I leaned against a cement blockade inside the prison, folding my hands in my lap to stop them from shaking. My entire body convulsed. I looked over at Bassam. "When we get back to the office, you tell them I didn't cry. Tell them," I insisted until he agreed. I needed them to know. I had not buckled. I had not broken down. I was intact.

A year later, after I had returned to Washington, Johnson,

who was at the Pentagon on a brief break from Iraq during the summer of 2005, decided to tell me the rest of the story. He said the Iraqi man who grabbed me first worked at the prison. He later told the Marines that he thought I was wearing a suicide vest, which would have explained the extra girth created by the flak jacket. A week after the incident, the man was murdered by insurgents, perhaps the guys who had grabbed me next. By exiting the prison and showing himself to the crowd, the man had exposed himself as an employee of the prison—an infidel working for the Americans.

I had the same concern for Bassam, who needed to leave the prison to tell Ghazwan to go back to the bureau without us. I was terrified that anyone lingering in the crowd would identify him, link him with the American the insurgents had tried to grab. Bassam took off his baseball cap, which would give him a bit more cover because he had been wearing one outside the prison. The Marines assured us that they would watch him.

After Ghazwan drove off without us, the Army offered Bassam and me a ride back to Baghdad in a Humvee. I had declined this option in the first place because of the threat of attacks on military convoys, but now, it seemed like the best choice. Johnson led us to a convoy, to a Humvee in line right behind a fuel tanker, a huge rolling target of lighter fluid. Resigned, Bassam and I crawled in the back of the vehicle. I pulled out my iPod and handed Bassam one ear bud while I tucked the other one in my ear.

We listened to Counting Crows, some Beth Hart, Cesaria Evora, and as the brown, barren landscape passed by in the window, I thought that now another poor sheep will have to die. Iraqi tradition dictates that a sheep be slaughtered and the meat distributed to the poor when someone escapes death. We had just slaughtered a sheep a week before when Dan and Falah were ambushed. The military dropped us off at a checkpoint, where a driver and guard were waiting to drive us back to the bureau. On the way, my mobile phone buzzed. It was Phil Bennett calling from Washington. "Are you okay?"

"I'm fine, Phil. I'm fine." I listened to my voice, listened to a person I did not recognize plead into the phone: "Please, do not make me come home," I told him. "I want to stay. Please, do not call me home."

I called Jenny after Phil and I hung up. My voice shook. "These guys tried to kidnap me!" I exclaimed. *Holy Shit! Kidnapped!* Although I could tell her the truth that I could not tell Phil—that I was rattled but also resigned—I did not tell her that I had begged him not to bring me home. I did not want her to know that I had gotten so close to terror, so far from her, and yet I could not bring myself back, could not take away her own fears.

I felt like I had made a rookie mistake, almost getting nabbed like that. Perhaps a more senior correspondent would have responded differently or had a different plan for leaving the prison. Perhaps I should have taken Abu Saif with me. Or a bodyguard. Even though I had vetted my departure tactic thoroughly with our Iraqi staff and with the military, it had been my reluctance to travel in and out of the prison without military escort that had left me vulnerable. I was mad at myself.

And at the same time, it felt so surreal. Had I been scared? Yes, after the fact, after I had time to realize what could have happened. Yet I did not want to leave Iraq. I wasn't ready. I did not want to go back to the newsroom defeated, to bide my time again unnoticed. There was so much of Iraq that I had not yet seen, so many facets of the story that I had yet to tell. Leaving would have been giving in, giving up, giving over to the terror. I accepted at that moment that it was not even a question of whether I wanted to stay. I had to stay. And if I were going to stay, I could not dwell on the possibilities of my fate. I reached inside, reached back to one thing that always kept me going, a gift from my devout parents. I trusted God. I trusted that this was where I had landed, at this moment in Iraq's history, for better or for worse, and I intended to wrap myself up in it and live.

I always knew it was her before she said anything, my "hello" met by a long pause, then the click click *of the satellite phone as*

it attempted to shrink the miles between us. Sometimes I waited for her to speak; other times, I shouted eagerly into the phone, "Jackie? Is that you, Jackie? Can you hear me?" When she left for Iraq, she promised to call me as often as she could. We usually talked every day, taking advantage of her journalist's access to the world outside Iraq. When she couldn't call, we emailed, often several times a day. As far away as she felt to me, it helped that I rarely went half a day without communicating with her, and we both understood what a privilege that was. But it also made her journey to Iraq seem closer, easier, than it truly was—at least for me. As long as I could reach her, she was within my grasp.

This phone call, though, was different—the pause longer, heavier, before I heard her voice. "Jenny," she whispered.

"What's wrong?" I asked, leaning into the kitchen counter where I had been cleaning breakfast dishes, steadying myself for whatever dark and unimaginable news she was about to share. I recognized that tone, the way she wrapped the letters of my name around a barely contained gasp. "Somebody tried to kidnap me," she said.

My world heaved. "Say that again," I said, even though I heard her the first time. Say it again and again and again. Say it until I begin to reconcile this bright Connecticut morning, happy and oblivious, with your world in Iraq. *"I fought like a dog," she said, the narrative steadying her shaky voice. "I kicked and screamed until the Marines finally rescued me."*

I tried to picture it: my thin sister, on the ground, her hands digging into someone else's dirt, scrambling for freedom.

"I don't understand," I stammered.

"I'll be okay," she said, shifting into protective mode. "We left the prison and are . . ." She stopped, interrupted by a loud voice. "Oh, no," she said, before the phone clicked, and went silent.

I stood at the sink, unsure what to do, how to go about the morning, the day, the rest of my life.

It would be hours before she would call again, and by then she was a new self, resolved, distant, yes, farther away than ever before.

CHAPTER 5

The bottom of the car vibrated under my feet. Abu Saif felt the unmistakable shudder, too. "Car bomb," he said, peering out the front windshield. We had not heard the sound of the explosion because the armored vehicle the *Post* used—an old jeep chosen for its speed and maneuverability—was sealed so tightly. Unlike the shiny white armored SUVs that foreign contractors and government officials drove in Baghdad, our car did not announce us. Painted a dull color, it was purposefully ugly to blend in with the other bandaged wrecks the working poor drove in Iraq. A security expert would be able to tell that the jeep was armored, but we hoped that the average person, or rather the average insurgent, would not.

Although we did not hear the bomb detonate, we soon saw a plume of smoke a half mile in the distance. "Let's go find it," I told Abu Saif and Omar 2, who was driving us back from the Mansour neighborhood in Baghdad where I had been interviewing people about the Abu Ghraib scandal. Omar 2 made a U-turn off the main roadway in central Baghdad and headed in the direction of the smoke, winding through narrow, residential streets lined with neatly constructed stone houses and metal gates protecting small courtyards, their brown plants undoubtedly baking in the summer heat.

The bomb had detonated on one of the main roads along the perimeter of the Green Zone. Under Saddam, cars did not linger on this road for fear of being picked up by police protecting the former presidential compound. Iraqis used to pray they would not get a flat tire on this road because it was sure to land them in jail on suspicion of plotting an attack against the government. One thing had not changed since Saddam was ousted. No one lingered yet on this road—not out of fear of arrest but out of fear of being blown up outside the two main entrances to the Green Zone: the Convention Center checkpoint and Assassin's Gate, so nicknamed because of the multiple car bombs that exploded in front of its stone arches. I sweated every time we drove past Assassin's Gate, my heart racing even faster when traffic jammed and slowed us down. At a standstill, I felt like a sitting duck surrounded by hunters' rifles.

United States soldiers had cordoned off the area around the blast, so we had to park and walk down the street to get to the wreckage, a charred hull of what had been an SUV for British security contractors. Two bodies remained in the vehicle, witnesses told us, although the soldiers had draped a black tarp over the side to block the view. According to the eyewitnesses, a two-vehicle convoy had just left the Green Zone from Assassin's Gate when the second vehicle exploded in a ball of fire. The soldiers would not let me pass a thick line of yellow tape to talk to the shopkeepers, so Abu Saif ducked through to interview them and try to sort out the facts. A butcher said he heard gunfire and believed that insurgents had shot the vehicle, causing its gas tank to explode. A bystander speculated the insurgents had planted a bomb in the road, an account the shopkeepers disputed; after all, it was the middle of the day. Someone would have seen something, they reasoned. Others described how the first vehicle swung around after the attack, scooped up two other men who were injured but not killed, and raced off with them. The soldiers suspected that the vehicle had been rigged with a bomb inside the Green Zone because of the way it had burned. This suggestion was even more disturbing than the idea of insurgents planting a roadside bomb in the light of day on a street crowded with cars and pedestrians. An inside job would prove that the Green Zone was infiltrated.

As was typical at a bomb blast, witnesses rarely saw the same thing, and in the bloody, confusing aftermath, the translators and I had to haggle for the truth, getting people to repeat again and again what they saw to make sure the details were still the same. We had to match what onlookers saw with what injured survivors experienced and somehow come up with what really happened.

The British Embassy later confirmed that two of its citizens—Mark Carman, a security contractor for Control Risks Group, and Bob Morgan, a petroleum consultant for the British Foreign Office—had died in the explosion, which investigators determined had been caused by a roadside bomb planted near the median. Every time we drove to the Green Zone, we had to slow down to avoid the huge crater in the road left by the attack on the contractors. Every time the car dipped, the image of the blackened car came into my head, and I thought about the men who had died. Pretty soon, out of habit, I began reaching for my St. Christopher medal hanging around my neck, and the motion of the car and my hand became the refrain of a deadly road. *Slow. Dip. Reach. Slow. Dip. Reach.*

By the end of the summer, I stopped going to bomb blasts like that one. On the rare occasion that I did, I kept my distance and did not hang around for more than ten minutes or so. The insurgents began targeting the rescue workers, American soldiers, and Iraqi police who responded to the scene of attacks with a second bomb or with sniper fire.

Our travel outside of Baghdad was completely suspended by this point as well unless we hitched a ride with the military. It was never really safe for me to identify myself as an American, but it became even more dangerous for our Iraqi staff to be seen working with a foreigner. We did not linger anywhere in public. If I wanted to talk to someone on the street, I sent one of our Iraqi staff members to do the interviews or I ducked into a shop for a few minutes and then ducked back out, not wanting to stay long enough to be identified.

I also stopped carrying my passport when I left the bureau and was learning how to lose my American ways, the smallest things that might betray me as a foreigner: swigging water directly from a bottle, walking too fast, or smiling too much. After all, Iraqis were suffering, the staff reminded me, as they coached me in the behavioral sciences of how not to be that proverbial tourist stomping around in a foreign land, talking too loudly in a floppy hat, black socks, and white sneakers. The staff taught me to wear long shirts that covered my behind and how to carry my purse on the crook of my arm just like my grandmother would. The large, black purse, which one of the guards bought for me, actually looked like something my grandmother had. It was engraved with the lettering "Mrs. Fields," making me imagine that I was carrying around a big cookie. On the streets, I was not supposed to laugh or look a man in the eye, lest he think I was a flirting whore. I disappeared into my Iraqi identity, even adopting an Iraqi name that the translators could use to summon me when we were outside. *Farah*, the Arabic word for happy. Farah, the fourth wife of Omar, the office manager. I was a homemaker, deaf and dumb, which would explain why I could not communicate if the insurgents ever stopped our car. When I was out reporting, I never told people on the street that I worked for *The Washington Post*. In some instances, I kept completely silent so as not to reveal that I spoke English. Most of the time the staff told people we were interviewing that I was from Canada or from Ukraine. Canada had not sent troops to Iraq, and although the Ukraine had a small contingent of forces in the country, it had a sizeable population of Muslims, including followers of a radical, extremist movement of Islam called Wahhabism, which were also operating in Iraq.

Huda and I went one afternoon to interview men outside a barber shop. Two of them were taking a break from visiting injured relatives at a nearby hospital. They needed a shave and a buzz cut. Huda and I both wore scarves, and we whispered in English to each other as she interviewed the men about the Iraqi soccer team competing in the upcoming summer Olympics in Greece. A little boy came out of an electronics shop with a dirty pitcher of tap water. He poured the water into a glass and handed it to me. I smiled and shook my head. I wanted to explain in English: *No. No thank you, little boy. I do not want to drink your dirty water, which will make me very sick. I cannot imagine someone in the United States making such an offer to a reporter who stops by for an interview. You are actually treating me like a guest, not a leech. But unfortunately your water is very, very dirty, and* . . .. He kept thrusting the glass at me, while the other men stopped talking to Huda and stared. Huda leaned over and hissed, "Drink the water. You're attracting attention. It's not polite to refuse." I threw it back in a single gulp and hoped *The Washington Post* truly appreciated the sacrifice. Huda wrapped up the interview and we hurried back to the bureau just in case I became ill, which I did.

On the day Iraqi television broadcast Ghazi Yawar would be the country's new interim president, I went out to talk to people on the street about what they thought of Yawar. Omar was with Rajiv covering the announcement, and Huda was off translating for Dan Williams. Bassam refused to leave the office because Rajiv had told him that it had to be staffed at all times. I tried to convince Bassam that there were obviously exceptions to the rule, and this was one of them, but he would not budge. He was terrified that Rajiv, Little Saddam, would get mad at him. So I took Muhanned, the security director, to translate. He spoke English well enough for this sort of man-on-the-street type of stuff, but he was nervous. He couldn't take his gun because our correspondents and translators did not carry weapons, a generally accepted rule of engagement by which most members of the press abided. Muhanned hadn't been on the streets of Baghdad without his pistol since he was fourteen. He kept reaching to his side as if reaching for a phantom limb. We went to one of my favorite cafés on a busy commercial street in the Karrada neighborhood, a tidy restaurant with a bright red awning, outdoor tables, and a great falafel sandwich. I had never been allowed to sit and eat at this restaurant for security reasons, but sometimes Falah would bring me a falafel while I waited in the car. Rajiv thought I was playing a game of chicken with my stomach by eating the raw lettuce and tomato that came on the sandwich, but Falah had assured me in his most sincere voice that this place was clean.

Falah parked the car at the side of the road near a homemade potato chip stand, and Muhanned and I went to the café to report. I wore a pink and brown Muslim headscarf and stood silently at Muhanned's side as he explained that I was a Muslim reporter from Canada. The guy behind the counter did not want to talk, but offered me a free soda, which I could not explain that I could not accept. At least it wasn't bad water. At first, people seemed very reluctant to talk to Muhanned. But they soon opened up, and Muhanned got some fantastic quotes, including one from the man slicing lamb off a spit who called the presidential selection "drama performed in front of the people." Back in the car, munching on the greasy homemade curry potato chips that Falah insisted I eat so that I would fatten up to find a husband, I quizzed Muhanned on how he was able to draw people out, never having reported before.

"I told them, 'You have to talk to us. There is no more Saddam. You are stupid to be scared. Talk!'"

I spit out a chip. "Muhanned! You can't bully people into talking to *The Washington Post*."

"Do not worry," he said. "I told them we are from the *Toronto Star*."

That was the last time I took Muhanned out as a translator. He could keep his gun from now on.

No assignment was easy in Iraq, particularly those involving interviews with Iraqi officials. Most government offices did not have working land lines. The top officials had mobile phones but did not give their numbers out. The only way to set up an interview was to show up and ask for one, which might take a couple of days or a week to get. If no one called us to confirm the interview, we'd have to traipse back to ask again.

For a story about Iraqi doctors being kidnapped for ransom, Huda and I went to the main teaching hospital in Baghdad to find doctors to interview. It took us two hours to reach the hospital, only two miles away, because of bumper-to-bumper traffic, another development of postwar Iraq. We showed up at the front door of the hospital and had to convince the security personnel that we were important visitors and needed to see the hospital administrator—we needed the administrator's permission to be on the hospital grounds. But the administrator's secretary refused to let us talk to him. She said we needed a letter from the Health Minister granting us access to the hospital. We had no such letter.

As we were leaving, we stopped in a lounge filled with young men in white coats. The head resident of the hospital was holding court when we walked in, and he stopped the conversation as soon as he saw us. Huda implored him to talk so we did not waste our trip. He refused to grant us an interview but suggested we might go upstairs to talk to more senior doctors. He said nothing about needing a letter, probably because he did not know we needed one. Taking this as permission from someone in authority, Huda and I ducked into a dirty stairwell and followed a stream of people up the stairs. The hospital was barren, and the secondhand smoke rivaled a bowling alley in Detroit. Patients wore their own clothes and three or four shared the same room. Female family members attended to them in place of nurses. We found a couple of doctors willing to talk to us about the problem they faced in the privacy of empty examining rooms: dozens of their colleagues had been kidnapped by criminals looking to extract a ransom. Other physicians had been kidnapped and killed. These two doctors were contemplating fleeing Iraq with their families. Under Saddam, doctors made about $20 a month. The new Health Ministry increased the pay to $200 a month. But even at that, they could not afford the tens of thousands of dollars in ransom many of the kidnappers were demanding. The doctors encouraged Huda and me to track down a surgeon whose children had been kidnapped. The kidnappers had demanded $200,000 in exchange for their safe return. The surgeon was not there that day, so we would have to come back tomorrow and start the process again. We never went. Other stories got in the way—political developments, attacks on police recruits, other kidnappings, murders, the shaping of the Iraqi army—and we had to move on.

I liked being out among ordinary Iraqis, even if I had to do my reporting in short spurts. It was the only chance I had to be a part of Iraqi life.

When I was in the car with Falah, he would often refuse to

speak English and would point to things we were passing, calling out the name in Arabic, which he then forced me to repeat. *Yaseer.* Left. *Yameen.* Right. *Sayyara.* Car. I tried to look nonchalant, and therefore more like a local, as I soaked in the sights of the city, the endless rows of shops, whose keepers often sold their goods in the dark when the power went out. Baghdad was a thriving capital, often a deceptive scene of normalcy, if one looked past the barbed wire, the American tanks, the Iraqi police officers with black masks shielding their identity from the insurgents. On those car rides with Falah, I focused on a different Iraq, one in which there were no car bombs, no shortages of drinking water, no power outages, no kidnappings. I trained my eyes on the colorful slide show of life that passed by the window. Students in backpacks holding hands as they went to school. Children playing soccer in the dirt median of the road. Trucks loaded with grapes and tomatoes. Scrawny sides of butchered beef hanging in shop windows. Cars decorated for weddings held on Mondays and Thursdays. Signs advertising mobile telephones. It is one of the beautiful mysteries of the human spirit—even in the worst of conditions, even when a country is falling apart at its seams (and there was no question that Iraq felt like it was falling apart), people did not stop living. Something deep within us says, don't stop. Take a breath. Keep breathing as long as your lungs will fill with air. Even with the flogging violence that hit like a strap time and again, people were still breathing, and I was riveted, in the backseat of that car, watching them collectively inhale, exhale.

The only way to find out how Iraqis really felt about what was happening to them was to ask. I can write that Iraq felt like it was falling apart because every Iraqi I met on the street, whether they supported the American invasion or not, told me that they felt like their country was falling apart, and they said it from the day I stepped onto Iraqi soil until the day I left. Sure, people talked about democracy and how brutal life had been under Saddam. But so many people could not fathom how things turned out after the Americans toppled Saddam. They didn't expect to be sitting in miles-long gas lines, where it often took a full day and night to reach the pump. How ironic was that, they asked, when Iraq was sitting on one of the world's richest oil reserves? Few mentioned the greatest irony of postwar Iraq, however. People could now actually complain openly about how bad things were. The whole time I was in Iraq, I grappled with this notion and perception that the press only reported bad news, that we only reported on Iraqis complaining about how bad life had become. People questioned why we did not find people who were happy about the invasion and happy that Saddam was gone. The truth is that when I went to talk to Iraqis about their lives, I did not set out to find people who supported one particular viewpoint or another. I tried to interview people of different economic and tribal backgrounds, both Shias and Sunnis, Arabs and Kurds, people who had benefited under Saddam and people who had suffered.

One of the problems was that most of the press was based in the Iraqi capital, which was where a good deal of the violence occurred. Not all of Iraq was as bad off as Baghdad. And not all of Iraq was bad at the same time. I liked to think of our Iraqi coverage in terms of the boroughs of New York City: if the Bronx and Manhattan were being hit daily by car bombs, if tourists from Iowa were being targeted for kidnapping in Queens, but Staten Island and Brooklyn were safe, what kind of story would we write? If we could go over the bridge to talk to people, we might write a story now and then about how life was pretty good still in Staten Island and Brooklyn. But the bulk of the coverage—and in my mind, the heart of journalistic responsibility—would be writing about the terror, the horror in the Bronx and Manhattan and Queens, the larger story about New York City itself. The same applied to Iraq.

The roads from Baghdad were so dangerous that we could not get to other parts of the country safely without the military. I could, for example—and did—go to a power plant in Baiji, north of Baghdad, to write a story about improvements to the electrical grid. To get there, I had to hop a ride on a military helicopter and dodge antiaircraft fire. I was not allowed to bring a translator with me, so I could not talk to any of the workers there. I would have preferred to go on my own but it was not an option. I hear the criticism cavalry coming already. Brave reporters face danger in the eye. Brave reporters tromp around the world's hot spots, risking their lives for the story. They did it in Vietnam. They did it in El Salvador. They did it in Kosovo. Indeed, they did. But Iraq was not like any other story. There is known violence and unknown violence, random violence and a noose already knotted and hanging in suspension for the fool who wants to get in a car and drive to Baiji. It would have been stupid and reckless, to my life and the life of the Iraqis traveling with me. So I took the limited option of traveling with the military, to write about power, to write about something other than violence.

In spite of the restrictions, I was hitting my stride by the end of June. David Hoffman, the foreign editor, had asked me to stay in Iraq through the end of the month, when L. Paul Bremer, the head of the U.S. occupation government, was scheduled to leave Iraq, handing over authority to a new interim government led by Ayad Allawi, an exiled Iraqi physician. This was not only big political news, but we expected a big increase in insurgent attacks aimed at disrupting the process. We expected as much because the U.S. military warned us things were probably going to get bad. I had agreed somewhat reluctantly to stay, not because I was afraid but because it felt like I had left Washington in the middle of the night the month before; I usually spend more time getting ready for a week's vacation than I had for my month in Iraq. If I was going to be away longer, I needed to cancel my cable and my cell phone. I wanted to visit my grandmothers in Illinois. And my supply of contact lenses was running short. Although the case against Jeremy Sivits had wrapped up quickly after he agreed to plead guilty, lawyers for the other six accused soldiers were vowing to fight their charges or convince a military judge to hold the remaining courts-martial outside Iraq. If I stayed on that story, it could be weeks or months between legal proceedings. The focus of the scandal had shifted back to Washington, where investigative panels were reviewing details of the abuse. That was fine with me. I was eager to write other stories from Iraq, stories about civilian life, reconstruction, whatever I could find. I did not want to be just the Abu Ghraib reporter. Rajiv and the editors were encouraging me to branch out, too.

By that summer, the *Post* was having a more difficult time getting people to volunteer for Iraq duty. The travel restrictions and the security measures under which we had to work took away from the experience of being overseas. Reporters had to weigh all the risks of being in Iraq with the opportunity to cover a big, moving historical story that editors in Washington cared about tremendously. For many reporters, the gamble just was not sufficient to justify a tour through Iraq.

Although I was not on the foreign staff, from the editor's perspective, there was an advantage to keeping me there: I was already there. I was also proving to be more of an asset than a liability—not just in terms of the stories I was writing. I was low-maintenance. I didn't complain. I got along and went along, respectfully deferring to the senior correspondents in the bureau, whose collective decades of experience in nearly every major conflict in world history humbled me. I spent a lot of my time studying these pros, how they tackled a story, what questions they asked. I didn't mind being the junior member of the bureau because no one treated me like one. And I knew I could do the job.

I pounded out the daily news story from my desk at night while Rajiv prepared a huge series to mark the hand-off of the government. I had moved from my flea-infested room to one right next to his. When I needed a break from writing, I played soccer in the hallway with the guards, running barefoot with the ball and trying not to trip in my skirt. Dan Williams left Iraq a few days after his close call on the Fallujah highway, and Rajiv and I were holding down the bureau with correspondents Doug Struck and Ed Cody until Karl Vick arrived. We were exhausted.

I woke up on June 27 and logged on to check my email. There was one from Jenny, with "CALL HOME ASAP" in the subject line. I opened it, and she had left her cell phone number with a message not to panic. "Just call me," she wrote. I did not panic. I assumed one of my grandmothers had died. Maybe it was twin intuition or maybe it was the careful way in which Jenny instructed me to call home but not to panic. Jenny picked up on the first ring. "Grandma Heinkel died," she said, referring to our maternal grandmother as we always had, distinguishing her from Grandma Spinner. I hung up a few minutes later and went to tell the guys in the office. My grandma was ninety-three. I had last talked to her a few nights before I left for Iraq. I had stood on the steps of the Inner Harbor in Baltimore, the twinkling lights of the boats blinking from the water, while listening to her garbled voice tell me to be good. "You were always the sweetest one," she told me, before hanging up. I turned to my friend, Suzy, who was standing next to me, and said, "She must have thought I was Jenny."

Jenny always had been the sweet one, the good one. In high school, I had parties in my grandparents' house while they were away, something that is shameful for me to admit as an adult. I just never liked doing things the way I was supposed to. I felt constrained by my strict upbringing, shackled by the idea that there was only one way to do things. That is why I left for California after graduating from college in southern Illinois. I just wanted to experience the antithesis of what I had always known. For God's sake, I didn't know what a bagel was until I was twenty-three. Grown up and long reconciled and even grateful for my upbringing, I was devastated that I had not told my grandmother good-bye in person before I left. I had confided to Rajiv that this was the main thing I worried about most, not saying good-bye to my grandmothers. I wanted to go home for the funeral, but the airport was shutting down in advance of the government hand-off as a security precaution.

Rajiv said I only had an hour or so to make a decision. I couldn't think. I went to my room, closed the door, sank to the floor, and sighed deeply. Of course, I had to go home. I got back up and went next door to see Rajiv. "Can you get me home?" Rajiv booked me on the last flight out before the airport closed. In Jordan en route to the United States, I watched CNN flash the breaking news: In a secret ceremony, Bremer had turned over governing authority to the Iraqis two days early. It was June 28. Iraq was a sovereign country, and my grandmother was dead.

I felt disconnected the entire time I was home. I sat stone-faced through my grandmother's funeral, never shedding a tear. I tried to cry. I loved her dearly, and we were very close. I saw my mother weeping, and I tried to cry for her. My mother was truly alone now. After my father died, she went to see my grandmother nearly every night, tucking her in, reading to her, praying with her. One of the last times I saw my grandmother, she was sitting in a wheelchair in a nursing home. She was tired and desperately wanted to take a nap in her rose-colored recliner. I left her room to find a nurse to help move her to the chair. I couldn't find anyone, so I went back to the room.

"Grandma, do you trust me?" I asked.

She nodded her head.

I reached down and put my hands under her fragile body, her skin so translucent that I could see the tapestry of her blue veins. I picked her up and carried her to the chair. We both weighed barely 100 pounds, and I struggled to keep her safely in my arms. She smiled at me when I put her in the chair and asked me to read from her Bible. She drifted off to sleep as I did. I cried on the drive home that day, but at her funeral, I could not force the tears. I held my mother up, as I had done when my father died, my arm steady across her shoulders as we followed the casket into the church. My voice did not break as I read my grandmother's eulogy to the pews full of family members and mourners.

Jenny kept watching me. I could sense her gaze but not her intuition. Something had disconnected, some sensor that had always enabled us to know in our gut what the other one was feeling, thinking. Months later I realized that I had disconnected the sensor on my own. I wanted to protect Jenny from the violence in Iraq, the threats against us. But mostly I wanted to protect her from my growing realization that I wanted to be in Iraq more than I wanted to be at home, safely tucked into my life, our life.

After we buried her next to my grandfather, in the same cemetery where my father was, we went back to the church for a potluck lunch. My relatives pulled their chairs up to my table. "Tell us what it is really like in Iraq." For more than an hour, I talked about Iraq, about the bombs, about Omar and Bassam and Abu Saif. I talked until my throat was raw, until I had emptied myself of my stories, hardly recognizing my own voice. I talked until I had nothing else to say.

It was a relief to come back to Iraq, to escape back into the story, to the comforting familiarity of the discomfort. I left an occupied Iraq and returned three weeks later to a sovereign one. Although American soldiers still roamed through the city, they were now almost always accompanied by Iraqi forces. The Baghdad mayor had started calling the shots on where the soldiers could put up barriers and what streets should be reopened to try to clear some of the horrible traffic congestion. The new interim government was up and running, and the new ministers now held their own press conferences in Arabic.

Bassam and I went to see the mayor of Baghdad, Alaa Mahmood Tamimi, for a story about a trash removal program in the city. Tamimi suggested we talk to his chief engineer, who had the numbers for how much trash was being picked up and how much U.S. taxpayer money it was costing. We roamed the dimly lit halls of the municipal building, with its dirty rest rooms and leaking pipes that pooled in the stairwells, soaking the hems of the long dresses worn by the city's female employees. We found the office and waited in a room for the engineer's secretary. She came to tell us the engineer would see Bassam. I got up, but she shook her hand at me and said, "No, only Iraqi," and with that led Bassam off to see the engineer. The Iraqis were taking back their country, such as it was.

Rajiv left soon after I returned for a much-needed break. He had been in Iraq almost eighteen months at that point, working at an incredible, almost bionic pace. Pam Constable came in from our Afghanistan bureau to help bridge the gap before Rajiv returned with two other colleagues. Pam was a huge animal lover who started a rescue operation in Kabul, the Afghan capital. She found a kitten in the parking lot at the Sheraton shortly after she arrived in Iraq and brought him to her room. Although I am severely allergic to cats, I somehow wound up kitten-sitting for Pam when she went out on assignment. My bathroom was cooler than hers, so the kitten made its home on my cool brown tile with a red and white checkered tribal head-covering for a blanket. I didn't mind. The kitten was a nice distraction from the miserable heat, although I drew the line the night Mr. Kitty hopped up on the dining room table for a romp while Pam cooed.

Summers in Baghdad are just awful. The mercury often tops 130 degrees, and without electricity to run fans and air conditioners, the whole city was in a heat funk. The hotel only had three to four hours of power at a time, as the government rationed the electricity. We bribed the hotel with cash to hook us up to the emergency generator to keep our fans and air-conditioning units running. Everyone else in the hotel was doing the same thing. The 800-amp generator had 2,000 amps worth of stuff plugged into it because the maintenance guys kept taking the bribes and hooking people up regardless of its limitations. It constantly maxed out and left us completely in the dark. Several mornings I took a shower by flashlight. Some nights we had dinner by candlelight. It was unbearable at night when we were trying to sleep. Most Baghdad residents do not sleep inside during the summer. They pull their mattresses onto the roofs of their houses to catch a breeze. We could not do that at the Sheraton. For one, the American snipers controlled the top of the building. And it would not have been safe with the barrage of mortars that headed in our direction.

I discovered something new about myself. I get cranky when the thermometer reaches 130 degrees. Pam and I took turns sleeping in the one cool spot in the office. I took the midnight to 3 A.M. shift and then from 6 A.M. to 8 A.M. I found that I could stay somewhat cool by taking a cold shower every thirty minutes or so. I'd take the shower in my clothes and, because it was so hot, they'd be dry in no time.

One night I could not sleep during my shift so I got up and

started working on the computer. Pam had not been sleeping much at all for about two weeks. She was miserable, so I offered her a motion sickness pill left over from a boat trip in the Galápagos Islands the year before. "The great thing about it is that it's not really a sleeping pill, so it will make you tired but you won't have that sleep hangover in the morning," I told her. She put it in the palm of her hand, eyed it for a moment, and then popped it in her mouth. Six hours later, while I was supposed to be on the office sofa sleeping, she stomped into the room. "Your pill didn't work!" she spat, and then went to curl up on the sofa. Uh, but it was still my shift. She was in my spot. I was supposed to have that spot for another two hours. I stopped grumbling at her in my head for a moment and listened in the dark. Pam was breathing deeply. She had fallen asleep. I smiled. Yeah, my pill didn't work all right. The next morning, she was still there when the translators arrived. They turned on the television. The cleaning crew came in and dusted and vacuumed. And Pam still slept. She slept for sixteen hours.

"My God," she said, when she finally woke up. "What did you give me?"

"I swear it was a motion sickness pill," I told her. "You must have been really, really tired."

Pam and I were in the office hanging out with the translators on August 1 when the hotel shook gently, a subtle rolling earthquake that jiggled the glassware but did not break anything. We went out on the balcony and saw a giant puff of black and white smoke rising in the distance. We had no idea what it was. I snapped some pictures, the smoke radiant against the cloudless blue sky with the sun setting in a pink blaze. We couldn't hear the shouts or the screams, the cries of anguish at the Lady of Salvation Church, one of four Christian churches struck by car bombers that night in coordinated attacks. A fifth church was bombed in the northern city of Mosul. At least a dozen people were killed and fifty wounded in the blasts.

Pam wrote the main story about the bomb blasts, and I wrote a smaller accompanying story. That night I told Pam that I would take the main story the next day, which would give me a chance to get out and do more street reporting. We had been trading off the daily story, and I was excited to have a chance at this one. I set out the next morning to find Christians to interview for the article. The nuns at the first orphanage I went to refused to talk to me—kindly, of course, even when I pulled the Catholic card and tried to do a wink and nod from behind my headscarf. No dice.

Ghazwan, the one Christian among our Muslim staff, was behind the wheel and took me next to a small convent in central Baghdad, not far from where one of the churches was attacked. We pulled up and rang the doorbell—these nuns did let me in. Inside their small compound was a beautiful garden with lush grass and purple flowers. The umbrellas providing shade to the flowerbeds advertised a German pilsner. Over glasses of cherry Kool-Aid, we talked about their life and how peacefully Christians and Muslims have always lived together in Iraq.

I asked the Mother Superior to show me the chapel, as I had not been inside a church since I left the States. It was a simple chapel with plain white walls and short wooden benches, but beautiful stained-glass windows and a hand-carved statue of Jesus and Joseph near the front. The chapel and convent were named for Saint Anne, Mary's mother. The convent was on a little side street in the middle of a Muslim residential neighborhood. After we left, we went across the street to interview the people who lived there. A woman answered the door in ordinary clothes and invited us into the parlor. She disappeared and came back in her full Muslim scarf and dress—Omar and Ghazwan were with me. She talked about how sad she was that the terrorists had attacked the Christians. She said she prays to the Virgin Mary because she likes the nuns and figures Mary has been good to them. All of the neighbors, in fact, expressed such dismay over the bombings.

As we were leaving the convent, an old woman in a very conservative Muslim covering ran out of her house. She grabbed me in a hug and began kissing me, telling me, "Oh, I'm so sorry they attacked you. I am so glad you are safe." She thought I was an Iraqi Christian visiting the nuns. She invited us into her humble cement house and offered to make me lunch. She had no electricity and sobbed through a story about how her sons had gone off to the Iraq-Iran war and never returned. Her husband had died and she was alone. She kept kissing me on the forehead and calling me her daughter. I assured her that I would come back to visit. I intended to keep my promise. But I never went back.

On the way back to the Sheraton, Omar and I talked excitedly about the story. I had such great material. I called Pam to let her know what I had. She decided to go out, too, and found a family who lived next door to the Lady of Salvation Church that had been attacked. In fact, she found three families living together, one Christian and two Muslim.

"Dammit," I told Omar after we hung up. "She's going to take my story. I just know it."

"Don't let her," he said.

"I won't! I was supposed to do this story."

We met on the steps of the Sheraton, and Pam threw her arm around my shoulder. "Isn't this great? I can't believe what I got!"

Back in the office, Omar whispered encouragement. "Don't back down. I know you. You will back down." And of course I did. It was not worth the battle. Pam had a great story. I knew she did not want to share the story with me. I didn't blame her. When you find a great story, you write it in your head, your material, from start to finish. I heard myself say the words, "No, of course, you take it. I'll write the news story and throw my nuns in there. You do the front-page feature. You have such great stuff."

As I walked out of the office back to my room, I shrugged my shoulders at Omar. There would be plenty of other stories. And I genuinely liked Pam. She is good people.

When Pam returned to Afghanistan a few weeks later, I was alone in the bureau, waiting for my reinforcements to come. By default, I was in charge, which basically meant threatening to rat the staff out to Little Saddam if they didn't stay in line. I marveled at the fact that in just a few months, Rajiv and the editors had enough confidence in me to leave me by myself. I also felt the weight of the responsibility. One morning my cell phone rang. A man identified himself as an Army major with the 1st Calvary Division in Baghdad. He asked for me by name and then asked me where I was located. I did not know if it was a trap, and I was reluctant to offer up the whereabouts of the bureau. I asked for his name and number so that I could call him back. I ran to the office to brief Omar and Muhanned. I called the number, and the major answered. "Look we have intercepted a bomb threat. We think there is a car coming to blow up *The Washington Post* bureau. It is a specific threat to *The Washington Post*. I need to know your location." I paused and let my gut instinct take over for my head.

"We're at the Sheraton."

"You're not in a house?"

"No, we used to be."

"Okay. I need to call you back."

I turned to Omar. "We need to get everyone out of the bureau, now. We need to evacuate."

"You go. We'll stay," Omar suggested.

"No. That's not how it works. Either we all go or we all stay. My life is not worth any more than yours or anyone else's in this bureau. We're leaving now, all of us. I am not kidding around. Move! Bassam, you, too. We're leaving."

As I turned toward the stairwell, my phone rang again. The Army major had more information. It appeared that the threat was to our former residence, not to the Sheraton. They had a description of a maroon sedan, a potential car bomber. We should stay on alert for a car of this type, but the threat did not appear to be imminent against our current residence at the Sheraton. A hurricane of relief pounded into me. That had been close, too close.

"Muhanned, round up the guards and drivers," I directed. "I want to be on the safe side. Check every room, under the beds, in the closets. Check the pantry. Look for anything that might seem out of place. I want to do this twice a day for the next week. While you get started on that, I am going to call

Washington and let them know what just happened." What had just happened? I did not have time to think about it. I did not want to think about it. I emailed Rajiv.

"Dude, you can have your bureau back now."

When my grandmother died in late June 2004, I couldn't help thinking that she died protecting Jackie, died giving her granddaughter a reprieve from the escalating violence in Iraq. My sister's unexpected two-week visit home at the beginning of July felt like a gift. For weeks I had been dreaming death, and when my aunt called to say that Grandma had died in her sleep at the nursing home where she lived in Illinois, I felt relieved to know I had been watching the wrong death play out in my dreams.

For years my grandmother had been predicting, and waiting for, her death. She wasn't so much morbid as ready. One Christmas, several years before she died, she asked my aunt Beth, her youngest daughter, to buy her a white blouse. When she opened the gift box, she smiled and draped the blouse across her chest. "This will be so nice in my casket," she announced. But she didn't die then. Eventually somebody took the tags off the blouse, and she wore it for several years before the embalmer slipped it over her bony shoulders and straightened the collar under her powdered chin.

I adored my grandmother. Had I been younger, had my father not been dead, had my sister not been in Iraq, my grandmother's death would have devastated me. But I'd spent so much time willing my sister to live that I felt at peace with a death that seemed to follow a natural order. My grandmother simply shrank away, yearning for heaven. My sister was in full color, looming large in my life, alive, and wanting to stay that way.

At the funeral, I shed no tears, not because I didn't love my grandma or because I wouldn't miss her terribly. Her death just made sense. Jackie agreed to give a eulogy and that made sense, too—the granddaughter fresh from war, speaking from the lectern, while the grandmother lay dead in the wooden casket at the bottom of the altar steps. In the last months of her life, when she had trouble recognizing members of her own family and when the present began to slip away from her, my grandmother remembered Iraq, remembered that my sister was there, and seemed to understand why.

When my family got up to follow the casket down the aisle into the waiting hearse, however, I panicked, groping for the pew to steady myself. In my dreams, it was my sister in that casket, and my husband had to carry me, too weak from grief to walk by myself. But this wasn't that dream, and I felt my legs plodding along. My eyes narrowed, focusing on my sister's back, her bony shoulders draped in black, her right arm slung around my mother as they walked. I focused on my sister, still alive, leading the rest of us down the aisle to the waiting hearse outside.

CHAPTER 6

Luma bounded into our office at the Sheraton, a trail of honeysuckle perfume stalking her as she rocked her head back and forth to the song blaring from her headphones. Luma only listened to American boy bands and the latest hit female artists crooning love songs, the lyrics enticing her to a different place, any place other than Iraq. Her blue Polo shirt was stretched tightly across her chest, and she wore her curly brown hair pulled back from her face to reveal the dangling earrings that dropped like golden tears. "Hi guys!" she exclaimed, her words a burst of happiness. The male translators beamed back at her, this firecracker whose personality sprayed little flecks of color around a room that had three TV sets tuned to images of carnage.

Rajiv hired Luma while I was away for my grandmother's funeral. Her English was terrible, but Abu Saif liked her, and that is what counted. Luma was the kind of woman that Abu Saif always dug—she was independent and beautiful, and she reminded him of the girls he dated during his college days in America. She was smart and a quick learner. A few weeks under his tutelage, and Abu Saif was convinced Luma would be a keeper. He also knew the office needed Luma; he knew I needed Luma. The testosterone in the joint could be choking, even if you discounted Omar, who did not have the typical Iraqi machismo. He was a girl's best friend, fashion-conscious and deep, a thinker and a dreamer. I could tell Omar everything, and I did, sharing news from home, my life there, my family. He could be very blunt and practical, and while he shared Luma's admiration for the American soldiers—whom he called his "brothers"—he detested her torrent of tears over a love song. Omar didn't cry. He allowed only that occasionally his eyes got some strange water in them. Omar did not believe in tears, but he did believe that a woman should dress for success even if the woman was in Baghdad under fire. One day, too hot to care that I was showing a little ankle, I dressed in khaki crop pants. When I showed up in the office, Omar clucked his tongue at me. "You know, Oprah says short women should not wear those kind of pants. They only make you look shorter."

Indignant, I backed out of the room in a huff.

Luma copied her style not from Oprah but from actresses in American movies and from singers in Lebanese music videos, where scantily clad women in fake eyelashes and thick black eyeliner danced to Arabic pop. When we went out, I dressed like an Iraqi to cover the fact that I was a Westerner, and Luma dressed like a Westerner to cover the fact that she was Iraqi. Once I told her that I liked her shirt, a black top with "Cool Chic" stenciled in shiny beads. The next day she brought me an identical one in white.

The Washington Post's office was Luma's little America. She could dress and act as she liked. At U.S. military bases, she also felt like she was on American soil. Luma, who was twenty-six when the United States invaded Iraq, ran a café for the soldiers on one Army base in central Baghdad, serving up sodas, light snacks, and a side dish of Luma charm. She wanted to distinguish herself from the other Iraqi women whom the soldiers encountered, the ones who wore scarves, the ones who looked Iraqi. Luma wanted the soldiers to see her as an American.

She listened politely one afternoon as I explained that if she wanted to go with me to a military base the next day, she needed to dress more conservatively. I would never ask her to wear a scarf. But I was hoping she would not wear that supertight top with the beads. And the flirting, well, perhaps she could tone that down, too. If she wanted to find an American husband on her own time that was fine. But not on mine.

"Why?" she wanted to know. "We are free."

"Well, it's just that it's better if the soldiers look at us first as reporters, then as women. It's just more professional."

"But why? You are free, too."

"Yes, free, in a sense," I told her, struggling to find words to articulate what I meant, to explain that the feminist in me was disgusted that I was even having this conversation with her. I was sad when I saw little girls dressed in long sleeves and long dresses, their heads covered, sitting at the edge of a swimming pool while their brothers splashed in the cool water. I had never felt more aware of my own femininity, and yet I also had never felt more of a need to hide my body, to be sexless, one of the guys.

"You know, it's hard because the soldiers aren't always used to having women around," I said, finally settling on an explanation. "And it's better if we don't attract that kind of attention."

She looked at me blankly, unable to comprehend the dress politics of the woman reporter in combat or of a Westerner in an Arab land. Luma had freed herself from the scarf and *abaya*. She was not about to be constrained by fabric.

"Just wear something normal," I said, "or I can't take you with me." I wasn't even sure what normal was.

I adopted Luma easily as my charge, a younger sister, a friend, a college roommate, someone to sing and dance with while doing the dishes—but I missed Huda when she left. Huda and I used to lock ourselves in the bathroom next to the kitchen, crank the music, and dance with the frying pans while singing to Counting Crows. Sometimes the guards came to try to watch us, and Huda slapped at them and shouted, "No, this is for us. Go away!" They scurried off and left us alone with our pot and pan dance partners. Huda had Luma's spirit, but she was also more conservative, religious. She didn't let anyone boss her around, but she felt strongly about covering her head to remove the temptation for men to look at her.

It was getting harder to find female translators because of the dangers of being on the streets and the long hours involved. Luma was a perfect fit. She was a divorced single mother whose daughter, Sarah, was mostly being raised by her grandmother so Luma could work. Luma answered to no one, unlike some of the other female job candidates we had interviewed who came with strings: brothers or husbands who wanted them to work in the office but not go out to report or young children who needed them at home by a certain hour to cook dinner.

After the U.S. invasion, Luma, whose older brother was a doctor, started an organization to help rehabilitate Iraq's health care system. She ran the organization, Nurses-Doctor Care Inc., from a rented house in the Green Zone. She had no experience, but Luma, who graduated from a private university in Baghdad with an English degree, was eager to make something of herself. She certainly did not need the money. Her family was well-off by Baghdad standards, though I never asked how they made their fortune. Luma and her family had suffered mightily but not uniquely under Saddam. Luma's father, Faruq, was a civil engineer in the government. In the 1980s, Faruq argued with a government official about the design of a building. With Saddam's consent, the official ordered Faruq to join the army and go fight against Iran. Luma was five at the time. Her father went off to war, and she never saw him again. He is presumed dead, but Islamic law does not allow someone to be declared dead officially until there is a body. Without a body, his wife cannot receive a pension, cannot settle his estate, cannot remarry. Luma and her family hated Saddam, hated what he had done to their father and husband. They loved America, particularly the freedoms it accorded women. Luma was a feminist even if she did not know the English word for it; had she known the word, she would have gladly accepted it for herself, spelling it out in beads on her tight T-shirts.

On one of her first reporting assignments, Rajiv dispatched Luma to a mosque to cover a Friday prayer service. We routinely covered these sermons by powerful religious leaders whose words had the intoxicating power to incite people to good or to bad. We could often hear the pendulum of the political pulse swinging through the words of the Imams, the powerful congregational leaders. None of our translators were regulars at Friday prayer. If they went, it was because they were on assignment. Their faith was as much cultural as it was spiritual. As a woman, Luma felt particularly oppressed by conservative Islamists. Her mother, who wore blue jeans, button-down shirts, and certainly no scarf, had no use for religious rites either. She forbade Luma to own a scarf and *abaya*. Luma borrowed mine to attend the prayer service and kept it in the office so her mother would not find it.

Luma came back from covering her first (and last) Friday prayer service with my scarf and *abaya* balled up in her hands. She threw the crumpled black material on the floor. "I want to burn this thing," she spat angrily. "I can't stand it. They treat women like animals."

I reached over to pat her on the shoulder. "It's hard being so ahead of your time, isn't it?" I said, trying to console her.

Every morning, I typed a vocabulary list for Luma to help her learn more English. Luma looked up the words she did not know in the dictionary and copied them into a notebook. I introduced Luma to a whole new world of words that she would need to be a translator in postwar Iraq. *Barricade. Blast. Suicide. Democracy. Barbed wire. Reconstruction. Insurgent.* Abu Saif coached her how to report and took her with him so she could watch him in action. He repeated what he had learned from Rajiv: "Write down exactly what someone says to you. Do not inject your opinion into questions. Put aside your own feelings. Go numb with impartiality." And he repeated what he had learned from me, passing down David Hoffman's words of advice like a journalistic genetic strain: "Do not close your notebook."

For her twenty-eighth birthday, Luma decided to throw herself a rock star party at the Sheraton. She urged me to invite the U.S. soldiers who guarded the hotel. I told her to do it herself. Luma and I were constantly battling over her relationships with the soldiers. She had already been jilted once by a sergeant she met in the Green Zone the fall of 2003. The two had a romantic relationship, and the sergeant proposed marriage to her. Luma's daughter and mother attended the engagement party. Luma was counting on the sergeant to be her ticket to a new life in the United States. Only he was already married. When Luma discovered that he had lied to her, she broke off the engagement. But she still sent emails to him back in Florida, where he had returned to his wife and children after his tour of duty ended. Luma still loved him, for all of his lies. That July, he was still promising Luma in his emails that he'd leave his family, come back to Iraq, retrieve her, and bring her to the United States. Luma was desperate to get out of Iraq, and she liked that the American soldiers treated her like an equal— wooed her, wined and dined her with visions of the future. Luma was ferocious but naive, with an idealized notion of a new life in America with her perfect new American husband. "What will you do when you get there?" I asked. "You'll have to start at the bottom. You do realize that you can't take your BMW with you. Are you prepared for that? Are you prepared to be an immigrant?" Luma had never wanted for anything but freedom under Saddam. I wanted to prepare her, protect her. She wanted to jump without looking down.

"There, over there. Look at him. Invite him. Please. Please. Pleeeeese."

"Luma, no. I am not going to walk up to some random soldier and invite him to your birthday party."

"Pleeeeese."

"Invite him yourself," I finally conceded, exasperated.

This went on for days leading up to the big event, which was held on her birthday, August 21, 2004. I sent out an email invite to our Western and Iraqi media friends, using the same Internet-based invitation I used back home to invite friends to barbecues and deck parties in Washington. For Luma's party, I asked our guests to bring their dancing shoes and their bathing suits but, please, to leave their Mahdi Army friends at home, a reference to Shiite cleric Moqtada Sadr's militia that had been battling American troops most of the summer.

Luma bought herself a birthday cake from the best pastry shop in town. The cake was the size of a large pizza, covered in white and chocolate icing with "Happy Birthday Luma" in both English and Arabic scrawled in white icing. Rajiv sprang for the food and the spirits, and our cook-of-the-moment, Haider, made kabobs from the grill. The meat sizzled over red coals, stoked by an electrical fan connected by a long extension cord that hung two stories up from my hotel room. The sparks from the coals flickered in the night air.

Of course, Luma's party had to include dancing, so she hired a group of disc jockeys that called itself the "Four Boys DJ." The four boys charged us $100 extra because we were foreigners and our party could be attacked, causing them to lose their equipment. The boys played cassette tapes of Whitney Houston hits all night, interspersed with Egyptian and Iraqi singers who crooned Arabic love songs. The guards and translators danced around the pool, shimmying to the music, shimmying to Luma's gift to them on her birthday, a party, an actual party where people were having fun and forgetting about life beyond the barricades for a moment. Because of the dangers of traveling at night, Baghdad was quiet after sunset. The restaurants and dance halls that had been filled nightly before the war were now empty. Our staff complained that they no longer had any fun. Their families were holed up in their houses, afraid of what lurked outside. I watched the staff dancing from a distance. Something seemed out of place. Only the men were dancing. Where was Luma? I spotted her dancing in a dark corner of the pool deck with two Iraqi teenage girls. "Oh no, no, no, no," I admonished them, walking over. I grabbed Luma lightly by the arm and pulled her in the direction of the dance floor, the real dance floor.

"You want to be American? You want to act like an American woman? You don't hide like that."

"But they'll all watch me dancing!" She was horrified. Men and women did not typically dance together in public places in Iraq. Over time I realized that Luma, as much as she did not want to be an Iraqi, could not deny that this was her country, this was where she learned her place in the world. She was fighting to emerge from the only culture she had ever really known. She was sitting at the side of the pool with her feet in the water, while the boys played. I didn't get it the night of her party, however, and told her so.

"I don't understand," I said. "You're wearing a tight shirt. You wearing jeans to show off your butt. And you don't want people to notice you? Tomorrow I'm giving you a new English word. It's called *contradiction*. Come on. There's safety in numbers. I'll dance with you."

We joined the circle, and everyone stared at her beautiful swinging body, just as Luma had predicted. She closed her eyes and let the music entrance her.

A few weeks later, I took Luma to Jordan, the quintessential coming-of-age road trip. It was my first real "out" from Iraq in two months. At first I wasn't sure whether I should take Luma with me. When I first mentioned it to her, she predicted that she would not get or need a minute of sleep the entire time she was gone. She intended to take advantage of every moment of her time away. I, on the other hand, needed sleep. The pace of our long stream of work days had exhausted me. I wanted to read and sleep and take in a movie and chill out. This was my vacation. I was not interested in partying every night and staying out late and dancing. Jenny and I talked about it on the telephone. She reminded me that I hate business travel because I can't stand going to a restaurant by myself. Plus, Luma could be my translator, helping me navigate the parts of Jordan that were not tourist-centered and therefore more accessible to an English speaker.

Luma and I were both on a Middle Eastern journey through Jordan for the first time. It was the kind of trip I had taken many times in the United States as a young adult. A friend in the passenger seat. A Big Gulp from 7-Eleven propped up against the gearshift. A bag of peanuts and a six-pack of beer in the backseat. I was nineteen when I tasted freedom for the first time, riding off to college without a parent on a southern Illinois highway in my beat-up Honda Civic hatchback.

Luma had to wait until she was twenty-eight to find her freedom in a rented Nissan on Wadi Araba Road to the Dead Sea. Until this trip, she had never been on vacation without her mother or a male relative. She had never worn a bathing suit at a beach where there were both men and women. For all her brashness, Luma had never been to a disco that served alcohol, never swapped telephone numbers with a dance partner, never cranked up the tunes in the car and wasted the cool air-conditioned air with the sunroof open, just because. She had never had a hotel minibar beer.

The first night we were in the Jordanian capital of Amman, she opened the refrigerator of our tenth-floor room at the Four Seasons hotel and discovered a shelf full of beer.

"We should have one," she declared.

"No, no, no," I objected. "Minibars are really expensive, and the accounting department will see this, and really, we just worked out in the gym." I looked at her eager face, a face that said, "But we're on vacation without our mothers!" Before we left, Abu Saif encouraged her to let loose and have fun. "There are no limitations," he said slyly.

For Luma, this trip was the ultimate freedom. She had been reading Victoria Lancellotti's *Here in This World*, a collection of short stories I had given her as a gift for her birthday about Western women who had no inhibitions, no traditions to shackle them, and she wanted to be just like them. Luma dreamed of a different life but could not see it in front of her. She told me at the airport that she had one wish—no, two: "I pray to the God for my daughter, mother, and brother. Then I pray to the God to make me an American."

I saw all of this in her smile as she held out a $6 can of Amstel Light. We each grabbed a cold one, turned off the lights, and sat on the floor to watch the moon rise over the twinkling city. I decided then that this trip would be my gift to her. I wanted everything for her that moment, every trip I'd ever taken, all the places I'd ever seen, all the nights I stood in a foreign land and lost myself in a new horizon. Luma stared out the window, dreaming.

We had traveled to Jordan by airplane. A week before we left, a plane was fired on by a surface-to-air missile, and Royal Jordanian temporarily suspended flights. We were on the second flight out since the ban had been lifted. A passenger moving through the security screening banged a piece of luggage against a fiberglass panel. I immediately ducked, as did about five beefy contract workers. Luma didn't miss a beat in the story she was telling. "Don't worry; it wasn't a mortar," she assured me before picking up where she left off. If I was giving Luma the trip of a lifetime, then she was reminding me to let go of Iraq long enough to enjoy it.

This was Luma's first airplane ride, her first exposure to the indignities of the war-on-terrorism airport search. A week earlier she had used diet pills to bribe the woman at the checkpoint to the Sheraton hotel to stop touching her "in a bad way." (She also asked her to "stop touching the little one, my friend, the one they call Jackie.") The woman, an Iraqi hired to frisk any females entering the hotel, had a habit of running her hands under our bras and squeezing our butts, kneading them as if she were preparing dough for the oven. As best as I could tell, the woman was simply doing a thorough check for explosives, but it was humiliating to stand there getting felt up while the American soldiers watched with smirks on their faces.

At the Baghdad airport, Luma set off a walk-through detector. When a security worker asked her to take off her shoes, Luma wouldn't budge. "I know how it is," she told him, wagging her finger. "First you ask for the shoes, then the pants! I will not." They waved her through. Passing through immigration, I handed an Iraqi security guard both of our passports. He looked at us curiously. "Which one Iraqi?" Great. I was in my headscarf, dowdy black pants, an equally dowdy button-down shirt, and horrid utility sandals. Luma, her hair recently cut like pop star Pink, wore tight blue jeans and a studded black belt. I had stopped caring about how I looked. I was hot and dirty all of the time. I had no time for fashion, no desire to pretty myself up. The hotel water had dried out my hair, which was long and stringy. My eyes were constantly red from the dry heat, and I could no longer wear my contact lenses for long stretches. I was a mess, and I knew it, but did that guard have to remind me?

Luma sat by the window for the spiraling ride into the sky. Her hands were shaking, and she couldn't sit still. She refused to look out the window and wrung her hands for the entire hour-and-a-half flight. "Wasn't that fun?" I asked, as we walked down the steps onto the tarmac at the Jordanian airport. Luma glared at me and clutched her stomach. I understood. My first spiraling flight into Iraq, I'd felt the same way.

At the Four Seasons in Amman, a luxurious, white-stone hotel, we dumped our bags in the room and went to have lunch at the restaurant in the lobby. Luma opened her menu. "Do they have wine?"

"Luma, it's not even two in the afternoon."

She shot me the same blank look as when I told her how to dress to go to a military base in Baghdad.

When the waitress came, Luma ordered a glass of house red and I had the house white. After months (for me) and years (for her) of the same Iraqi food, the same rice, the same tomato, cucumber, and green pepper salad, we could not wait to sink into something else—lentil soup, smoked salmon, and cottage cheese for me and grilled cheese and fries for Luma. After a sip of wine, Luma held the glass in front of her and pushed her face closer to mine so I could better study her. "Am I drunk yet? I don't feel drunk." She ordered a second glass, drank it, and then asked again: "Am I drunk yet?" I patiently explained the difference between being buzzed, tipsy, and drunk, her first vacation lesson. "You don't want to get drunk," I said. "Keep it at tipsy. I don't want to have to carry you up to the room." Iraqi women generally do not drink in public. When Huda and I made a run to the liquor store to buy wine for a party at the bureau, she went into the store with me, but would not touch the bottles. Luma had no religious qualms about drinking, and for a reason that both saddened and amused me, seemed to think that drinking alcohol made her more American. She had her first glass of wine only a few months before the trip to Jordan. It made her feel free to be able to drink, to do as she pleased. She was a college student on her first spring break.

After lunch, we whisked off to the Mecca Mall, a large,

multistory, indoor shopping center in the heart of Amman. Aside from the garish clothing and abundance of headscarves for sale, the Mecca Mall could be any mall in America. I was in search of jeans, black shoes, and maybe a new shirt. As much as Luma modeled herself after the Western image of women, she was disappointed to discover that Jordanian women, succumbing to the pressures and ideal of woman-as-twig, tended to be much smaller than those in Iraq. The saleslady in one store asked Luma if she wanted to try a size 27 pair of pants.— 28, 29, 30, 34? The sales lady ticked off the sizes, and Luma shook her hand after each. "How about a 44?" Luma was very quiet when she left the store. "I am fat!" she cried out. "I need to lose weight. I don't feel fat in Iraq. I have never felt fat. But I am fat!" Luma was not fat. She had the body of a young woman who had a baby, who eats healthfully, and does not obsess about diet and exercise. For the rest of the trip she continued to talk about diets and exercise and asked me to come up with a meal plan for her.

That night we made plans to go for sushi with a *Post* translator whose house had been bombed in Baghdad. He was now living in Jordan with his family and working for Scott Wilson, the *Post* foreign correspondent based in Amman. I had not yet met Naseer but heard he was quite the character. He was a former minder for Saddam, who had minded Rajiv and Anthony Shadid before they no longer needed an escort from Iraq's Information Ministry, which controlled the access foreign media had to Iraq under Saddam.

Luma decided we needed to dress up for the night: tight pants, cropped shirts. I wore my new jeans, purchased at the Mecca Mall. The jeans were a nice fit; I could wear them in the bureau without feeling like a floozy. "What do you think?" I had asked Luma, swirling around when I stepped from the dressing room. "Well," she said, "do you think they are tight enough?" Now back at the Four Seasons and getting ready for our evening out, she was not pleased with my shirt selection, a sleeveless orange T-shirt. "Jackie!" she exclaimed. "We're not going to the office." She pulled a shirt out of her suitcase and handed it to me. After I put it on, she showed me how it could be adjusted by pulling two strings, revealing the desired amount of cleavage. "There! Now you look like an American."

With that, we set off for dinner with Naseer to a sushi restaurant at the top of the Howard Johnson Hotel in Amman. After dinner, we walked around the corner to Nie, one of Amman's hottest night spots, filled with trendy Jordanians and their foreign friends. We didn't have a reservation, and the bouncers flipped their hands at us to go away. Naseer leaned in. I heard him say, *"Washington Post."* The bouncers waved us in to a posh, velvety drinking spot turned dance spot after the beautiful Jordanians got wild with alcohol. Luma decided she wanted a cocktail, so I ordered her a cosmopolitan. She guzzled it. "Am I drunk yet? I do not even feel tipsy." She ordered another one from the bartender. While she looked away, I leaned in and told him to go easy on the alcohol. Every time a man would come over to talk to us, Naseer, who had become a very drunk minder, shooed them away. I wasn't used to this sort of big-brothering and Luma, two cosmos to the wind, would have none of it either. She wanted to talk and flirt, and not with Naseer, who kept insisting on walking us to and from the bathroom lest we talk to anyone else. We made a break for it and ditched Naseer when he turned to watch the dance floor. Naseer called Luma on her mobile phone while we were in the taxi on the way back to the Four Seasons. I could hear his foul screams through the receiver. "Fuck you guys! Fuck *The Washington Post.* Fuck everything!"

We had hurt his feelings, and I felt bad about that. It was not easy to go from being an important Saddam man, to an unemployed Saddam man, to a well-connected Saddam man working for *The Washington Post*, to an unconnected man without a country, to a man in a bar whose female charges had ditched him. But really. We needed no minding. We were just trying to have a little fun.

The next morning Luma woke up with her first hangover. "See," I scolded her with a smile. "That's why I told you not to get drunk."

In Baghdad, Luma and I had decided that we would spend most of our trip in Jordan at the Dead Sea. I needed a resort, a beach, where I could read and think of anything but Iraq. Luma had told me that we could borrow her uncle's car to get from Amman to the Dead Sea, about an hour away. But the morning we were planning to leave, she said the plan had changed because her uncle was worried that she did not have a driver's license. Instead, we would borrow Jamal's car. Jamal was an Iraqi engineer Luma knew from Baghdad who was in Amman for a few months to escape the violence. I wasn't sure how this was better, given that Luma still had no driver's license. It turned out that Jamal did not have a car to lend us but he did have a contact at the Avis rental car agency in Amman. There, Jamal disappeared into a back room while we went to a garage to look at rows of four-door sedans. Back in the office, I could not understand a word of what was being negotiated, but whatever it was, it took two hours, and I ultimately had to hand over my District of Columbia driver's license and credit card. To repay Jamal for this "favor," we allowed him to take us to lunch at Whisper's, an air-conditioned restaurant near the Four Seasons that had a giant fish tank near the bar. It also had a salad bar, so I was content to munch on lettuce while Luma and Jamal talked in Arabic. I tried to read the conversation by gesture and picked up that Jamal had a thing for Luma but she was not interested at all. Another hour later, we had to go to the supermarket to gather provisions, to the 7-Eleven for sodas, and to the gas station to fuel up. We went to two different gas stations, each one rejected by Jamal for its inferior fuel. By the third gas station, I was irritated and sullen that we had wasted the day on these travel arrangements.

Finally, we had a full tank of gas, and Luma plunged our Nissan into the chaotic traffic and we were off, weaving and dodging and honking through the streets of Amman. Luma looked over at me. "What's wrong?"

"Nothing. I just need ten minutes."

I closed my eyes.

"Okay, here's the thing," I said after sorting through my thoughts. "In Baghdad, when everything takes so long, so be it. My time there seems endless. But this is my vacation, my five days. We wasted a morning arranging transportation, and I just wanted out of the city. In Washington, I have Rehoboth, this beach in Delaware where I go during the summer to escape the city. I didn't grow up in a city, so I need space. In Baghdad, I have no space at all, no sanctuary, no reprieve except that hot, miserable kitchen where I can bake."

She nodded. I was never sure how much of what I said Luma actually comprehended.

"I just need order," I continued, closing my eyes again.

I ducked in the passenger seat while Luma piloted our great adventure. As the road opened, revealing the wide brown vista of the Jordan Valley on each side, I opened my eyes and saw that we were now barreling down a hill, straddling the center lane. It's one thing to get a late start on your treasured vacation; it's quite another to die before you make it to the beach. "Luma," I asked meekly, "is it difficult to get a driver's license in Iraq?"

"Oh, yes," she said.

"The test is hard?"

"Test? There is no test. You pay a bribe. Twenty-five thousand dinars!" (About $17 in 2004.)

"Luma," I said quietly, pleading. "You know I never ask anything of you. You know this. But please, I don't care how long it takes us to get to the Dead Sea. Please, please drive the speed limit. . . Do you know you're driving on the shoulder?"

"What's a shoulder?" she asked innocently.

At the first military checkpoint, a sign that we were getting close to the Israeli border, the soldiers addressed Luma in Arabic. She pretended not to understand and asked him to speak in English. They waved us through.

"Why did you pretend?" I asked.

"I don't want to be Iraqi for this trip. I need a vacation from it." Fair enough, I thought, as we drove past camels grazing in brown fields. We both needed an escape. We drove and drove, until it came to us on the right: a patch of sparkling, extraordinarily blue water beneath the mountains of the West Bank on the other side. The Dead Sea. I'd never felt so alive.

I spotted the sign as I gazed out the window at the sea. "Look," I pointed, to a brown sign with an arrow. "Baptism site." I wondered, could it be? Was this where Jesus was baptized?

"Do you mind if we go find it?" I asked. Luma did not mind at all and turned right on a narrow asphalt road. Then there it was. "Site of Jesus' Baptism." My eyes welled up with tears. I understood in an instant why Muslims cry and plead and pound their chests on pilgrimages to holy sites. I needed this moment to understand. I felt so close to my faith at that moment, to the bareness of it that lay in front of me, behind a gate and a ticket booth. I had spent months in Iraq learning about Islam, the similarities between it and Christianity. Huda read to me from the Quran to show me that true Islam did not support the violence in Iraq. She was desperate for me to understand, to take this understanding back to the United States with me. I found it easy to talk openly about religion with our Iraqi staff. They knew that I had grown up in a religious household, that faith had been and remained an important part of my life. In a secular American newsroom, journalists tend not to talk about their beliefs. We are supposed to be objective or at least private, even when it comes to matters of the soul.

I remember when I first came to the *Post*, a colleague in the southern Maryland bureau blurted out that only ignorant, uneducated people believed in Creation. "Really?" I said, turning around in my chair to face him. "Because I believe in Creation. Do you think I'm stupid?" He turned red. "No, I'm sorry, it's just that, I didn't know you were, you know, a church person." A church person! Well, yeah, I guess I was. But what did that mean? That I was intolerant, evangelical, out to convert the world? I was not on a mission. This was just who I was. After that, I never felt comfortable telling my colleagues that I tried to go to church every Sunday, that I was not a fanatic, that I felt quite normal, that the thing inside that kept me level was my faith in God. I didn't feel comfortable until I came to the

Financial staff and sat in a pod of four other young women, two of whom also went to church every Sunday. It was no big deal.

The baptism site was closed that afternoon, so Luma and I pledged to come the next day. The heat and humidity were nearly unbearable when we drove back the next morning. The site where Jesus was reportedly baptized (Israel claims its own spot on the other side of the Jordan River) is now actually a dry riverbed with steps leading to it. The Jordan River is a few hundred feet away. We traipsed behind our English-speaking guide to the river, a meandering body of green water. Luma asked the tour guide to find us an empty water bottle, and she filled it while we sat with our feet in the warm water. "My mother will want some of this," Luma said, while dipping the water bottle in.

"That's a great idea," I said. "Mine will, too."

Later that night when we were hanging out in the swimming pool at our resort, Luma turned to me, beaming, and asked if I felt happy. "Happy? No, better than happy," I told her. "I feel safe." She nodded, and we leaned our heads back against the tiled pool wall and watched the sun drop behind the mountains in Israel.

Luma had two glasses of wine every night at dinner, enough to put her soundly to sleep when she returned to our room. I was a little worried that she was drinking so much but decided she was simply taking advantage of the fact her mother wasn't around. She was on spring break in Florida. Each night, I made her drink a cocktail of water and ibuprofen before tucking her into bed. While she slept, I wrote from our balcony and called my mom and Jenny and talked to them until the weight of sleep dragged me under. I needed them to hear my voice, happy and safe for a change. Too often when I called home, our conversations were interrupted by the buzz of helicopters overhead or sirens in the distance or loud bangs. After I hung up, content that Jenny and my mom could fall asleep not worrying about me for a change, I snuggled under the covers, leaving the balcony door open to the night air and the twinkling lights of Jericho in the faded distance.

We spent three days at the Dead Sea and then took the

long way north back to Amman, up the winding, terrifyingly narrow highway to Mount Nebo, and then on to Madaba, famous for its Byzantine mosaics.

The morning before we left, Luma told me she wanted me to hear "the whole of her story." When she was eighteen and in college, Saddam's sadistic son, Uday, invited her to a party. She knew better than to refuse. Uday had a reputation for taking what he wanted, including countless young girls, even brides, newly wed. At the party, Uday gave her a drink. Luma remembered nothing more. She woke up the next morning in his bed. She had been raped. She sobbed as she told the story, then ran into the bathroom to cry even more. I was stunned, sickened by what she had told me. A while later, Luma came out to apologize to me before continuing the story. "Don't apologize, please; don't apologize," I told her as she slumped on the bed.

A relative who was at the party recognized Luma the next morning and told her mother what had happened. Luma's mother kicked her out of the house and refused to speak to her for two years while Luma lived with her grandmother. Because she had been raped, Luma was ruined as far as her mother was concerned. One aunt never spoke to Luma again. Luma thought perhaps there had been a mistake. She tried to reach Uday. His advisers told her that she could have an operation to restore her virginity. Luma declined. She had heard that women often showed up for the procedure and were raped again or killed. She was bewildered.

"How did you feel when you heard that Uday had been killed by an American bomb?" I asked.

"I didn't believe it," she replied.

"Not even when they showed the bodies on television?"

"Maybe then."

"Do you feel justice? Did you feel happy?"

Luma turned her head to the wall at my questions.

"It didn't change anything," she said quietly.

As we drove away from the Dead Sea, I tried to explain she had done nothing wrong. "A woman has a right, even if she is married, to refuse her husband," I told her. "You were raped, Luma. You were not bad. You are not bad."

She stared out the window as I steered the car up the narrow switchbacks to Mount Nebo.

"You're the first person who ever told me that I did not do anything wrong," Luma said, her voice hushed.

"Luma, you did nothing wrong. I am so, so sorry that happened to you. You did nothing wrong."

We made it to Mount Nebo and a small monastery at the top of the hill, where Biblical history says God sent Moses to see the promised land of Israel before he died. At the top of the mountain, Luma and I looked, too, to the land Moses saw, to Israel across the wide valley of the Dead Sea.

We walked into the church. "Do you feel that?" Luma said, her eyes wide. "Do you feel it?"

"Yes," I said. "I feel that every time I walk into a church."

She sat alone on a bench near the altar, "saying my wishes," she told me as we walked back to the car.

We had planned to stop to sight-see in Madaba but Luma immediately noticed that most of the women wore long dresses and headscarves. Luma was still in a spaghetti-strap shirt, appropriate at the Dead Sea and the disco in Amman but not Madaba, she concluded. "Where did all these bin Laden come from?" she asked nervously.

She reached into her bag to pull on a long-sleeved shirt, and I took off my fishing cap and threw it in the back of the car. "Get out of here as fast as you can," she instructed me, and I floored the Nissan and headed back to the modern city of Amman.

Luma and I did not talk about the "rest of her story" again. But I saw her differently. She was a real survivor. She had every reason to give up, to be swallowed up by what had happened to her. But she had not. She had chosen to embrace life, to be free. Now she had to survive her new freedom in Iraq, which was still being delivered to her in a swirl of blood and violence.

By the pool at the Four Seasons, Luma had confided how scared she was that she would be killed before she could leave Iraq with her daughter.

"Promise me, you'll make sure Sarah gets to America if something happens to me," she asked.

"Of course, I promise, but let's not talk like that. You're going to get out."

We hatched a plan for the future. After I returned to the United States, she and her family would apply for visas. It was a long shot but perhaps Luma's whole story would help them get asylum somewhere. If they came to the United States, Luma would stay with me or with my sister. I had already talked to Jenny, who was completely agreeable. Sarah would attend school with my nephew Aidan. Luma could help baby-sit Sarah and Aidan in the afternoons to earn money. Eventually, she could get her own apartment, or I might have enough saved up to buy a house for all of us.

"I don't want to die before it happens," Luma said, eyes hidden behind dark sunglasses.

"You won't," I assured her. But we both knew it was an empty promise.

I was tanned and rested when we touched down again in Baghdad five days later. I could never have imagined such a journey. I had watched Luma live.

"Welcome to Baghdad," the flight attendant chirped. Luma scowled. "Don't welcome me home," she said.

An hour later we climbed into the armored car that took us back to our drab hotel. I sat in the back and watched the grim postwar landscape pass us by—the wreckage, the dusty terrain, the garbage piled up against barbed wire. In the passenger seat, Luma blinked back tears.

"I hate this country," she said. "Look at the tanks. Look at the guard rails," which were mangled by roadside bombs. "I just want to close my eyes and someone will wake me up in the morning and say, 'Come on, here is your flight.' I don't want to be here. I just want to live normal."

Back at the hotel, Luma came into my room to thank me for

taking her to Jordan. She started to cry again. "I was free," she choked and buried her face in my shoulder. "You were Luma," I said, wrapping her in a hug. "You were free."

During the next few days, Luma became more quiet. She started coming in late and falling asleep at her desk. She blamed it on late-night squabbles with her mother, on Sarah being sick, on worrying about everything. She talked about how much she hated Iraq. She fought with Bassam, who didn't think she should deny her country, as bad as it was.

Omar was in Jordan—our trips had overlapped by one night. He planned to return about a week after Luma and I got back to Baghdad. I promised to make macaroni and cheese for the four of us: me, Luma, Omar, and Bassam. It was their favorite dish, and they always requested it when I offered to cook for the bureau. Bassam, Luma, and I waited on our floor for Omar to emerge into the Sheraton lobby. We giggled and shoved one another, laughed and waited for our little family to be back together again. Luma seemed happy, alive again. Perhaps this was all she needed, I wondered, looking over at her.

Omar strolled across the lobby. *"Ente when?"* I called out to him, proud of my Arabic. *Where were you?* Bassam and Luma burst into giggles. *"Enta when! Enta when!* You called him a woman," Luma said after she caught her breath.

We dished up our macaroni and cheese and took our plates to the deck by the pool. We opened a bottle of Jordanian wine, toasting our adventures on a perfect September night in Baghdad. We were four friends, so full of life, so full of possibility. Luma and I shared our stories from Jordan. I told them about Iyad, the twenty-two-year-old Jordanian I met at a dance club one night. The next night Iyad took me out for a drink. At the end of our "date," Iyad asked me if I would cook for him when I came back to Jordan. He looked so innocent, his body muscular and toned from his job at a health club. Iyad was a university student. He was doting, polite. He sent text messages to my Jordanian cell phone, ending with "MWH," or kiss. "Where will I cook for you?" I asked playfully. "In your mother's kitchen?" Iyad still lived at home. Iyad was so, like, twenty-two, and I was so not. "Why do you care so much about age?" Omar asked, as I recounted the story.

"Omar, he was twenty-two!"

"So?"

Luma decided to pipe in. "She isn't very free for an American. But she has the right."

Fox News was having a loud party at the other end of the deck. The music blared from a speaker. One of their producers cooked hamburgers from the same spit our cook made kabobs on for Luma's birthday party. We wanted no part of it and declined an invitation to join them. We just wanted to lose ourselves in our own night.

Pfffft.

The first mortar sailed over our heads. We barely glanced up. It seemed too far away.

Pfffft.

The second mortar shot over us. We looked up.

"That was close," I said, the words barely out of my mouth before a large crack and flash of fire exploded over us. We looked at one another for a split second, a collective recognition on each of our faces. We were going to die together.

"Oh my God! Run! Run!" I don't remember whose voice it was.

The revelers at the Fox party sprinted toward the door ahead of us. Luma, Bassam, Omar, and I ran behind them. We ducked into the dark atrium of the hotel. People were nervous, shaking. Omar had shoved Luma and me into the middle of the pack of bodies to better protect us from the attack.

We waited, breathing hard, sweating together as the rockets exploded outside. Our guards found us there and berated us for not running after hearing the first mortar. It was Combat Zone 101. *Stupid! Stupid!* I heard myself say in my head. *Stupid!* I had let my guard down. For one night I had crept into the dreams of my Iraqi translators, losing myself in their hopes, losing myself. And I could have died. I could have died right there, and Jenny would have been devastated—all because I wanted to feel normal for one night, all because I wanted to bring Jordan

back for one night. I called her and then my mother. I choked
on the words as I recalled what had happened, how we all
thought we were going to die. I tried never to sound frightened
when I called my family or friends. I knew they worried
enough. And the fright I often felt in Iraq usually stayed just
below the surface anyway, a necessary survival tactic to keep
from being scared all of the time. Even when I was scared, I
found it difficult to articulate. I was flat. But not that night.
That night I was terrified, more scared than I had been outside
of Abu Ghraib when the men tried to grab me. "We thought
we were going to die together," I told Jenny again and again. "I
kept thinking, please God, make it fast. I want to wake up and
see Heaven."

Back in the lounge on the *Post* floor of the hotel, Omar, Luma,
and Bassam dragged on cigarettes, their hands still shaking.

"Give me one of those," I said, while they stared. I puffed
amateurishly, coughing whenever I inhaled. I had only smoked
one time, back in high school before a trumpet solo at a high
school basketball game. I messed up the solo, and my father was
furious when he smelled the smoke in the car. I blamed it on a
Canadian exchange student who could be forgiven for smoking
because she was a foreigner and thus afforded some sort of
amnesty from my American father. I vowed never to smoke cigarettes again. I had not, until that night.

Omar and Bassam left shortly after to return to their homes.
Our night, the magic was ruined. Luma and I finished off the
wine and then played soccer in the hallway, bruising soccer that
left us tumbling and wrestling. She broke my glasses. I knocked
the breath out of her when I shoved her to the ground in a play
struggle.

Bruised and broken, we crawled to my room, as the guards
watched, amused and concerned at our erratic behavior.

Luma decided to spend the night, and as we drifted off, I
realized the spell of Jordan had not only broken, it had broken
Luma.

I woke up the next morning to a tremendous blast that
shook the hotel. Oh my God. Not again. Luma had slept

through the sound. I reached over and shook her awake.
"Luma, get up! Get on the floor!"

She looked at me in a daze and then the second explosion
went off. This time we both dove to the floor. I could hear the
guards running to the room. I got up and flung it open.

"We're okay. We're okay!"

A second later, Luma's cell phone rang. It was her mother. A
car bomb had blown up outside her mother's house across
town; we had not heard that explosion. Fortunately, her mother
was staying with Sarah at Luma's home in a different Baghdad
neighborhood. Her mother was frightened. The house had
been destroyed. In a panic, Luma stuffed her clothes into a plastic sack and asked our night driver, Rifaat, to take her home.

I never saw her again.

*When I first saw a photograph of Luma, I thought she looked
dangerous. Not dangerous like a hooded criminal with small
penciled eyes who is out there somewhere calculating more
harm. No, with her big brown eyes and wide smile, Luma
looked dangerously alive, a woman dancing hard through life,
her arms flailing in uncontained fervor, unconsciously taking
out people on the sidelines, people trying to live safely and
unnoticed in the shadows of war, people like my sister.*

*"I don't know if I should ask Luma to go to the Dead Sea,"
my sister confided to me in the weeks before her vacation. "She's
just so . . ." she paused. "She's just not careful."*

*"Then don't take her," I warned, suddenly angry at this
woman I'd never met. I wanted to love the Iraqi staff just as my
sister did, to sympathize with their hard lives and desires, but
that love had limits. "Take Huda instead," I said. Beautiful
Huda. Poetry-loving Huda. Safe Huda. So when my sister told
me a week later that Luma would accompany her, I could barely
contain my irritation. "I'm so happy she'll get to go with you," I
lied.*

"I wish you were going, too," Jackie said.

I did, too. Only a few years before I accompanied my sister, at the age of thirty, on her first trip abroad to England. I couldn't wait to show her Oxford, where I had spent a summer studying while in college. It was the only place I ever lived that my sister hadn't seen. I needed her as witness to my life, at times to make that life real, at others to make it less lonely. We also were the quintessential road sisters, perfectly tuned to each other's moves and thoughts. When Jackie graduated from college, I was the one who journeyed with her on the four-day trek west to Los Angeles, squeezed in alongside all of her possessions with just enough air to belt out John Denver songs as we rolled along in her Chevy Nova. She would live in California, and I would live in Pennsylvania, the longest stretch of miles ever to separate us—until Iraq. At the airport, she walked me to my gate where we said good-bye. I turned around for one last glimpse of her before I boarded my plane, and there she stood, two fingers raised in a "V"—"V" for victory. Conquer the distance, that gesture said. Conquer the life lived well. For years after, whenever one of us left on a journey, we would flash that sign.

In my mind, I saw them off, Jackie and Luma, first waving good-bye as they barreled down the dangerous airport road, waving good-bye as they boarded the old Iraqi Airways jet that would take them to Amman, waving good-bye as they set off in a rental car toward their resort on the Dead Sea. My sister would call at each leg of the journey, sounding happier than I'd heard her in months. I knew Luma was, in part, responsible for the joy in my sister's voice, and I would grow to love the dangerous Iraqi woman whose freedom came in her refusal to play it safe. I was grateful that she and my sister could share a journey of their lifetimes.

But for now I stood on the lip of the photograph, wistful and anxious as I watched them go, my own two fingers raised in a "V"—"V" for victory, and for peace.

CHAPTER 7

The cluster of guards and drivers made a ring around the drying rack in the laundry room of the bureau, where a former palace cook for Saddam Hussein washed our clothes. Um Hussein, no relation to the former Iraqi president, was in her sixties, widowed and alone. Her newborn son, Hussein, died ten days after his birth, leaving Um Hussein childless and an outcast. The whole point of being a woman in Iraqi society was to grow up, get married, and raise a family of sons and daughters, who would, in turn, grow up and take care of their parents. Like Falah, Um Hussein was constantly prodding me to eat more. She was convinced I had not found an acceptable suitor because I was too thin, and she wanted to spare me her fate.

When I first met Um Hussein in May 2004, she was working as one of two daytime cooks. She and Um Mohammed, a housewife in her fifties, came to the Sheraton around 8 A.M. to fry eggs, make tea for breakfast, and prepare lunch for the staff and correspondents. After they cleaned up the dishes and sometimes caught a catnap on the sofa in the kitchen, they went home. No one could stand Um Hussein's cooking. She and Um Mohammed took turns making lunch, and the drivers and translators groaned when they heard Um Hussein was cooking her greasy beans in red sauce, soggy French fries, and flavorless stews. Fortunately for Um Hussein, Saddam's palace staff never knew which of his dozens of opulent palaces the former president would show up at for dinner each night. As Saddam scurried, paranoid and secretive between his residences, the chance that he might taste Um Hussein's cooking was fairly remote.

Um Hussein, came to the *Post* through Khalid, our senior

translator who had worked for the Planning Ministry under Saddam. Um Hussein had the body of a toy Weeble but was too solid to wobble. She shuffled her feet under her long skirts, sweating and panting. When she hugged me, she picked me up and carried me a few steps across the floor, even though at five feet three inches, I towered above her. Although Um Hussein was eligible for a government pension, the new interim Iraqi government lost her paperwork. As a former palace worker and Baathist tied to the former regime, Um Hussein was not on the priority list of civil service workers the new government wanted to compensate. I found her crying in the kitchen one morning after she had tussled with a security guard outside the ministry office where she went once again to try to get her check. Um Hussein did not want to work anymore. Her body was tired, but without her pension check, she could not survive without her salary from the *Post*. "Can we help her?" I asked Omar, who raised his eyes back at me. *We can try*, they said. *But if we go to the ministry and try to inquire on her behalf, they will find out she works for an American company, and then she will be targeted.*

Um Hussein had a washing machine in a little room off the kitchen in our new bureau, a residence in Baghdad we moved to in October 2004 after fleeing the diminishing security at the Sheraton. In the move, Um Hussein lost her cooking privileges, which made her more bitter about her lot in life. We simply couldn't stand any more of her food, however, and the move allowed Karl Vick the opportunity to shift her responsibilities to the laundry room. Karl, who became the bureau chief when Rajiv left Iraq for good in September 2004, tried to soften the blow by buying Um Hussein a washing machine for her own house after she quit in protest. It worked. Um Hussein was back within a couple of weeks, her own clothes tidier than ever. Although we provided Um Hussein with a clothes dryer at the bureau, she was too scared to use it, even after I spent twenty minutes one morning showing her how it worked and explaining that it was not going to blow up despite the fact that it shook rather violently while on. After she wrung out the clothes, Um Hussein spread them across a laundry rope or on

several metal drying racks, which is where I discovered some of
the staff gathered that morning. I wondered what the fuss was
and squeezed in for a better look. They were silently staring at
my thong underwear, which Um Hussein had daintily arranged
on the top of the drying rock. I fled the kitchen and ran upstairs
to Karl's room.

"You want to buy a ticket?" I asked, bursting in.

"What's that, Spinno?" Karl said, looking up from his laptop.

"Apparently they're selling tickets to see my underwear in
the laundry room."

Karl laughed. He was used to me ranting about the indignities
of being the only woman in the bureau aside from the Ums.

I loved the Ums, my term of endearment for Um
Mohammed and Um Hussein. I especially loved hanging out
with them in the kitchen. They made me feel like I was still part
of the world of womenfolk. They worried when I did not eat,
when I came into the kitchen for lunch and lifted a pot lid, only
to put it back and walk out without even a scoop of rice. As a
vegetarian, I could not eat their chicken and beef dishes. Sometimes I made myself a tuna sandwich, scraping the fish out of a
can and tucking it into the pocket of Iraqi bread. I had added
fish and eggs to my diet in Iraq to keep from getting anemic,
which I constantly battled even in the United States. Um
Mohammed always watched me make my lunch and then tried
to make it for me the next day, adding her signature splash of
vegetable oil. Like all good Iraqi cooks, the Ums believed in oil,
and often after I ate their food, I was sick for hours until it left
my system, one way or another. Omar used this as leverage to
get the Ums to take seriously his directive not to cook my
food in meat broth, which they routinely did, passing it off as
vegetarian nonetheless. "You are making her sick," he told
them, while they listened sadly, hanging their heads. "It's okay,
you aren't used to someone like me," I interrupted, hoping they
understood my tone if not my words. But it was hard to hide the
fact that I was pale and shaking, having just thrown up their
meat-laced rice. The first time I tasted one of Um Mohammed's
rice dishes, I recognized it immediately as "dirty rice," U.S.

southern-style rice with liver pieces. "Oh, I can't eat this," I told Um Mohammed, handing her the plate back. "This is dirty rice."

"Um Mohammed rice nooooo dirty!" she said, walking away insulted.

"No, no," I called out after her. But it would have been futile to try to explain.

The Ums wanted to wait on me like they did the men in the bureau, but I didn't want to be waited on. Over time, they got used to me joining them in the kitchen to make my own lunch, and sometimes lunch for Omar, who liked when I served him pizza made from the Iraqi bread *samoon*, topped with grated mozzarella and tomato sauce. The Ums often made me soup or beans and called me into the kitchen to see. "Look, Jackie," Um Mohammed would say, lifting the lid on the small pot. "No meat, no chicken." Sometimes, if I was not on deadline or out reporting a story, I sat in the kitchen with them and helped snap green beans or slice tomatoes for lunch. Um Mohammed's younger sister, Wijdan, a kindergarten teacher by training, was the better cook of the two. She believed in presentation: lemon wedges tucked around her salad, paprika sprinkled decoratively around her hummus. The two sisters gossiped in Arabic while they worked, occasionally joined by Um Hussein, who shouted out her two cents from the laundry room.

We had not needed a laundress at the Sheraton because the hotel staff provided laundry service. To keep track of the clothes, the laundry staff wrote the number of our rooms on each article of clothing in permanent blue ballpoint ink. Each time I changed rooms, I got a new number. On my favorite peach button-down shirt, they scribbled "103," the number of my first flea-infested quarters. When I moved to 109 next to Rajiv, someone simply crossed out 103 and wrote "109" above it. By the time I got to 116, the writing went about one-third of the way up the shirt. Omar was furious when he saw what they had done. He sent the shirt back and admonished the laundry staff to remove the numbers. He threatened to call the hotel management and have them fired. I thought this was a little extreme and told Omar so. I kind of liked my souvenir shirt from the Sheraton. But Omar dismissed me. "I know my people," he said, using the same phrase as Abu Saif. A few hours later the shirt came back scrubbed clean of the numbers, with an apology from the manager of the hotel laundry service. It seemed they did not know what to do with a woman's shirt, which did not need to be tucked into a pair of trousers like a man's shirt would be. I looked closely at the shirt after the laundry manager scurried down the stairs. I burst out in laughter. "Look what your people did," I said, showing it to Omar. "They scrubbed so hard they put a hole in it." Omar scowled.

I had little, if any, privacy in the bureau. I accepted this begrudgingly. Once Um Mohammed walked in on me in the bathroom after I had just stepped out of the shower. I was looking in the mirror trying to determine if my butt was still in shape after not running for months. She just stared. "Um Mohammed, please get out!" I implored, as I tried to cover myself with my hands. She continued to look. "Niiiiice, Jackie," she said before backing out and closing the door. Great, I thought, knowing how much Um Mohammed wanted to fatten me up. That meant my butt was bigger!

I had tried to lock the bathroom door the first time I took a shower, but the lock stuck, and I ended up having to crawl through an open window onto the roof and shout for the guards to let me in through another door. Although the bathroom window was tinted, making it virtually impossible for anyone to see in, the guards wanted to be certain that my honor was kept intact. They had the handyman put up a sheet over the outside to provide one extra shield. The handyman stapled the sheet so securely that I would not be able to escape if the lock stuck. So I had to leave it unlocked and hope that someone did not barge in.

Mine was the first room in the new bureau to get curtains. Mohanned was worried that the Iraqi guards on the roof of the *Time* magazine house next door would spy on me through the large glass windows of my bedroom. We were not getting mortared at the house like we had been at the Sheraton, so I actually started sleeping in my bed in shorts and a T-shirt rather than the long-sleeved shirt and pants I wore during the day. It had been easier in the Sheraton to flop down on the carpet fully dressed. Inevitably someone would come to shake me awake to head to the stairwell, and one night I was so exhausted that I refused to go. "Here, I'll just sleep here," I said, getting up from the center of the floor and lying back down in a little alcove in front of the bathroom. "No, Jackie, no," one of the guards said, reaching for me but not allowing himself to touch my wrist. "Fine!" I said, getting up and grabbing my pillow. "Rajiv isn't here. I'll sleep in his room." My room was in the front of the hotel, and the guards thought it made a better target for mortars. The guards let me into Rajiv's room, which faced the Green Zone in the back of the hotel, and I curled up on his bed and slept for another three hours. At dawn, I got up and returned to my room, only to be awakened by another explosion. This time I needed no prompting from the guards. I took my pillow back to Rajiv's room and stayed there until I started my day.

At the new bureau we were far more worried about being overrun by insurgents than being attacked by mortars, but we were not immune from bombs. One morning in December, a car bomb exploded on a nearby street, shattering all of the windows in the bureau. It was just after dawn. Sabah, our night security chief, hurried Karl, Anthony, and me to a safer spot behind the stairwell. I was in the shorts and white T-shirt I had slept in, so Sabah took off his leather coat and draped it around me. There was nothing he could do about my bare legs so he stood in front of me to block the view of the other staff.

To most of the male Iraqi staff, I was somewhere between girl and woman, frozen in prepubescent adolescence, no doubt made easier by the fact that I looked young and played sports. As a woman, I would be a sexual creature, grown up, marriage material, someone's potential wife and lover. As a girl I could still be a sister, an innocent daughter. I learned how to recognize the difference and act accordingly. Whenever I hugged a male member of our staff, which was rare, they made sure to call me sister, to repeat it during the seconds of the hug so that it was clear to any observer and even themselves that this was a familiar hug between brother and sister. I found myself suppressing the woman inside of me the longer I was in Iraq, adopting the Iraqi view of myself as an asexual creation. I adopted it so thoroughly that when I arrived back in the United States, it took me months to feel comfortable wearing shorts in public. I felt practically naked in spaghetti-strap shirts after covering my shoulders for so long.

In spite of the occasional indignities in Iraq, it seemed easier to be a female correspondent than a male one. My male colleagues had a harder time getting Iraqi women to talk to them. I could talk to both sexes, particularly if I had Luma or Huda with me. As the security situation in Iraq worsened, I also found it safer to be a woman. As long as I wore my scarf, I blended in in a way that my American male colleagues could not. The drivers did not mind shuttling me to and from the Green Zone. They felt safer, too, with me in my Muslim garb. If we ran into trouble, an Iraqi man would be less likely to confront me directly. I could pretend to be so righteous that I would not dare return the gaze of a man who was not my male relative.

It took some practice. I am not shy by nature. I am guarded, but I have a healthy sense of myself. My mother took a social beating from the pastor's wife of our church when I was sixteen and took my first real job as a peer counselor at the Planned Parenthood in my Illinois hometown. At that time, I had no clue of the politics of Planned Parenthood, no idea that it might seem strange for a straightlaced Lutheran teenager sheltered by a parochial school education to work there. I only knew that my job entailed talking to young women about self-esteem and self-respect. Whenever I saw that pastor's wife, I glared in defiance. And yet, in a moment I am deeply ashamed to admit, I also joined my friends in protesting two of our female high school classmates who wanted to wear pants to the senior prom. I was on the prom committee and, swept up by the intolerant peer pressure of 1984, I actually gave an interview to my hometown newspaper declaring that the girls were trying to ruin the prom. After college, I fled Illinois to a job in Los Angeles, in part because I wanted to see and experience what I supposed was the antithesis of everything I had known growing up in the Midwest. For the first time, I felt as if I were seeing the world uncensored, finally testing the social theories that had been handed to me as scientific—or religious—fact. The years I spent in California made me a broader thinker, a more tolerant human being. I emerged from my time there grateful for my upbringing in the Midwest, for the foundation of virtue and goodness that my parents and my community taught me. It took me years to figure out that I did not have to abandon those ideals in order to accept different people and ideas, to look at the world as a journalist should try to do, with a blank slate. *Tabula rasa.*

It is often difficult for people who are not journalists, trained or born into it, who do not think like journalists, to understand that it is possible to put aside your feelings, to go numb with objectivity, as Rajiv encouraged Abu Saif to do. It is not easy. How could I not react when I saw such senseless disregard for life, suicide bombers who had no concern that their victims were innocent bystanders, children? How could I feel nothing when I saw a soldier wounded, bleeding, scared? All of that violence made me sick to my stomach, and it made me mad. But I could not allow those feelings to affect my reporting. I still had to understand why it was happening, why the insurgents were so angry, why there was so much hatred, why people could still have hope. Obviously, as journalists, as human beings, as people of the world, we are innately biased. There is no such thing as a truly blank slate or blank mind. We are shaped by where we have been, what we have seen, and what we have been taught. The trick is to accept this but at the same time not to abandon the pursuit of the blank slate, to take a deep breath and say, "Okay, I'm going to ask questions, not debate, not pursue a thesis, not go into this with any notion of what I might find." If journalists simply abandon the pursuit as an unreachable ideal, we will never be able to see past our own perceptions to find stories and to listen to people, whether we agree with them or not.

This was particularly difficult when it came to my relationship with Iraqi women. On the one hand, I detested their obvious second-class place in larger society, though I recognized that this varied from family to family. I gritted my teeth in silent fury after seeing a farmer driving by in a pickup truck—his wife riding in the back with the sheep, he in the protected cab, alone. Luma never hid her fury. During lunch at the Four Seasons in Amman, she spotted a man sitting at a table with a woman we presumed was his wife. The women was completely covered in a *burqa*, a fuller version of the *abaya* that did not allow us to see her face.

"Look at that dog, that pig, making his wife wear that thing," Luma spat. "She can't even eat!"

"Luma," I said softly, "I don't really like to see that either, but we can't judge them. I mean, maybe she wants to wear it."

"No woman wants to wear that. And that's easier for you to say! No one makes you cover up."

"Well, no one makes you cover up either," I reminded her.

"Not yet!"

During the nine months I was in Baghdad, I noticed more women wearing a scarf in public, even in neighborhoods like Karrada and Monsour, which were fairly secular before and after the war. Bassam and Omar said their own mothers, who never wore a scarf before the U.S. invasion, started to wear one to go to the market, fearing the growing influence of conservative Islamic leaders, particularly in the Shiite south of Iraq, and of the radical extremists behind elements of the insurgency. The scarf had become a protective accessory for women in Iraq. In an interview for a story about the trend, Fadhil Shaker, a psychology professor at Baghdad University, said women wore the scarf to hide or take shelter, to protect themselves. And the scarf, Shaker said, was the best protection. "Women believe the scarf will be the wall to prevent people from looking at them." I understood this idea well. I was not obligated to wear a scarf in Iraq, although one could certainly argue that fear of not wearing one took away the choice of doing so, a viewpoint that many moderate Iraqi women expressed to me. It was also my choice to dress modestly within the hotel and in our bureau. Even if I hated the societal rules, I felt compelled to respect them.

"So why won't you wear short sleeves," I asked Huda on one of my first days in the bureau. "Why do you wear the scarf? You seem —I don't know, pretty modern."

Huda, a devout Shiite, did not wear the scarf out of fear; she wore it in devotion to God. Huda said she believed that women should cover their hair to hide their beauty from the temptations of men.

"But, don't the men have some responsibility to suppress any inappropriate feelings?" I asked.

"They are too weak," she said.

Deep down, I did not understand. Her explanation seemed absurd to me, but it was her faith. It did make me wonder how close Huda and I could get. This difference felt like a bridgeless chasm. I wondered if she considered me ignorant or unholy, in some respect, for not wearing a scarf. I was afraid to ask, afraid of her answer. In the end, I needn't have worried. Her scarf, my bare head made no difference. We belonged to the universal sisterhood of women, a sisterhood that embraced me—at least for the most part.

Rifaat, our night driver, and our night security chief, Sabah, delivered me to the airport in January for a flight to Kurdish-controlled northern Iraq, a safer, faster way to skirt Baqouba and Kirkuk, two Iraqi cities festering with insurgents. The road to the airport was the most dangerous in Iraq, and I held my breath every time we had to drive the mile-long stretch that ended at a military checkpoint. Once I made it to the checkpoint, I still did not feel totally in the clear because the checkpoint itself was a target for suicide bombers. We had to shut off our engine and wait for bomb-sniffing dogs to clear us before waiting in another line to be inspected. Rifaat, who was a driver for an Egyptian import-export company before the war, sang religious songs every time we neared the checkpoint. His humming and singing unnerved me. He was supposed to be the calming flight attendant, assuring me that the bumps were just turbulence. Instead, he was acting like a man preparing to die.

On a busy day, it could take up to three hours to get through the checkpoint. Once we made it to an open-air bay, we had to get out of the car and go through a personal inspection before being allowed to board the bus to the airport. Even though Rifaat and Sabah were not coming with me to the airport, they helped me carry my suitcases to the inspection table. There was one table for men and one for women, on the obvious assumption that a respectable Iraqi woman would not want a man rummaging through her intimates. The women who conducted the luggage inspections usually wore headscarves and spoke little English. They were contract employees for the security company that provided airport security. With gloved hands, the inspector poked around in my suitcase, pulling out my toiletries and feeling through my clothes. At the bottom of the suitcase, she found a tampon. She held it up to me inquisitively. "It's a tampon," I told her. She shook her head. The word meant nothing to her. She began to unwrap it. "Put it down!" I whispered through clenched teeth. Rifaat and Sabah sensed something was up and moved closer to check out my cotton missile. The inspector still had no idea what she was holding. Finally, unable to communicate and desperate to end my humiliation, I shouted, "Woman bleeding! Woman bleeding!" She blushed and shoved it back into the suitcase. "For God's sake," I muttered, as I batted Rifaat and Sabah away.

I carried my own suitcases to the bus.

Sometimes she would call as the security guards were at her door, insisting she follow them to the stairwell at the Sheraton to wait out the attack. Other times I wouldn't hear from her until hours afterward, when she was allowed to return to her room. Thousands of miles away in D.C., the bombs sounded like muffled heartbeats, a background cadence to my own pulse, drumming in terror. Somehow it would have made sense for my sister's calls to rouse me from my own sleep, but she lived nine hours ahead of me and when the nightly mortar attacks began in Baghdad,

it was often late afternoon in Washington. I often retreated under a blanket to talk to her, my eyes closed against a sun that seemed too bright for her urgent whisper.

In late September, at the end of a brilliant, near-perfect autumn day, she called sobbing. I struggled to make out what had happened as she led me in panicked refrains: "We almost died." "We stood in a circle." "The heat burned our necks." "God." "Allah." I couldn't make sense of what she was telling me. "Slow down," I ordered. "Say it slowly." But she couldn't. She was gasping in horror at what she had narrowly evaded. For the first time, I think my sister understood the real possibility of her dying in Iraq. I understood it, too, in her garbled panic. Back in her room, alone, it was also the first time she had come undone. I was the only witness. By the next day, by the next story that appeared in the Post, she would be herself again, composed and in command. Only I understood the widening gap between the lines of her public words and that abyss of fear into which she was falling.

"Did you feel it, Jenny?" she asked suddenly. "I know you must have felt it."

I knew what she was asking. Did "Twin Power" kick in, that inexplicable connection that allowed me to feel what she did even when I wasn't there? Throughout our lives, whenever one of us was in danger or in pain, the other inherently knew. If I had the flu, her stomach would ache. Once, when I injured my knee in a softball game, her knee throbbed for days. Several years back she was in a car accident and broke her arm. At the very moment the accident occurred, I was leaving a message on her work voice mail, telling her to check in because something didn't feel right.

Now she had almost died. Had I sensed it? Had my world stopped for just a moment as the mortar blew by her head?

"Of course, I knew it," I reassured her. "You're my twin."

But after I hung up the phone, I remained under the blanket, too ashamed to face the daylight. I hadn't felt anything at all.

CHAPTER 8

"Spin, it's pretty bad here."

Karl Vick was on the phone from Baghdad. He had reached me in my room at my hotel in Amman, where I was packing and repacking for my trip back to Iraq the next day, rearranging the winter clothes I brought with me from Washington. I had agreed to stay in Iraq through the end of the year, and in exchange, the editors flew me back to the United States for a short visit with my family in early October. My return ticket to go home for good was now stamped for January 9, 2005, eight months after I arrived for my short summer tour.

"I want you to know what you're getting into," Karl told me. "A journalist was kidnapped outside of our hotel. Everyone is shaken up. You don't have to come. It's your decision, and no one is going to second-guess you."

In the two weeks that I had been gone, the violence in Iraq had escalated to a punishing, daily barrage of car bombs, kidnappings, and assassinations. U.S. security officials were reporting up to seventy attacks a day across Iraq, attacks on American military convoys, foreign contractors, Iraqi police and government workers and civilians who ended up in the wrong place at the wrong time. On October 14, 2004, a suicide bomber detonated himself in the Green Zone Café, killing five U.S. security contractors and proving just how vulnerable the Iraqi capital was. If the Green Zone wasn't safe, what was? A day later, John Markinus, an Australian journalist for the SBS network, was ambushed and kidnapped about 500 yards from the front of the Hamra Hotel, where we were now bunking at night while waiting for our new residence, a house, to be ren-

ovated. Markinus was released unharmed a few days later, but
the incident shocked the journalists who lived in the Hamra.
We no longer trusted anyone—hotel staff, translators for other
media organizations; anyone could be a potential tipster to
the insurgents, a spy, a *mujahideen* opportunist. On top of that,
a mortar shell had narrowly missed our new house the day the
translators began setting up the office there. Karl had moved us
out of the Sheraton in part to escape the mortars, but it seemed
we were once again on the mortar flight path, this one between
the insurgents and the Iraqi Interior Ministry bunker.

Karl had been in the Sheraton by himself on October 7
when a mortar hit an empty room on our floor, shooting flames
and glass into the driver's lounge next door where Little Naseer
was playing billiards. No one was injured in the fiery attack,
which I witnessed from a TV screen in the *Post* newsroom in
Washington. I was meeting with David Hoffman when *Post*
national security correspondent Dana Priest interrupted us
with the news. David flicked on CNN, and I showed him the
floor where the *Post* bureau was located, my finger tracing
each of our rooms and the office across the TV screen. "Right
there, where that palm tree caught fire. You can see the floor
through the flames." David rushed off to call Karl. I rushed off
to call Omar. I was elated to hear his voice. "Don't worry. Be
happy always," he said, adding, "We're waiting for you." Within
a few days, the staff completely dismantled the Sheraton
bureau—computers, televisions, Internet cables, and satellite
dishes—and moved to what we hoped would be a safer place.

When Karl called me in Amman, I could hear something different in his voice. He was trying to warn me. Warn me about
what? He couldn't predict what was going to happen in Iraq. In
fact, that seemed to be the very point he was making. *It's bad,
kiddo, and I have no idea how much worse it's going to get, and you
need to know that coming in.* Karl has always been one of my
favorite people at the *Post.* We worked together in the Mont-
gomery County, Maryland, bureau when I first started at the
newspaper. Karl left Washington in 1997 to become the *Post's*
Nairobi bureau chief in Africa and then went on to Turkey. He

was in the Kurdish-controlled area north of Iraq, which borders Turkey and Iran, when the United States invaded in 2003. We had not seen each other since he left for overseas, and we reunited in Baghdad during the summer of 2004, seven years later. Beyond his admirable journalism, his beautiful story-telling, Karl was just an all-around nice guy, a fellow Mid-westerner who grew up in Minnesota and Wisconsin, the son of a Lutheran preacher. He had a wry sense of humor, and nothing ever seemed to faze him, which is why his phone call startled me. I tried to read between his words, but I knew I had already made up my mind.

"Karl, I've come this far. I'm not turning around."

It sounded profoundly braver than it actually was. You cannot fear what you cannot see, and I had no idea what was to come. It was only later, looking back on the last three months of 2004 in Iraq, that I paused to contemplate, putting myself on a chessboard, my fingers barely brushing the top of my head. *Do I move ahead? Do I turn around?* I appreciated that Karl was giving me a chance to back out. He had never questioned my judgment, never tried to talk me into taking a dangerous assignment.

"Okay, Jacks," he said. "See you when you get here tomorrow."

I showed up at our new residence the next day and found Karl sifting through a catalog of bathroom fixtures. In between reporting and writing, keeping people alive and accounted for, Karl had to put together an office and a house. I had not yet taken off my coat when Karl asked me to follow him up the stairs for a walking tour of the gutted bathrooms. He wanted my advice on toilets, tile, and light fixtures. The house was not inhabitable yet for sleeping, so after picking out some faucets, I grabbed my luggage and carried it to the Hamra, where Karl and Steve Fainaru had rooms on separate floors. Although I was now in the same hotel with Hannah Allam, of Knight Ridder, and Huda, I missed our old floor at the Sheraton, missed the family-style dinners and having the staff a few feet away. We worked in our new hotel rooms with our doors closed, for security, or in the house, careful to scurry back to the hotel before dark. In the Sheraton, we worked under an open-door policy. The guards patrolled the floor and pounced on strangers who wandered into a room looking for directions or for the *Post* office. Even fellow journalists learned to stop at the guard desk before a visit. The guards did not trust anyone who was not "*Washington Post*" and tackled people without hesitation.

I was miserable in the new hotel, cooped up, scared. Many mornings I was blasted from my bed by the crack of a car bomb in a nearby square. My heart pounded as I walked briskly down the hall, past Karl's room to a balcony where we could see black smoke rising from the street. As bad as it was for us, it was worse for the Iraqi people. This was becoming their daily reality: waking up to carnage, losing relatives and friends. It was difficult to detect just when things had changed, just what had changed, but Iraq felt different in October 2004. I felt different.

My trip home had been a disappointment. I spent much of it thinking about Iraq. I felt angry and disconnected from my friends. Why close the broken circle, I wondered, only to have to rebreak it in a few weeks when I left again? I felt bad about this because my friends had been so supportive while I was in Iraq, sending long, encouraging emails. My closest friend Suzy stayed up until 2 or 3 in the morning her time in Jersey City, New Jersey, so that when I got up in Baghdad, I wouldn't have to greet the morning alone. A few hours later, Jenny would be up at dawn with Aidan, leaving me only a few hours of isolation if I wanted to connect with a familiar voice. I followed my running crew, Jamie and Kathleen—"The Five-Mile Hoes" as we called ourselves—as they trained for a marathon that I had planned to run with them. And yet back home, so close, physically there, I felt so very far away. I couldn't stand the questions: *You're going back! For how long? How long are they making you go back for?* One by one they emailed. *Don't go. You can't go. You shouldn't go.* I hated these stupid pronouncements. Why not? The idea that I had volunteered to return to Iraq, to stay longer and longer was unimaginable to most of my friends. Of course the *Post* wasn't making me do anything. But how do you tell the people you care about, how do you look at them and say,

I'm choosing Iraq over you. I'm choosing risk, disease, and pain over Friday night happy hour at Hamburger Mary's, over kayak rides down the Shenandoah and the beach house we rent every summer, over dance clubs and movies and barbecues. I'm willing to give all of it up because it means more to me to skirt death than to feel alive with all of you. I was too tired to explain, too focused on summoning the mental courage to leave everyone I loved behind again. So it was easier to stay away.

A few days before I left Washington to return to Baghdad, I went to the doctor for a quick checkup. My blood pressure was twice as high as usual. The student-doctor at George Washington University Hospital, the only place where I could find a last-minute appointment, expressed alarm. "Are you worried about anything?" she asked. "Well, no, not really. I am going back to Iraq this weekend. But I'm not worried."

She listened to my body, which was ratting me out, and prescribed Zoloft and Klonopin, antianxiety medications. I dutifully picked up the prescriptions, with no intention of ever taking them. I don't even like to take cold medicine and usually ride out the winter flu and other ailments nonmedicated. I threw the bottles in the bottom of my suitcase and left them there. Who wants to be in a daze in a combat zone? That seemed like a good way to get killed.

But I was anxious back in Baghdad, with our office broken apart and scattered. And I missed Luma. I was hurt and angry that she left without explanation, that she lied about taking a new job with the U.S. Army, which Omar deduced through short telephone exchanges with her. I would have supported her, whatever she had decided to do, but she had been moonlighting for the Army in her last few days with us without telling me. On our last assignment together in September, we went to Abu Ghraib prison to interview Iraq's human rights minister, Bakhtyar Amin, who was meeting with detainees being released. Luma was cranky and tired and kept dozing off in a meeting with Lt. Gen. Miller and a pack of journalists invited to the prison for the morning. I was embarrassed and covered for her, telling Barry Johnson, Miller's spokesman, that her daughter

had been sick all night. I whispered to Luma to leave the meeting, and she went back to the media bus and sacked out.

Omar and Abu Saif reached her by telephone a few days after
she simply stopped coming to work. In one conversation, she
claimed to be stuck in Sadr City, the Shiite slum in Baghdad,
unable to leave because of an Army operation. She gave us a
detailed account of the military assault, my first clue that she had
started to work for them as a translator. She knew too much for
a citizen holed up in her aunt's house, observing a military
operation from behind a closed curtain. Luma would not take
my telephone calls or answer my emails. I was furious. She
wanted to send a family friend to return her *Post*-issued telephone and press badge. Through Omar I ordered her to deliver
them in person, to resign to Rajiv in person like a professional,
like the professional I had created. She ignored me. I moped
around for days like a jilted lover. My translator had dumped me
for the U.S. Army! Eventually, I made peace with the fact that
Luma was not coming back. When I returned to Baghdad in
October after my visit home, I sent a bag of presents to her
house with Ghazwan, our driver, but she never acknowledged
them.

I did not leave the bureau for more than a week after I
returned in early October. Karl dashed out for quick trips to the
Green Zone, but we mostly stayed put. Other journalists in our
little part of Baghdad had been targeted for kidnapping, followed on the same roads we used to leave the hotel, which did
not amount to much more than some concrete barriers and
unreliable Iraqi soldiers who only did their jobs when they knew
the snipers guarding the Australian Embassy were monitoring
them with high-powered binoculars. The Iraqi soldiers were
not there to protect us. They were part of a special police
force for foreign diplomats, a cadre that did not include us, the
journalists.

I missed going out to the streets to report. I had carved this
little part of the Iraq story out for myself, leaving the big political stories to Rajiv and then to Karl. I preferred talking to and
writing stories about ordinary Iraqis. In September, Bassam and

I hung out on location with a TV crew for Al-Sharqiya, a new Iraqi satellite network that sprang up after the war. The crew was shooting for its new hit series, *Labor and Materials*, a reality show that follows the rebuilding of a war-damaged house. Al-Sharqiya also was preparing a drama series called *The Looters* about families who grew rich off the spoils of ransacking after the U.S.-led war. Another show, called *Iraq's Most Melancholy Home Videos*, captured reactions of Iraqis watching footage of former neighbors now living abroad. It was the kind of story I loved, a story about Iraqi culture, Iraqis trying to get on with their lives. I didn't like writing about death and bombs all of the time. I wanted to find moments of triumph and happiness, of progress in Iraq. But when I returned in October, I returned not to an open world of progress but to a cage. We were scared of being followed, scared of being ambushed, and ultimately, scared of our own fear.

I steadied myself the way I always had, with a soccer ball and a dinner party. Instead of cooking in the makeshift Sheraton kitchen, with Little Naseer to help and the translators darting in and out to watch and gossip, I cooked alone in my room with Mexican ingredients brought from home: canned crab quesadillas, guacamole, black beans, and rice. I also asked Karl to post a guard on the floor of the hotel at night so I wouldn't have to worry about somebody coming to kidnap me in the middle of the night while we were isolated from one another. I spent the nights writing stories pasted together from reports gathered by our Iraqi staff, my only access to the war outside my window, and making tea for the floor guard, Huday, who implored me not to be so stingy on the sugar. He came back every hour looking for more tea, and I enjoyed the company. I had found some Arabic flash cards in a box in the bureau and practiced my new vocabulary on Huday, who patiently corrected my pronunciations.

I returned in October, the Islamic fasting month of Ramadan, the ninth month of the religious calendar in which Muslims believe that God sent the holy Quran to the prophet Mohammed. Muslims in Ramadan fast from sunrise to sunset, breaking the fast with a prayer and meal celebration called *iftar*. U.S. military commanders warned us that Ramadan would likely stir an increase in insurgent attacks. Islamic martyrs believe that their afterlife riches will be enhanced if they die on a holy day. I fasted during the day with the staff, out of respect and to test my self-discipline. Sometimes the hunger won out, and I sneaked a soda and a granola bar in my room, careful to brush my teeth so the translators wouldn't smell the sin on my breath. On the days I did make it, I was ravenous by the time we gathered around the *iftar* table in the bureau kitchen, tiny plastic containers of take-out Iraqi food scattered about. The staff munched on hummus, bread, cucumber salad, beans and rice, kabob. I was the only woman at the table and stood with everyone else, elbowing my way to the vegetables. The Sunnis broke the fast first, digging in while our Shiite staff waited for a minute longer, piously observing the fast one tiny bit longer than their Sunni counterparts. It was good-natured. There were never any religious tensions between our staff. Sometimes I joined in with the Sunnis, and other times I waited with the Shiites. "I have to be objective," I told them.

One of the stories we were tracking during Ramadan was an upcoming military operation in Fallujah. U.S. fighter planes had been hitting the city almost nightly, dropping huge bombs from the darkened sky. On October 14, based on a tip from the U.S. Marines, CNN reported that the assault on the city had already begun. In fact, it had not, and the Marines were only using the network to test the insurgents, to see what kind of reaction they might get in response. CNN had to back off the story, basically recanting it. The network was furious, and it made all of us in the press wonder about what other disinformation the military had spread. We did know that an assault was coming at some point; the Iraqi government was under intense pressure to resolve the "Fallujah problem" before upcoming national elections in a few months. Karl and Phil Bennett, the foreign managing editor, had been talking about how we would cover the military operation. Steve Fainaru, the *Post* correspondent who was in Iraq primarily to embed with the military, was wrapping up his second long assignment and was due to return to the United States in time for his son's birthday. When Karl first mentioned the possibility of my covering the assault, I balked. I had limited embed experience, and this did not seem like the best one to wet my feet. The U.S. military was planning a decisive combat operation on the city, intent on retaking it from the insurgents. Frankly, I was scared to death—of Fallujah, of being in battle, of not knowing what the battle would be. I hemmed a bit in a telephone conversation with Phil but ultimately agreed to go. I was up for the assignment, they assured me. Whether or not I agreed with that assessment, I knew they had no one else to send. At least I'd be getting out of my Baghdad prison.

I called to talk with Emily Messner, the foreign news aide, before I left. Emily was our godsend, fielding requests for prescriptions and contact lenses, coordinating packages from home that she sent with incoming correspondents, clipping articles for the Iraqi staff, patching in telephone calls to relatives and editors. Before we hung up, Emily mentioned that she had talked to my mom recently. "My mom?"

My hands were trembling as I dialed my sister. She picked up the phone on the second ring. I could barely speak. "You, you would not believe what Mom did!" I shouted into the receiver.

"What? What's wrong?"

"She called Phil Bennett. She called the foreign editor of *The Washington Post* to ask if I was okay!"

"Get out. She did not." Jenny burst out laughing.

"It's not funny," I said. "I'm just mortified. I can't believe that she actually did that. It's bad enough he thinks I'm too chicken to go! But Mom?"

Later that night, I felt terrible about my outburst, even though I had directed it at Jenny and not at my mom. This was so out of character for my mom, who supported me no matter where I went, what choices I made, what worry I caused her. If she was that scared—scared enough to pick up the phone and make sure that Phil knew what he was doing, sending her daughter into Fallujah—then she must have been terrified, absolutely terrified. I called her. "Look, Mom, it's going to be okay," I said, reassuring her, even though I doubted what I was saying myself.

I packed my gear on October 26, the night I was due to leave for the Marine base near Fallujah. I wanted to spend the last night with our staff, celebrating *iftar* and saying good-bye. Karl and I fought. Our Western security consultants were adamant that we leave the new bureau before dark to return to the hotel; I implored Karl to let me stay. Our Iraqi guards had a detailed plan to protect me if insurgents overran the house. I practiced jumping into my hiding spot in the freezer. I trusted our Iraqi guards more than the private company we had employed for security consulting. The Iraqi guards loved me like a sister. I knew they would die to protect me. And on the night I was headed to Fallujah, I wanted to be with people I loved, not sitting in a hotel room by myself, contemplating my new lonely life inside the walls of the Hamra Hotel, isolated and sad. "If the insurgents are watching, they will see me walking with my luggage when I come back to drive to the Green Zone. I'm more of a target than if I just stayed here!" But Karl wouldn't budge. So I trudged back to the hotel to wait until dusk, when it was time to drive to the Green Zone to meet up with the other press corps for our ride to Camp Fallujah.

At the Green Zone checkpoint, an Iraqi guard searched my backpack and gear, pulling out every item I had carefully packed, examining it and returning it into my bags. My photographer friend Stephanie Kuykendal, who was a *Washington Post* intern in 2001, was in front of me, her camera equipment scattered about, as she, too, tried to repack in the dark. Stephanie was in Iraq with her husband, Stefan Zaklin, also a photographer. She worked for the Corbis photo agency, and Stefan worked for European Pressphoto Agency. Stephanie and Stefan, who met in college at the University of Missouri, were regulars at the *Post* bureau, coming over for dinners and attending Luma's birthday party in August. Stefan was already embedded with a Marine unit in Ramadi, another insurgent stronghold northwest of Fallujah.

This was Stephanie's first major military embed assignment, too. Most of the rest of the Press Corps that had assembled with us in the Convention Center were grizzled veterans of the Iraq invasion and of other battles, including the civil war in Bosnia, another dangerous assignment in which journalists were targeted, robbed, and killed by mortars and sniper fire. Our group in Fallujah had dodged bullets and death all over the world. Anne Garrels, the senior foreign reporter for National Public Radio; Ned Parker of AFP, who was embedded during the 2003 invasion; Scott Peterson, a seasoned correspondent for *The Christian Science Monitor* and photographer for Getty Images; Matt McAllester of *Newsday*, a Pulitzer Prize–winning reporter who was jailed in Abu Ghraib by Saddam's secret police on espionage charges just before the U.S. invasion; Michael Ware, the Baghdad bureau chief for *Time* magazine; Kevin Sites, a cameraman for NBC. In all, more than seventy journalists had signed up to embed with the 1st Marine Expeditionary Force to cover the Fallujah operation.

We had no idea when the battle would start or what it would look like when it did. The Iraqi government was still negotiating with the city leaders to avert a battle, but those negotiations were for show. We understood that U.S. and Iraqi forces were going to retake the city, one way or another. At the Green Zone landing pad, I lay on the cool cement, my head on my knapsack, watching the stars. It was so peaceful, with a bright moon to illuminate our Chinook helicopter on the flight to Fallujah. There is a calm that descends on the eve of a battle, whether that battle comes the next day or, as it did for us, the next week. I was resolved—afraid, but resolved. But I also knew that I was certainly headed to a killing field. Insurgents. Marines. Soldiers. People were going to die; that was certain. Mingled with my resolve was a terrible sadness.

We landed at Camp Fallujah in the middle of the night, only the moon and the blue glow sticks of the "Night Walkers"—the Marine landing crew—to guide us in. It looked like the press was invading the camp. All of us were shuffling along with our gear, packing the buses that drove us to two large tents, one with a dirt floor and one with a wooden platform. We shoved in together, men and women, taking the dirt floor tent and leaving the platform tent for the rest of the Press Corps who were coming on later flights. Stephanie was on one of those.

I picked a cot closest to the front of the tent, for the air, and tried to sleep, as the steady saw of snores rose around me. I thought about Jenny and my mom, thought about my dad sleeping on a cot in a tent in Vietnam. I talked to him in my head: "Can you believe it, Dad? I'm going to cover a battle. I'm really scared. Were you scared? Did you think about Mom all of the time or was it too hard?" I kept talking to my father, talking to his ghost, until I finally drifted off into fitful sleep.

The Marines were anxious to ship us off to our units, to the various companies where we would spend the battle. The morning after we arrived, we packed into a utility room at the camp's fitness center to find out our assignments. The reporters were anxious, too, anxious to see who would be with an artillery unit, infantry unit, armored tank unit. I didn't feel any deep longing to be on the front line. I had been in Iraq long enough to realize that the front line of the war was really a snake that stretched from the traditional battlefield front all the way to the rear, to the support and supply units. The Marines warned us that this would not be a pretty battle; the odds were good that some of us in the room would be shot or killed. First Lt. Lyle Gilbert, a lanky, by-the-book Marine who was our main point of contact through the public relations shop at Camp Fallujah, delivered this news solemnly and sternly. I wondered if mine was the only heart racing in the room. I felt like a big chicken. There was not a single part of me curious about what war looked like up close. Plus, I was worried about making sure that I could see the larger battlefield, to write broad pieces about how the battle was going. I didn't want to be in a foxhole only able to see in the limited radius around me. *The New York Times* had sent two reporters and a photographer to cover the battle. Dexter Filkins, the *Times'* chief correspondent in Baghdad, would be at the front, recording the gripping, hand-to-hand scene of combat. Bob Worth would be farther back, able to put Filkins's reports into the larger context of the battlefield. Then there was me, alone, not even a *Post* photographer to accompany me.

I got my assignment, an infantry unit that would be one of the first into battle. I felt no thrill. I did not count myself lucky. Instead, I was filled with dread. Matt McAllester and James Hider of the *Times* of London were furious that they had not received infantry unit assignments, meaning they would most likely be assigned to a headquarters or support group for the battle. I considered a headquarters assignment ideal, even if it was a softer place to see the battle, so I offered to exchange my spot. Gilbert agreed. It was a trade-off. I would give up the cohesion that comes with hanging out with a single unit for the battle, sharing the war experience with one group whose story I could tell throughout, an endless yarn. On the other hand, by hooking on to headquarters, I could cover the battle with multiple different units—support, artillery, and infantry. I would miss recording what it felt like and looked like to roll into Fallujah the night the battle started. But then I would actually know when it started. I didn't want to screw this up for the *Post*. If I was risking my life for this story, I wanted to get it right, to do it better than anyone else, to deliver. I called Karl. He backed me up immediately. Good thinking, he said, when I explained what I had done: tried to save myself and the story. After talking to Karl, I settled in with the others, waiting for the battle to begin.

I filed my first story October 27 from "near Fallujah," the dateline required by the Marines to keep us from disclosing our actual location. Marine Brig. Gen. Dennis J. Hejlik, deputy commander of the 1st Marine Expeditionary Force, reflected the gung-ho attitude of the Marines at Camp Fallujah. American forces had not been in the city since April 2004 when the Marines backed off an offensive under pressure from the White House. It was a sore point for the Marines, many of whom believed that the insurgents would never have gripped control of the city if the operation had continued. In the months that followed, Fallujah, 40 miles west of Baghdad, became the most dangerous city in Iraq, a hotbed for Wahabi Islamic extremists. Abu Musab Zarqawi, the al Qaeda–linked terrorist leader in Iraq, was rumored to be in Fallujah. Though military intelligence could not confirm his presence, intelligence officials certainly believed that elements of his network operated from Fallujah. With the rising postwar insurgency and the most deadly attacks linked to Zarqawi and his network, *Fallujah* became synonymous with everything bad in Iraq. It was the Abu Ghraib of the country, a lawless place of torture, terror, and murder, a place where foreigners who were kidnapped went to be beheaded, to die. "We're going to go in there and whack them," Hejlik declared, earning his battle nickname from the press: "Whack 'Em Hejlik."

While we waited for the battle to begin on a day still unknown to us, I settled into my new quarters at Camp Fallujah, a sprawling base on the outskirts of town, which the Marines had occupied since March 24, 2004, replacing the Army's 82nd Airborne Division. The camp was the base for the command of the 1st Marine Expeditionary Force, or I MEF, in military short-term. It had a chow hall with two hot meals a day, showers, flushing toilets, two fitness centers, a PX to buy Cokes and peanuts and DVDs, a barber shop, and laundry. It also got hit regularly by mortars and rockets, maiming and killing Marines playing a little off-duty football, squatting in the portable toilets, or walking to the PX. We had to wear our flak jackets and helmets when traveling around the camp. I listened intently when I walked, listening for a mortar shell that might whistle by, the incoming sirens that directed us into a bunker to wait out an attack. One Marine was killed in a bunker when a rocket slammed through the tiny opening on the side, a lucky shot from an insurgent firing off a round on the perimeter of the camp. We never knew who he was. The Marines were very protective of their casualties and did not typically tell us how they died, which, Gilbert explained, would only give the insurgents information about the effectiveness of their attacks. We only knew that a Marine was killed in a bunker because we were there when it happened.

In spite of the dangers and restrictions, I was delighted to be out of Baghdad. I reported my own stories near Fallujah and didn't have to rely on a translator. I roamed the camp looking for people to write about. I walked everywhere. I felt free. When the incoming fire got really intense, I simply slept with my flak jacket over me, a heavy-duty blanket. The Marines set up a media tent for us, and we wrote stories from there. It was a good gig. The tent had electricity, so we could plug in our laptops and hook up our satellite dishes, running the cables through the flaps on the tents and pitching the dishes in the proper southeasterly direction to pick up a signal. In the lead-up to the battle, part of the camp and surrounding forward operating bases were on light restrictions, meaning we had to cut our white lights so the insurgents could not easily spot us under the dark of night. The Marines glided easily through the dark, while we civilians stumbled over stones and potholes. I realized that I did not have the proper gear for the battle and spent a couple of hours at the Post Exchange outfitting myself with special eyewear (mandatory to roll out on a mission), black cotton T-shirts, a pocket knife, foot powder, insulated socks, a knit hat, and long underwear. It was cold in Fallujah as October rolled into November, and I was unprepared for the chilly winter desert nights. I slept with cardboard under my sleeping bag to ward off the cold, borrowing the idea from the homeless who sleep on the streets in Washington.

I tried to get a sense of how the troops felt about the impending fight. They talked big, about their desire to see action, about wanting to go in and kill the bad guys, about getting it over with and going home. The bad guys were trying to kill them, after all, and already had.

At the field hospital at Camp Fallujah, Dennis Astor, a U.S. Navy corpsman 3rd class, wanted back in the fight but first had to work up the courage to go outside by himself at night. "That's the only thing that bothers me." Astor was injured on October 31 when a suicide bomber blew up next to his military convoy near Fallujah, killing eight Marines and injuring nine others, the deadliest single attack on Marines at the time in

The author washing dishes after cooking Friday dinner, a tradition she started in the bureau. June 2004.

Luma at the Dead Sea in Jordan on her first "road trip" outside Iraq. September 2004.

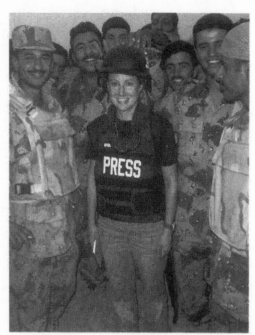

With Iraqi Army soldiers on the eve of the U.S. Operation to retake the city of Fallujah from insurgents. November 2004.

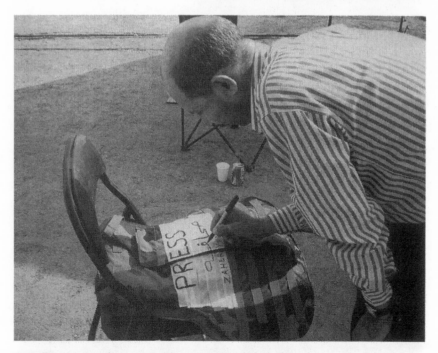

An Iraqi journalist writes "Press" in English and Arabic on his flak jacket in preparation for the U.S. battle in Fallujah. October 2004.

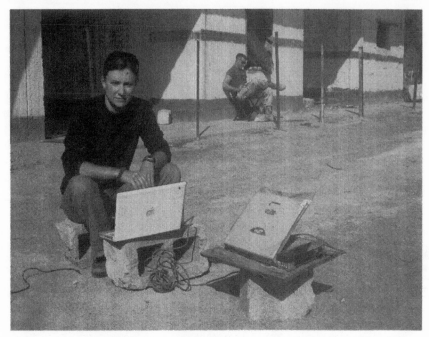

The author at her "office" near Fallujah. Reporters use small satellite dishes to send reports from Iraq. November 2004.

A U.S. Marine gunner during the battle for Fallujah. November 2004.

U.S. soldiers with Army Task Force 2-2 hang American flag
on a former Iraqi military building outside Fallujah
during the battle for control of the city. November 2004.

An American soldier set up his cot beneath a mural of Saddam Hussein
in a former Iraqi military compound outside Fallujah. November 2004.

Hannah Allam, the Baghdad bureau chief
of Knight Ridder news agency (left) and the author
prepare Christmas dinner. December 2004.

An Iraqi woman casts her vote in the Kurdish village of Salahuddin
in the country's first democratic elections in nearly fifty years. January 2005.

The author dressed as
an Iraqi Muslim to go
to the disputed city
of Kirkuk, where
foreigners were targeted.
January 2005.

Cloud formations near a U.S. military traffic checkpoint
outside Baqubah, Iraq . November 2004.

Men gather for prayer at a mosque in Sulaymaniyah
in the Kurdish-controlled north of Iraq. February 2005.

A U.S. Marine searches Iraqi residents of Fallujah who returned
to the city after an American assault. February 2005.

The author and her twin sister, Jenny, after Jackie
returned from Iraq. March 2004.

2004. "I'm just afraid my friends are going to pop up outside, and I'll see them, see my dead friends." Astor was a medic with the Marine Battalion Landing Team 13 based in Kaneohe, Hawaii. The unit had been in Iraq only two weeks when it was hit. "It was a bad day," recalled Marine Staff Sgt. Jason Benedict, of West Milford, New Jersey. His face and arm were burned. "We had no losses before that."

The platoon was riding in the middle of a truck, sitting back to back on sandbags, a protective measure against an attack. Benedict said he didn't see the bomber and only remembered hearing a loud noise and then looking to his right where a column of Marines had been sitting. "There wasn't anybody else," he said. "There was just smoke."

As soon as the car bomb exploded, insurgents began firing weapons and rockets at the convoy, he said. The heat from the truck began setting off ammunition and mortar rounds in the packs on the truck. Benedict said the attack was clearly coordinated between the bomber and the fighters hiding in the fields off the road. "There were a lot of hard lessons learned," he said. "We know the tactics and techniques used by the insurgents. We're more alert to our enemies hiding among the locals. I think that's why everyone was mad at first. There was no way the locals did not know what was going on." But he added, "We know you can't get angry with the locals, the regular people who want freedoms. It's the insurgents." Benedict said the unit was eager to return to duty and participate in the battle for Fallujah. "We're anxious to get back and go back in. Nobody wants to remain here."

Astor knew he would be left behind because his burns were not healing fast enough. "It's hard to get over it, but you just have to." His buddies from his unit would come to visit at the hospital and Astor would tell them he is fine. But "deep inside, every now and then you still see the faces of your dead friends."

I am not a soldier, so I could not relate to this thing inside of them, this desire to fight. Yet I felt a sense of duty and obligation to tell their stories, too. It was the same obligation I felt for writing an Iraqi's story. The politics of the war aside, the politics of the Fallujah battle aside, I was there to chronicle the human side of what was happening, the people caught up in what was happening in Iraq, for better or for worse.

The press corps was obsessed with the messiness of what we were about to witness and experience. Even the veteran combat journalists expressed concern. I spent an afternoon with Anne Garrels, one of the few reporters who remained in Baghdad when the war started in 2003. I looked up to Anne, admired her courage and her reports from all over the world. I was surprised to hear that she, and many of the others, was scared, too. Before she shipped out with her Marine forward unit, she wrote her husband's telephone number in my black leather journal. "Call him, if . . . just . . ." she instructed me, trailing off. Paul Wood, the BBC's Middle East correspondent, gave me his editor's telephone number. We wrote our blood type on tape and stretched it across our flak jackets. I put a picture of Aidan and Jenny and her husband, Peter, in the lining of my helmet. Before I rolled out of the wire, the guarded perimeter of Fallujah, I wrote my name and blood type on my hand (in case my head got blown off) and on my neck (in case my arm got blown off).

While the Marines were preparing for their battle, I was preparing for mine, trying to figure out how to cover it from the best spot. I asked Gilbert if I could hang out in the Marine command base the night of the battle. I promised not to report what I was seeing until it was cleared so as not to compromise the operation. We had strict rules that forbade us from disclosing troop movements or reporting battle plans ahead of an advance. If we violated the rules, we would be sent packing back to Baghdad on the first available flight. The Marines never censored what we wrote or forced us to clear our copy before we hit the "send" button to our news organization. But they did read carefully what we wrote or aired, monitoring it for breaches of the rules. In a feature story about the Night Walkers, the Marines responsible for the helicopter landing zone at Camp Fallujah, I wrote about their sense of pending battle. Troops were "cleaning their weapons, drilling, lining up at the barbershop for haircuts, turning in a last load of laundry and stocking up on cigarettes, foot powder and cases of soft drinks at the Post Exchange." Further into the story, I quoted Staff Sgt. Randal Southern, a reservist with Marine Air Control Squadron 24, based in Fort Worth, saying that sixteen helicopters had landed one night in a four-hour period, an indication that something was up. Gilbert came to see me the next morning after reading the story online. I should not have written the number of helicopters, which would tip off the insurgents about the amount of air activity at the camp, he said. "Okay, but don't you think that's going a little overboard?" I responded. "I mean, the insurgents can hear the helicopters. We can hear them all night long from our tent. I can count them myself."

"No numbers, Jacks," he said.

"Fine."

It was not worth pushing him, and frankly, I had no interest in putting Marine lives at further risk. Gilbert knew that. In just a few days, we had forged a bond. I was not a troublemaker and, really, had no reason to be. I was getting what I wanted without being pushy, at least so far. Gilbert had made me the POC of the press corps, short for "point of contact." I changed it to "petty officer in charge." My duties included signing people up for trips and gathering blood types and Social Security numbers for trips outside the camp. I was like the den mother of a giant Girl Scout troop of journalists.

I was polite and not pushy, a tactic I found to be much more beneficial when dealing with the military. At the same time, I told Gilbert which stories I wanted to cover—not the other way around. I pushed for access, and sometimes got it and sometimes did not. I knew that if I were not going to cross into the city with a Marine unit, I had to be in a position at least to write authoritatively about what my colleagues were seeing on the ground. I was in a unique position at the headquarters—able to interview U.S. and Iraqi commanders. I formed a little pact with James Janega of the *Chicago Tribune* and Tom Lasseter of Knight Ridder to exchange information about what we were seeing from the front and side and rear. I sent them text of the briefings the generals gave at the camp, and they let me know if it fit with what they were seeing from their foxholes.

I needed another correspondent to help to cover this battle. I called Omar. "Will you come to Fallujah?" Omar never resisted a chance to mingle with his brothers and readily agreed when I pitched the idea. The trick was getting the Marines to accept him. We were not technically allowed to bring our Iraqi translators with us because there were only a limited number of people the Marines could accommodate, so I told Gilbert I wanted to fill our photographer slot with an Iraqi. I instructed Omar to find a camera, any camera at the bureau, and make sure he knew how to use it. Most of our Iraqi staff used cheap digital cameras or camera phones to snap photos—this would be a big tip-off to the Marines that this was no real photographer. The fact is that I wanted Omar the Iraqi, not Omar the photographer. I wanted Omar, *The Washington Post* correspondent. Omar arrived two days later, his gear stuffed into my purple and white hiking backpack that I had left behind. He had a leather camera bag slung over his shoulder. That night, he tucked into a borrowed sleeping bag in the cot next to mine, and I felt safe and secure. Omar was going to be my secret weapon. I had already hatched a plan to ditch the Marines and join up with the Army to cover the fight from a tactical operation center nearer the front. Omar would stay behind with the Marines and also act as a liaison with the Iraqi press corps, who were embedded with Iraqi troops. No American media had access to the Iraqi soldiers. Between the two of us, I was determined we would cover the entire battlefield, as if we were our own media army.

The U.S. Marines had invited Iraqi journalists to cover the battle, and six of the hundreds registered with the occupation government agreed to come. The military only trusted the Iraqis so much. They embedded three of them with Iraqi forces and two with American forces. For U.S. troops, an Iraqi, no matter if he were a journalist, was a potential traitor or insurgent. They knew they needed the Iraqi journalists to cover the pending Fallujah battle. The Iraqi journalists were eager to be there, to help record the battle, but they were ill-prepared. I went to the PX and bought what I needed to survive, backed by the *Post* dollars that sent me there. The Iraqi journalists came to Camp Fallujah without a change of clothes, boots, sleeping gear, or flip-flops for the shower. Omar and I adopted them informally, outfitting them with my extras and with donations from the others in the Press Corps. The Marines set up some laptop computers for them and gave them donated blankets, grumbling that they had urged the Iraqis to bring their own gear. But how would the Iraqis have known? The most time many of them had spent around the military was on one-day trips to see reconstruction projects. They did not routinely embed with the military. I had a vague idea that I needed to pack for a camping trip, but the process was foreign even to me, an American reporter. I could only imagine how different it was for the Iraqi press, even those who were not recent converts to the profession. When Saddam invited journalists to view a military operation, he put them up in the top quarters, provided and bribed them with the best amenities. Saddam wanted the Iraqi journalists to feel that war was comfortable, that "the boys" from home were being taken well care of. This was part of the spin. The American military provided a completely different perspective, one in which the journalists would come to battle and face it as soldiers, with all the discomforts of sleeping in a dirt-floored tent, under the mortar shells, in the mud. Most of us who remained in the camp moved into the wood-floor tent, which was slightly more comfortable and equipped with heat. The Marines assumed that we Westerners had no problem sleeping in mixed-sex tents, but the Iraqis wouldn't stand for it. They stayed in their all-male bunk, even though it was uncomfortable. I spent a good deal of time coaching them through satellite issues, loaning my computer, picking up their trash, bringing them juice. I hated whenever I saw a foreign reporter dismissing an Iraqi journalist—their sometimes silly, rambling questions, poor etiquette in a press pack, lack of experience. We may have out-equipped them and more often than not out-reported them, but this was their country.

Mudhir Karim Zuhairy, of the U.S.-backed *al-Sabah* news-paper, came to cover the battle in a blue sweater vest and gray trousers. He came without a computer. Or a telephone. Or any means of communicating with his editor. But he came. A spry man who kept his graying hair cropped short, Zuhairy described how his two wives and three children cried the night before he left for Fallujah. They were terrified for him, and tears welled in Zuhairy's eyes as he described the emotional parting. Because of his English skills, Zuhairy was the statesman of the Iraqi press corps in Fallujah. He brought questions and requests to Omar and me on behalf of the others. "Of course it will be dangerous," Zuhairy told me. "There will be killing. But I am ready for any-thing. I want to take the truth from Fallujah to the people." For a story I wrote on the journalists, Hakim Ateah Jaber, who stud-ied film at Baghdad University and was a correspondent with al-Iraqiya television, told me he loved war. But when I pressed him if he was prepared to get close to the action, his eyes widened. "I love peace," he said, before rattling off a list of words in En-glish to emphasize his point. "I believe in peace. Democracy, authority, government, system."

We knew the battle was getting closer because the chow hall was emptier at night, a sign that most of the troops based at the camp had moved into positions closer to the city. The hospital at the camp was preparing for casualties, bringing in stacks of body bags. The Marines and Army had cordoned off the city, putting up barricades and warning through loudspeakers that any men under forty-five caught in the city would be detained. The *Post* still had a stringer inside the city who helped us eval-uate the truthfulness of what the Marines were telling us (that most of the city of 300,000 had emptied in the weeks leading up to the assault) with what he was seeing (the same—a mostly empty city).

My photographer friend Stefan and I were preparing to visit the field hospital, Bravo Surgical, the afternoon of Novem-ber 4, one of the countless pending-assault stories that we were trying to crank out in the days before the battle, which we knew was now imminent. Stephanie had shipped out with her

Marine unit days earlier, and Stefan had just come in from Ramadi to join up with an Army unit. He was waiting for his embed assignment, and we passed the time together, teaming up for several stories so that I could focus on writing and not on photographing. Stefan's mobile phone rang. We were both surprised he got reception. It was getting more difficult to call out, as the military scrambled the signals. A Fox News producer who was already at Bravo Surgical was on the line. Stephanie had just been brought in. She was in a Humvee that rolled over a gas-infused roadside bomb. The force of the blast slammed her camera into her mouth, pushing her teeth back toward her tongue. Stefan raced across a small dirt field to the hospital, pushing his way past the military guard instructed to keep the press out. Stephanie was already in surgery, alert but sedated as a dentist worked on her mouth. She told Stefan to take pictures, to record what was happening. Later that night she was evacuated to another hospital in Balad, in central Iraq. She and Stefan agreed that he should stay to cover the battle, so he did. They had come this far. There was no turning back. I got that.

Stephanie was the first reporter injured in the lead-up to the battle. When it was all over with, her injuries—from which she has fully recovered—ended up being the worst. But we didn't know that the night of November 6, a Saturday night, the night the Marines took us to the Iraqi camp where newly trained soldiers were preparing for their part in the battle. The interim Iraqi defense minister, Hazim Shalan, gave a rousing speech to the Iraqi soldiers surrounding him. The soldiers danced and cheered and thrust their rifles into the air, as Shalan shouted: "This is the first time in the history of Iraq we have seen people being slaughtered like sheep under the umbrella of Islam. Your conscience and families call for you. They call for you to liberate this city." At some point during the speech, the curious Iraqi soldiers, some of whom had never been so close to a Western woman before, reached out to touch me—first the top of my helmet, then my arm, and then my butt. They came at me again and again, reaching and grabbing as I shouted and slapped at them. I pushed my way out of the circle. They followed, and I found myself in the arms of a Marine, who opened a Humvee door and shoved me in. "You better stay in there," he said, while I peered out the window, indignant. *Well*, I thought, trying to console myself, *if they die tomorrow, at least I gave them one last treat.* Later, as the sun was going down and we went to see another group of soldiers, I chatted at the edge of the circle of Iraqi soldiers with Gen. David Petreus, a former commander of the Army's 101st Airborne who was in charge of training Iraqi security forces. For the Iraqi troops, Fallujah would be the first real test of that training. We stood in the light of one of the Humvees. When we finished talking, Petreus warned me to stay close to a U.S. soldier. "Watch her," he asked one of his bodyguards. As with the Iraqi press, the U.S. military only trusted their Iraqi counterparts so much.

The next morning, November 7, we learned that Iraqi and U.S. forces had stormed Fallujah General Hospital overnight, taking the hospital by force. It seemed that the battle for Fallujah had begun. Col. John R. Ballard, commander of the Marine 4th Civil Affairs Group based in Washington, said the military had been planning for weeks to secure the hospital as a prelude to a potential battle. "We've surrounded it to protect it," Ballard said. "The key word here is to protect." Gilbert had denied my final request to be in the Marine operations center for the start of the battle, and now I did not know if this really was the start or not. Some media outlets were reporting it was, and certainly the visit from the Iraqi Defense Minister to the Iraqi troops the night before would suggest that it had begun. But no one would give us a straight answer. I knew it was time to head for the Army. Originally, I had planned to go into the city on the night of the battle with the Navy's elite Seabee Engineer Reconnaissance Team. I had spent quite a bit of time with the Seabees at Camp Fallujah. Lt. Chris Neish, who was in charge of public affairs for the Naval Mobile Construction Battalion 4, took me under his wing. He loaned me a Navy sleeping bag when I told him that I was freezing at night in my summer liner. My dad was a Seabee in Vietnam, and for Neish and the battalion commander, John Korka, that made me family, even though I was a journalist. I also felt some comfort in the idea that I might go into the battle with the Seabees, whose engineers would be one of the first units into the city. In the end, though, it didn't work out for me to ride into the city with the Seabees, at least not the first night. So on November 8, I hitched a ride to an abandoned Iraqi military training center on the outskirts of town where the Army's First Infantry Division Task Force 2–2 had located its tactical command center. Capt. Erik Krivda, a wonkish Army officer in charge of the center, graciously invited me in, giving me a cot in a bombed-out building filled with bats, and allowed me to ride out the battle with him. I made him the same promise I made Gilbert—that I would not disclose troop locations or battle plans in advance. Krivda, who was from Gaithersburg and seemed to know what a *Washington Post* promise meant, agreed to my request. Yes, he told me, the whole hospital raid had been a setup, designed to fool the insurgents into thinking that the Marines intended to breach the city from the eastern side of the city along the Euphrates River. The Marines had not divulged this to the media, leading us to believe at the time (and misreport) that the battle may already have started at the hospital. In fact, Krivda said, the battle would start that very night, November 8, just after sunset. I knew hours in advance what was going to happen, and I wrote a small story that I could send electronically as soon as the first Army and Marine units charged into the city. At just after 7 P.M. Iraq time and 11 A.M. in Washington, the radio in the room cackled. The battle had started. I called Washington, with Krivda's consent. Fred Barbash, who was on our continuous news desk and responsible for getting news onto our website, answered the phone. "We're on. We're on. The battle has started," I told him. The *Post* was going to tell it first, and I was excited that washingtonpost.com gave me the outlet to get the news to our readers well in advance of the paper copy that would land on their doorsteps the next morning, but, even more important, before TV and radio were able to report that the assault had started. The Army intelligence officer in the room next door intercepted the call. "Not yet! Not yet! The Marines are not in yet." I called Fred back. "Hold up. Wait until I give the go-ahead again." A few minutes later, Krivda consented again. I phoned Fred, as the city rocked with loud booms. "Now! Now!" The waiting was over. The battle had finally started, and thousands of U.S. and Iraqi troops pushed into the insurgent-held city in the largest military operation in Iraq since the U.S.-led invasion the year before. U.S. Marine and Army units entered Fallujah from the north, their armored vehicles crawling over huge dirt mounds that insurgents built around the city. Fighters dug positions as the U.S. forces moved forward and raced between buildings as the troops advanced, crawling into holes cut into the backs of buildings.

On the third day of the battle, I asked Krivda if I could hop on a supply run to go into the city, to get closer to the front. U.S. forces had pushed into the heart of Fallujah, encountering roadside bombs, rockets, and gunfire in trying to wrest control of the city from insurgents. The Army and Marine units that had entered Fallujah from the northeast and northwest on that first Monday night had fought their way to the city center by Tuesday. Soldiers with the Army's 1st Infantry Division had made their way to the southeastern part of the city, a neighborhood of factories and warehouses where they expected to find guerrillas waiting for them. Instead, the district was relatively quiet, though the units reported being fired on by women and children armed with assault rifles. "There were multiple groups running around shooting at us," said Air Force Senior Airman Michael Smyre, twenty-six, of Hickory, North Carolina, an airstrike spotter attached to the 1st Infantry who was wounded when a rocket hit his armored vehicle. "You could see a lot of rubble, trash everywhere. It was real nasty looking." I wanted to see it for myself. I have no idea where my fear went, but it was gone. Now that I had a sense of what was happening, I wanted to get closer to the action. Omar was monitoring the Marine command a few miles away at Camp Fallujah. From a gunshot-pocked window of a Humvee, we rolled into Fallujah—into the city. Guns crackled from the neighborhoods, and the streets were strewn with dead bodies. The city looked destroyed. Nearly every building showed some sign of damage. For the next few days, I went into the city once or twice a day with the 2–2, as they pushed farther south, fighting insurgents. The troops encountered hundreds of civilians who remained in the city, riding out the assault by hiding in their homes. A man named Abu Saad hunkered in his house with his father, brother, and nephew, praying out loud to drown out the sounds of the bombs. I found Abu Saad at a school in the city, where he had gone to find food.

On November 13, Ayad Allawi, Iraq's interim prime minister, declared the city liberated. The city had been destroyed—and not just by U.S. artillery and airstrikes. Insurgents rigged homes to blow up when U.S. troops entered. They threw grenades as troops stormed into buildings.

This was a close-up battle, urban combat. Many of the insurgent fighters, particularly the foreign fighters in the southern part of the city, wore uniforms. They hung bricks from their hideouts—a marking for weapons drops. The insurgents hid in homes and mosques and fought U.S. troops from there. U.S. troops fired back, in some cases destroying the mosques. In spite of the declaration of liberation, fighting in Fallujah went on for months.

The city itself was in ruins. A week after the battle I returned with the Seabees. Our green Humvee rolled up to the mangled railroad line on the northern edge of Fallujah, at the very spot where the first U.S. and Iraqi forces had broken into the city in a shower of bullets and mortar shells. Pen and notepad in hand, Equipment Operator 1st Class William Seado of the U.S. Navy jumped out and started to inspect the tracks. As he walked around a tanker car, Seado, thirty-one, of Custer, South Dakota, noticed a black wire strung across the metal rails. He followed it to the tanker, where he found two sandbags filled with mortar rounds. Seado, a member of the Navy's elite Seabee Engineer Reconnaissance Team, raced back to the Humvee, which was parked only a few feet from the tanker—well within what is called the kill zone of the improvised explosive device, or IED.

"Let's get out of here," he said, as he cranked up the engine and sped off. "There's an IED on the track." Navy Lt. Jeffrey McCoy, the convoy commander from Youngstown, Ohio, who was sitting in the passenger seat, grabbed the radio handset to warn the other team members.

"I've never seen you move that fast, Seado."

"I intend to get out of here with my butt in one piece, sir."

U.S. officials had promised to rebuild Fallujah after the offensive, and now the Seabees were there to make good on it, beginning the first survey of the damage to the railroad tracks, which U.S. airplanes broke apart with 2,000-pound bombs. But keeping that promise—in a city rigged with booby traps and explosives, with insurgents still fighting back in some neighborhoods—proved way more difficult than the Seabees anticipated. Their mission that day was supposed to be fairly simple—get in, take some measurements, snap a few pictures, get out. That didn't happen.

After Seado discovered the bomb on the tanker car, the convoy quickly but gingerly backtracked across a muddy field dotted with land mines. Then the team spent nearly two hours securing the area around the rigged tanker before moving to another section of damaged railway. There the Seabees spied the blue wire of a second bomb, forcing another quick exit. At a third stop, a group of Marines advised them to park behind a dirt berm because snipers were firing from a bank of houses a short distance away. The vehicles rolled over the berm and onto a flat area where construction stakes marked another batch of mines.

"These insurgents are really making things inconvenient," McCoy quipped. As in other parts of Fallujah where U.S. forces have battled insurgents, the railway was more extensively damaged than the Seabees had expected. "It's pretty bad," Seado said. "I was hoping it wouldn't be that bad, but it's going to be a lot of work to rebuild."

The city was messed up, not only by airstrikes and ground assault but by years of neglect. After the battle, even the dogs had started to die, their corpses strewn among twisted metal and shattered concrete in a city that looked like it forgot to breathe. The aluminum shutters of shops on the main highway through town were transformed by the force of war into mangled accordion shapes—flat, sharp, jarring slices of metal that no longer obscured the stacks of silver pots, the plastic-wrapped office furniture, the rolls of carpet.

Black smoke rose from buildings across the city as U.S. artillery continued to bombard insurgent positions and weapons bunkers a day after commanders declared that the city had been liberated. On a cinder-block wall near the Othman bin Afan mosque on the main east-west highway that divides the city, someone had scrawled: "Islam came back again." But there was no one to welcome it right now, and no one to receive it. And if the brave holy warriors are living long lives, as another graffiti scrawl proclaimed, they were not doing it at the deserted Arch of Victory Square, its metal monument arch and the painting of Saddam Hussein crumpled months ago by a roadside bomb aimed at a U.S. convoy.

Artillery was very important in this battle, and the central highway through town bore the singed, pockmarked evidence. To minimize danger to ground troops, artillery batteries struck suspected insurgent targets before the infantry went in. Airstrikes and mortar fire added to the pressure. Whole blocks were battered this way. Broken glass, furniture, pipes, and other debris were piled on the sidewalks. Fallujah looked like a city from which everyone had simply walked away. A fruit and vegetable stand near the Arch of Victory Square was abandoned, but it still had brown woven baskets neatly arranged on a rack of shelves. The city smelled like dust, ash—death. A few blocks from the fruit stand, the decaying, burned corpse of a bearded man in a black tribal robe lay on the street, arms extended.

U.S. armored vehicles took up a position at the end of some city blocks, while soldiers and Marines on foot skirted booby-trapped buildings and unexploded bombs and mines to search every house, every building, looking for insurgents.

As Brig. Gen. Dennis J. Hejlik, deputy commander of the 1st

Marine Expeditionary Force, was touring a western neighborhood near the neck of a bridge that crossed the Euphrates River, a firefight erupted between Marines conducting the house sweep and insurgents hiding on a narrow street. The sound of the skirmish intensified, and Hejlik walked toward the crack of guns and bang of mortars. "Come on Marines!" he bellowed, leading the way down the pathway. "No, no, Marines," I muttered to myself. "The other way! The other way!" I got behind the biggest Marine I could find and trailed behind Whack 'Em Hejlik. His security detail and aides followed behind him, guns at the ready. Hejlik watched for a while and then returned to his vehicle. Asked how the battle was going, Hejlik looked out at the deserted street. "This is what we do," he said. "This is what we do well."

Later, as the sun set and he prepared to return to a military outpost outside the city, Hejlik said he was pleased with the outcome of the battle and the way American troops were taking care of the city until its residents could return. "What I saw out here is a bunch of professional Marines and soldiers who were protecting the property of the Iraqi people," Hejlik said. "But they continue to whack the bad guys." In the distance, an artillery shell whizzed through the air and landed with a bang, a sound that honking vehicles might have drowned out had there been any traffic. Instead, there was only silence. After the sun set on the purple horizon, there was nothing to see at all.

Exhausted on the ride out of the city, I fell asleep in the back of the Humvee, curled up as the gunner fired from the turret, the bullet casings falling around my feet. The sound was deafening, but I was too tired to care, too tired to react. If I died, I reasoned, I could sleep. I just wouldn't wake up.

I went back and forth between the Marine and Army units, following that frontline snake. I wrote stories about the men and women who manned the fuel pit, the ammo yard, the artillery guns. I wrote about the supply troops who drove food and water to the front, dodging roadside bombs and gunfire to get there. More than fifty U.S. troops were killed in the official five days of the battle and hundreds were wounded. Medics and surgeons who treated the wounded said the injuries were unusually devastating, most of them the result of close-range explosions. "They're just horrific injuries," said Chief Petty Officer Damon Sanders, head of the shock stabilization team. "We saw an increasing amount of shrapnel wounds. Typically there are one or two people who take the brunt of the blast, and the rest of the guys take shrapnel." Sanders of Temecula, California, said the injuries sustained were more severe than those typically suffered in Iraq, largely because the insurgents had been in control of the city for months and were ready to fight. "When you're waiting, you give the enemy time to set up. When they're running, they can't do as much."

Marine Lance Cpl. Davi Allen saw little action in the first days of the offensive. But after a week, after the city had mostly been secured, he and his platoon—part of the 1st Battalion, 3rd Marine Regiment—were clearing houses in one of the northern neighborhoods that troops swept through at the start of the offensive. After going through about fifty houses, Allen of Cloverdale, Oregon, was looking around the small living room of a residence when he heard gunshots coming from the kitchen. He looked over and saw a grenade roll into the room. The house's windows had bars on them, and the grenade was too close to the doorway for Allen to make a run for it. He had no choice but to ride it out. "I balled myself in the corner and waited. It blew up behind me." Two Marines were injured and one was killed in the attack. Medics brought Allen to Bravo Surgical with twenty-four pieces of shrapnel in his backside.

The pace of covering the battle, of seeing the devastating injuries, of watching troops injured and killed, of watching insurgents blown to shreds, of seeing the city destroyed, of trying to capture all of it, exhausted me after weeks and weeks. I wrote two stories some days, the main battle story and what I called my "soldier stories." I drank six to seven cups of coffee each night after dinner to stay awake until 2 or 3 in the morning. I crashed on my cot, only to wake up at 6 or 7 to start the day all over again. Omar often stayed up with me, writing his own accounts based on interviews with Iraqi soldiers and generals. I reported on the battle for CNN International and MSNBC, going live from a satellite truck parked at Camp Fallujah. I described the battle for ABC News, for NPR, and *The NewsHour With Jim Lehrer*. Back home, my family followed these reports, listening to my voice, catching glimpses of me, tired, dusty, and dirty. "I don't like her hair," Grandmother Spinner declared one night upon seeing me talking into a microphone in front of a concrete bunker. I hadn't showered in days. The first time I did a live spot on television, the producer asked if I had brought any makeup with me. Makeup? To a battle? I consented to applying some ChapStick—but that was it! "You should at least comb your hair," Omar chided. I licked my fingers and patted it down. "Satisfied, Oprah man?" I asked, grinning.

The Marines allowed us to use the laundry facility, and Omar and I took our dirty T-shirts and muddy pants to get cleaned. The laundry facility was staffed with foreign subcontractors who worked for KBR. Some of them were Iraqi, but most were Filipino. As Omar handed over his laundry, he exchanged greetings with one of the Iraqis in Arabic and then gave instructions for his laundry. One of the contractors barked at him: "Only English! No Arabic." Omar blushed, startled.

"Excuse me?" I said. "You're going to tell him he can't speak his language in his own country? That's bullshit. This isn't your country!" I turned and stomped out with Omar at my side. A day earlier, Omar had gone into the city with a Marine civil affairs group. I was still with the Army, and Omar was eager to see the city for himself, so I encouraged him to go on the trip. Whenever the press went into the city, we usually rode in armored Humvees for extra protection since we didn't have a weapon to defend ourselves. As Omar got ready to climb into a Humvee, a Marine ordered him to ride in an open-air truck with other Iraqis who worked as translators for the military. Omar refused and continued to get into the Humvee. "I'm with *The Washington Post*," he said. "This is where I ride."

I remained in Fallujah until November 22—almost a full month. Omar returned to Baghdad ahead of me; I wasn't ready to go back. I had grown used to the guns and bombs, had grown mostly numb to the fear. Things weren't any better in Baghdad. Karl had even temporarily closed the bureau for a day or two and ordered the staff not to come to the house for fear that they would be targeted or lead the insurgents there. The translators refused to stay home and came to the office anyway. They were terrified about what this meant, that the *Post* might be pulling out of Iraq, that they would lose their jobs, that the story would not get told. "Look," I had told Omar. "You tell everyone that the *Post* is not leaving Iraq. You are the office manager. You calm people down. Karl is doing what he feels he has to do to keep you safe. Your lives are his responsibility. But I know more than you do. I know that the *Post* is not leaving. We are not abandoning the Iraq story. Tell the drivers. Tell the cooks. Calm people down." In a sign of solidarity, I listed all their names at the bottom of a Fallujah story that day. With all of the precautions our Iraqi translators took, they refused to give up this right to receive credit for their contributions to stories. They coveted bylines and counted newspaper copies sent from Washington like poker chips. It amazed me that the insurgents had so far never made this link. But I suppose this was the one way they could acknowledge that yes, they were journalists for *The Washington Post*. They could see it for themselves, merit of their existence in black and white, not erased or left out in conversations with friends and family. I called Omar. "See, we're in this together."

On November 23, the Army began pulling out of Fallujah, leaving the city to the Marines. I prepared to leave, too, to head with the Army to Baqubah, another insurgent hotspot in eastern Iraq. The night before I left, I walked the dusty road to Seabee camp and left the donated sleeping bag on Chris Neish's desk. I no longer needed a flashlight to get around. The base was as familiar to me as any place I had known. As the sound of artillery rounds exploded in the distance, I wondered what it would be like to walk down a quiet street, unafraid; if I would ever walk down a street and feel that way again.

✦ ✦ ✦

Jackie was everywhere during the Fallujah fight: on TV, on the radio, in the newspaper. Everywhere but home. I wanted to shake people on the subway during my morning commute and tell them that the voice they were reading in the paper belonged to me. To most readers, "Jackie Spinner, Staff Writer," was an invisible body behind a column of words. But when my newspaper landed on the doorstep each morning, Jackie Spinner landed too, her story proof that she was still alive.

My sister joked about how much she was "pimping herself out" to the media during the battle, but I lived for each trick she turned, standing in front of the television during The News-Hour *on PBS, my ears pressed against every crackling word, my hand brushing the static to touch the still image of her face on the screen. Once, while driving and listening to her give an interview on NPR, I had to pull over into a parking lot until my heart stopped racing. I didn't hear a word, only her voice: steady, smart, and alive.*

Jackie's public appearances helped ease the new fear I felt when she told me she would be embedding with the military. Even though she was often in danger while reporting in Baghdad, it wasn't the same kind of danger she faced while traveling with the U.S. military. I knew she was becoming increasingly depressed, cooped up in the Baghdad office and unable to do much hands-on reporting. As much as I sympathized, I was secretly happy, lulled into thinking that as long as she stayed in that office, nothing would ever happen to her.

The afternoon before my sister left to cover the battle, she called to say good-bye. I thought of the final moments of my father's life, when he lay gasping for breath in the bedroom he shared with my mother. During his battle with cancer, I'd rehearsed his funeral many times but never the last words I would utter into his ear as he lay dying. What had I said then? What do I say now?

"I just want you to know," I started to tell my sister as my two-year-old son began tugging at my arm. "Aidan, please," I begged, trying to forgive him for not understanding but desperate to keep talking, to send my sister off to battle with something

of significance. I held the phone above Aidan's reach and tried to call for my husband, but in the commotion, I disconnected the phone. In the end, my good-bye was nothing more than a scramble of grunts, a tug-of-war with the living.

CHAPTER 9

Army Staff Sgt. John Casey put a great deal of thought into creating the ideal military checkpoint. In November 2004, a car bomb blew up at a checkpoint outside of Baqubah, a city of about 300,000, located 35 miles northeast of Baghdad. One soldier was wounded in the attack, prompting Casey to create a better plan for how his platoon would inspect civilian cars. It started with what he believed was the perfect spot: a muddy patch of road off a narrow highway flanked by a deep ditch filled with reeds and several mounds of dirt, natural obstacles that would slow a vehicle trying to ram his soldiers. On November 23—one day after I left Fallujah for Forward Operating Base Warhorse, where the 3rd Brigade, 1st Infantry Division was headquartered, I headed out on patrol with Casey and his platoon, soldiers with the 263rd Armor Regiment. The guys did not seem all that happy to have a reporter tagging along; it was typically hit-or-miss with soldiers—some tolerated reporters and even liked the publicity while others saw us as a nuisance, inept warriors, or simply bad-news messengers to the folks back home.

The goal of the traffic checkpoint was to keep traffic flowing, Casey told me, as soldiers from his platoon stretched wire across the roadway. "That way," he said, "the bad guys don't see a big line of cars and get away." One of his soldiers waved a beat-up white car off the highway. "Car coming in," the man nearest the road shouted. "Car coming in," Casey repeated. The refrain echoed in my head like the pulse of a familiar song—*car coming in, car coming in*—as I watched the car ease off the road.

For the nine months he had been in Iraq, Casey, of Cedar-town, Georgia, had one primary mission: catch the bad guys. Diyala province on the eastern edge of the Sunni Triangle, where the platoon patrolled, had plenty of bad guys to catch. Since the Fallujah battle in the western Anbar province of Iraq, U.S. troops had noticed more insurgent activity in Baqubah.

Atop the Humvee closest to Casey, a gunner scanning the surrounding farm fields with binoculars yelled down: "Hey, boss, there's a guy in black picking up something. He's about a kilometer away. He's got a black plastic bag. He's picking up something." Casey reached for the binoculars. "Let me look." He stared through the lenses into the field. "He's picking up turnip greens," Casey said, handing the binoculars back to the gunner. "It's that time of year—collard greens and turnip greens." The gunner spotted another man. "He's walking like Moses," the gunner shouted.

"He's just a herder," another soldier muttered.

U.S. troops in Iraq could be a crude, insensitive, elephant-stomping lot—not every single soldier and not every single encounter between an American and an Iraqi. But many of the soldiers I encountered couldn't stand the place or the people and had absolutely no appreciation for the primitive culture of rural Iraq. Some of them acted like American goons, just as the Iraqis saw them. The soldiers typically described the tribal robes Iraqi men wore as "man-dresses" and the men themselves, regardless of whether they had earned the title, were called *haji*. To Iraqis, a *haji* was a man who had been to Mecca, but the American soldiers did not bother with that distinction. An Iraqi man approaching a military checkpoint was more often than not a "*haji* in man-dress." I often winced watching the way many of the soldiers and Marines (you learn quickly never to insult a Marine by calling him or her a soldier) interacted with the Iraqi civilians, laughing at their dress, their language, their food, their way of life. All of it was fair game. But this behavior was not going to win hearts and minds. It was especially rankling to watch the way they treated our Iraqi staff, some of them former military officers who outranked the insulting young American privates who pushed them around. I could see the shame on the faces of our staff, and I felt it with them.

At the same time, I understood clearly that the soldiers could not tell the good guys from the bad guys. A bad guy could look like a good guy and come alongside a seven-ton truck full of Marines and detonate the vehicle with deadly consequences. Soldiers busted down doors looking for weapons because insurgents and Saddam loyalists blended into the civilian population, and often, the good guys were not willing to rat out the bad guys. Under Saddam, the people of Iraq learned to look the other way, to mind their own business, to ignore their neighbors' screams. If you went to the police station looking for a family member, odds were good you would be arrested, too. American troops were trying to weed out their attackers within this mind-your-own-business culture. And they were trying to do it as outsiders. In the same vein, to insurgents and Saddam loyalists, Westerners were Westerners. In war, there's no time for nuances, on either side.

Yet, some of the soldiers I met did try to understand the part of war that exists somewhere in the gray, between good and bad, friend and enemy. "I don't blame them," said Spec. Eric Mulkey of Dallas, the medic assigned to Casey's platoon, as he bent over the engine of a car examining it for explosives. "If there were some weird Iraqis running around my country, I'd plant something by the side of the road, too. I think it's messed up, but I don't blame them. We're in their country." The hood and driver's-side door of the car Mulkey was inspecting were both missing, prompting laughter from the soldiers when it rolled up to the checkpoint. The soldiers had no way of communicating with the Iraqis they waved into the checkpoint because they had no translator with them. I taught them how to say *car* in Arabic. *Sayyara*, I said, pointing to the car, just as our driver, Falah, had taught me to say the word.

Duty at vehicle checkpoints can be one of the most boring, tedious jobs that soldiers are asked to do in Iraq. But it also can be one of the most dangerous. The soldiers stand in the open, exposed except for their body armor, vulnerable to rocket attacks and suicide car bombers.

I hadn't asked what we were doing when the platoon rolled out that morning. Before Fallujah, I would have asked a ton of questions, then weighed the risk of the mission with the story I would get. It was ingrained in me from months of reporting in Baghdad. We did not just leave to go out on random report-ing assignments. We calculated. I had stopped calculating in Fallujah. The part of my brain that processed fear just shut down, and now, standing in the field with the soldiers, exposed and hoping not to get blown up by a car bomber, I wondered if it was time for a break. I wondered if Fallujah had hardened me too much. I had grown used to the feel of the flak jacket, the extra 20 pounds that it added to my frame. I wore special glasses like the soldiers—eye gear, they called it. It was supposed to stop blinding shrapnel, and a lot of convoy commanders would not let you roll out with them if you did not have your eye gear. Inside the Humvees, I had a narrow view of the pass-ing landscape. I always sat in the back, usually wedged in like an extra piece of baggage between the rifles and the ammunition boxes. Sometimes I picked up the empty bullet casings that lit-tered the floor and stuffed them in my pocket—souvenirs for little cousins back home. The vehicles smelled like sweat and diesel, a portable auto mechanic shop that had not been prop-erly vented after a long summer. I sat there wondering if my new courage, or perhaps new numbness, was a sign that I was becoming a better reporter, or a mentally unhinged human. It was becoming harder, I surmised, to be both war reporter and human.

I was the only reporter in Baqubah, alone in a little trailer on the edge of Warhorse. After the battle in Fallujah, Capt. Mar-shall Jackson, a public relations officer at the Baqubah base who had followed the 3rd Brigade units that had taken part in the assault on Fallujah, had invited me back to Baqubah. When I first got there, I climbed on the sandbags piled against the trailer to place my satellite dish on the roof. I strung the cable into the trailer through a missing thread of caulking around the door. I was grateful for the quiet, for not having to stuff plugs into my ears at night to drown out the snores of my tent companions. For nearly six weeks, I had changed clothes inside my sleeping bag. I stood naked, giddy in my private trailer, letting the cool air wash over my body. I felt like dancing. It was so quiet in Baqubah. The base had not taken a direct incoming hit in a few weeks, although the town and surrounding villages were festering hideouts for insurgents. The week before I arrived, bands of insurgents stormed police stations in Baqubah and a nearby village. U.S. warplanes dropped two 500-pound bombs on insurgent positions, and four American soldiers and twenty insurgents were killed in a two-hour firefight.

I told Capt. Jackson that I wanted to write a couple of stories during my week at Warhorse. Reluctant to go back to Baghdad, to the intensity of our collective fear there, I mostly wanted to rest. I felt more of a random target with the military. If something happened, it wasn't aimed directly at me. Something about being specifically targeted—about knowing there were people out there lurking, waiting to pounce on a Western journalist—was its own, more direct kind of psychological terror. At least on a military base, I could go for a run, wear T-shirts and cargo pants, eat familiar food, and wear my dad's fishing hat instead of a scarf. Jackson was not pushy about getting me to write stories to publicize the actions of his soldiers. He had been through the battle of Fallujah, too. We were both exhausted, physically and mentally. Jackson was a wise-cracking cop from Ohio, recently married and nearing the end of his yearlong deployment. In introducing me to the top command, some of the officers asked how long I was staying. "Until she finds a husband," Jackson quipped, three times, until I told him to knock it off.

When working alongside the military, I had the same access to the soldiers as a male correspondent would, and neither the Army nor the Marines restricted me in any way. I got to do and go wherever I wanted. But I always felt a bit disconnected, a little bit like everyone knew there was a woman in the room.

"Sorry, ma'am," they'd say when they cursed. At first I'd offer this stock reply: "I don't fucking care if you curse." They recoiled at my vulgarity. I was a woman. I had to be tough enough to pee in a Gatorade bottle in a moving vehicle with a bunch of guys around me, but I should watch my mouth.

The Marines were especially tough. A gunnery sergeant at Fallujah informed me that only lesbians joined the military. I studied his face to see if he was kidding. He was serious. The gunny then went on a small tirade about how women did not belong in the military, how they were not tough enough, how they did not belong anywhere near a war zone. Perhaps he forgot that I was a woman in a war zone, walking down the road of a war zone with him. Sometimes hanging out with the troops felt like being the only chick in a frat house. The homoerotic, machismo nature of the military didn't really bother me. I tuned it out. I could not pretend to be a warrior, to have that warrior mentality, because I wasn't, and didn't have it. What bothered me was that being a woman made it difficult for me to connect with the soldiers, and therefore, made it more difficult for me to tell their stories. I am sure that I got some to talk to me because they were simply eager to talk to a female for a change. But mostly, I got blank stares when I asked x and y. I always felt like I had something to prove. Fortunately, this was not the case with the commanders, who tended to view me through more gender-neutral lenses.

There is a perpetuating myth that being embedded somehow limits access to a story because the military tells us what to write, only shows us what they want us to see. That was not my experience. But what I did find is that the story was more complete when I was able to work both sides, even if I relied on an Iraqi stringer to get the civilian side while I was with the military. For example, our stringer inside Fallujah during the battle reported that the military was using chemical agents that melted people. Our stringer quoted doctors who described treating people whose skin was falling off. I took those reports to the Army, which confirmed that they were firing white phosphorous rounds, which create a screen of fire that cannot be extinguished with water. So between the Army and the witness statements, we were able to match the reports.

I preferred to take my own translator with me when I embedded with the military. Our translators were journalists and translated verbatim. Many of the Iraqi translators who worked for the U.S. military seemed to tell the soldiers what they wanted to hear or were reluctant to pass on "negative" information. They wore the uniforms of the soldiers, and many were gung-ho about the U.S. Army, defending it when civilians tried to speak out. By taking one of the *Post's* translators with me, I could get a clearer picture, a more accurate sense of the interaction between U.S. troops and civilians. This grew more necessary as increasing violence made it impossible for me to travel independently to many parts of Iraq. In many cases, we had no choice but to embed even though it was not ideal. The ideal is to stand on both sides of the story, from the military perspective and the civilian perspective. Embedded, without the ability to step off and step out to report from the other side of the gun, we had to rely on our stringers who lived and worked in the communities where we were embedded. In reality, there was nothing new about the criticism of embedded reporters. And as embedded reporters, we have to constantly challenge ourselves, to make certain that we keep our distance, that we do not become too attached to our units, that we still ask questions, broad questions of the battle in general, not just our tiny, personal part of it.

On patrol in Baqubah with Casey's platoon, we went to check on some Iraqi National Guardsmen who were manning a vehicular checkpoint just outside the city. We did not have a translator with us, and the soldiers had difficulty communicating with the Iraqis, who seemed to be waving cars through without ever checking them. Back in Baghdad and in Washington, U.S. military leaders were expressing great confidence in the Iraqi security forces. But Casey had to wake up some of the Iraqi soldiers, who were sleeping instead of securing. This was the advantage to embedding: the military could not hide when things went wrong or were going wrong. Politicians in Washington could say how great things were going, but on the ground in Iraq, riding around in a Humvee with soldiers, no one could hide the fact that soldiers were constantly getting attacked by improvised explosive devices. Riding around in the Humvee with Casey and his team, I saw children who raised their thumbs at the soldiers, and I also heard the pings of rocks from other kids expressing a different reception of the Americans. I never felt like the military was steering me in one direction or the other. I was never censored. But I also did not always feel that information was forthcoming. That was not the case at Warhorse. Col. Dana Pittard, the battalion commander, ran an open shop. He was honest about the challenges in Diyala province, which were numerous. Under Saddam, Baqubah was a garrison city. The 41st Armored Brigade of the Republican Guard was based there, and after the U.S. invasion, troops emptied the base of its weapons and disappeared into the population. When the U.S.-led occupation government disbanded the Iraqi military, Baqubah turned into a city of unemployed former soldiers and Saddam loyalists with a massive amount of weaponry that were now trained on U.S. and Iraqi troops.

The one connection I had with the soldiers—a connection that I might have been able to exploit in order to get them to open up to me—I simply couldn't use, and that was our shared nationality. We were all American, but they were soldiers and I was a journalist. In Iraq, playing up being an American meant making a political statement of a sort. Soldiers embraced their passport, their flag. As I journalist, I did not. In addition to my desire for neutrality in the story, identifying as an American in Iraq could get me killed. I didn't become a journalist to serve my country; I became a journalist to serve the story. Dying for my country was not as noble as dying for the truth. Understandably, it is much easier for patriots to rally behind American troops with their blatantly American identity. It is less easy to support journalists whose political views are stereotypically supposed but generally invisible, whose mission is, at least in patriotic terms, much less glamorous.

Inwardly, I remained an American, grateful that I had gone to Iraq under one of my country's basic values—freedom of the press. But outwardly, if it appeared to the American public that I had abandoned my country, so, too, I often felt that my country had abandoned me. I was constantly beaten up by readers who sent emails accusing me of being anti-American because I did not write glowing stories about the liberation of Iraq and of its liberators. During my months there, I heard a lot of criticism about how the press never reported the good things that were happening in Iraq. The fact is, we did. I know it was disheartening for the soldiers to see and read the barrage of so-called negative news to come out of Iraq when they were toiling in the villages, trying to make peace, trying to make progress. From some of their foxholes, life was improving for the Iraqis. The problem was that the foxholes are just that— narrow windows that offer a very limited view of progress in general.

From my vantage point, I could see more broadly that the pace of progress was slow, that large parts of the country were erupting in violence, with dozens and dozens of attacks every day. This wasn't a vantage point from the hotel bar. This wasn't a vantage point from just talking to other reporters. I had limited access to other reporters, particularly as our extraneous travel was cut by the threat of kidnapping in the summer of 2004. My stories came from the streets, from seeing for myself, from listening more than talking, from simply observing. An Army combat photographer once asked me why we didn't write more about the schools the soldiers were helping to rebuild. I listed all of the stories about the rebuilding that my colleagues and I had written in the year after the war. The problem was that by late 2004, it had become too dangerous to get to those schools. "I have the same thought you do when you roll out of your base every morning," I told him. "I hope that whatever I do that day makes a difference because I have no guarantee that I am going to make it back to my hotel alive. So I essentially have to decide what story is worth my life. If it is a choice between covering a horrific bomb that kills forty-seven

Iraqi civilians or a pencil distribution at a school, I am going to choose the bombing." In that context, he seemed to understand. We were just two human beings trying to find meaning for our existence in a really screwed-up place.

When the press is constantly writing about what is going wrong, your existence seems futile. I got that. I got it every time a reader sent a nasty email accusing me of bending the truth, of not working hard enough, of reporting the story of Iraq from my hotel bar. If you're there, risking your life, you want someone, anyone, to understand why you are there. For many of the soldiers I met in Iraq, it was not just an obligation. They wanted to make life better for the Iraqi people, and they felt a deep commitment to it. I felt an equally deep commitment to reporting the truth, whether it made people uncomfortable or not. Americans do not seem as interested in facts as they are in the filtered news that reaffirms their beliefs or what their favorite pundits are repeating. In the face of hard evidence, if the evidence does not fit their politics, they will challenge the message and the messenger. I had no message to deliver from Iraq except what I saw, what I experienced, and what I heard. But for some of our readers, depending on the story of the day, I was either for or against the war, for or against the occupation, for or against the soldiers.

After one story about a U.S. raid on a private home in Baghdad, in which soldiers humiliated an Iraqi man in front of his mother, causing him to go crazy and turn against the Americans, Internet bloggers went on the attack, posting such comments as this one, which referred to my story as an "article by Jackie *Spinner* (yes, that's her real name—not a parody, as it should be in this case)." The blogger, Roger L. Simon, went on to say, "The Jackie Spinners of the world arrive to be told what's going on (in a language they quite frequently don't know) . . . We, the consumers of news, are always left to deal with the writer's prejudices." As the blog string continued, Lola—bloggers tend to identify themselves by their first names only—chimed in that she was not surprised by the account because "this is what happens when the management cuts their budget for foreign correspondents to the bare bones. And you end up with garbage like this. Where have all the best correspondents gone?" Richard had the answer: "Maybe she was scared shitless to go out on the streets of Baghdad, and she picked up this tale hanging out in the hotel bar."

The story incensed people because the subject of the article, a man named Imam, was disturbed that soldiers had placed the Quran on a collection of soft pornography they discovered under his bed. In the story I failed to explain adequately just how big an insult this was to a Muslim man—for his sacred text to be placed atop his pornography and, perhaps more important, to be thus shamed in front of his mother. Readers thought I made the story up. In fact, I found out what happened because Imam lived next door to one of our translators. Imam had been a supporter of the Americans until the night of the raid, and his single encounter with American soldiers turned him against the occupation. This sort of incident happened time and again across Iraq, as soldiers, instead of winning hearts and minds, broke them by acting like invaders. The point was lost on the readers who disagreed with the story. The fact that I had graduated from Berkeley was my final indictment. "Jackie Spinner appears typical of the people drawn to elite journalism," Jay decided. "A graduate of Berkeley with an interest in identity politics and ethnic grievance—what kind of shape would you expect her to give to that malleable perception, reality?"

Amid these attacks, another blogger, Sharon Johnson—the mother of a soldier and herself a volunteer police reservist from Minnesota—sent me emails of encouragement. Sharon's son, Al, was serving in Iraq for the New Hampshire National Guard. "I hope that you are able to ignore the yapping from the right wing today," she wrote. "I'm one of them. But I think they are treating you unfairly." Sharon's emails, which continued after her son returned home in January and continue still, kept me from the edge.

Whenever I read the blog attacks, my blood pressure rose until I felt like I was being choked by words. The American public, it seemed, had no idea why I was in Iraq. It is not that I wanted their praise. I remember a sign on the door of my college newspaper that read, "A newspaper's success is measured by the number of people pissed off at it." I don't run from controversial stories just because bloggers or anyone else might take a crack at me. After all, the very principle of free speech that sent me to Iraq gives people the right to criticize what I write. I'm fair game. It was something more: these attacks seemed so personal. They were not aimed at my stories. They were aimed at me, Jackie Spinner, a woman at war, who has a twin sister, a mother, and a family back home counting the days until my return. Why was I even in Iraq, searching for the truth, putting myself at risk, if the American people did not trust what I was delivering? I could take the criticism sitting at home in Washington, in my comfortable chair, with my comfortable life. But it really burned into me in Iraq.

In some ways, it also started to unravel me. I could not find a way to keep from taking the attacks personally. Sharon tried to put it into perspective. "As the mom of a prison guard in Iraq, I have been intensely, maybe obsessively, aware of the media's bias in reporting on the war. I'm sure that each and every reporter in Iraq feels they are bettering humanity. No one wakes up and says, 'I'm going to make the world a worse place today.' Even the terrorists. Jackie, you are caught up in this whole cauldron of intense emotion of people wanting to 'support the troops,' many of whom are their sons, brothers, wives, moms, or kids down the street. They can't figure out whether supporting the troops means rooting for the war or protesting for the troops to come home. The media play a convenient scapegoat in the release of emotions." She was right, of course. During Vietnam, the military and the public, to some extent, blamed the media for the war's negative coverage. The military believed that the critical reporting lost the war, building the foundation for future mistrust between the press and the military, the military and the public. But in the war zone, right in the middle of it, it was hard to separate myself from *the media*. With the troops, I didn't feel like *the media*. I felt like me, one reporter searching for the truth, with a duty to deliver that truth to a readership that sometimes didn't think the truth necessary or that didn't like the version I witnessed. In Iraq, I didn't have my usual defenses—my family, the sound of the ocean, running as fast as I could until the sound of my racing heart oddly calmed me—to deal with criticism of my work.

One of the most likeable commanders I came across in Iraq was Pittard, the commander at Warhorse. He and his XO gave me complete access to anything I wanted to write about. They seemed to get *the media*—whatever that collective label meant—get why we were there, why we had to be there.

Pittard was an avid runner, and on Thanksgiving Day 2004, he made sure that his soldiers had a chance to compete in a Turkey Trot, the traditional 5-K run that marks the start of the holiday across the United States. I had not missed a Turkey Trot in almost a decade, and I was thrilled to have a chance to run one in Iraq. The race started like any other, with the pop of a gun and the sudden slap of tennis shoes on hard mud. The sun had just started to peek above the purple horizon, and the air was cold, New England cold. The strand of runners, most in black shorts and matching gray T-shirts and windbreakers, curved past a pair of guard towers, a column of sandbags, rusting Iraqi helicopters, and the ammo depot. In a wide, 3.1-mile circle, we ran—lungs burning, hearts beating. In a place where death comes suddenly around the bend, we ran for no particular reason except to feel alive. I was terrified of finishing last, beaten by these hardened warriors of the Big Red One. I had nothing to worry about. I finished near the front of the pack, running respectable seven-minute miles. After the race, I walked back to my trailer, not eager for a cold shower. There was no hot water in the women's shower trailer and, because there were so few women on the base, it seemed there was no one to complain to about it. I blasted the heat in my trailer instead and logged on to my computer to send Thanksgiving greetings to my family back home. I noticed I had an email from the sergeant who had been engaged to Luma until she realized he was already married. *That's strange*, I thought. *I wonder why he's contacting me on Thanksgiving.* I opened the email. The sergeant was actually copying me on an email to Luma's brother. "Dr. Ali," it began. "If what you told me is true, you need to get this reporter (Jackie Spinner with *Washington Post*) to conduct an investigation NOW. Accident like this does not happen. No one should have a gun to someone's head. I know of Jackie because Luma sent me her story in *The Washington Post*. I have asked other people to assist with this matter. I will call you tomorrow in the AM." My heart sank. What was I reading? What had happened to Luma? I scrolled down and looked at Ali's original email:

Plz . . . call me at my phone now. lumma is dead plz
hurry and call me

I gasped. Was this real? Was Luma really dead? Shot in the head? Where? How? Why? I called Ali. His English was not much better than his sister's. I pieced together that Luma had been shot the day before, November 24, at the Army base in Baghdad where she worked as a translator. Ali was still trying to get her body from the morgue in the Green Zone. He did not know what had happened. The Army told him Luma was playing with her gun and shot herself. Ali refused to believe it. I called an Army sergeant Luma knew. He confirmed that she was dead and said she had been upset and shot herself. I was having a hard time breathing. I knew Luma was depressed when she got back from Jordan, but I could not imagine her taking her own life. I could not imagine her being so careless with a gun, either. She had her own pistol, and she knew how to use it properly. Her brother had showed her. It did not make sense. I called Ali again, trying to steady myself for him. "How's your mother? How's Sarah?"

"I haven't told them. I can't tell them, yet."

"Oh, Ali. I'm so sorry. Luma, she was like my sister. I'll be back in Baghdad soon, and I promise you, I will help you find out what happened."

After hanging up, I wrote a small notice about Luma's death and sent it to the editors. I am sure that I called Omar and Jenny because telling them would have forced me to exhale, but I do not remember the conversations. Trying to slog through the day, I forced myself to go to Thanksgiving dinner at the dining facility, forced myself to eat the instant mashed potatoes and the canned green beans. I was too shocked to cry, too battle-hard from Fallujah to confront her death. Something must have been lost in the translation. She could not be dead. She was not dead. I would straighten it out once I got to Baghdad. I needed to go back, but not yet. I had one more stop on my tour of the worst places in Iraq. I hopped on a flight two days later and left Warhorse for Camp Victory, just outside Baghdad. From there, I caught a ride to Camp Kalsu, a Marine base south of Baghdad in an area known as the "Triangle of Death."

For a moment, sitting on a bench at Victory waiting for my ride, I realized how easy it would be to call the guys in the bureau to send a driver to pick me up. Within an hour, I could be back in the bureau, standing in a hot shower, letting the past seven weeks wash off of me, letting go. My ride pulled up, and I jumped in. "Do you want to be famous?" I asked the truck driver, getting out my notepad, prepared to record his story.

When I uttered this catchphrase, soldiers and Marines would talk to me. I loved walking into a room and asking the question. "Who wants to be famous?" It was my way of letting the soldiers and Marines know that I was interested in their stories. Everybody in Iraq had a story that needed to be told to someone, anyone who would listen. I was the ear, channeling back to their family and friends and supporters in the United States.

Marine Lance Cpl. Bryan Vitalo, the truck driver in charge of ferrying me and hundreds of gallons of fuel to Camp Victory, was racing the sun to the horizon, his choirboy voice singing along to Michael Jackson's "Thriller," which was pounding from the portable speakers lodged against the windshield of his seven-ton truck. After the sun goes down, the insurgents come out, attacking the military convoys that pass through the dangerous stretch of Highway One that we were on. Among their preferred targets are trucks—like the one we were in—that haul huge, vulnerable trailers full of highly flammable fuel. But as long as the sun is up, the convoys generally pass through without getting hit with mortar shells, bullets, or bombs—*generally*, because there are no certainties out on the road.

In the pink hue of the setting sun, a white pickup truck roared along a secondary road that follows the main highway, where Vitalo was fifth in the line of military trucks carrying supplies to his home base in northern Babil province, Marine Camp Kalsu, our destination. Vitalo, his head slightly cocked, followed the pickup with his gaze. Was it a suicide bomber? Or just a harmless civilian headed home? The pickup sped past and disappeared, and Vitalo turned his head back to the highway and tapped his hands against the wheel to the beat of the music.

Vitalo was a member of the Transportation Support Detachment assigned to the 24th Marine Expeditionary Unit. To get my mind off the potential hazards of the road, I asked Vitalo if it was okay to interview him for a story. I didn't want to waste the ride. Vitalo, twenty, was a self-professed singer and dancer from Freehold, New Jersey, whose dance idol is pop rocker Justin Timberlake. He said he lets his mind wander elsewhere when he's on the road. Sometimes he thinks about his girlfriend, sometimes the clothes he wants to buy with his Marine paycheck, sometimes his 1996 Volkswagen Jetta back home, a car he nicknamed "The Smurf." If sent back to Iraq on a second tour, Vitalo thought he would have enough money to buy The Smurf a new engine. "I try not to think about what could happen in the next thirty seconds," he told me, his eyes never leaving the road. "If you stay on your toes too long, it is bad. You go to bed and you can't turn it off."

When he first came to Iraq, Vitalo had a picture of what the country would look like: "Everyone thinks it's a big dirt hole." But since he began logging miles on his truck, Vitalo has seen a different Iraq, one with marshes, irrigated fields, palm trees, and canals. "Shame on me," he said quietly. "Some places are pretty. It's nothing like you would imagine. It makes me a better person being here." With the sun dipping lower and the countryside blurring into long shadows, the convoy picked up speed. Vitalo accelerated to about 65 miles per hour. The truck can go up to 85, he said, but that's too fast to maintain control. "I could hit it, but we'd probably die." Vitalo learned to trust the drivers behind him and in front of him. "There are guys who will freak out and guys who will hang out of the truck shooting." But that's not what he wanted to think about, and that's certainly not what I wanted to think about. Suddenly, in front of the truck, there was an explosion of white. "Are those tracer bullets?" Vitalo asked, peering into the dark. "Hey," he said, "they're fireworks. It's fireworks." He turned up the music, and I felt myself relax, for just a moment, as we watched the celebratory dazzle of, perhaps, a wedding party.

I spent a week with the Marines at Kalsu, putting off my return to Baghdad as long as I could. November rolled into December, and I no longer truly felt fear. Not even when a mortar slammed into the Internet café, nailing the computer terminal where I had earlier been filing a story, and injuring dozens of soldiers. I had gone into the café for warmth. It was so cold in Iraq now that I found it difficult to file my stories from my satellite dish set up outside on a concrete bunker. The tent I shared with a group of female Marines had no heat, and I burrowed into my sleeping bag at night to ward off the chill. To get to my quarters, I had to walk by a large white tent, singed from the fire of a mortar. A mortar hit the tent a few weeks earlier, and it sat eerily empty, the flaps waving in the breeze, no word of what happened to its former occupants. Kalsu was hit so consistently with mortars and rockets that we were not allowed to enter the dining facility without our vests and helmets. One afternoon I was in the Porta-John when I felt the shudder of a mortar slamming into the ground. I bolted out of the Porta-John and raced to the concrete bunker near the public relations shop of Capt. David E. Nevers and Staff Sgt. Joe Espinosa. The bunker happened to be the one where I had placed my satellite dish. Huddled with the Marines under the concrete, I realized I still had Internet access. "Anybody need to Yahoo?" I asked, passing the computer around.

Kalsu was not an easy place for the Marines who lived there. It was isolated among the palm groves and farm fields. The commander at Kalsu was Col. Ron Johnson, the head of the 24th Marine Expeditionary Unit. Like Pittard at Warhorse, Johnson was an affable leader, respected by his men and good with the press. One morning in December, Johnson invited me to go on a patrol in the village of Haswah, 25 miles south of Baghdad. A few weeks earlier insurgents had stormed the police station in the town and ordered the men to leave. Minutes later, they blew up the station. Johnson's Marines had since set up a security command across a garbage-strewn canal running alongside the ruined police station. Our foot patrol meandered through a marketplace without incident. Johnson stopped to talk to vendors and bought green-skinned oranges, a tin teapot, and two small rugs. The man who sold him the oranges said he was frustrated by the lack of business. "The people, when they see the Marines, they are scared to go shopping," the fruit vendor told Johnson. Another man selling chickens complained that the Marines had closed the road that runs in front of the market. Johnson promised to open the road the next day, but he told the man who sold him the teapot, "When I open the road back up, don't let the people stop" their cars alongside the market.

As the Marines patrolled the center of town, groups of young boys approached them, asking for money, their gloves, even the cheap ballpoint pens tucked into their flak jackets. The Marines talked to the boys and exchanged short English phrases until an Iraqi National Guardsman in a black ski mask ushered the children away. "Yalla, goom," he said. Come on, go. They hurried down the street, and we got back into our Humvees and drove away.

The next day, I climbed into another truck for the ride back to Baghdad. This time, I made no attempt to interview the driver. The singing Vitalo who delivered me to Kalsu had been reprimanded after my article was published. Vitalo had broken the rules, playing music while driving. I felt awful about it, even though I learned that his reprimand only entailed a few extra duties. Still, I wasn't going to take the chance on getting anyone else in trouble. I was ready to go back to Baghdad now, ready as I would ever be. I would only be there for a few days before heading out of the country for a short trip to Budapest. I had been gone almost eight weeks. I was no longer afraid, but I also no longer felt all that real. I was eating and breathing and walking and running. But I was functioning on autopilot, and I had no idea how to switch it off.

✦ ✦ ✦

For the most part, we are a family of teachers, churchgoing Lutherans, and card-carrying Republicans. My sister and I are exceptions, and that often means being drawn into contentious political discussions, generally at the dinner table, after too much wine, on Christmas Eve. We shrug off accusations that living on the East Coast, converting to Catholicism, and having too many degrees has turned us soft—that is, liberal. We've come into our own, on our own, defying easy categorization.

Once my sister decided to go to war, she stopped talking about it, stopped analyzing or politicizing U.S. involvement. I knew that was her way of preparing herself to see Iraq, to listen to its people, to hear the stories of U.S. soldiers as objectively as possible. She's always been that way, aspiring toward an objectivity, a capital-T Truth that the philosopher in me thinks impossible but the sister in me deems heroic and admirable.

When criticism of Jackie's work began in earnest, after she had been in Iraq for many months, she was livid, sending me links to blogs where people were berating her. "Why do you care?" I asked. "They're dimwits. They're nothing."

"Because I'm here," she told me. "And they're not." She beseeched our brother Tim, a conservative, to respond to the bloggers, to speak to them as one conservative to another, to defend his sister's honor. It incensed her that she had been lumped into this category of "liberal media." And I think it shocked her to realize that some readers would have cheered her kidnapping or death.

Even among our own extended family, there were rumblings of discontent about Jackie's presence in Iraq, and that hurt her more than the public criticism. These were the people she'd grown up with, who knew the person behind any label. One cousin accused her of denying Christ, just like Peter did, when she dressed as a Muslim woman to avoid being recognized as a Westerner.

To show our support, my immediate family rallied around our troop of one, hoping that she heard our shouts above the others. No yellow ribbons. No bumper stickers or car magnets. No protests or demonstrations on city corners. Just private, urgent, deliberate love.

No matter what we thought of the war, we understood our troop's mission: to be our eyes and ears in Iraq. We weren't there. She was.

CHAPTER 10

Luma was dead. The afternoon I returned to Baghdad from Camp Kalsu, Luma's brother, Ali, brought me a picture that proved it, shaking me from my disbelief. In the black-and-white photo, her head and shoulders protruded from a body bag. There she was, undeniably dead. Her brother still had few answers from the Army about how Luma had died. Ali, who was finishing his last year of medical residency in Baghdad when the United States invaded Iraq, refused to accept the explanation that his sister had shot herself. He had examined Luma's wounds himself, then had an Iraqi doctor perform an autopsy. According to the doctor's report, the bullet entered her skull from the left side, shattering the bone at close range and exiting near her right temple. Ali noticed burn marks where the bullet first struck, indicating that Luma was shot at close range. But Luma was right-handed. The bullet path from the left meant it was nearly impossible that she had pulled the trigger. If she hadn't shot herself, who had? And, more important, why?

Ali told me his mother wanted to see me. I was one of the few friends Luma had had before she died; it was too dangerous for her to tell her Iraqi friends where she worked, so they slowly drifted apart. I wanted to go to the gravesite, but nobody in the bureau thought it was a good idea. The cemetery where Luma was buried was located along a route used by insurgents. Instead, Ali brought me a video so I could see the grave. I watched it solemnly, still finding it difficult to believe that she was dead. At night, I dreamed that the photograph of Luma's body was just that, a dream, until I woke up and remembered. When her mother arrived at the bureau, Omar came to fetch me from my room. I walked into the living room and found a woman dressed in a religious robe, her head completely covered. She wore no makeup, and her bare face was wrinkled. The last time I had seen Luma's mother, she had been wearing jeans and a tight shirt. She wore flashy lipstick. What had happened? Sarah, Luma's daughter, was with her, but Sarah was shy, withdrawn, nothing like the outgoing little girl Luma had described. The family still had not told Sarah that her mother was dead, but she knew. She saw her mother's picture in a cabinet in the *Post* bureau, a Walt Whitman poem printed beneath it. It was a shrine. While her grandmother and uncle had not noticed, little Sarah had. She knew not to ask a question for which the answer would be too painful. We sat across from one another, sharing short exchanges while Omar translated. "Thank you," Luma's mother told me. "Thank you for receiving our family."

"But of course! Your daughter was like my sister. I loved her like my sister."

"I know, but, Luma told me that she shared her story with you," her mom said, referring undoubtedly to Luma's rape. "And, well, we are grateful you will accept our family."

I wanted to spit at her in rage. Her daughter was dead! She had been raped, and it wasn't her fault! And yet this woman was still blaming her daughter after her death. I wanted to hate her but I couldn't. She moved to leave, and I grasped her in a hug. She sobbed and dug in her robe. "Here," she said, pushing an earring into my hand. Luma had been wearing it when she died. She also gave me a picture of herself, Sarah, and Luma, tiny little glamour shots, smaller than a wallet-size photo.

"You are a sister to us now," Ali said as he left. I felt the weight of his words pressing into me. "You must help us find out what happened. Why did she die?"

With this question unanswered, I left Baghdad and flew to Amman the next day for a ten-day vacation in Budapest. I was heartsick for Luma, furious at her mother, and mad at Iraq for being such a messed-up place. But mostly, I was tired. I collapsed in a chair in the waiting room at Queen Alia airport outside Amman, waiting for a morning flight to Paris to connect to the Hungarian capital. Someone was shaking my arm. I opened my eyes and looked up in a daze. It was a flight attendant. I had fallen asleep so hard that I didn't notice the plane had boarded, leaving only me in the waiting area. "Oh, my God," I sputtered as I opened my eyes. "I'm so sorry. I was . . ." I picked up my backpack and raced down the walkway to the plane. Typically I am a light sleeper, unable to fall alseep amid the slightest noise. In Iraq, consumed by fatigue, I fell asleep anywhere, whenever I had the chance. Still, the fact that I had crashed so hard in the middle of this busy airport really surprised me even though nobody was shooting at me and no bombs were exploding outside. I was always so careful about listening to my body, and yet while it was shouting its exhaustion at me, I was too tired even to hear it. I wondered what else I might have missed.

I desperately needed the break in Budapest, to be in a place where I could move about unafraid, not looking up or over my shoulder. I had taken a poll among the Fallujah press pool during the battle about where to go for a holiday. It was nearly unanimous: "Budapest," they echoed. Inexpensive. Lively. Great food. Culture. And, most important, it was not Baghdad. But I didn't want to be alone. My friend Suzy agreed to meet me in Paris; from there we would travel together to Budapest. After arriving in Hungary, we took a train to the southern countryside and then a bus to the north near the Austrian border, crisscrossing a landscape with its own war wounds, scarred but healing. Hungary was getting ready for Christmas, and I felt more homesick for my family and for the holidays than I had in Baghdad, where there were few visible signs to remind me of the season. The snow and cold, the twinkling Christmas lights, the carols—it hit me in Hungary that I was not going home for the holidays, that I was going to be in Iraq. For the first time in seven months, my homesickness swallowed me deeply.

At Camp Kalsu, before I left on my vacation, the soldiers had showed me all of the Christmas stockings and packages that strangers were sending them from various church groups,

Rotary clubs, and Girl Scout troops in the United States. A Marine gave me one of the stockings as a gift, and I was grateful for this piece of home, even more grateful when I was able to dig into it for food a day later. Falah, Dhia, and Sabah were meeting me at the military checkpoint near the Baghdad airport after the Marines dropped me off a few days before I was to make the trip back to the airport to leave for Hungary. Just as our Iraqi drivers and guards were passing through the checkpoint, a car bomb went off in the middle of the airport road, and the military sealed it off. We were stuck at the checkpoint until the road reopened in one hour, maybe two; no one could tell us for sure. I opened the stocking and passed out beef jerky, peanut butter crackers, and candy bars to tide us over. We shared the treats with strangers in the parking lot, divvying up all that we had. While we waited, I showed the drivers and guard a photograph I had taken on the Humvee ride back to Warhorse after hanging out with the soldiers at the vehicle checkpoint near Baqubah. Gazing out the dirty window in the backseat, I had spotted four small, spindly clouds. The sky was a vast empty blue except for these clouds. They looked like angels. I took a picture for my mom, to show her that the legion of angels she prayed for were indeed watching over me.

"Look at this picture and tell me what the clouds look like," I instructed Falah, Dhia, and Sabah. Dhia peered at the computer screen, his mouth full of a Snickers bar.

"Angels. Those are angels."

"Sabah, what about you? What do you see?"

"Birds."

"And Falah?"

"Bombs. They are about to fall and kill you."

We laughed nervously at our morose Falah, whose outlook on life had skydived since the incident with Dan Williams on the highway from Fallujah. Falah, who had always been one of our most cheerful Iraqis, dedicated to God and to his family, now considered himself a dead man. The fact that he was still alive only meant that he had successfully outsmarted the demons that chased him. His neighbors were after him. The insurgents were after him. The Americans were after him. Everyone and every force in Iraq was trying to snuff out the life that was Falah. Karl had taken Falah to see an Army psychiatrist in the Green Zone. Falah was very public about his fear, how the close call with the shooting insurgents had nearly undone him. He was becoming a ghost of a man, sleepwalking through his days because he could not close his eyes at night. He was angry, prone to sudden outbursts. He wanted to stay busy to keep his mind off his fear, but we were afraid to go out with him, afraid that he had become so unsteady that he would unravel at the wrong moment.

I worried about Falah while I was in Hungary. I checked my email every day, scanning it for news reports from the guys in Baghdad, and obsessed over how I could uncover the truth about Luma's death. Even in this cold country, bedecked with Christmas jewels, I could not fully pull myself from Iraq. I was afraid that if I did, I would not have the strength to go back.

While I was in Budapest, David Hoffman called to ask if I would consider applying for bureau chief when Karl left to go back to Turkey in February. I had no idea how to respond. I talked to him about it in the cold, shivering outside an antique photo store on a crowded Budapest street jammed with shoppers. On the one hand, I was deeply honored that he asked. I was witnessing my own metamorphosis into a real foreign correspondent. I had been the most junior member of the bureau and now David was asking me if I wanted a shot at running it. "Here's the thing, David," I told him, after promising to think it over. "I don't want you to ask me because you have no one else to ask. I want you to ask me because you think I'd be the best person for the job." I knew David was having a hard time filling the spot, and I didn't want to be the bureau chief he pulled up triumphantly from the bottom of the barrel. I really needed to think about it, to think about how much more time I could spend away from home, how much more my sister and my family could endure. I knew my presence in Iraq put a tremendous strain on them. How selfish was I being by agreeing to stay in Iraq, month after month, while they worried? This question gnawed at me in the dark Hungarian night while I listened to David's even, patient voice on the other end of the phone. I decided to figure it out once I got back to Iraq. I had Christmas presents to deal with first.

I was delighted to be able to go shopping in Hungary, enjoying the simple act of walking through a store, lingering over teacups and shiny ornaments. In Iraq, by December, whenever I needed something, I had to send Falah for it. I hoped that in spite of my absence, my friends and family would hold these gifts and know that I was thinking of them. I routinely shopped online while I was in Iraq and imagined the recipients opening their doors back in the United States to the surprise of an unexpected package. *She hasn't forgotten me*, I imagined them thinking. Perhaps it was also a way for me to say, *Don't forget me. I'm still here even if you can't touch me.* My nephew, Aidan, was the main beneficiary of my Internet shopping sprees. Whenever I had a close call, I sent Aidan a gift with his favorite Thomas the Tank character on it. During the battle for Fallujah, my brother-in-law Peter collected an unusually large box from the mailman. He opened it to discover a Thomas beach towel, a Thomas toothbrush, a Thomas pillow, and a Thomas dinner plate and cup. "I don't even want to know what happened," he told me, when I called to see if the box had arrived. To be honest, I couldn't even remember. The specifics of my near-death experiences had begun to blur, taking shape in Thomas the Tank back home.

As journalists in Iraq, we did not have access to the military postal system, so it was impossible for our families to send us mail. Jenny had sent me off to Iraq with fifteen notes to open each week that I was in Iraq. I kept them in a drawer in my desk in the bureau and opened one every Sunday. Sundays were days of ritual in my family when I was growing up. We went to church, then had dinner together, usually a bucket of KFC picked up on the way home. Dad watched Nascar races Sunday afternoons. Mom sat on the right end of the sofa, never the left, and scanned the grocery ads until she dozed off. We kids had quiet time in our rooms, reading, napping, or doing homework.

At night, we often visited my grandparents, who inevitably had the television tuned to Lawrence Welk. In Iraq, Jenny's letters were my ritual. Each envelope contained a picture and a goofy note designed to make me laugh. One picture captures my parents at a New Year's Eve party, my mom sparkling in a silver crown. Another shows me dancing with my brother at a wedding. In another I am wearing a home-stitched Little House on the Prairie dress. These photographs were innocent moments of an all-American childhood, recollected in a place where many mothers keep their children inside for fear of the violence lurking on the other side of the door. I felt both fortunate and sad. Because I stayed in Iraq longer than any of us imagined, the letters eventually ran out. The first Sunday I had nothing to open, Omar handed me an envelope with a picture that showed the two of us, smiling together on a cliff along the front of the Tigris River near Saddam's hometown of Tikrit. "Be happy, always," he had written on the back of the photo, recording his mantra for living.

I could not mail letters home easily. On visits to military bases, I often scrawled a short postcard or letter to my family, sending out my correspondence through the free military system. I was never sure if I was technically allowed to do this but reasoned that my fellow taxpayers probably did not mind if Grandma Spinner got a postcard once in a while, courtesy of the Department of Defense. I also sent letters home through other correspondents traveling in and out of the country, an informal courier system that I tapped when I could. Email made it easy to keep in touch, but I liked the idea of writing letters home as my father had done in Vietnam. As kids, my siblings and I pored over these letters by flashlight, pulling them out of the Navy locker in the closet under the stairs where my father stored his "Vietnam stuff." He never talked about Vietnam. We learned about it through his letters, reading them aloud while wearing pieces of his Navy uniform that had also been stored in the trunk. My father's close friend Mike Smith was an Army ranger in Vietnam, assigned to a unit of Vietnamese mercenaries. He talked about his experience more than my father ever had. In one email shortly after my attempted kidnapping outside Abu Ghraib, Mike wrote to let me know that he supported my decision to stay in Iraq. He confided that he wished he were in my shoes. "As you know, I was a Ranger," he wrote, signing off. "And the way we always said good-bye to each other and give them something to think about is this: Don't worry. If you get in trouble, I'll come get ya. That is the promise we all gave to each other, and that is my promise to you." I knew he meant it. The night my father died, Mike helped carry my father's body out of the house, fulfilling his last act of friendship by shouldering his buddy to the waiting hearse. I wanted to believe the impossible in my most terrified moments, and so I did: if something ever happened to me, Mike would come get me. He would rescue me from my captors, or he would shoulder my body home, just as he had done for my father.

In Hungary, no one at the post office in the northern town of Sopron spoke English, so I had to mime my way through the process of mailing Christmas presents home. I gestured to the postal clerk that I wanted the packages sent by air. "Like this," I said, flapping my arms like a bird. Most of the other packages piled up behind the counter were wrapped in burlap potato sacks, not boxes like mine. I shrugged and laughed. At least my Christmas cards would make it. Those I had entrusted with Suzy, who planned to mail them once she arrived back in the United States.

In the Middle East, I had learned how to communicate without words. In a perfect world, the *Post* would send only Arabic speakers to Iraq, correspondents who did not need a translator and who could understand the subtleties of language. We certainly accept people more familiarly when we understand them, our mutual language an understood common ground. When reporters are sent overseas on long-term assignments, they take the time to learn the language of the country where they will be based. But that was not possible in sending reporters to Iraq. I did not have a year to spend learning Arabic. When the *Post* needed me to go, I had to go, with or without a proficiency in the language. It was not ideal—for me or for our coverage of the Iraq story—that I did not know Arabic, but it was the best we could do. The one good outcome was that it had made me less intimidated to be in a place where I did not speak the local tongue. I learned other ways to communicate: gestures, facial expressions, body language. I learned to read language in a way I never had, silent and wordless. For example, I had been able to deduce at the restaurant in Amman that Luma's friend Jamal had the hots for her, and she in turn was rebuking him. The only phrase I ever made sure to learn before going to a new place where I didn't understand the language was "I'm a vegetarian." So I had no qualms about flapping my arms in a crowded post office to make a point.

When I wasn't flapping in Hungary, I was wrapping my arms around the little things I had missed while in Iraq—enjoying a glass of red wine and a bowl of minestrone soup in a warm café crowded with people; shopping for office supplies; hiking. I literally ate my way from north to south, devouring anything with cottage cheese, my favorite food, which I could not get in Baghdad. Being in Iraq had awakened a greater appreciation in me for these little things. I bought pickles with giddy abandon, skipped down the street, and smiled at strangers without worrying if they were hiding a bomb underneath their clothes.

It was a fleeting freedom. I returned to Iraq in mid-December, to a country still bleeding. The violence had picked up in advance of the Iraqi national elections scheduled for January, and we still could not go out and report freely. On the upside, the renovations for the house were mostly completed, so I felt like I was actually coming back to a home. I played basketball in the driveways with the staff in the mornings, just like I had with my father growing up. For a baseball fix, we tossed oranges in the backyard. Our guards, who grew up playing soccer in the streets of Baghdad, ruled at that sport. But I was the queen of our backyard baseball field, and they often recoiled, shielding their faces with their hands, as I hurled an orange at them. After four or five good throws, it usually exploded in a pop of squirting orange juice. I had been able to spend very little time outside when we lived at the Sheraton, and I enjoyed the outdoor space at the new bureau. I couldn't go to a park or walk down a road or go for a run, but I had a swing set and a backyard baseball field, and it was enough for now. Besides, I still had my kitchen.

Rajiv had put me in charge of the cooks shortly after I first arrived in Baghdad in May. He was tired of dealing with it. Rajiv had a fiery relationship with our night chef, Muhnthir, a former restaurant cook. When I first arrived in Iraq, Muhnthir had just left the *Post* for a better-paying gig at the much larger CNN bureau next door at the Palestine Hotel. Muhnthir preferred cooking for forty instead of four, and he needed to express his culinary talents in three meals a day instead of one. The larger job was more prestigious for Muhnthir, even if it was more work. When he left, Muhnthir lied and told Rajiv he was going on vacation. One of our Iraqi staff later spotted him at the Palestine. Rajiv saw this as a major act of betrayal, but instead of just letting Muhnthir go, he spent weeks begging Muhnthir to come back. Toward the end of his eighteen-month tour in Iraq, Rajiv was growing more impatient with bad food. One of his few comforting constants was a decent meal at night. Muhnthir knew what Rajiv liked to eat and did his best to please our Little Saddam. The replacement cooks Muhnthir offered when he left for CNN were subpar by Rajiv's standards, and often Rajiv would walk into the dining room at night, take a look at what was on the table, declare it "slop," and walk out. The slop was typically overcooked French fries, meat swimming in flavorless tomato sauce, dried-out chicken legs, hummus, and more hummus. Muhnthir ended up coming back for a week to try to appease Rajiv, but he could not swing both jobs. Muhnthir told me he would come back later that fall when his job with CNN was up. Until then, he brought us his friend, Haider, a restaurant chef in Baghdad. Rajiv did not like Haider's simple, Iraqi-style food. Muhnthir had trained in Lebanon in a Western-style kitchen, and his cuisine reflected that experience. Muhnthir made curries, hamburgers, and pasta in a Bolognese sauce. Haider made meat stews and rice dishes, Iraqi staples that

Rajiv had grown sick of. With Omar translating, I sat down with Haider one afternoon to go over a meal plan that I hoped would make Rajiv happier, including hamburgers and pasta, and curries like Muhnthir had made. I also pleaded with Haider to make a lighter, vegetarian dish for me at night. For a few days, Haider complied, making grilled fish and mashed potatoes, salads, and plates of vegetables. But he couldn't keep it up, and soon he was back to making Rajiv's "slop." I seemed to be the only one who liked his cooking.

I started cooking myself on Friday nights when Haider had the night off. I did it initially for selfish reasons. The take-out plates of small Iraqi appetizers that Rifaat, the night driver, brought for dinner often made me sick. The first Friday night I cooked, I slipped into the kitchen around 4 in the afternoon and scanned the cupboards for something I could throw together for dinner. The kitchen was disgusting. It was a converted hotel room, equipped with a stove, a freezer, and a refrigerator. Rajiv was obsessed with making certain the Ums did not make us sick with sloppy kitchen hygiene, but it was difficult to get them to cook differently than they did in their own kitchens. Muhnthir had been rigid, donning plastic gloves and forcing Little Naseer to wear them, too, when Little Naseer chopped the vegetables. But no matter how hard Muhnthir tried to keep our kitchen halfway up to code, it was always dirty. I found some macaroni noodles on a shelf, cheese in the refrigerator, and some very lean hamburger meat typical of feed-starved Iraqi calves. Someone had thrown the meat in a plastic bag at the bottom of the freezer, where it became stuck in warm, then frozen blood. I whipped up meatloaf and macaroni and cheese as our curious translators came in to watch me in the kitchen. Correspondents didn't come to Baghdad to cook. No one seemed certain what to make of this. Omar took pictures as I chopped, stirred, and sweated in my Super Girl T-shirt.

Little Naseer was supposed to have the night off with the cook but refused to leave and instead pitched in. I learned my first Arabic words as Little Naseer pointed to various vegetables and told me the Arabic word. *Thoom.* Garlic. *Busal.* Onion. *Fil-*

fil. Pepper. I made veggie burgers and corn bread from scratch. Huda came in to help that first night too, but I had to watch her at the stove. She was tempted to fry everything in too much oil. "No oil!" I shouted when I saw her pouring oil over my healthy veggie burgers. "You have to use a little oil, Jackie," she admonished. "No, not with my food," I insisted. I was convinced that one of the reasons I was sick day after day was, in part, because of the heavy oil in the food. The Ums were killing me, trying to fatten me up and turn me into marriage material. If they didn't succeed, the dirty water would surely finish me off. During one particularly bad spate, I counted that I had vomited at least once for about seventeen days straight.

The biggest challenge of cooking in Iraq was finding ingredients for my creations. Several of the larger grocery stores in Baghdad stocked American and foreign foods, but the stock was still limited. Fortunately, I had been able to scout the stores before it became too dangerous for me to go out shopping myself, so I had an idea of what was available and what was not. "Bassam, do you guys have basil?" I asked one afternoon while compiling the shopping list to give to Falah. Bassam's English vocabulary did not include basil. I tried to describe the plant's appearance and taste, but we were not getting anywhere. I moved on to green onions and again struck out. Part of the problem was that our all-male staff had limited experience in the kitchen. If I were asking for spark plugs, no problem, but a green plant called basil? I found a picture of a basil plant and showed it to Bassam. He recognized it. "Oh, that is *reehan*." From then on, whenever I needed something from the store that the staff had never heard of before, I printed out a picture and attached it to the shopping list. My cooking was also limited to what ingredients were in the markets that month. Lettuce was a winter crop. So were green onions. But no matter what time of year, Iraq seemed to have an abundance of tomatoes, green peppers, and cucumbers, a combination that Iraqis ate together as a cold salad with a splash of lemon juice and vinegar. The open-air vegetable stalls were deemed too dangerous for me to go to myself. Falah would drive by them slowly as

I scanned the produce from the windows. "Oh, cauliflower! Oh, look, spinach! How come nobody ever buys spinach?" "What is spinach?" Falah wanted to know. I had to go home and print out a picture and send him back to the market with his cue card.

Without fail, I made dinner every Friday night that I was in Baghdad, running through a mix of ethnic themes: Mexican, Cuban, Thai, Chinese. Bassam, Abu Saif, and Omar always stayed late on Friday nights for dinner. We invited our Western and Iraqi friends, turning Friday-night dinners into festive dinner parties. Sometimes when Rajiv walked away from the "slop," I made us dinner then, too. "Why don't we make something else?" Rajiv would ask and then often disappear into his room to work, while "we" went into the kitchen to make dinner. I had no problem making him dinner if it made him happy. I looked at it this way: a happy bureau chief translated into a happy Jackie. Often after dinner Rajiv would turn to me and say, "Spin, something sweet tonight?" That meant, Spin, how about making me cookies or brownies? I usually obliged, eager to do my part for the cause. Everyone had a role. If mine was to make sure Rajiv had cookies, I was going to do it. I hesitated only once, after a small kitchen mishap. When I turned on the stove and leaned in to light it with a match, a ball of flame shot out of the oven, singeing my hair and eyebrows. The sound of the fireball brought Dhia and Baldy running down the hall and into the kitchen. Dhia sniffed. "You smell baked," he announced. I looked down at myself. I wasn't burned, but I had no hair left on my right arm. Rajiv had heard the commotion, too, and walked into the kitchen. "What happened to the brownies?" he asked. I glared at him. "You're okay, too, right?" he responded sheepishly. Baldy answered for me. "Mohammed Baldy. Jackie Baldy." I refused to light the stove again and always called one of the guards in to do it during subsequent baking adventures.

By August, word had started to spread about my Friday-night dinners, and Rajiv and I struck an informal deal: I would not write the news story on Friday nights so I could spend the three to four hours in the kitchen preparing food. I never knew exactly how many people to expect. If news broke, atten-

dance was down; if it was quiet—no big bombings or clashes—
sometimes twenty people would come for dinner. By the time
I tacked on an extra six or eight to make sure the guards had dinner, I was usually cooking for at least thirty people. That would
have been challenging in the most ideal conditions, but this was
Baghdad. Most everything had to be made from scratch. On
Mexican night, I roasted the tomatoes, green peppers, onion,
and garlic in the oven, then threw them into the blender to
make salsa. Little Naseer helped me shred cheese by hand. Miracle Whip? That would have been a miracle. I made mayon-
naise from scratch, whipping the eggs and canola oil into a
frenzy with a whisk.

When the power went out, we finished by flashlight or candlelight. Sometimes we had to duck into a stairwell, abandoning dinner preparations until the threat of a mortar attack
passed. The heat in the kitchen was unbearable; often the temperature soared past 100. I didn't understand why Rajiv would
not put an air conditioner in the kitchen for the Ums. One
night, after he helped flip quesadillas on the stove, he remarked,
"It's too hot in here!" *Mmm, hmmm, Little Saddam,* I thought to
myself. *This is what life is like from the other end of the whisk.* One
Friday night I went into the kitchen two hours before dinner
and found the hamburger meat and fish I had requested from
the market still in the freezer. I was dismayed, thinking this
rock-solid meat would never thaw in time for me to cook it. But
because the kitchen was so hot it thawed in twenty minutes, sitting on the counter. Little Naseer and I had to drink multiple
bottles of water to stay hydrated while we cooked. I was spent
by the time we carried the food to the table on silver trays.

We always started the meal with the reading of a poem,
blessing our meal with the one thing we all shared: a love for
language. Bassam, a poetry aficionado, usually stood at the
end of the table and read my selection for the night. I tried to
tie the poem to the theme of the dinner, emailing my sister in
the hours before dinner, asking for her to send pronto a good
poem, fit for a wartime dinner party, written by a Chinese or
Mexican or American poet. On the night of my last dinner in

Iraq, she sent a poem she had written about the two of us, about love "bound back together." Mostly, though, we settled on my favorite, the Chilean poet Pablo Neruda. I had brought two collections of his poetry to Baghdad with me. We also read Iraqi poets, Chinese poets, American poets. I taped each poem to the wall after dinner, and after several months, the poems covered the wall of the dining room like wallpaper, with the date of each reading noted at the bottom.

I loved these dinner parties, loved the one time in Iraq that I felt like I was really giving of myself. When we shared the table together, our Iraqi staff felt like they were part of the family, equal participants in our news operation. I would never have considered excluding them—in fact, their presence made the parties. Abu Saif entertained us with stories of his romps around the world as an Iraqi Airways pilot and engineer. I picked up strays at press conferences and invited them to dinner. After Charlie Crain, a freelance writer for *USA Today*, told me that the paper made him pay for his own meals, I insisted that he start coming around for dinner on Friday. He became a regular. A U.S. soldier even showed up one night in August. He was one of the snipers who guarded the roof of the Sheraton. His name was Mark and he was from upstate New York. He was twenty-three, lonely, and scared to be in Iraq. This was his first adult dinner party. He also had never eaten Indian food before, which is what I had made that night. He sat with his rifle slung over his shoulder, his skinny little self squished between a well-traveled, bearded reporter from Reuters and a South African journalist, while we passed around bowls of chickpeas, lentils, and curried chicken. He looked shell-shocked during the entire meal, but he ate every bite.

In December I set out to prepare the bureau for the holidays. Many Iraqi families, whether Christian or Muslim, celebrate Christmas, often with trees and family dinners. "We need a tree, guys!" I proclaimed the afternoon I came back from Hungary. With only a week before Christmas, Ghazwan, our lone Christian staff member, took charge of the tree-buying mission. Omar threw himself into our Christmas preparations. He and

Ghazwan went out one afternoon to buy Christmas decorations for our spindly pine tree. They came back with plastic sacks filled with cheap ornaments imported from China, tinsel, lights, and stockings. On the afternoon we decorated the tree, I set up my laptop on the dining room table with a Web camera attached. The tiny device beamed images from one computer to another. While visiting my sister and her family in their new home in Maryland, my mom sat in front of another computer and watched us decorate the tree. We could see her on our screen, staring at the image of nine Muslims, one Iraqi Christian, and one American, loading our tree with ornaments. "Look, Mom, this for you," the drivers would say, dangling ornaments in front of the Web camera, placing them on the tree, then turning around to beam at the digital image of my mom. "Hi, Mom," Dhia said into the computer. "How are you? We are taking good care of your daughter. Merry Christmas."

A few seconds later, my mom's voice crackled over the computer. "Thank you!" After lamenting the lack of garlands to my sister one day, she reminded me of the construction paper garland strands we used to make as kids. I spent an hour that afternoon cutting strips out of the Iraqi newspapers. My scissors cut through stories of car bombs, kidnappings, and errant mortar shells. I strung the slivers of destruction around the tree. "A symbol of hope," I told Omar.

During my last trip to the United States, I bought Christmas presents for everyone on the staff, knowing I would not be able to do so once I was in Baghdad. The staff bought presents for me and Karl, too, and the packages began piling up underneath the tree. The Ums offered to make the staff traditional Iraqi *dolma*, grape leaves, onions, potatoes, and tomatoes stuffed with rice, meat, and spices. "Well," I told them, through Omar, "how about you make that for our staff lunch when we open presents on Christmas, and I'll make dinner for Christmas night." I had grown to love *dolma*, but it wouldn't be Christmas without green bean casserole.

I wanted to re-create a Midwestern family Christmas in Iraq. Back in the United States, it was going to be a hard

Christmas for my family. Since my maternal grandmother had died in July, my mother would be celebrating and grieving and also worrying about me in Iraq. I missed my family, but home was starting to feel more distant. My life seemed so entrenched in Iraq. These Iraqis were now my family, too, and Iraq was as familiar to me as any other place I had known.

Iraqi Christians were preparing for the holiday with a great deal of dread. Attacks on Iraq's Christians had increased in previous months, as insurgents targeted churches, Christian businesses, and their owners. Some Christians who had openly worn crosses on chains around their necks began to hide them under their clothes. Crosses dangling from the rearview mirrors of cars disappeared. Iraqi Christians, a small community of 800,000, had lived peacefully among the Muslim majority for hundreds of years. That peace now seemed fragile, in jeopardy, as Christmas approached.

With that in mind, Abu Saif and I decided to scout out a church to attend on Christmas Eve. The first church we went to was surrounded by American Humvees, so we kept on driving. Abu Saif was concerned that this attempt at protection made the church an even bigger target because the insurgents might see it as an opportunity to attack the Americans, too. We didn't want their presence to attract the attention of the insurgents, so we bypassed it. Several priests sent us packing for just the same reason, unwilling to expose parishioners to the added danger of an American reporter inside. We drove to another couple of churches, knocking on locked doors until the priest at the Virgin Mary Church on Palestine Street in eastern Baghdad agreed to meet with us. His parishioners were making last-minute preparations for the Christmas Eve service. They erected steel barricades in front of the main gate to keep potential car bombers from getting too close to the church. Several young men rehearsed how they would search strangers for hidden explosives. The church had hired a security director from its own flock a few months earlier. The man said he had walked to the church that morning with his hand over his heart. "We are frightened," he confided, his blue eyes looking down at a desk covered with passages from the Bible and images of Mary, the mother of Jesus. "People are frightened to come to church."

It was the first time in as long as even the old women could remember that Iraqi Christians prepared for the Christmas holiday with heart-thumping sadness and dread.

Many Christmas Eve services were canceled or changed to daylight hours, and police cars guarded the churches on Friday night. Priests expected to deliver their Christmas messages to nearly empty churches. People shopping for presents, decorations, and trees did not linger on streets for fear of being targeted by insurgents.

The thin-faced priest at the Virgin Mary Church said he would find a way to deliver a message of hope for the people who dared to attend Christmas Mass.

"This Christmas will be difficult," he told me. "People are dying every day. Every house has casualties. Every house is crying, and the church cannot celebrate when people are crying. Our happiness will only be the birth of Jesus Christ and the hope that he will bring peace back to our country."

He clasped his hands and smiled reassuringly at me. "I am not afraid," he said. "I am sitting here. I am not frightened."

I asked him for his name, but he was afraid to give it.

As we left the priest in the parish house, Abu Saif and I discussed our plan to return that night. "Just a minute," Abu Saif said, dashing off for the door to the church. He peeked in, looked around, and then returned to pick up our conversation.

"What were you doing?" I asked, puzzled.

"I wanted to see where we would sit. I wanted to find a place where there would not be so much glass when the bomb went off."

We decided that we would need three cars: me in the armored car, an armed guy in the second car standing outside and acting as a spotter, and a translator in the third in case a bomb went off. Someone would need to cover the news. We did not talk about what would happen *if* a bomb went off, but *when*.

I came back and discussed the plan with Karl. He was worried. "Talk to David," he told me. I called David Hoffman and discussed the plan with him. He was uneasy. It seemed like an awful big risk to take for the story, David told me, but ultimately it was my decision. I had no idea what to do. I mean, I was rattled but at what point was the fear impairing my judgment? I knew other reporters were going to churches. I also knew that our security procedures were some of the most stringent in Baghdad. Then I thought of all the people going to church with me, because of me: Ghazwan, Abu Saif, three drivers, Omar or Bassam outside waiting. No, I couldn't do it. I couldn't put them all at such risk. "Karl, I think I have enough for a story without going to church," I told him.

"It's your decision, Spinno," he said, but I couldn't help wondering. Had I done the right thing? I hated this second-guessing. I filed my Christmas story with what I had. The story reflected the sadness and dread of people too scared to go to church. I was one of them.

After I sent my story to Washington, I cheered myself in the kitchen, making spinach lasagna and meatballs for Christmas Eve dinner. Karl had invited a few correspondents over and, after we ate, we put the Christmas classic *It's a Wonderful Life* into the DVD player and waited for the little bell to ring. It was a quiet night. No bombs went off. The empty churches in Baghdad were spared.

Our Christmas was filled with music and laughter and the sounds of wrapping paper ripped from packages. Karl and I sat in the living room, surrounded by presents and our Iraqi family. The staff, eager to turn a tomboy into a proper lady, presented me with jewelry—gold necklaces and bracelets, silver earrings. My bounty included five watches, two necklaces with a "J" pendant on them, four bracelets, a solid gold cross in a red-cloth-lined box, a spinning glass manger scene, and a giant pink bunny that sang "Twinkle, Twinkle Little Star" when you pressed its paws. I was touched by their generosity, by the way they threw themselves into "my holiday."

"This is your holiday," Dhia told me, explaining why I had

to be the one to climb the ladder and place the star at the top of the tree.

We now shared this day together, shared wishes of good cheer and of peace. I thought of how many times I had seen that phrase—"Peace on Earth"—around the holidays back in the United States. *Peace on Earth indeed*, I thought, as I grabbed each of our Iraqi staff in a Christmas hug.

Karl spent the day writing the Christmas story, and per a deal we had made, I spent the day in the kitchen. Hannah Allam and Huda came over to help with the preparations. Our American security adviser offered to stir the gravy after I pulled our thirty-pound turkey from the oven. I wore all of the jewelry the staff gave me for Christmas as I made homemade cream of mushroom soup for the green bean casserole. We ended up with quite a feast: turkey, mashed potatoes and gravy, corn pudding, green bean casserole, broccoli and Velveeta cheese (which my sister had sent back with me in October, anticipating my need for it during the holiday). The only thing missing was the fruitcake. Hannah made cookies that did not turn out quite right because the electricity went off while she was baking them in her hotel. She had intended them to be a festive red but the only food coloring she could find in Baghdad had expired. Part of the turkey was undercooked, so Karl had to cut around the pink parts. The mashed potatoes turned out slightly runny, more the consistency of pudding. But we had our Christmas miracle when Muhnthir showed up with a traditional yule log. We were a family, and we did what families do when estranged relatives show up for Christmas dinner. We welcomed him and the green frosted log with open arms. Peace on Earth.

✦   ✦   ✦

The last Christmas my father was alive, he skipped the candle-light service we always attended as a family. He thought he had the flu. A few weeks later we learned it wasn't the flu but cancer, already spread too far for him to be saved. We missed him at church with us that Christmas Eve, but we didn't long for him. We had no idea that he would be dead in less than four months. Had we known, the service would have been wrenching. Instead, we brushed it aside as a disappointment, a temporary interruption in our family tradition.

With a few exceptions, we were one of those lucky families rarely apart at Christmas. There was that near miss of mine when I lived in Minnesota and was forced to work late on Christmas Eve. Too broke to travel or to take any time off from work, I settled in for a lonely, self-pitying holiday. But my sister would not hear of it. She booked a hotel room for me halfway between Minneapolis and Chicago, where my family would be gathering for the holiday, and I set out in a blizzard, blindly following my twin's love to a Super Eight just outside Madison, Wisconsin. I knew my sister's gift was as much for herself as it was for me, but still, I was ashamed that she had to pay for my hotel room. Although we had both graduated with master's degrees the previous year, I was struggling to make ends meet while she was finally earning a "grown-up" salary at the Post. "I'll pay you back," I promised.

"No way," she protested. "From now on, think of me as your Sugar Sister!"

Sugar Sister went into overdrive in Iraq, surprising us with treats she ordered online and had shipped to our door. My son acquired enough Thomas the Tank engines to outfit a day care. I began to dread the UPS man, knowing that what he carried up our path represented a brush with death in Iraq. While on vacation in Hungary, Jackie called to tell me she had bought presents for all of us and was shipping them home for me to distribute. She hoped the package would arrive in time; she needed it to arrive in time. It did—on Christmas Eve. All of the once carefully wrapped packages lay in a jumble on the bottom of the box, the paper torn from where customs officials had opened them. There weren't any tags left to identify the receivers. There were tubes of paprika, chocolates, calendars of lovely but unidentifiable Hungarian meals, and bottle openers—all trinkets, really, but trinkets that said, "I touched this and thought of you. Don't forget me."

That night, during a candlelight Mass in Maryland, I sat next to my mother, my arm around her shoulder, as much to steady her as to steady myself. When the congregation rose to sing "O Come All Ye Faithful," my mother and I could not will ourselves to rise. Weighed down by seven months of worry and a future of unknowns, we sat and wept, struggling to sing, struggling not to lose hope.

CHAPTER 11

The fish were dying. Falah had stocked the backyard pond at the bureau with goldfish, but after a particularly cold week near the end of December, the fish were sick, paddling lethargically in the stagnant, cold water. Falah needed to get them to a warmer climate or they would certainly die. He asked me if I would take them in, and I agreed, so he bought an aquarium for my room and filled it with warm water, rocks, and a wheel that spun a kaleidoscope of psychedelic colors. Falah wasn't convinced that bringing the fish inside would save them, but he remained hopeful.

"Let them see your face," he instructed. "Be kind to them."

Great, I thought. *More death. Just what we need to ring in 2005.*

Karl and I celebrated New Year's Eve in the bureau by ourselves, poking at a dinner neither one of us really cared for. We had a new cook, Abu Haider, who was hit-or-miss. Abu Haider had been a chef for Iraqi Airways. Standard jokes about airline food aside, I used to tell our dinner guests that Abu Haider's former employment meant that he was one of Iraq's better professional cooks. Iraqi Airways chefs catered to visiting foreign airlines, so Abu Haider had dabbled in all different kinds of cooking. While flying, he had studied Chinese cuisine in China and Italian cuisine in Italy. But Abu Haider also had crossed Saddam or his men at some point; he declined to go into the details, only acknowledging that he was imprisoned in Abu Ghraib. There he was tortured. The torturers concentrated on Abu Haider's hands, his most important cooking utensils. They were now mangled, making it difficult for him to chop effectively. Nonetheless, I loved the way Abu Haider treated Little

Naseer like an apprentice, not like his personal slave as Muhnthir had done, and Little Naseer thrived under Abu Haider's tutelage. When Abu Haider called in sick one night, I asked Little Naseer to cook. "You've been watching these guys for two years," I told him through Abu Saif. "You can do it."

"Abu Saif," I continued, "tell Little Naseer that some day I am going to come back to Baghdad, and he will be running his own restaurant. Tell him to keep his head up. He may be a small man. But that does not mean he cannot be a great man."

Little Naseer blushed, proud but embarrassed, as Abu Saif translated. I have always believed that if you tell someone he is great, he will rise to this greatness, especially if he is devoted to you, as Little Naseer was devoted to me. His dishes were simple, but Little Naseer had a secret weapon. Every night, it was his job to clear the table. He knew what food we left untouched and what food we devoured. The first night he cooked, he made our favorites, relying on memory to make a baked potato and a tomato and green pepper casserole for me and chicken and French fries for Karl. From then on, whenever we needed a fill-in chef, Little Naseer stepped in. I had brought Arabic-language cookbooks back with me from Amman during my trip to Hungary. Little Naseer's life in the bureau improved tremendously when we hired Abu Haider. Muhnthir had come back in December but then left to go on a religious pilgrimage, or so he claimed. I fought with Muhnthir, imploring him to bring a replacement quick. It wasn't his problem, Muhnthir told me.

"But you are the chef! Your job is to make sure we eat. If you can't do it, you have to find someone else." Muhnthir ignored me. I threatened to fire him, diplomatically. We couldn't allow someone to leave too ticked off. Muhnthir knew where we lived. He knew our security procedures, our get-out-of-Dodge escape plan, and my hiding spot in the freezer. Muhnthir also knew that I picked up the slack when he didn't show up. I could not eat the take-out the guys brought because it made me sick, so I fixed my own dinner. I felt selfish making something only for myself. My Midwestern grandmothers would have been ashamed if I had cooked but not shared. Muhnthir knew nothing of my grandmothers, but he knew that something, in this case guilt, translated into my covering for him and cooking for the bureau.

As soon as Muhnthir left on his pilgrimage, we hired Abu Haider. He was a polite man with a large round face who constantly dabbed at the sweat on his balding head while he cooked. He stayed in the kitchen with Little Naseer, teaching him how to cook, kindly directing him to chop, stir, and bake. Abu Haider struck out more often than not, overcooking vegetables and refusing to quit adding his Iraqi touches to foods we requested, rendering them unrecognizable and usually inedible. But he was loyal, and that counted.

"It's lonely here, isn't it," Karl asked, as we picked at the New Year's Eve dinner.

"Yeah, the holidays have been hard. And I'm exhausted."

We stirred the food around our plates—cold, undercooked potatoes, mushy beans.

"Karl, I'll be your friend," I teased.

"I have a friend!" he exclaimed.

We smiled warily and pushed back our chairs from the table. I went back to my room to write a story about what a bad year it had been for Iraq, the kind of story that conservative readers would no doubt label "Liberal Media Propaganda." It was hard to fight that kind of criticism. My stories unapologetically reflected the despair of the Iraqis I interviewed. I was more self-conscious when it came to my own despair. Cooped up, sad, and missing home, beaten down by the violence, I tried hard not to project my personal depression on the Iraqi people. Earlier in the year, when it was still safe to travel in Iraq, we could find glimpses of normal life to report to our readers. There were villages untouched by the war, others trying to rebuild primarily with the help of the U.S. military. But by December 31, 2004, it was difficult to find these upbeat stories. Soldiers I talked to were merely trying to stay alive as well. As 2005 rolled in, for the most part, Iraq was a miserable place.

When the clock turned to midnight on New Year's Eve, I returned to the kitchen to make popcorn for the guards and for Karl and several of his journalist pals who were watching a movie in the living room. As soon as it struck midnight, I took a large bowl of popcorn out to the guards. "Happy New Year!" I shouted, eager to embrace the possibility that it would be a better year. "Get back in the house," one of the guards yelled, turning his back to me and my words of cheer. "You're going to get hit by a stray bullet." Indeed, the neighborhood had erupted in gunfire as Iraqis took to the streets shooting off their guns in celebration, their own popping corn of optimism.

A few days later I awoke to a strange odor. I went to the fish tank and found three of the fish floating belly-up. As Falah instructed, I had kept vigil in front of the tank, letting the fish see my face and hear my voice wish them well as they prepared to depart for that great pond in the sky. They learned the sound of my voice and came to the front of the glass when I tapped. Sometimes Omar or Bassam would join me at the tank, and we would watch silently as the fish struggled for life. I was merely hospice care by this point, enacting an allegory that seemed to represent Iraq itself. I often felt as if I were watching a country struggle to throw off its death wish and get back on its feet. Yet, as an outsider, as a care worker but not a player, I could only stand aside and watch things unravel. Day after day, we wrote about sadness and grief. And day after day, it was beginning to be more difficult to find joy. We were all running on fumes toward Iraq's first democratic elections, which were scheduled for January 30, 2005. I hoped we would all make it.

With a sigh, I gingerly put the dead fish in a net and carried them from my room. I stopped in the office where the translators were sitting.

"Come on guys," I announced, "we're going to have a funeral."

We traipsed outside to the garden where Dhia, one of the drivers, dug a hole. Translators, cooks, and guards all gathered around while I read from the Bible, Psalm 69, chosen for its reference to water, then swung rosary beads and Muslim prayer beads over the fresh mass grave, making up the ceremony as I went along, much as a child does when its first pet departs for hamster heaven. We repeated this scene each time another fish died until all twenty or so were properly buried. Falah promised to bring me more fish, healthy fish. I really liked having the fish. They were good company, and the hum of the filter at night lured me into sleep, a bubbling lullaby. But really, I couldn't take one more thing dying in front of me. After the final funeral, I cleaned out the aquarium, discarding the buckets of cloudy water into the toilet. By the time I was done, I was soaked in the smelly water and had to change clothes.

I woke up the next morning with a terrible headache and a fever. My head pounded as I staggered dizzily to a cabinet in my room where I kept a bottle of ibuprofen. I reached down to open the cabinet, tugged on the door, and fainted, pulling the door off its hinge as I tumbled down. When I came to on the floor, I was soaked in sweat and unable to move.

"Karl," I called out in a whisper. But I knew he would not be able to hear. Karl slept with earplugs in the room next door. Only the loudest crack of a car bomb could rouse him from his exhausted sleep.

I pressed my cheek onto the floor, trying to cool off, and fell into a fevered stupor. Abu Saif found me a few hours later on the floor and helped me into bed. The Iraqi staff summoned a doctor they trusted, and he came to the house. I was having a hard time breathing, and my ribs were aching where I fell on the cabinet door. The doctor blamed the fever on a bad case of the flu and shot me up with morphine before I could object. By night, I was hallucinating, and my fever had spiked to 104 degrees. Karl called a doctor he knew at the U.S. military hospital in the Green Zone. The doctor agreed to see me, so we set out for the Green Zone. The emergency room was mostly quiet, except for the cries of a Marine with kidney stones and two Iraqi civilians who appeared to have burn wounds from some sort of explosive device. The doctors took blood for tests and pumped me with two bags of saline, rushing to fix me up so we could leave in time to make the 11 P.M. curfew that forbade traffic on the streets. Being out after curfew was dangerous. Iraqi police patrolled the streets, and we didn't quite trust them not to turn us over to the insurgents. The hospital released me with a plastic bag of painkillers and instructions to drink plenty of fluids. The diagnosis: flu and dehydration. Nothing unusual had turned up in the blood test, and there was no time for an X-ray. Because I was too weak and dizzy to walk, a soldier rolled me out in a wheelchair to a waiting Humvee that took Karl and me to the Green Zone perimeter, where our drivers were waiting for us. We sped back to the bureau, racing the clock through the dark streets. We were stopped once but waved through when Dhia explained he had taken his sister to the hospital. I was in the backseat, curled up in a ball.

Karl forced me to take a few days off to recover, which I was reluctant to do. As the only ones in the bureau during the first weeks of January, we were extremely busy preparing for the upcoming election and making sure we had the proper credentials to cover them. Because he had not had a break in months, Karl also planned to go out for a few days for a short vacation in Egypt. So I had to hold down the bureau on my own for a few days until Anthony Shadid returned. And the violence was unrelenting. Bombs went off like alarm clocks around the city most mornings, awaking Iraqis to another bloody day. We had to cover these attacks and then send in reports to *The Washington Post* website. Days were spent tracking the political news and reporting whatever else happened. By night, we took turns writing the daily newspaper story. The *Post* had published at least one story from Iraq every day, with very few exceptions, since the U.S. invasion in 2003. With only one or two reporters in the bureau at a time, the pace was especially grueling. I felt terrible for Karl, already exhausted and now having to pick up the slack for me. I worked from bed for a few days. Omar went into caretaker mode, making me hard-boiled eggs for breakfast. The guards gave me a two-way radio that I could use to communicate with the translators downstairs because I was too weak to walk down to them. My call sign was Wife-4.

"This is Wife-4, does anyone read me?"

"We hear you Wife-4, come in."

"What is the latest from Mosul? Have we heard from the stringer? Could I have some water?"

Up and down the next few days with the fever coming and going, I remained frustrated by how sore my ribs were. I had to hold my side whenever I walked down the stairs to keep the pain from buckling me over. I knew this wasn't the flu. My ribs felt broken or at least cracked, and I blamed the water from the fish for causing my illness. It was too much of a coincidence that I got sick the morning after handling the water from the Tank of Death. Both David Hoffman and my financial editor, Jill Dutt, encouraged me to leave Baghdad to go to Amman to get medical treatment, but I was too weak to travel. And I had good days as well as bad days. I was still writing stories. One night, ten days after I had initially collapsed, my fever shot up, and I could no longer take the pain. I struggled to get down the stairs. Abu Saif was at the bottom talking to Omar. I was close to tears.

"Abu Saif, something is wrong. I can't breathe."

I slumped down the wall to the floor.

Abu Saif lifted me up. It was too late to go to the Green Zone. Someone would have to take me to an Iraqi hospital. Abu Saif called Huda, who was nearby at the Knight Ridder bureau where she now worked. She came as soon as he called her. I would need a female translator to go with me into the emergency room. With Anthony in the car, too, we set off for a Christian hospital in Baghdad, a place the guys thought might not be as infiltrated with insurgents. It was a gamble, for them and for me. But nobody felt we had a choice at this point. My fever had spiked too high. Huda ushered me into the emergency room. She found a doctor and whispered to him. They led me to a private room. She had quickly determined that he was a "friendly," a military term in Baghdad for someone who is on your side. The doctor spoke excellent English. He encouraged me to take off my scarf and to describe what was happening. He wanted to X-ray my ribs but said I would have to come back the following day to do that. He thought the ribs, cracked or bruised, were causing the spiked fever. He filled out a prescription for an antibiotic and some sports medicine cream and left me with Huda. "Put on your scarf," he advised before walking out.

"What's happening?" I asked Huda.

"Shhh," she said. "The woman who is coming to give you your medicine cannot be trusted. Do not speak English to her. If she asks you a question, grab your throat."

Before I could protest—I was leery of getting a dose of medicine when I didn't know what it was—a woman in a white coat walked in with a huge syringe. Huda pushed me over on my side and hiked up my long black skirt. I started to protest, but Huda shushed me quickly. I was going to have to lie there and take this big needle. After the shot, Huda massaged the serum into me, and I was too sick to register the humiliation. As soon as the woman walked out, I asked Huda what she had given me. "Valium," Huda said. *What's up with these Iraqi doctors and their sedatives?* I thought. *They think they're the answer to everything!*

As we walked into the waiting room where the drivers and Anthony were waiting for me, I excitedly told them, "Well, I'm alive!"

"Shhh, no English, no English," Huda said, dragging me, loopy and stoned, out to the waiting car.

Later that night, after tucking me into bed, Huda, her scarf tucked neatly around her head as usual, backed out of the room with a smirk. "I saw your butt! I saw your butt!" she sang in amusement.

"How fair is that?" I complained. "I've never even seen the hair on your head."

Then I passed out.

We decided it was not safe for me to return to the same hospital for the X-ray, just in case someone at the hospital had tipped off an insurgent about my appointment.

Hannah Allam had mentioned to Lt. Col. Barry Johnson, the Army detention operations spokesman, that I had been sick. Barry called to see if he could do anything.

"Yeah, I need an X-ray," I told him. "Can you get me to Abu Ghraib?" It was difficult for civilian journalists, even Americans, to get medical care in the Green Zone. Karl, who knew a doctor there, was still in Egypt. Plus, we were only supposed to use the Green Zone hospital if we had a life-threatening injury. I didn't think some sore ribs and a fever would qualify, particularly when the doctors at the hospital were treating soldiers with horrific injuries caused by roadside bombs and other explosions. I felt bad about taking up their time.

During several earlier visits to Abu Ghraib, I had interviewed doctors and nurses who worked at the field hospital there, and I knew it was a first-rate medical facility with a caring staff of soldiers. On top of that, I had met the head doctor when we were both in Fallujah for the battle. Perhaps he would remember me and hook me up. I told Barry Johnson that I would go only if I could find a story there, too. I didn't want to owe anyone a favor, even though I knew that Barry and the medical team at Abu Ghraib would be doing me a huge favor, story or no story. Still, I wanted a professional reason to make the trip out.

I met up with Barry at Camp Victory for the convoy ride to Abu Ghraib. I thought of the risk I was taking, riding out along the dangerous stretch of roadway to Fallujah just to see a doctor, for the fourth time. I could barely get in and out of the Humvee and had a painful, bone-jarring ride to Abu Ghraib, with the heavy flak jacket banging against my ribs. Barry took me right away to the medical facility once I arrived, and I finally got an X-ray, a full checkup, and a diagnosis other than the flu. My ribs were not broken, but when I fell, I had burst some blood vessels behind my ribs, causing a pool of blood to form. The doctors told me there was really nothing I could do except wait for the blood to disappear into my body and for the antibiotics to take care of the resulting infection. I was relieved and grateful. That night, Barry took me to the prison dining facility, and I gorged on iceberg lettuce. "What I won't do to get some lettuce, right?" We laughed, and for the first time since that morning I fainted, I felt like I was going to be okay.

Back in Baghdad, I turned my attention to getting ready for the national election, a historical moment for Iraq and a crucial political step toward true self-governance. Iraqis would go to the polls to elect local leaders and a 275-member national assembly charged with writing a new constitution. More than 14 million Iraqis, including those overseas, were eligible to vote, but insurgents were threatening widespread violence on Election Day, prompting the government to issue a three-day curfew leading up to it. The Iraqi government and its independent election commission planned to issue special badges for journalists so that we could get around the curfew. Initially, the Iraqi Interior Minister required that our vehicles carry a special sticker and that our drivers and translators provide their home addresses on applications for the badges. We refused and, along with a small group of other Western news organizations, signed a letter of protest. By giving up the home addresses of our Iraqi staff, we were allowing the ministry to create a database of Iraqis who worked for foreign companies. In the wrong hands, the outcome could be deadly. We knew the Iraqi government was corrupt because we had been forced to bribe it: for weapons cards, passports, residency permits. Low-level government employees routinely shook us down. Twice I went to the ministry's representative set up in the Green Zone's Convention Center to plead with them to give us credentials without turning over the home addresses. I explained how dangerous it was. No one would budge. Fine, I told Omar, back in the office. I showed him how we could scan their passports and national identification cards into the computer, and then using a simple photo software program, adjust the numbers and names of the street addresses, to create doctored copies. I wasn't proud of this. I didn't want to have to do this, but the corrupt government was inviting disaster, and there was no way we were going to put our staff's lives at risk. Fortunately, the revolt among the Western press worked, and the ministry retracted this part of its requirement. We no longer had to register our drivers and vehicles. But the translators, if they were to go to the polls with us, would still have to turn over their information to the independent election body. We had no reason to believe this body was corrupted although the translators still worried about how thoroughly their workers had been vetted and who would have access to the database. Ultimately, the translators decided to fill out the applications rather than miss covering the elections. We then had to turn to the issue of the curfew. It would be too dangerous for the translators or any of our staff to travel to and from their homes during the elections, so we booked hotel rooms near the bureau for them.

Karl, back from his vacation in Egypt, decided to dispatch me to the Kurdish north of Iraq to cover the election from there. This was the biggest story since the U.S. invasion: the political future of Iraq was going to be determined. No one knew how many Iraqis would turn out to vote or just how violent the day would be. For once, we had a full bureau to cover the story. Cameron Barr, in from Washington, would embed in the Green Zone, where the election results were going to be announced. Anthony and Karl planned to anchor our coverage in Baghdad. Steve Fainaru was already embedded with the U.S. military in Mosul in northern Iraq. And Douglas Struck, the *Post* correspondent based in Canada, was heading to Najaf in southern Iraq. I had willingly pushed back my return to the United States once again so I could help cover the elections, which felt like the epilogue to the U.S. invasion even though the "story of Iraq" would continue *ad infinitum.* No one expected that the election would end the violence or put a halt to the insurgency. Nor would it be the final step in the political journey. The newly elected government would be in place for only a year. If the process worked as planned, Iraqis would go to the polls again in a year after adopting a new constitution and framework for a more permanent government. The first election would only offer uncertain closure, but it was closure nonetheless. Or so it felt to me at the time.

I needed closure for Luma, too. And it came, eight days before the election. The U.S. Army announced that it had charged two soldiers with killing her. Their court-martial was scheduled for January 22. We knew no other details, just that these two soldiers had been implicated. The press release that the Army sent out did not name Luma. I knew other media outlets would receive the release without knowing that our Luma was the Army "interpreter" for whose death the soldiers were allegedly responsible. I sent out the word to as many of the other reporters as I could, hoping to get as much coverage as possible at the court-martial. I excused myself from covering it because I was too close to Luma and her family, and Doug Struck agreed to cover it instead. Still, I wanted to go to the court-martial and asked Omar if he did, too. It seemed important to have a member of our Iraqi staff at the proceeding, which was held at Camp Liberty, an Army outpost near the Baghdad airport. Luma's brother told me that he would not be there. He thought it was too dangerous to bring the family to an Army base. I promised to tell him what happened, every detail.

On a rainy morning, just after the curfew lifted at 6 A.M., Doug, Omar, and I set off for Camp Liberty to find out, finally, the circumstances of Luma's death. *The New York Times* and Knight Ridder both sent reporters. There was no other media attention. A dead Iraqi translator who worked for the Army was not big news in the grand scheme of what was happening in Iraq. I had made this very kind of calculation many times, weighing the risk of traveling this airport road for whatever story waited at the other end. But this was not any story. This was Luma's story. And it had come to an end.

As the court-martial proceeded, we learned the details of that final chapter. On the morning of November 23, Luma was in a break room at the Army base in Baghdad where she worked as a translator in a detention facility for suspected Iraqi insurgents. Luma's job was to help Army interrogators interview the prisoners. Her supervisors were impressed with her skills. She translated exactly what the prisoners told her, word for word— a good reporter. Only two other people were in the break room with her that morning, Spec. Charley L. Hooser and Spec. Rami M. Dajani. By Hooser's account, they were "joking and horseplaying." Dajani handed him a gun that was in a filing cabinet. Hooser put it to Luma's head and pulled the trigger. They were horrified when the gun went off. Dajani said he assumed the gun was not loaded when he handed it to Hooser, and Hooser said he assumed the same. They were all friends.

He did not mean to kill Luma. Because they were scared about their careers, their families, and their future, the soldiers said they initially lied to Army investigators, claiming that Luma shot herself.

Hooser, the triggerman, pleaded guilty to involuntary manslaughter and filing a false report. Dajani pleaded guilty to being an accessory after the fact and filing a false report. The men cried in court as they recounted what had happened. They cried in asking the court to be easy on them. They cried for their families, for their futures, now certainly broken. In a plea deal with Army prosecutors, Hooser was sentenced to three years in prison. Dajani received eighteen months. Both men were ordered demoted to the rank of private and dishonorably discharged from the military.

As we left the courtroom, I turned to Omar. "At least she got justice. I can't bring her back. But at least we got her justice."

"Justice?" he asked. "They were her friends. Luma would have hated this."

I knew he was right. Even though she lost her life, Luma would have been crushed that her friends had been punished for it. I only hoped that if the soldiers had been telling the truth—if they had all been horsing around and joking in the moment before she was killed—Luma had died laughing.

Three days later I left for the Kurdish north with answers to Luma's death but no peace. Luma's daughter Sarah disappeared after the court-martial, and despite our efforts to find what became of her and her family, we never heard from them again. My promise to Luma that I would look after her daughter haunted me as I headed north. The highway to the Kurdish territory passed through the eastern edge of the restive Sunni Triangle, around Baqubah, where soldiers had set up the checkpoint to catch bombers. The road went on to Kirkuk, an oil-rich city deep in ethnic tensions that had only deepened leading up to the elections. Ethnic Kurds, Arabs, and Turkmens all claim a right to govern Kirkuk. Many Arabs and Turkmens were fearful that if the Kurds prevailed in the election the city would be subsumed in the Kurdish region of northern Iraq, which has been outside control of the Iraqi central government since 1991.

With the approach of the elections, tens of thousands of Kurds who were driven out of Kirkuk when Saddam held power were returning to vote. Under the Arabization campaign, which the Iraqi Baath Party initiated in 1963 and Saddam pursued with vigor after seizing power, Kurds in Kirkuk and surrounding villages and towns were replaced with Arab settlers. The return of the Kurds to vote angered the Arabs, who believed that the ballot was being stacked against them. The tension between the factions had erupted into violence in advance of the election—Kurdish political party offices had been attacked, polling stations were bombed, and government officials feared assassination. I had no interest in driving through the middle of all of that or in putting one of our drivers—most of them Arabs—in danger.

Instead, we decided to send Omar 2, the driver, alone in an armored car. He would be fine without an American at his side. I would fly, hopping on a nongovernment organizational flight used by the U.S. Agency for International Development. I had never been to the Kurdish-controlled north just beyond Kirkuk. The Kurds had a decade of semi-self-rule to practice democracy, and the area was considered one of the safest and most peaceful in Iraq. That had not always been the case. While in power, Saddam exercised brutal authority over the Kurds, razing their villages and, during the 1988 Anfar campaign, attacking them with chemical weapons. Human Rights Watch/Middle East estimate that more than 100,000 Kurds lost their lives under the Saddam regime.

When I showed up at the Baghdad airport for my flight to Irbil, the capital city of the Kurdish region, an immigration officer demanded to see my visa. "A visa? I don't need a visa to go to another city in the same country!" I told him, but the man insisted. I called Abu Saif back in the office and asked him for help. Perhaps he had a connection at the airport that I might be able to use. I wondered if the immigration officer was just trying to shake me down for some cash. We had run low on money in the bureau, and I only had a small amount to spend in Kurdistan. I had to borrow $1,000 from Bassam just to cover my expenses. I quickly did the math in my head. I could afford to pay the officer about $20, on the small side for a bribe, but that was it. I tucked the bill in my passport and showed him again where I had a visa to enter Iraq. He pushed my hand away and started speaking in Arabic on his two-way radio. I didn't know if he was calling the police, so I picked up my bag and fled outside to the curb. I called our drivers and asked them to turn around and pick me up at the airport checkpoint. In the meantime, Abu Saif had contacted a director of Iraqi Airways, which was starting flights later in the month between Baghdad and Irbil. The plane was making a test run later that day. Iraqi Airways would hold the plane for me for a few hours if I could get my papers straightened out. In fact, I could not. I needed a residency permit to leave Iraq. Even though I was not leaving Iraq, I had exceeded my six-week temporary visa the Iraqi government issued had allowed. Most journalists lived in Iraq on these expired visas until it was time to leave and then got the proper residency permit required for a longer stay. The immigration officers at the airport only cared if we had the residency permit stamped in passports, not whether we had violated our visas while in the country. It was a hassle to get the residency permit. We had to turn over our passports and then come pick them up a few days later. It was an uneasy feeling, knowing that the Iraqi government could hold our passports hostage until we paid whatever fee the low-level employee working the counter wanted to charge to give it back. I didn't have time to play the game. I only had a few days left before the election and needed to get to Kurdistan to cover it. So we bribed another ministry $100 to get the proper stamp that should not have cost me anything. With the stamp, I was finally off to the Irbil the next afternoon on a chartered flight.

I hired two translators while I was in Kurdistan. One, Shereen, was a former Iraqi Airways flight attendant who had worked in our Baghdad bureau until she was threatened by Saddam loyalists for working with Americans, forcing her to relocate to Irbil, her hometown. Kurdistan is controlled by two rival political parties, the Kurdistant Democratic Party (KDP) and the Patriotic Union of Kurdistan (PUK). Irbil is in KDP territory in the northern half. That made Shereen KDP. I needed a PUK translator, too—someone who lived in PUK territory. Karl had used a translator from Sulamaniyah in the southern part of the Kurdish territory during the U.S. invasion. So I hired Sarok, too, and paid him to meet me in Irbil. I paid both Sarok and Shereen the going rate of about $50 a day, which, along with our hotel bills, ate up most of my cash. I had to skip dinner most nights because I could not afford to eat. Iraq was a cash-only business, though I was able to pay Sarok part of his fee by having Karl transfer money from his bank in Turkey to a money shop in Sulamaniyah.

In Kurdistan, I was broke but free—free to walk the streets without worrying about getting kidnapped. I threw my scarf in the bottom of my bag and left it there. During the entire nine months I had been in Iraq, I had never gone out to eat in a restaurant, a reckless and risky venture almost two years after the U.S. invasion. The first time Sarok invited Omar 2 and me to eat at a small diner in Irbil, I balked. "Are you sure? Is it safe?"

"Of course," Sarok said, laughing. "You are in Kurdistan now. You are free."

The election credentials I had from the Iraqi Interior Ministry and the Independent Election Commission of Iraq did not work in this part of Iraq, a sign of just how autonomous the region was from the central government in Iraq. The Kurdish regional government issued me a whole new set of credentials. I also had to get a special credential from the KDP. Of course, this credential would not work when I went into PUK territory, so I had to get a separate permission letter from its party press office when Sarok, Omar, and I traveled to Sulamaniyah after the election.

Even though I had flown to Kurdistan to bypass Kirkuk, Karl and Anthony wanted me to get into the city before the election to test its mood. The *Post* had not had any reporters in the city for months, and our reports of the escalating ethnic clashes and insurgent violence were mostly coming from our stringer there. For the trip, I donned my most conservative *abaya* and scarf. Omar 2 and Sarok were scared of being caught with an American, which could get them killed on the spot. Although Omar 2 was Arab and Sarok was an ethnic Kurd, they immediately struck up a friendship. Both had sons named Mustafah and both had been in the Iraqi air force. Sarok was a conservative Muslim but he was open to showing me the mosque in his hometown. He was an ideas man, constantly scribbling in his notebook questions and thoughts to recall later. Sarok believed in the future, believed in the possibility of it. "Try to be like me, the optimistic guy who never loses his faith and trust in God for a better future and a safe shore," Sarok advised Omar and me. "We live in bad times but believe me when I say after rain comes sunshine, after night comes daylight, after war comes peace, and after darkness comes light."

Shereen was working full-time for a development company in Irbil and could not be with us all of the time. So we left her behind on the trip to Kirkuk. On the hour-drive to the city, I stuffed all of our identification into my bra. "Anything with English on it, hand it over," I told the guys. Into the backseat came Sarok's reporters' notebooks and a letter introducing him as a *Post* translator. Omar handed me his *Post* driver's identification. "Geez, guys, I warned you not to bring any of this stuff!" I admonished, though managing to stuff every bit of it under my bra until the straps, straining from more weight than they had ever held, burned into my skin. Even if the car or the guys got searched, no one would dare touch my chest.

On the outskirts of Kirkuk, we saw a large line of men selling black-market fuel. I could not resist the irony of a fuel shortage in one of the richest oil fields in Iraq, so I instructed Omar 2 to pull over so I could interview one of the entrepreneurs. Sarok leaned between the front seats.

"Not here, Jackie. This is not a good spot. I will bring him to you."

Sarok jumped out of the car and, through the window, I saw him talking to one of the men selling gas from a plastic jug.

They walked back to the car together. Sarok opened the back-seat door and the man slid in next to me. Through the tinted windows, no one would be able to see that an American was interviewing him through her Kurdish translator.

Zaka Omar was fifty-one, a thin man whose clothes smelled of gasoline. He had dark, sad eyes with dark circles underneath them. Zaka Omar sold gasoline on the black market. Four years ago Saddam's government gave Omar, an ethnic Kurd, a choice: change his legal ethnic status to Arab or leave Kirkuk and his family home behind. "I had no money," he told me. "I didn't want to leave, so I changed to Arab."

I asked Omar how he felt about the election. He smiled and dropped his face. "I will participate in the election honorably and with . . . a Kurdish spirit. We are very thirsty for these elections, just like someone is thirsty for water."

His response was typical of the Kurds I met and interviewed before the election. They were elated at getting a chance to vote and being able to send their representatives to the central government in Baghdad.

We arrived safely back in Irbil, where Sarok and I found a small group of men campaigning for the KDP along a busy street in the city's Tajil district. The party bosses invited us to join them the day before the election on a campaign romp through the city. We hopped on and took our seats, unsure of our destination. Shortly afterward, cars surrounded our bus and people waved the yellow and red flags of the KDP. Adnan Ismael, the party boss who had invited us along for the ride, raced to the back of the campaign bus and frantically pulled aside a dark blue curtain so he could see out. Hundreds of honking cars were following behind in an impromptu rolling celebration through the ancient city. Passengers hung out of vehicles, shouting and waving the yellow flag of the KDP and the red, white, and green flag of the Kurdish region.

Ismael turned from the window, a stunned look on his face. Inside the bus, a group of aging, bewhiskered former guerrilla fighters struck up an old revolutionary song. Their eyes brimmed with tears as they sang in husky voices: "Our flag is waving high in the sky. We are still alive. The Kurds are alive. There is no cannon that will break our will."

"We were dreaming for this day to come," said Ismael, the KDP leader for Irbil's Tajil district, who darted back and forth to get a look at the scene unfolding on every side of the bus. "Now we will all choose our representatives for the future. Every Kurd wishes to see this day."

I looked over at Sarok. He had grabbed the KDP flag and was waving it out the window, tears in his eyes. "I will never forget this moment," he told me.

Outside the window, a car pulled up with a young man inside. "American? You American?" He screamed the question. I panicked. I should have worn the scarf. I was in trouble. But the man only smiled back. I had been leaning out the window taking pictures while Sarok hung on to my legs. He had merely assumed, correctly, that I was from America. "Welcome, American! Welcome to Kurdistan. We love you."

I turned away from the window to keep my composure. It was the first time since I had come to Iraq that I felt welcomed, that I felt the happiness of the people for the American presence in Iraq, for the presence of a journalist documenting Iraq's history.

The entire city felt alive with anticipation as candidates and their supporters blasted old Kurdish songs from loudspeakers at party headquarters, waved to passing cars from plastic chairs lined up on sidewalks, and raced through the streets in caravans with flying banners. "Someday," Sarok told me, "everyone in Iraq will have this."

In many other parts of Iraq, voters were anxious for the election, fearful of insurgent violence and doubtful about the political process. But not in Irbil, where there was a sense that something big was about to happen. It was as if the whole city had turned out for a wedding party.

On the bus with us, Raqeeb Shekhan, a retired *peshmerga* of the Kurdish militant force, did not try to conceal his pride. He sang along with the revolutionary songs, and he waved his Kurdish flag out the window His sun-wrinkled face beamed.

"We waited for this a long time. We've ached for this freedom. We want to be like the rest of the world."

For the election, Kurdistan had the same restrictions in place as the rest of Iraq. Polling centers were heavily guarded, and we could not travel between provinces without a placard on our car that identified us as journalists. Omar 2, used to the violence in Baghdad, did not want us to be caught off guard by a false sense of security. On January 31, 2004, two suicide bombers detonated themselves in both the KDP and PUK party headquarters in Irbil, killing sixty-seven people, according to news reports at the time. Unsure of what might happen on Election Day and fearful of being out in our vehicle on desolate streets, we left the car behind and walked the streets of Irbil just after dawn.

The day before, I sent Shereen out to look for a donkey cart that we could hire to get around. Team Kurdistan, which is how we had begun referring to ourselves, did not initially believe that I was serious. "Look," I told them. "*The Washington Post* has sent me to cover the elections, and I intend to cover the elections. If we have to do it by donkey, we will do it by donkey." Shereen could not find a donkey cart in the city, so she drove a short way from Irbil to find a farmer. She spotted a small boy of perhaps nine or ten leading a donkey down a narrow dirt road. Shereen sped up alongside him. The boy frightened at the sight of Shereen, who was a strikingly beautiful and modern woman with bright pink lipstick and long curly eyelashes shaded behind dark Jackie O sunglasses. "Wait, I want your donkey!" Shereen screamed, as the boy hurried the donkey into a narrow alley where Shereen could not follow. Still, she had a sighting. Shereen knew where we could go on Election Day if we had to.

People lined up at the polling centers early to vote. Once they voted, they dipped their finger in purple ink, a voter fraud measure that would become the most powerful image of the election. In symbols of hope, Iraqis who voted proudly displayed their purple index finger. In Baghdad, Omar had dispatched Falah to the polling center near his house. He had elected to stay home during the election for fear of raising suspicions from his neighbors about where he was during the three-day curfew. Falah told his neighbors that he quit his job working for the *Post*. Instead, to explain where he went every day, Falah claimed he was going to the auto shop he owned in Baghdad. He tried to show up once in a while so that if the insurgents checked up on him, his alibi would hold. Falah had no intention of voting. The insurgents in his neighborhood had threatened to attack the polling center and retaliate against anyone who did vote. He dreaded leaving his house, but Omar had told him to cover the polling center, so he went. The only people there when he arrived were foreign journalists, including a TV crew that thrust its camera on Falah. Not wanting to divulge the real reason he had come to the election center, Falah told the TV crew that he wanted to be the first in line to vote, that he believed in the new Iraq. Then Falah walked into the polling center and reluctantly cast his vote. Afterward, he went home and cut at the ink with a razor blade until his finger was raw and bleeding. Throughout the day, CNN ran the interview of Falah declaring that he wanted to be the first in Iraq to vote. Any insurgent who might have missed him on CNN got a chance to see Falah on an election spot that Iraqi TV ran for days after the election. "I'm a dead man," Falah told me, recounting the story.

"Well, you already knew that," I replied, reaching to pat his hand.

No one expressed such fears of reprisal to me in Kurdistan. Voter turnout was one of the highest in all parts of Iraq. When the votes were tallied days later, turnout in Kurdistan ranged from 82 to 92 percent. The overall turnout in Iraq was 58 percent, or 8.55 million of the 14.66 million registered voters. In some parts of Iraq, including the western Anbar province that included Fallujah, only 2 percent of people went to vote. As a result of the high turnout in Kurdistan, Kurds were able to win 25 percent of the seats on the national parliament, ensuring their voice in establishing the future of Iraq.

We had no numbers on Election Day, but it was clear that the Kurds had come out in force. People waited in line for two hours to cast their ballots. After monitoring the polls in Irbil,

Team Kurdistan set out by car to find the donkey that Shereen had spotted the day before. We found the boy and his donkey in a dirty, unpaved village just outside of Irbil. We asked the boy's mother if we could rent the donkey to go to the polling center in a nearby village. "Just take it," the woman said, smiling. "But you won't need it. Everyone is driving."

We had come this far—at least we could get a picture. Omar 2 held the donkey as I climbed on. Shereen and Sarok clamored to get into the picture. *Snap.* We had our souvenir from Election Day. The woman asked if we would take a picture of her with her brood, some twenty children—relatives and neighbors—who gathered around her. Though she did not ask for a copy of the picture we printed one for her the next day, and after I left Irbil Shereen took it to her.

We had been to nearly a dozen polling centers that day, but we decided to hit one more. We ended up in a small farming village a few miles away. In the pursuit of a story, reporters look for leads—that one moment or scene that will capture the essence of the moment and draw the reader into the story. I found mine in the back of a white pickup truck where Adhima Mustafa and five female relatives were huddled together. Mustafa wore a green velvet dress and her head was wrapped in a dark scarf more common in the villages. The women had set out at dawn to cast votes near their home, but the ballot boxes were already full. The women finally ended up in this small farming village, nine hours after they set out. That was how badly they wanted to vote. I thought of voter turnout in the United States—how few people go to the polls even though they are free to do so. I thought of all the things Americans take for granted, that I had taken for granted. No matter what else I covered in Iraq, I knew no story would ever touch me the way this one had. I only wished Luma had been alive to share it.

I returned to Baghdad by car. I just wanted to get back and did not want to wait to find a flight, so Omar 2 and I decided to risk it. We hatched our return plan. Falah's wife was from Kirkuk and had not seen her mother in more than a year. So Falah drove his wife and one of his daughters to Kirkuk from

Baghdad to visit for a day. Muhanned, the security chief, went with them. Omar 2 and I met them in Kirkuk, a short drive from Sulamaniyah. We had gone there from Irbil to take Sarok home and to visit his family. I rode back to Baghdad with Falah and his family. Omar 2 and Muhanned followed us in the armored car. Whenever we got to a checkpoint, Falah shouted, "Sleep!" We would then pretend to be dozing, figuring the police would not bother sleeping womenfolk. We repeated this routine on the four-hour return trip to Baghdad, where we arrived safely. Falah seemed to have found his steady hand again, now that he was completely resigned to his fate.

All of our staff in Baghdad had made it through the election, even though Bassam and Omar had prepared for the worst. The night before the election, they shared a bottle of wine in their hotel room near the bureau and said good-bye to each other. In fact, the violence throughout Iraq had been less than anticipated. Although insurgents launched 260 attacks against targets of all kinds in Iraq—including 109 polling places—the casualty count was relatively low in comparison: 45 dead and 100 wounded. It had not been the deadliest day in Iraq. Perhaps Sarok was right about the future of Iraq, the possibility that peace would come. I had a touching email waiting from him when I got back to the bureau.

Hi, my good friend, how are you? I pray for your health and safety. I miss you so so much. In the midst of the sound of explosions, blood, screams, mistrust and betrayal that is all happening in this country, your bravery and sweet presence to shed a light on truth was really surreal. And guess what? You were the LIGHT! And believe me when I tell you that this light strengthened my optimism even more . . .

In fact, Sarok had strengthened me. His unwavering optimism, his unwavering belief in the future, his dedication to his country in the face of violence deepened my commitment to the Iraq story. I had promised my family that I would return to the States after the election. But how could I leave now? I had to stay, to touch this cloud of hope hovering over Iraq, over me.

✦ ✦ ✦

When Jackie and I were young, we often spent nights at our paternal grandmother's house, especially after her husband died and she needed the company. Before she turned in, she would pad into our room and tuck the covers close to our chins. "Be careful," she insisted. "You be careful, too, Grandma," we echoed back. "All right, then," she nodded, "but you be careful." My sister and I lay in the dark pondering our grandmother's words. Be careful of what? We hadn't even known to be afraid and now, unsure what dangers prompted our grandmother's warning, we became afraid of everything: suffocating in our sleep, burglars lurking outside the window, the ghostly creaks of the floorboards. Sometimes it took hours to relinquish our vulnerable bodies to sleep.

When Jackie left for Iraq, my childhood terror came creeping back. I recognized it at once: a fear so large it could not hold its own shape and swallowed everything. Because I was trying to be strong for Jackie, to hide from her my own nightmares, I never told her. But she knew. "Listen," she told me one day, "I promise I'll be careful."

And she was—until the fish began dying and she got sick. One afternoon while I was at the park with Aidan, she called. "Put Aidan on the phone," she choked, struggling to breathe. I couldn't get a good signal, so Aidan and I climbed to the top of the jungle gym. "Bye, Aunt Jackie," he said solemnly before the phone cut out. I grabbed Aidan's hand and ran home. But there wasn't anything I could do when I got there except wait for the phone to ring again. It did—two days later. She sounded worse than ever, breathless and delirious. I knew something was terribly wrong, and I urged her to go to a military doctor. "You can't go on like this," I pleaded. Her voice suddenly sharpened. "I'm not going home."

I didn't want her to come home. I just didn't want her to die in Iraq. I hung up the phone and sat at my husband's desk, trying to figure out what to do. His computer was in front of me, and I logged on to my email account. My fingers hovered above the keys, arched over the significance of what I was about to do. I remembered how angry and mortified Jackie had been when our panicked mother had called the Foreign Desk earlier in the year, and I had commiserated. "Oh, how could she have done that?"

"Dear Emily," I typed, addressing the assistant on the Post's *Foreign Desk. "Jackie is very ill. She will never leave Iraq until she is told to leave. Do what you want with this information. But please don't tell Jackie."*

I turned off the computer and headed over to Jackie's apartment to water her plants, unable to shake my guilt. Not only didn't I trust her anymore, I didn't trust myself. Was I just being paranoid?

It made me feel better to be in my sister's apartment, but I moved around like a ghost. I sat on her couch and stared at the blank TV screen. I opened and closed the refrigerator. I lay in her body's curve on the bed, watching the blades of the ceiling fan twirl in lopsided strokes. In her closet I fingered her shirts, her shoes, leaning in for long, deep breaths of her familiar scent.

The night my father died, my grandmother came to say good-bye to the last of her three sons. She left her walker at his bedroom door and stood beside him. "I love you, son," she told him. "Be careful." He promised he would. Hours later, he was dead.

CHAPTER 12

"Bassam," I called out one cold morning in February. "Let's go swing."

Back from Kurdistan for only a week, I was already feeling cooped up again. It was depressing not to be able to walk down the street to talk to people in the open or even to buy my own groceries; yet I felt selfish complaining about losing control over what I ate when people were getting blown up and dying, when our staff feared for their lives every time they came to work, when U.S. soldiers and Iraqi police did not have a choice between staying inside or getting out to face the danger. My job was not nearly as difficult or dangerous as theirs. I ran from the insurgents that they chased down. Reminding myself of this kept me from dwelling on my loss of such luxury items as fresh air. Still, this was the hardest part about being in Iraq. I managed better than most, in large part because of my relationship with the staff. When the power went out and we were shut off from the rest of the world, unable to do anything but wait for it to come back on, I got out the Monopoly board. Or grabbed the soccer ball. Or pulled one of the translators away from the laptop and went to the swing in the backyard, where, pumping our legs like children to see who could go the highest, we forgot for a moment where we were. The sky was blue, the air crisp. I took a deep breath and closed my eyes, until a helicopter roared by, rattling the windows and reminding me where we were. We never stayed outside long. I felt vulnerable in the open air, where any sniper could take a shot at us over the garden wall, but for a moment or two, I simply breathed.

Bassam and Omar were coming into their own as journalists by that February. They were no longer simply translators, and they knew it. They began resisting the very title of translator, finding it degrading to be introduced as such. For them it implied they were merely drones, exchanging one set of words for another. Omar dreamed of being a journalist. "What I care about is my steps to being a journalist, and this is the only thing," he once told me. "This is the red line in my life, and I will defend it by any means." Omar was always the first one in the office. He never asked for a raise. I imagined him on the sinking *Titanic*, a musician playing as the ship slipped into the frigid waters, staying behind as the others scrambled off the ship to safety.

Bassam was not as sure about what he wanted to do. He did not have journalism in his blood the way Omar did. In the fatigue following the election, Bassam decided to leave the *Post* for a job with more predictable hours at a government ministry. We talked about his decision on the swing and then later back in the bureau. I knew he was mostly feeling unappreciated. It was hard for the guys. They had lost all of their friends. They worked twelve hours a day, and when they went home, they were too tired to socialize. Not that it would have been safe for them to travel the streets after dark to see their peers anyway. Before the U.S. invasion, young Iraqis met in cafés, parks, and clubs. These places were either closed now or emptied out after the sky drew its shades. Bassam and Omar also got ordered around a lot, often bearing the brunt of the stresses that the American reporters were feeling being far from home. They hated being talked down to, not trusted, their opinions discounted. Not all of the *Post* correspondents who passed through the bureau were sensitive to this. Abu Saif felt the most beaten down, now running around to get quotes after once flying planes all over the world. He embraced his new career when he felt appreciated. But if he sat at his desk day after day while the other guys were sent out to cover the news, he talked of quitting, of going back to the air. As soon as one of his stories hit the front page, he would come back to us emotionally because he felt important again, useful. Bassam was a tougher case than Abu Saif because he was just starting his career. He fell into journalism, and with pressure from his family to quit, no wife or children to support, it made it easier for him to dream of a different life, of starting out somewhere easier, safer.

"I know it's tough, Bassam, but you are a good reporter," I told him one particularly tough day. "What can I do to convince you to stay? There would be no *Washington Post* Baghdad bureau without you and Omar and Abu Saif. We could not do our jobs. It's your life. You have to decide what you want. But do not leave because you feel like you're not making a difference. You are."

Nobody from Washington called to tell me that I was in charge in February when Karl left to return to Turkey. The role of interim bureau chief was handed to me without official word from Washington. That meant extending my stay once again, to the frustration of friends and family back home. As bad as it was in Iraq, I had to be crazy for not wanting to leave, they surmised. Only my sister seemed to understand, or at least she sounded convincing when she told me she supported my decision to remain. Although I had decided not to apply for the bureau chief job, I wanted to make sure that the bureau was intact for the next chief. It was looking more likely that the *Post* would have to hire an outside candidate for the job. I had fallen in love with these Iraqis—their commitment to the *Post*, to journalism, to recording their country's history. I wanted to make the transition as smooth as possible for them.

I was also eager for the chance to lead the bureau, to show that I could do it. I had not had a chance to manage a staff since my days as the editor of my student newspaper, the *Daily Egyptian* at Southern Illinois University. I loved being the editor, not the power that came with it but the responsibility. I remember when the *Daily Egyptian* was selected as the top college newspaper in the state, beating out our rival, the *Daily Illini* at the University of Illinois. I climbed on top of my editor's desk and gathered the staff around me, more than fifty student journalists of all levels of talent and commitment.

"I want you to scream at the top of your lungs for one minute," I instructed. "Scream for all of those people who never believed that you could get here. Scream so that they can hear you wherever they are." For one minute, the newsroom was filled with the roar of those screams. I heard the voices of people who would spend the rest of their lives searching for a moment like this again. I heard the voices of people who would never get there. But for one minute in their lives, they had it, this knowledge that they had been on the top.

The morning Karl left and handed me the sword—a real sword that the bureau chiefs passed to each other ceremoniously—I asked the staff to gather in the backyard. They had been waiting for this day, begging me to apply to be Karl's permanent replacement. I was a kind, comforting presence for them. But I could not give them my permanence. I had to get home eventually, and I was burned out from working seven days a week, from getting only a few hours of sleep at night, from worrying about getting nabbed and beheaded. I could give them a few weeks, carrying the bureau on my shoulders until the end of the month.

They assembled in the backyard together, drivers, guards, the Ums, and translators.

"Hold hands," I instructed. "Come on, everybody. Grab the hand of the person next to you."

I waited until they linked together.

"We are now in a circle, united. We are not united for me. We are not united for you. We are united for *The Washington Post. The Washington Post* is counting on each one of you. I will only succeed because of you." Everyone looked back solemnly. I heard a few murmurs of "We're behind you boss," and "Go, chief." It was as if I were a preacher and these were my faithful congregants.

"Now we are going to shout '*Washington Post!*' Shout it loud. '*Washington Post!*'"

Washington Post! Washington Post!

That was enough. No need to attract the attention of the insurgents.

"Now, I have an order, my first order as bureau chief. Every day, every single day for five minutes a day, you will come out here and swing. Ums, put down your spoons and come swing. Drivers, take a swing on the way in or out. Everybody is going to swing and forget where they are and look up at the sky and remind ourselves that we are alive even in the midst of this chaos. We are alive."

They stared back at me.

"Come on guys, it was an order. Um Mohammed and Wijdan, you go first," I told our lunch cooks. "I'll take my swing-of-the-day with you." The ladies hopped on and we pumped our legs together. After everyone had a swing, we traipsed back inside to work. Bassam and I needed to track down politicians who could give us a sense of who the new national leaders would be. This was the big story following the election, the political jockeying for the top seats in the new government.

We headed out to try to find someone to interview at the Kurdish Democratic Party headquarters in Baghdad. A man answered at the gate but told us that we would have to come back in a few days because the party leaders were meeting in Kurdistan. Shut down, Falah turned the car around and headed back to the bureau. We passed a large parking lot where Falah told me that men brought their mistresses to teach them to drive. Although it was a public lot, opportunists had set up a gated fence and charged people the equivalent of $1 or so to get in.

"Falah, can we swing in?"

Bassam looked back over the seat.

"Are you serious?"

"Totally, if it's safe. I want to drive. Do you know how long it has been since I've driven a car?"

"Sure thing, chief," Falah said, turning the car into the lot. He paid the man a few bucks and drove to the center of the lot. I was in my Iraqi disguise, so no one would have noticed from the street that I was an American. Falah hopped out, and I climbed into the driver's seat. We spun around and around while I relished my new freedom. I was bureau chief. I couldn't believe it. I was in charge of this operation. I was overjoyed, until it hit me: I also was now responsible for keeping everyone alive, for keeping us on top of the biggest news story in the world. I pulled the car over and handed the keys back to Falah. We had work to do.

Before Karl left, I had made one trip back to Fallujah to see the city now that the Marines were back in. I knew it would be my last trip out of Baghdad before I left for good in March. Once Karl left, I would have to turn my attention to the political jockeying for leadership positions in the newly elected government.

Fallujah was calm, but the Marines were still battling pockets of resistance in the city. Although "officially" the fighting had ended the second week in November, Marines continued to take small-arms fire and dodge roadside bombs. I decided to go on a foot patrol, to get a ground view of the destruction and of the piecing together. When we hit the center of the city, the Marines jumped out of their armored vehicles on a quiet dirt road with mounds of crumbled bricks, twisted metal, and debris on both sides. Within minutes, the patrol from the 3rd Battalion, 5th Regiment, Weapons Company was surrounded by dozens of hands pulling at their arms and reaching for their pockets.

"Mister, mister," little voices chirped, as a swelling group of twenty children pushed one another out of the way and called for pieces of chocolate. The older, savvier ones would grab a baby, borrowing one from a stranger if they had to, hold it up, and say, "Baby, baby," in English, an effort to get more candy from the Combined Anti-Armored Team.

Lance Cpl. Richard Setterstrom, who still had a piece of shrapnel in his leg from a December 12 battle with insurgents, moved beyond the children and past badly damaged houses, each one marked with a red X to indicate that it had been cleared of weapons. "It's weird walking by a house that we burned and seeing a family in it now," he said.

"See that house?" said Lance Cpl. Michael Catalano, pointing across a large puddle of rainwater and sewage to a brown, two-story structure, its sides blackened from smoke. "A Marine died there."

The relative ease with which we walked through Fallujah was nearly as jarring as the sudden blasts of gunfire during the battle. The biggest change for many was the presence of civilians. By the time ground troops roared into the city in November 2004, most of the residents had heeded warnings and fled. Three months later, tens of thousands of people had swarmed back in, but it was not clear how many had stayed. The city was in ruins.

Many of the returning families marked their houses to let security forces know that they were inside. Crude cardboard signs scripted in a borrowed language hung on gates that were broken by advancing troops. "Family in said," one sign read. "Hear family," read another. Many residents also flew white flags fashioned from torn pieces of cloth, soccer jerseys, or kitchen aprons.

When the Marines first started patrolling the streets, residents were standoffish and rarely smiled or waved. Children were the first to approach the Marines, and once they learned that the Marines would give them candy, footballs, and soccer balls, they began swarming the patrols: "Saddam bad, George Bush good," one boy said, repeating a phrase he used to get candy from them. It usually worked.

Another small girl had learned to follow the Marines throughout their hour-long patrol, pausing to shed crocodile tears when she did not get a piece of "chocolata, mister." She tried to pick my pocket. I swatted her hand. "*Haram,*" or sin, I rebuked. She simply smiled and ran to a Marine ahead. "Chocolata, mister?" she asked, peering up at him.

One man, Hatam Jasim Hussein, stopped the Marines while we were on patrol to show them a pile of empty artillery shells in a muddy field littered with trash. He said he was happy the Americans were there. "We're all very happy, everybody," he told us, pulling his leather jacket tighter around his gray *dishdasha*. "We're relaxed. The Americans protect us. We feel safe." But he pleaded for more help rebuilding his house, which had burned during the offensive. "What about fixing the town? We need to fix the city." The Marines acknowledged they had a small window to show the Fallujah residents that help was on the way to rebuild the city, or they would risk losing their already tenuous support.

Karl and Anthony left Iraq a week after I returned from Fallujah. I was alone in the bureau until Caryle Murphy arrived from Washington in mid-February. In May, I had bought a box of Q-tips for my trip, 172-count. One hundred seventy-two. I remembered wondering at the time what 172 days in Iraq would be like. *Good thing, I'll never know,* I thought, sure I would be home long before my box ran out. Each time I agreed to stay for another month and then another, I looked at that box of Q-tips until one day, I finally pulled out the last one. By the time I became bureau chief, the box had been empty for months, and as charged as I was about my new role as interim bureau chief I was starting to run on empty, too. I was overextended, jumpy, and starting to lose it. One night, alone in the bureau after Anthony and Karl left, I was convinced that the insurgents would come get me, and nobody in Washington would find out about it. I tried to sleep, moved to Karl's empty room, then to Anthony's, then back to mine. In my sleep-deprived state, I reasoned that by moving between rooms, I could fool the insurgents.

Rajiv and Karl had been excellent role models. Both had this knack for juggling the journalism and the logistics of the bureau. I hoped I could live up to the standard. It was an incredible amount of work and responsibility. Security was our foremost concern, for the American correspondents and for the staff. Then the story. And somewhere between, the health and welfare of everyone. Um Mohammed wanted us to hire "her boy" as our cleaner. She needed surgery on her hand. She needed a loan to go to Jordan to see her husband, who was in the hospital. Um Hussein wanted a raise. Baldy's father had a rare eye condition, and no doctor in Iraq would operate. Could we get his father in to see the Americans, he implored. Khalid needed a credit card to pay the lawyer in Canada who was helping him emigrate. Ghazwan stopped coming to work for a week after his brother-in-law was kidnapped. He was afraid that the insurgents would come after him, too, and he would lead them to us. The generator kept breaking. Falah got into an argument with one of the Iraqi staff at the *Time* magazine house over who had paid the fuel man for the week. It blew up, and two days after I became bureau chief, I had to lead a delegation of our staff over to *Time* to sort it out. I brought cookies and passed them out. Friends? They shook hands uneasily. Friends. We could not afford to have neighbors who were enemies. In spite of our intense security procedures, the guards kept leaving the kitchen door open, enabling anyone to come in or out. I had Omar put up a sign in English and Arabic. "Anyone who leaves this door open will be fined $5."

I was desperate for Caryle Murphy to arrive, bringing me the necessary cash to meet payroll, pay the diesel man, pay the contractor building the guard shack on the roof, and get back in the black with the man we paid not to kill us. I had borrowed money from Falah just to buy groceries. "Hello!" I emailed my friend Jessica back in Washington. "We're *The Washington Post*!" I could not understand how we were just scraping by. I also had to fire a new female translator we had been trying out for a month or so. Karl and Anthony both advised that she be let go. Neither volunteered to do it. I sat the translator down in my room and explained as nicely as I could that her English was not suitable and her presence in the bureau had become a little disruptive. She had ordered the guards to wash their own dishes at night. It was a nice thought—after all, I had squabbled with my own brother about this over the years—but, I told her, "if they are washing and not guarding, it is a security concern." I offered to pay for her to attend a language-training course in Jordan. "Work on your English, and then come back and see if the next bureau chief will hire you," I told her. I was nice. We hugged. She cried, thanked me, and kissed my cheek. The next day she showed up for work. Her English was so terrible she did not realize I had fired her.

Falah refused to discuss my pending departure. With tears,

he turned to me after I brought it up for a second time. "I don't want to know when you are leaving," he said. "I just want to come in to the office and you are not there."

It was wrenching to think of leaving these people, this place I had grown to love even as I hated the violence that encapsulated it. And yet, I could get out. I could leave. I never forgot that. Even the times when I was terrified and depressed, caged and fighting for air, I knew I was in Iraq by choice.

The last week in Iraq was a blur of farewells and parties, a final Friday-night dinner, with all the staff favorites—macaroni and cheese, mashed potatoes, tacos, hashed browns. Nothing fit together, but those were the dishes the translators had selected, and I was not going to deny them. I had nine suitcases filled with Christmas and farewell presents from the staff; summer, winter, and spring clothes accumulated over nine months; battle gear from Fallujah. We hired a man to drive the luggage to Jordan; it would not have to go with me. March 1, March 1, March 1. I had not been so fixated on a date since I counted down the days to get my learner's permit to drive in high school. I would leave March 1.

I had a difficult time getting interviews with anyone in the Iraqi government for two final stories I wanted to write. I had Omar and Bassam keep calling, pestering, imploring, but we got nowhere. I did not want to spend my last few days stuck in the bureau, but I was stuck, unable to get out and interview anyone. Two months later, when Omar came to the United States, I found out why. As a favor to a State Department employee in the Green Zone, I agreed to give an informal talk to some Iraqi journalists about how *The Washington Post* covers the story of Iraq. It seemed like a nice way to leave Iraq, giving something back to the emerging Iraqi press. Abu Saif and Caryle Murphy came with me to the international press center. We told the journalists that the discussion was off-the-record, meaning it was simply a discussion between colleagues. I talked about the need to be objective, how it would win journalists the trust of both government leaders and their readers.

Unbeknownst to any of us, a journalist for the newspaper

Baghdad Today was sitting in the back of the room, not partici-
pating in the discussion but scribbling some notes. The next day,
I was the lead story in the newspaper. The story itself was not
damaging to the *Post*. It quoted me as saying that the *Post* had
"no friends and no enemies." I had been trying to explain how
important it was not to take sides, with the American military or
with the Iraqi government. The newly freed Iraqi press was still
learning how to separate themselves from their nationalistic
feelings of pride while covering their new government objectively. At the bottom of the story, the reporter wrote that I could
get identification and permission to work in Iraq but Iraqi
journalists could not get the same in America. This was not true,
of course, but the implication was that I could go undercover in
Iraq and work as a spy. "You are dangerously famous," Omar
told me after showing me the story. I was furious at the reporter
for not telling me that she was writing a story, for not checking
the facts of the discussion with me, for not understanding that
off-the-record *meant* off-the-record. I knew it was the mistake
of an untrained journalist, of someone just grappling with what
a free press meant. But it also could get me killed.

The next day our insurgent informant, the guy we paid not
to kill us, asked Omar if that young woman he knew from the
bureau—that would be me—was named Jackie Spinner. The
insurgents were willing to pay someone $5,000 to let them
know where I lived. With that information, they could try to
kidnap me. Omar did not tell me about this at the time because
he and Muhanned, the security chief, knew I was rattled about
having my name in the lead story of a newspaper aligned with
Prime Minister Ayad Allawi. The whole point of my discussion
with the Iraqi journalists was that *Post* reporters did not align
themselves with anyone.

"No, we have no Jackie Spinner here," Omar told the
informant. "That is not her name."

So for my remaining days in Iraq, Omar instructed the
other translators not to follow through with my requests for
interviews outside of the bureau. Instead, they would keep me
inside and hopefully safe.

"You had no right to keep that from me," I told Omar when he eventually confessed why I had not received the interviews I requested.

"We were protecting you."

"Don't ever do that again. I have the right to make my own decisions about safety. And Washington had the right to know there was a price on my head." My words were harsh. I did not want to hurt Omar's feelings, but I was the chief, not the sister or the friend or the wife. I was the bureau chief, and if the staff had been withholding information from me, even out of well-meaning concern, it could compromise our security. What else had they not told me? I stayed in Iraq because I knew the risks. Or so I thought. It was vital to know all of them.

I decided to throw a party for the staff before I left, something to unify them and distract them from the ongoing violence, which had paused around the election and picked up again. Omar 2 hired a popular Iraqi singer. This would be no DJ affair. I wanted the real deal for the staff. The stringers came in from all over Iraq. The singer set up in the living room, pushing aside our sofa and chairs to make room for a dance floor. Abu Haider made traditional Iraqi dishes, *dolma*, rice, and kabob. We sprinkled the dining room table with Tootsie Roll Pops, and the staff sucked on beers and lollipops as the singer crooned in Arabic.

This was my farewell gift to myself as much as it was to the staff. Our Iraqis had rare chances to party since the war. To sing. To dance. To drink bootleg beer. The circle of dancers surrounded our Fallujah stringer, who was in a crouch in the middle, holding the bureau chief's sword as he kicked his feet in an Iraqi jig. The drivers gyrated up to the singer, throwing dollar bills at him. Several times, I nervously ran outside to see if anyone could hear the music. It was so loud inside the bureau that no one could talk. I just knew we were sending up an audible flare to the insurgents. Come get us! Happy Iraqis and Americans defying your terror! Hello! Here we are!

On March 1, finally meeting a deadline to exit, I walked out the door of the bureau for the last time. I was exhausted from staying up late the night before with Bassam and Omar, squeez-ing out our final minutes together in the bureau. Little Naseer hung out with us, too. We sat on the floor of the living room in the dark, blasting the Iraqi national anthem. I listened to the guys sing along, my heart thumping with the beat, my heart thumping for a country that had crept in and did not want to leave.

Omar went along for the ride to the airport, even though I asked him not to, pleaded with him not to risk the dangers of the road to see me off. He would not listen. He pulled on his dark shades and got in the front seat. No one spoke. We pulled in line at the military checkpoint and silently waited as the cars in front of us inched toward the bomb-sniffing dogs. I looked at my watch. I only had about an hour to get to the plane, and I still had to submit my bags to a search and catch a bus.

"I'm not going to make my flight."

"There's still time," Omar reassured me.

Another fifteen minutes passed. I could not make this trip again, could not go back to the bureau to say another round of good-byes, to hear the chorus of *habibti*— the strongest Arabic term of endearment for a woman.

"I'm going to walk."

I reached into the front and grabbed the walkie-talkie to tell Muhanned, who was in the chase vehicle behind us.

"Muhanned, I'm walking. I cannot wait in this line any-more."

Omar protested.

I opened my door and grabbed my knapsack. Muhanned came behind me with his pistol.

"Let's go," I said, and I ordered my legs to move across this last stretch of road, past the waiting cars, the would-be suicide bombers, the soldiers, the shepherds, the mothers walking their children to school, the old ladies bartering for bread in a mangled landscape that had swallowed Luma before she found her country. Ahead of me was an airplane that would take me back to the United States, to my life, to my twin, to every person I loved and had left to come to Iraq. I blocked out the

sounds around me, the honks of impatient cars, soldiers order-
ing drivers to lift their hoods, the crunch of tanks rolling past.
I went numb with relief and sadness as my sandals kicked up
dust and the tails of my headscarf flapped in the breeze like a
waving flag. I did not look back at Omar waiting in the car
behind me, waiting for the freedom I had at the other end of
my journey. I did not know if I was at the beginning of the end.
I only knew that I had to keep walking.

*In the weeks following Jackie's return from Iraq, I stopped
expecting life to return to normal. I knew it never would, at least
not for a long time. Two weeks after she arrived back in the
States, she accompanied me to San Francisco, where I attended
an academic conference. I had been looking forward to our trip
for months, remembering our long weekends together when she
was in graduate school at Berkeley. Mostly, I looked forward to
spending time alone with her without having to share her with
my family or her friends. After ten long months, we had a lot of
catching up to do. Now that she was safe and didn't need me to
pretend that everything was okay, that I was okay, I could tell
her how afraid I had been, how sure I had been that she was
going to die. It was a selfish desire but I desperately wanted to
leave behind my fear and move forward. We could move forward together.*

*The trip did not go well. During our evening dinners
together, my sister drank too much wine, talking angrily and
loudly about the morons around us. I tried to hush her, but she
lashed out at me, too. When I pointed to her shaking hands
wrapped around her third glass of water in ten minutes, she
pushed herself a little farther from the table, farther from me.
In the hotel room we shared, she refused the bed, opting to
sleep in the closet instead. I fell asleep to her tapping on the computer, emails sent to "the guys back home." Home. Iraq.*

*As the weeks and months wore on, I began to realize that
whatever Iraq had given my sister, had given all of us, the war*

had taken more. I thought back to the night we had collected her from Dulles, how we had arrived far too early because we wanted to be there the moment she came through customs. At last she emerged, skin brown from the Iraqi sun, too thin from a diet of rice—and fear—and from her recent illness. She was dressed all in black, her headscarf wadded up in one of the nine suitcases she pushed. We chattered all the way to the car, but after the first minutes of frenzied conversation, we fell into silence. Aidan beamed in wonder at the woman beside him, who was gazing out the window, her tired face lit by the northern Virginia cityscape.

"Tell Aunt Jackie you love her," I nudged my son.

"Love you," he parroted.

"Tell her thanks for coming back to us."

"Come back," he said, his tiny hand reaching for her in the dark.

My own hand cuts through the dark, reaching, still reaching.

CHAPTER 13

I was home, but I had never felt so lost, so uncertain of where I was headed.

The morning after I landed at Dulles International Airport in Virginia, I staggered into the *Post*, sleep-deprived and unshowered. I wandered the maze of cubicles to reach my desk in the Financial section of the newsroom. The metal plate with my name on it was missing. In the weeks that followed, I obsessed over this detail, sure that it was a sign that I no longer had a place in the newsroom. My feet ached from the mile walk to work in leather shoes. I had worn flip-flops in the bureau in Iraq, T-shirts, and ink-stained khakis. These stiff, professional clothes felt like a uniform. I was a reluctant ant, getting back in line.

As I recounted stories with my editors, I swore at my bosses like the best of the Army guys I'd been hanging around. I wasn't a solider but a bad-ass war correspondent, my outward bravado demanding immediate assurance that there would be life after Iraq. Primarily, I wanted a new beat at the *Post*. I wanted to write about something meaningful, to find a story, an assignment, that I could embrace like I had embraced the story of Iraq. I was not certain what that story was, just that it had to be out there and that I should beallowed to cover it.

"Don't worry," the editors said in response to my queries about my next assignment. "Take a break. We'll talk about it after you have had some time off."

This was not what I wanted to hear. I wanted to hear, "We promise that you will not have to go back to writing about derivatives and special purpose entities and obscure financial instruments. We pledge that we will do right by you, that we will not forget what you have done or what you have sacrificed, ever."

In reality, newspaper editors have notoriously short attention spans. They remember you if you are in front of them. While I was grateful to have time off to rest, I was afraid of being forgotten. I had seen it happen to other reporters. It had happened to me at other times in my career. But more important, in order to heal, I needed to hear their reassurance of purpose and direction waiting for me at the other end. If I went back to the same life I had lived before Iraq, it would be like Iraq never existed.

Back home, I relished the freedoms I had lost in Iraq. I spent hours in the sandbox with my nephew, running the trucks across his Maryland desert. I bought a house, and I settled in to spend the summer writing about Iraq. I feasted on cottage cheese and smoked salmon. I planted a vegetable garden and tended to the weeds. I had all the appearance of a normal life again, of a woman back from war, starting over, moving on. I walked the aisles of the grocery store, amazed at the bounty of produce. There were eight different kinds of beans! I tried to embrace America, but I resented it, too, resented that so many people went about their days oblivious to the struggles in Iraq. America was at war, but so few really had to sacrifice. At a café one afternoon, I tried to block out the voice of a young woman recounting some water cooler drama on her cell phone. I willed her to shut up, but she did not. I wanted to punch her into submission, but I did not. Instead, I left my cup of tea and uneaten sandwich and walked out into the sunshine. Did anybody know? Did anybody care? Halfway across the world, people were suffering, Americans were dying, Iraqis were dying. I suddenly hated these drones who called themselves Americans, who went about their day complaining about such stupid inconveniences like traffic, just as, I acknowledged, I had once done. I could not bear to turn on the television, to the reality TV shows, the obsession with the Michael Jackson trial. Celebrities competing to lose weight? Give me a break! "Get a life," I screamed at the TV before I unplugged it.

Behind the walls, between the rows of orange spring flowers I planted, I felt like I was going crazy, driven mad by the unknown of the future and the known dangers I had escaped in Iraq. I curled up in a ball, fighting nightmares of insurgents chasing me with swords. I jumped when the toaster popped, when a door slammed unexpectedly, when a fork rattled to the ceramic floor of the kitchen. Helicopters nearly undid me; at the sound of the swirling blade, my pulse raced and I started to sweat. I knew this was simply postwar trauma, but I still wanted it to make sense, to understand what was happening to me. I did not want to talk about this with my colleagues who had been in Iraq because I feared their judgment of me as weak, feared the silence that might follow my question, "Is it just me?"

The week after I returned, I was supposed to fly to Illinois with Jenny to celebrate "Christmas in March" with my family. The morning we were scheduled to depart for the airport, I refused to walk out the door of Jenny's house in Maryland. "Go without me," I pleaded to her. "I cannot get on that plane." I had not slept in three days. Instead, I called friends, inviting them to the party that was my nervous breakdown.

Jenny and her husband, Peter, left for the airport, then turned the car around. Jenny bounded up the steps, crying and angry—not at me, she later told me, but at what was swallowing me. "I'm not going without you," she shouted. "I don't care if you don't want me here. I'm staying." A few days, I begged, just a few days and I'll be able to go.

A few days later, I took a deep breath and traveled to Illinois, hoping to slip in quietly, without the fanfare of a hero's welcome. Barely holding on, I didn't feel like a hero; I felt like a fraud. We pulled up to the house where I grew up. My mother had planted a huge sign that stretched the length of the yard, welcoming me home from Iraq. I mustered gratitude until I truly felt it. Even the family bowling alley welcomed me home on their marquee. "Now I know I've made it!" I exclaimed when we drove by it.

But I couldn't shake my anger, which initially targeted the yellow ribbons hung around town, the bumper stickers and ribbon car magnets that were not meant for me. I did not deserve them. The soldiers did. But I had also gone to war, had survived and hobbled home, mentally broken. For many people, the soldiers were heroes; the journalists, scum. My rage boiled; I had no control over it, no explanation for it, no experience in how to deal with it. Eventually I wasn't just angry at the yellow ribbons; I was angry at everything. When a car blocked my alley and I could not park behind my apartment in Washington, I calmly walked upstairs, grabbed a box of eggs, and pelted the car from the second-floor deck until the neighbors started to come outside. I scampered back inside, shut off the lights, and sat trembling, waiting for the police to come. They never did, and the next day, I made sure to bury the empty egg box at the bottom of the trash.

Twice in the months after I came home, I got up in the middle of the night and peed on the floor of my bedroom. I was horrified the following morning when I realized what I had done, stepping into an unusual wet spot. *What the? Oh my God. I must have . . .* This behavior was obviously a holdover from being embedded with the military, from all of the times I peed in the dirt, in the sand, under the cover of night. Still, I was too ashamed to tell anyone until I read Katherine Skiba's book about being embedded with the 101st Airborne. Skiba, a reporter for the *Milwaukee Journal Sentinel*, described how her husband caught her answering nature's call in the hallway outside their bedroom one night shortly after she came home from covering the invasion. It was the first time that I felt what I was going through might be normal. I wrote Katherine an email, admitting that I had done the same thing and thanking her for making me feel less crazy.

Supportive as my friends had been while I was in Iraq, I could not bring myself to see them once I got home. I wanted to tell them about Iraq, and yet I didn't. I only wanted people around me who I thought truly understood this person I had become, this person who was reluctant to embrace her old life for fear of forgetting her most recent one. I felt crazy and messed up, yet I knew that I had escaped Iraq with barely a scratch. The only physical scar I brought home was a tiny, half-moon tear on my right index finger. I cut it on a piece of glass when a car bomb exploded not far from the bureau, blowing out nearly every single window, door, and pane. Little Naseer had been the one to find me, my finger dripping in blood as I stared at it in shock. As much as I braced myself, prepared myself for physical danger in Iraq, the sight of my own blood stunned me. It took months for this tiny sliver of severed skin to heal, months before I could twist the cap off a bottle of soda or grasp a softball. And yet, I still had a hand. I was incredibly lucky.

I shunned my friends in favor of my family because they asked no questions and surrounded me in unconditional love. Even when I retreated from them emotionally, they were there, waiting for me to return. In many ways my family saved me. I went back to the womb and cradled in their unflinching love and support, tried to find myself again.

In the weeks after I returned home, I talked a lot with Allen Petty, the truck driver from Texas I had first written about in May. I had gone back to visit Allen and his family when I was home to visit in the fall of 2004. Allen told me that at night, after their work was finished and the desert moon had risen over their camp, some of the civilian truckers who hauled military supplies across Iraq would gather at their base in Kuwait and watch videos. They watched the same three clips again and again, fast-forwarding through some scenes, rewinding to replay others, pausing to stare at the screen. In each, they noted the way the victim's hands were bound. They counted the seconds between the time his neck was cut open and when he stopped struggling. They would tie each other up and practice how to escape a similar fate at the hands of anti-American insurgents. Allen told me he soon was able to calculate how long it took a beheaded man to die: "Between seven and fifteen seconds."

Allen had spent the summer of 2004 in Iraq, dodging roadside bombs, mortar fire, rocket-propelled grenades, and bullets as he drove his unarmored flatbed between U.S. military bases. He had lived that unnerving fear of being kidnapped by men in black hoods. And he was earning no more than he made driving a truck in the United States, with an extra run to Mississippi thrown in. He came home to Texas on a break in September and never went back. "I didn't tell my family it was getting so bad," he said. "But I talked to God, and He told me it was time to come home."

He came back a broken man, his wife, Sylvia Petty, confided to me when Allen went to pick up the kids from school. "He brought the war home. His character changed. He is at the bottom of the barrel." I felt a strong affinity for Allen, who, like me, felt he had returned from Iraq to the same life he had tried to escape. He paid a much higher price, though, because he didn't have a job. His former employer would not rehire him. He was jumpy, nervous, and depressed, and he seemed crushed by the weight of having failed to provide for his girls. The girls looked up at their father and asked when he would find a job. He couldn't look back at them. "Nobody wants your daddy," he told his daughters.

During Allen's first weeks and months in Iraq, the couple found ways to cope. Allen didn't tell his family everything he was going through; Sylvia avoided the news. Allen sent money home, and Sylvia repaid her mother about a third of what they owed her. Sylvia planted flowers outside the corner house on Main Street that they rent from her parents. She bought the children treats and planned a cruise for the family. She was able to afford more healthful food for herself and the children. She lost twenty-five pounds, and her face was tanned from working in the garden. Allen bought handcrafted wedding rings in Kuwait. He purchased a laptop computer so they could communicate by email and instant message.

After Allen returned home, Sylvia said she knew he was hiding his fear from her. But at least "he knows where the enemy is," she said. "For me, the fear is everywhere. That fear of the unknown has to be the worst feeling in the world." Sylvia said the children were initially excited when they heard their father was coming home. But soon, she said, the meaning of it sank in. "The kids are just so heartbroken," Sylvia said. "Naomi, she is really super-smart. Over breakfast, when she found out, she said: 'It's over, isn't it? We're not going to get our house. What are we doing wrong?'"

It was late September when we visited, and the air was just starting to turn crisp. As Allen sat in an overstuffed chair and turned his head toward the window, Sylvia twisted her hands in the fold of her shirt, hiding the fingernails she had clipped the night before. While Allen was away in Iraq, she had her nails manicured for the first time since they were married. Her husband went to Iraq with hopes of earning money for a house, but Sylvia had smaller dreams. She wanted her refrigerator to be full, her girls to have blankets on their beds, her rotting teeth to be fixed. She wanted to be able to afford to take two-year-old Lydia to the doctor for a persistent ear infection. She wanted to look nice for her husband. The night before, she and Allen had argued. They both were frustrated, uncertain about what lay ahead.

Sylvia was thinking about starting a home jewelry business. Allen offered to get a job at McDonald's. "I said, 'I can't see you in a silly hat flipping burgers,'" Sylvia recalled. Allen was considering going back to work overseas, but only if he could be gone for thirty days at a time—and not be in a war zone. He recently had read about job opportunities with UNICEF. The family was living on about $80 a week in child support that Sylvia's former husband sends for the older children. "I know it's not right," Sylvia said, "but we don't know what else to do."

Sylvia wants her husband to understand what it was like to be left, to care for the children alone, to manage their dreams, to watch it all disappear. "I knew it was over when the water hose broke," she said. "The neighbors saw the flowers outside dying. The water hose breaks, and you can't get a new one. We're back to barely making it."

Allen doesn't want to talk about what happened. He spends the nights when he cannot sleep looking at the pictures and video footage he took in Iraq. There's the one of a buddy waving as he passed Petty's truck on an Iraqi highway. There are images of burning limbs, bleeding bodies, dead civilians, dead soldiers, rubble. He stared at each photo as he showed them to me. Then he pulled out a hand-printed sign that someone had put up near the lounge where the civilian contractors hung out in Kuwait. He wrote it down because it spoke to him. It read: "I got no medals, patches or awards. . . . No one knows us; we're just hurting, bleeding and dying. We're just contractors."

Days after he returned from Iraq, Allen said, he felt a tingling in his chest. He struggled to breathe. Sylvia took him to the hospital, where he was kept for a week while doctors ran a battery of tests. They said he had a heart abnormality that was probably there before he went to Iraq but had gone undetected. As we talked, one of the girls banged a chair and Allen jumped. He pulled the baby to his chest. "I forget what she looks like, and then I see her, and she's beautiful," he said. "She has these curls. It amazes me." He looked off. "My mind wanders. I'm here, but I'm not."

I called Jenny from Texas. "He understands, Jerky," I told her, using our pet name for each other. He made me feel more human. I was so disconnected from everyone else. I had gone to Iraq to find a story. Coming home, I became the story, a battered, beaten half soul of a human. I knew Allen got this.

I felt tremendously guilty for the Iraqi staff I had left behind with kisses and hugs and no promises for a future. It was as if I had personally invaded Iraq and then left under the cover of dark. Be patient, I told them, like I really understood. Patient for what? I was going home to the land of the plentiful, to peaceful nights, clean water, electricity, and super-sized meals. I know they dreamed of the day I would return. I hated myself for leaving them, for being so selfish to want my life back, my old life. What life did they have?

From Baghdad, Bassam sent me an email.

> By the way, I don't know what is happening to Little Naseer. Oh my God, he behaves like a teenager. He bought a special CD of love songs, and he said that it's for your sake. Moreover, he gave me a letter this morning and asked me to translate it for you. The letter says:

To my love Jackie,

I miss you so, so much. Being away from me breaks my heart. I promise u that I will learn English and I'll show you my love then. I swear by God if I put my love on a mountain, the mountain will fall. You are the best woman. I pray and ask God to make you succeed because I love you from the depth of my heart. My heart and my soul are in your hands and I think of you day and night.

You are the most beautiful flower I ever seen in my life.

I was relieved two weeks later when Omar emailed to let me know that Little Naseer was now smitten with the new cleaning lady. I was off the hook.

Three months later, after a quiet Washington summer, I still do not know where my journey will next lead me. I only know that I must get up in the morning, put my feet on the floor, hope there is no wet spot, write, live, breathe, move. Sometimes the needle of my compass spins east toward Iraq and sometimes it settles on Washington. Mostly, it just spins, a silver blade whirling furiously in a circle, pointing everywhere and nowhere.

EPILOGUE

Six months after I left Iraq, I returned in mid-September 2005, unable to resist the hypnotic pull of the country, the people, and the story. On the way in from the airport, I shared a taxi ride to the checkpoint with Louise Rouge of the *Los Angeles Times*. We were both old-timers now, and we knew the drill. As the driver sped us toward our waiting vehicles, we pulled our headscarves out of our satchels and disappeared under the black fabric.

"Are those Iraqi sandals?" I asked, pointing to Louise's feet. She had been wearing nicer, red balletlike slippers in Jordan.

"Yes, I bought them here."

"Dude, they are so ugly. They're perfect!"

"I know," she said, grinning.

The taxi driver picked up speed as we neared the parking lot where our drivers always waited for us. We were barreling down the airport road now, and I looked over at Louise. "Where's he going? Is he going to stop?" The panic set in quickly at the imagined scenario: this guy was actually an insurgent, and we were going to being kidnapped.

"Hey," I yelled at the driver, tapping him hard on the shoulder. "Slow down!"

The driver looked surprised but slowed the car. He pointed at a statue of a winged man that hovers over the entrance to the Baghdad airport. Oh. The parking lot had moved. We weren't being kidnapped. I smiled sheepishly at Louise.

"There he is," I told the taxi driver, pointing to the *Post* bodyguard, Baldy, who was standing in the middle of the road, scanning the passing vehicles for me.

"The bald guy with the belly. That's my guy!"

As soon as the taxi stopped, I jumped out, and Baldy scooped me up in a hug.

"Sister, sister, we have been waiting for you."

I had been waiting, too, ever since I walked out of the bureau in March. *Feeh*, the guys had told me, their made-up greeting for "good-bye." *Feeh* was like my coded "t" and "me, too," with Jenny to say we loved each other. *Feeh* meant: *We are all in this together and we both know that there is a chance we will never see each other again. Be safe. We are more than friends. We are brothers and sisters. We may have fought today. I might have let you down. But I love you. Come back to me.* The drivers and guards ended each telephone conversation, each dispatched errand, each good-bye at the end of the day with this simple word packed with meaning. Feeh.

Me, too, I had told Jenny when I left this time. I felt selfish for leaving her again. The first time, I had no idea how hard it was going to be on her, how hard it had been. But this summer, writing together, reading how sad and scared she had been, I knew she would be in pain. And full of this knowledge, I still returned. A few days before I left, as I was packing and emailing Jenny excitedly about seeing Omar and Bassam and the rest of the gang again, she sent me a reply. "You've already left, haven't you?" she wrote. "But you never even really came home!" She was right. I had been stuck emotionally between the two places for the summer, and now I was leaving for another couple of months; in fact, I had already mentally left. I had packed a new box of Q-tips, stocked up on contact lens cleaner and disposable lenses in preparation for being gone. But something inside also told me I had a finite time to give to Iraq this trip. For Jenny's sake. For my sake. For my sanity. The morning I left for the airport, I thought better of the new 176-count box of Q-tips that had become a symbol of my extended stay during the last trip. As the taxi driver bleeped his horn for me outside my Maryland house, I hurriedly took the box out, grabbed a handful of swabs, threw those in the bag, and left the rest of the box in my bathroom cabinet. There, that's more manageable, I thought to myself. It calmed me down.

David Hoffman was sending me back to cover the trial of Saddam Hussein, which was scheduled to begin October 19, only a few days after Iraqis were due to vote on a new constitution that would set the framework for a government without Saddam. I had been telling David for months that I was willing to go back if he needed me. I was relieved more than anything when he finally asked.

Baghdad looked the same as I had left it, although the American presence in the city was not nearly as obvious. White Iraqi police pickup trucks loaded with blue-uniformed recruits raced through the city, guns pointed at passing vehicles. They shot wildly and randomly when they got spooked. The streets did not feel any safer, and the Western press was still largely locked down in their bureaus. We were able to get out a little more to report, but the trips were calculated, the risk of kidnapping still a constant threat, particularly at what had become one of the most dangerous places in Iraq, the entrance to the fortified Green Zone.

The week after I returned, the Iraqi Army took over control of this checkpoint, which was not a positive development for most of us who pass through this gate. Like us, the Iraqi soldiers fear car bombers, and for good reason. A suicide bomber detonated at the entrance on October 4, killing ten people. Although access to the checkpoint was supposed to be limited, the Iraqi security forces let just about anybody in who waved a piece of plastic. Drivers sometimes waved prepaid phone cards, and with a flip of a hand, the security forces allowed them to pass. Knowing this, I'd grown increasingly wary of the moments I was exposed at the checkpoint. We used to get dropped off at the entrance, with only a few feet to scurry. After the Iraqis took over, we had to walk several blocks, trying to blend in, trying not to rush too much but mindful that a bomb could go off at any moment. When I went to get my press credentials updated in September, I walked quickly to the Iraqi army soldier who was part of the perimeter security. He demanded to see my passport. No problem; I had it. Then he proceeded to argue with me. I had no idea what he was saying. I understand Arabic for "Walk straight ahead. Go left. Go right. Are you a journalist?" But he was shouting something different. I looked to our security chief, Muhanned, who was a few feet away, ironically, for security reasons. I'm supposed to look like an ordinary Iraqi when I walk to the checkpoint. Insurgent-repellent. If Muhanned were by my side, I might look like a VIP or what I began to refer to as VIT, Very Important Target.

I had spent the drive to the Green Zone thinking about what fun I had been having in the bureau in the weeks since I returned. We had a freelance reporter, Kimberly Johnson, staying in the house with us. Kim and I were instant buddies. She embraced Iraq the way I did, embraced life in Iraq with complete abandon. We spent hours sliding down the banister of our curling stairwell, playing football with the guards at midnight in our *abayas*, swimming in our headscarves, gobbling ice cream cones with chocolate sprinkles while swinging in the backyard. The night before I had decided to climb the tree in the backyard. I desperately needed these moments to feel like I was not in the middle of a bloodied country, to feel happy and free of the routine fear. On my last tour, I called these moments my "oasis of joy." But I was having second thoughts on the drive to the Green Zone about having such drastic ups and downs—the up of feeling safe in the house and the terror once I left it. And it was terror. I watched carefully, waiting for car bombers, expecting the sudden blast, accepting at once that I might die and also fearing it. Since coming to Iraq for the first time in January 2004, I realized that absolute freedom was simply not being afraid to die. The terror of death is so restricting, and in some ways in Iraq, I had become closer to this freedom than in any other place, in the world or my life. Toward the end of my last tour, I had grown so unafraid, so resigned to my fate. But on that drive to the Green Zone, it hit me. This was stupid. I was a fool. I could die! The feelings were absolutely paralyzing. So when I was confronted at the Green Zone, standing out there vulnerable for a good five minutes while the soldier shouted at me, I went into a panic. "*Amerikiya! Amerikiya!*," the soldier shouted. I wanted to strangle him and yell, *Go ahead and get on a bullhorn and tell the freaking insurgents. Perhaps one of them has missed your rant.* But I did not, and the soldier finally let me in. Inside the barbed wire, I was mad. It was the same feeling I had had after the kidnapping attempt at Abu Ghraib. I did everything I could to keep myself protected, to hide in Iraqi clothes, but I am not Iraqi. When I left the bureau that morning, I realized I was wearing my orange flip-flops. I held up our caravan while I raced upstairs to put on my cheap, painful Iraqi sandals. What was the point? *Amerikiya! Amerikiya!* I tugged off my scarf as soon as I reached the first checkpoint inside. Usually, I wore it until I got deep inside the Green Zone to the Convention Center. What the heck, I told myself. I could have worn jeans and a baseball cap and I would have been just as identifiable. *Amerikiya!* I was shaking so badly I could barely hold on to my ID card as I handed it to the Georgian soldier at the first internal checkpoint. I was short of breath and jumpy for the next thirty minutes until I finally calmed down, my head swimming. It was sobering to realize that I had not yet conquered the fear of death. When we drove back to the bureau, Omar 2 asked me if I wanted to drive when I passed into our secure compound. I just shook my head. I was too scared and it seemed stupid.

I was depressed until Friday night, until I threw myself into cooking spinach lasagna, spaghetti and meatballs, and minestrone soup. Bassam read a poem by the Italian poet Antonella Anedda, about the innocence of language. We had extra guests at the table. My friends from other news organizations were pouring back into the country for the referendum and Saddam's trial, and the familiarity of their faces, the comfort of friendships forged in a war zone lifted my spirits.

Nope, I told myself, looking around the table, seeing friends, both Western and Iraqi, eating Italian food by candlelight, gathering in spite of everything. I could not stop dreaming and living and throwing footballs. Iraqis had not put their lives on hold. They were still going to the markets, going to school, driving to checkpoints, getting out and walking in to their jobs. Earlier that day I had told our house manager, Isra, about

Grandma Spinner, who has buried her husband and her three sons, her parents, and both of her siblings. Grandma has every reason to wake up in the morning and shake her fist at God, and yet she does not. After dinner, as I scrubbed the dishes, I felt closer to my grandma than ever, felt closer to her in Iraq than I had at her ninety-fourth birthday party in August in Illinois. I felt her resolve breathing inside of me, as I scraped the lasagna pan and swirled clean water through the wineglasses. We have a shared faith in the future—me, Grandma, Jenny, Bassam, Abu Saif, Omar. Whatever side of the globe, wherever we are in our own journeys, whatever our faiths, whatever the flags that flutter in our respective homelands, we have nothing else but this hope. So we hold on tightly, our hands grasped together in one wish.

Feeh.

Jackie Spinner
Baghdad, Iraq
October 10, 2005

ACKNOWLEDGMENTS

The recounting of this story was possible only because of the tremendous support of *The Washington Post*, including *Post* company chairman Don Graham, who told me that no story in Iraq was worth my life. I know he meant it.

Thanks to Managing Editor Phil Bennett and to Foreign Assistant Managing Editor David Hoffman for giving me a chance to go to Iraq. They had my back, and it kept me alive. They valued our Iraqi staff just as much as the American correspondents on assignment in a borrowed country. This reconfirmed my belief that I work for the best newspaper in the world.

Also, thanks to *Post* Financial Assistant Managing Editor Jill Dutt for loaning me to Phil and David and continuing to support me even though I was no longer writing business stories for her.

I left my girl-pod in the Financial section behind when I went to Iraq: Renae Merle, Sara Goo, and Yuki Noguchi kept me in the loop, feeding me newsroom gossip and offering words of encouragement.

David Ignatius offered to write the foreword to this book without hesitation. He got behind me at the beginning of my career and stayed there, championing and encouraging.

Todd Doughty, a lifelong friend from Southern Illinois University, put me in touch with my agent, Jeff Kleinman of the Graybill & English Literary Agency. Jeff immediately embraced this project. The people at Scribner in New York seemed instinctively to "get" my story. I have never had a better editor than Lisa Drew. She took a chance on this first-time author and patiently guided me through the process.

I am grateful for the advice of *Post* colleagues who went before me or who stayed behind and encouraged me, a freshman of war reporting. With thanks to Dana Priest, Tom Ricks, and Brad Graham.

To the curious reader, this must seem like a Oscar acceptance speech, without the stars. In fact, some of the best foreign reporters passed through *The Washington Post* Baghdad bureau. And yet, they treated this B-list actress as an equal. Their names are associated with some of the best foreign reporting in the word: Ed Cody, Pam Constable, Dan Williams, Anthony Shadid, Scott Wilson, Caryle Murphy, and Doug Struck. Iraq would not have been the same without them. Special thanks for the leadership and friendship of Rajiv Chandrasekaran and Karl Vick. They were my heroes, and my pals.

The Washington Post owes everything, most of all, to its brave Iraqi staff, to the translators and bodyguards, drivers and cooks, who risk their lives embracing our mission—the never-ending quest for the truth. When my words failed me most, it was in describing the commitment of our translators: Omar Fekeiki, Bassam Sebti, Naseer Nouri, and Khalid Saffar. They are true *Washington Post* correspondents.

I owe special gratitude to Suzy Garber, a fellow nomad who never needed a compass. In Jersey City, she shifted her sleeping pattern to make sure she was always there for me. Also, though they were not always sure I should be in Iraq, Mai-Trang Dang and Cathy Crowley helped me home.

Thanks to Damien Bouillard and Kevin Bliss for giving me a place to write in Rehoboth Beach, Delaware, a comforting, familiar place where I could talk to the waves and heal while I wrote.

It is impossible to list all of the people, church congregations, and prayer lists that lifted me up. I felt every one.

My family loved me unconditionally: to my mother, Donna Spinner; my brother, Tim Spinner; my grandmother, Cloe Spinner; my godmother, Beth Abbott, and my uncle Elmer Abbott; my aunts Phyllis Spinner and Carol Burke; the entire McGahey clan—John, Peg, Johnny, Michael, Chris, Peter, Laurie, Lisa, Scott, Courtney, and Caitlyn. They never abandoned me.

Finally, my twin sister, Jenny, has my deepest love and respect. Some people come into this world alone. I am grateful I heard her beating heart before I had the words for it. I would have no story without her.

ABOUT THE AUTHORS

Jackie Spinner is a staff writer for *The Washington Post*, where she has been a reporter since May 1995. She was a winner of the 2005 Distinguished International Reporting award from the Washington-Baltimore Newspaper Guild. Before working at the *Post*, Spinner contributed to the *Oakland Tribune*, the *San Diego Union Tribune*, the *Decatur Illinois Herald & Review*, and the *Los Angeles Times* TV magazine. Spinner grew up in Illinois, the daughter of a pipe fitter and a schoolteacher. She lives in Maryland.

Dr. Jenny Spinner is an assistant professor of English at St. Joseph's University in Philadelphia, where she teaches writing and journalism. Her columns and critical and literary essays have appeared in the *Hartford Courant*, *The Washington Post*, *Newsday*, *Decatur Illinois Herald & Review*, the *Oxford Encyclopedia of American Literature*, on NPR's *All Things Considered*, and in numerous small magazines. She lives in Pennsylvania.

13592000R00189

Made in the USA
Lexington, KY
08 February 2012

Raves For the Work of
MAX ALLAN COLLINS!

"No one can twist you through a maze with as much intensity and suspense as Max Allan Collins."
—*Clive Cussler*

"Collins is a master."
—*Publishers Weekly*

"Collins has an outwardly artless style that conceals a great deal of art."
—*The New York Times Book Review*

"Max Allan Collins [is] like no other writer."
—*Andrew Vachss*

"Collins breaks out a really good one, knocking over the hard-boiled competition (Parker and Leonard for sure, maybe even Puzo) with a one-two punch: a feisty story-line told bittersweet and wry…nice and taut…the book is unputdownable. Never done better."
—*Kirkus Reviews*

"Entertaining…full of colorful characters…a stirring conclusion."
—*Detroit Free Press*

"Collins has a gift for creating low-life believable characters…a sharply focused action story that keeps the reader guessing till the slam-bang ending. A consummate thriller from one of the new masters of the genre."
—*Atlanta Journal Constitution*

"For fans of the hardboiled crime novel...this is powerful and highly enjoyable reading, fast moving and very, very tough."
    —Cleveland Plain Dealer

"Strong and compelling reading."
    —Ellery Queen's Mystery Magazine

"Intelligent, witty, and exciting."
    —Booklist

"Masterful."
    —Jeffrey Deaver

"Collins makes it sound as though it really happened."
    —New York Daily News

"An exceptional storyteller."
    —San Diego Union Tribune

"A gift for intricate plotting and cinematically effective action scenes."
    —Jon L. Breen, Twentieth Century Crime and Mystery Writers

"So vivid and colorful that it's like watching a movie [and he] gives the reader a front-row seat."
    —Cozies, Capers & Crimes

"A compelling talent."
    —Library Journal

"Nobody does it better than Max Allan Collins."
    —John Lutz

The ex-gangster walked into the trees, heading toward the yawning white expanse of frozen water. I followed behind, nine millimeter in one hand, sawed-off in the other.

As we wound through the pines, the snow got deeper, ankle deep in places. Finally, at the snowy edge of the wooded shore, Harry came to a stop, and half turned.

"Go on, Harry."

Harry frowned. "Go on? What the fuck, 'go on?' "

"Keep walking."

"Where?"

I gestured with the shotgun, toward the lake.

Harry followed the gesture, eyes tight, and it took a few seconds for him to absorb the meaning. Somehow, though, he couldn't turn his confusion and apprehension into words.

Harry looked at the lake, then at me; the lake, me.

His voice seemed even higher pitched than before, almost childish, his wide eyes buggy behind the lenses. "What...what if the ice gives, under me? I mean...it's gonna get thin, farther out I get...."

"We'll keep the stress to a minimum."

"How?"

"I'll stay put," I said...

The Last
QUARRY

by **Max Allan Collins**

A HARD CASE **CRIME NOVEL**

A HARD CASE CRIME BOOK

(HCC-023)

First Hard Case Crime edition: August 2006

Published by

Titan Books
A division of Titan Publishing Group Ltd
144 Southwark Street
London SE1 0UP

in collaboration with Winterfall LLC

Print edition ISBN 978-0-85768-370-0
E-book ISBN 978-0-85768-641-1

Design direction by Max Phillips
www.maxphillips.net

The name "Hard Case Crime" and the Hard Case Crime logo
are trademarks of Winterfall LLC. Hard Case Crime books are
selected and edited by Charles Ardai.

Printed and bound by CPI Group (UK) Ltd, Croydon, CR0 4YY

Visit us on the web at www.HardCaseCrime.com

For Jeffrey Goodman—
who brought my killer
to life

"Any victim demands allegiance."
Graham Greene

THE LAST QUARRY

One

It had been a long time since I'd had any trouble sleeping.

Not since the fucking shelling was keeping me awake, a lifetime or two ago. I'm not by nature an insomniac. You might think killing people for a living would give you some bad nights. Truth is, guys in the killing biz? Just aren't the type to be bothered.

I was no exception. I hadn't gone into retirement because my conscience was bothering me. I retired because I had enough money put away to live comfortably without working, so I did. And for a while that retirement had gone well. I'd invested a little and was living off the gravy; I'd even been married for a while, which had worked out fine.

For a while.

Currently I was deposited in an A-frame cottage with a deck onto the frozen expanse of Sylvan Lake, somewhere in Minnesota, only it's not called Sylvan Lake and maybe it's not Minnesota, either. I was staying at the only resort on this side of the lake, Sylvan Lodge, but I was not a guest—I ran the place. Or, anyway, did when it wasn't off-season.

Once upon a time I had owned a resort in Wisconsin

not unlike this—not near the acreage, of course, and not near the occupancy; but I had *owned* the place, whereas here I was just the manager.

Of course I didn't have anything to complain about. I was lucky to have the job. When I ran into Gary Petersen in Milwaukee, where he was attending a convention and I was making a one-night stopover to remove some emergency funds from several bank deposit boxes, I was at the loosest of loose ends. The name I'd lived under for over a decade was unusable; my past had caught up with me, back at Paradise Lake, where everything went to hell in an instant: my straight business yanked from under me, my wife (who'd had not a clue of my prior existence) murdered in her sleep.

Gary, however, had recognized me in the hotel bar and called out a name I hadn't used since the early '70s: my real one.

"Jack!" he said, only that wasn't the name. For the purposes of this narrative, however, we'll say my real name is Jack Keller.

"Gary," I said, surprised by the warmth creeping into my voice. "You son of a bitch...you're still alive."

Gary was a huge man—six six, weighing in at somewhere between three hundred pounds and a ton; his face was masked in a bristly brown beard, his skull exposed by hair loss, his dark eyes bright, his smile friendly, in a goofy, almost child-like way.

"Thanks to you, asshole," he said.

We'd been in Vietnam together.

"What the hell have you been doing all these years, Jack?"

"Mostly killing people."

He boomed a laugh. "Yeah, right!"

"Don't believe me, then."

I was, incidentally, pretty drunk. I don't drink often, but I'd been through the mill lately.

"Are you crying, Jack?"

"Fuck no," I said.

But I was.

Gary slipped his arm around my shoulder; it was like getting cuddled by God. "Bro—what's the deal? What shit have you been through?"

"They killed my wife," I said, and blubbered drunkenly into his shoulder.

"Jesus, Jack—who…?"

"Fucking assholes…fucking assholes…."

We went to his suite. He was supposed to play poker with some buddies but he called it off.

I was very drunk and very morose and Gary was, at one time anyway, my closest friend, and during the most desperate of days.

I told him everything.

I told him how after I got back from Nam, I found my wife—my first wife—shacked up with some guy, some fucking auto mechanic, who was working under a car when I kicked the jack out. The jury let me off, but I was finished in my hometown, and I drifted until the Broker found me. The Broker, who gave me the name Quarry, was the conduit through whom the murder-for-hire contracts came, and, what? Ten years later the Broker was dead, by my hand, and I was out of the killing business and took my savings and went to Paradise Lake in Wisconsin, where eventually I met a pleasant, attractive, not terribly bright woman and she and I were in the lodge business until the past came looking for me, and suddenly she was dead, and I was without a life or even identity. I had managed to kill the fuckers responsible for my wife's killing—political assholes, not wiseguys—but otherwise I had nothing. Nothing left but some money stashed away, that I was now retrieving.

I told Gary all this, through the night, in considerably more detail though probably even less coherently, although coherently enough that when I woke up the next morning, where Gary had laid me out on the extra bed, I knew I'd told him too much.

He was still asleep. Like me, he was in the same clothes we'd worn to that bar; like me, he smelled of booze, only he also reeked of cigarette smoke. I reeked a little, too, but it was Gary's smoke: I never picked up the habit. Bad for you.

He looked like a big dead animal, except for his barrel-like chest heaving with breath. I looked at this man—like me, he was somewhere near or past fifty, not the kids we'd been before the war made us worse than just men.

I still had liquor in me, but I was sober now. Too deadly fucking sober. I studied my best-friend-of-long-ago and wondered if I had to kill him.

I was standing over him, staring down at him, mulling that over, when his eyes opened suddenly, like a timer turning on the lights in a house to fend off burglars. He smiled a little, then it faded, his eyes narrowed, and he said, "Morning, Jack."

"Morning, Gary."

"You've got that look."

"What look is that?"

"The cold one. The one I first saw a long time ago."

I swallowed and took my eyes off him. Sat on the edge of the bed across from him and rubbed my eyes with the heels of my hands.

He plopped down across from me with those big paws on his big knees and said, "How the hell d'you manage it?"

"What?"

"Hauling my fat ass onto that Medivac."

I grunted a laugh. "The same way a little mother lifts a Buick off her big baby."

"In my case, you lifted the Buick onto the baby. Let me buy you breakfast."

"Okay."

In the hotel coffee shop, he said, "Funny…what you told me last night…about the business you used to be in?"

I sipped my coffee; I didn't look at him—didn't show him my eyes. "Yeah?"

"I'm in the same game."

Now I looked at him; I winced with disbelief. "What…?"

He corrected my initial thought. "The tourist game, I mean. I run a lodge near Brainerd."

"No kidding."

"That's what this convention is. Northern Resort Owners Association."

"I heard of it," I said, nodding. "Never bothered to join, myself."

Not by nature much of a joiner.

"I'm a past president," he said, obviously proud of that. "Anyway, I run a place called Sylvan Lodge. My third and current, and I swear to God everlasting wife, Ruth Ann? Maybe I mentioned her last night? Anyway, Ruthie inherited it from her late parents, God rest their hardworking Republican souls."

None of this came as a surprise to me. Grizzly bear Gary had always drawn women like a great big magnet—usually good-looking little women who wanted a father figure, Papa Bear variety. Even in

Bangkok on R & R, Gary never had to pay for pussy, as we used to delicately phrase it.

"I'm happy for you," I said. "I always figured you'd manage to marry for money."

"My ass! I really love Ruth Ann. You should see the knockers on the child."

"A touching testimonial if I ever heard one. Listen… about that bullshit I was spouting last night…"

His dark eyes became slits, the smile in his brushy face disappeared. "We'll never speak of that again. Understood? Never."

He reached out and squeezed my forearm.

I sighed and smiled tightly and nodded, relieved. Killing Gary would have been no fun at all.

He continued, though. "My sorry fat ass wouldn't even be on this planet, if it wasn't for you. I owe you big time."

"Bullshit," I said, but not very convincingly.

"I've had a good life, at least the last ten years or so, since I met Ruthie. You've been swimming in Shit River long enough. Let me help you out."

"Gary, I…"

"Actually, I want *you* to help *me*."

"Help you?"

Gary's business was such a thriving one that he had recently invested in a second lodge, one across the way from his Gull Lake resort. He had quickly discovered he couldn't run both places himself, at least not "without running my fat ass off." He offered me the job of managing Sylvan.

"We'll start you at 50K, with free housing. You can make a tidy buck with damn near no overhead, and you can tap into at least one of your marketable skills, and at the same time be out of the way. Keep as low a profile as you like. You don't even have to deal with the tourists, to speak of—we have a social director for that. You just keep the boat afloat. Okay?"

"Okay," I said, and we shook hands.

Goddamn I was glad I hadn't killed him....

Two

Now, here I was a little more than six months into the job, and a month into the first winter—off-season, settled in. My quarters, despite the rustic trappings of the cabin-like exterior, were modern—pine paneling skirting the room with pale yellow pastel walls rising to a high pointed ceiling. Just one A-frame room with bath and kitchenette, but a big room, facing the lake, which was a mere hundred yards from the deck that was my back porch. Couch, Dish TV, plenty of closet space, a comfortable bed. I didn't need anything more.

During off-season like this, I could've moved into more spacious digs if I liked, but I hadn't bothered. My first summer and fall at Sylvan Lodge had been a real pleasure. Just a short jog across the way was an indoor swimming pool with hot tub and sauna, plus a tennis court; a golf course, shared with Gary's other lodge, was an easy drive. My duties were constant, but mostly consisted of delegating authority, and the gay chef of our gourmet restaurant made sure I ate well and free, and I'd been banging Nikki, the college girl who had the social director position for the summer, so my staff relations were solid.

But the cold months had come, and in this part of the world that was fucking cold indeed. Everyone except a maintenance guy, José, was gone, and even he didn't live on site; Nikki was back blowing frat boys and probably posing for a *Playboy* college-girl spread, and I didn't even want to know what my gay chef was up to. Gary was off with Ruth Ann down in Florida, where his "winter" home was, and I was up here, keeping an eye on things—like making sure a moose didn't get inside the restaurant and take a dump or something.

In short, I had nothing to do. The only managerial instruction I'd given José since we closed for the season was to keep the pool and hot tub and sauna going, for my personal use.

So for the past month, boredom had started to itch at me…and for the past few nights I'd had trouble sleeping. I sat up all night watching satellite TV and reading paperback westerns; then I'd drag around the next day, maybe drifting to sleep in the afternoon just long enough to fuck up my sleep cycle again that night.

It was getting irritating.

At about three-thirty in the morning on the fourth night of this shit, I decided eating might do the trick. Fill my gut with junk food and the blood could rush down from my head and warm my belly and I'd get the fuck sleepy, finally. I hadn't tried this before because I'd been getting a trifle paunchy, with this easy job, even more so since winter kicked in.

In the summer, at least, I could swim in the lake every day and get some exercise and keep the fucking spare tire off. But with winter here, I'd just let my beard go and belt size, too. I tried to make myself do laps in the pool across the way, but mostly I sat in the hot tub and drank Coca Cola and thought about my past. I wasn't sure why—it wasn't the kind of past you got anywhere with by thinking about it. The only thing I knew for sure was, this winter was making me fat and lazy and, now, fucking sleepless.

The cupboard was bare so I threw on my thermal jacket and—since I was alone on my stretch of Sylvan Lake—took the ten-mile ride to the nearest junk food. At this time of night a shabby little convenience store, Ray's Mart, with its one self-service gas pump, was the only thing open fifteen miles in either direction.

The clerk was a heavy-set brunette named Cindy from Brainerd. She was maybe twenty years old and a little surly, but she worked all night, so who could blame her.

"Mr. Ryan," she said, flatly, as I came in, the bell over the door jingling. She was engrossed in a telephone conversation and this effusive greeting had been both an effort and a concession to a regular customer.

"Cindy," I said, with a nod, and I began prowling the place, three narrow aisles parallel to the front of the building. None of the snacks appealed to me—chips and crackers and Twinkies and other preservative-packed delights—and the frozen food case ran mostly to ice-cream sandwiches and popsicles. In this weather, that was a joke.

I was giving a box of Chef Boyardee lasagna an intent once-over, like it was a car I was considering buying, when the bell over the door jingled again. I glanced up and saw a well-dressed, heavy-set man—heavy-set enough to make Cindy look svelte—with a pockmarked, Uncle Fester-ish face and black-rimmed glasses that fogged up as soon as he stepped in.

He wore an expensive topcoat—a tan Burberry number with a red-and-black plaid scarf, the sort of pricey ensemble that required a small mortgage—and his shoes had a bright black city shine, barely flecked with ice and snow. His name was Harry Something-the-fuck, and he was from Chicago. I knew him, in my former life.

I turned my back.

If he saw me, I'd have to kill him—I was bored, but not that bored.

Predictably, Harry Something went straight for the potato chips; he also rustled around the area where cookies were shelved. I risked a glimpse and saw him, not two minutes after he entered, with his arms full of junk food, heading for the front counter.

"Excuse me, miss," Harry Something said, depositing his groceries before Cindy like an offering on an altar. His voice was nasal and high-pitched; a funny, childish voice for a man his size—it went well with the Uncle Fester face. "Could you direct me to the sanitary napkins?"

Cindy winced, phone in hand, annoyed by this intrusion. Harry was not a regular customer.

She said, "You mean Tampax?"

"Whatever."

"Toiletries is just over there."

Now this was curious, and I'll tell you why. I had met Harry Something around ten years before, when I was doing a job for the Outfit boys in Chicago. I was never a mob guy, mind you, strictly a freelancer, but their money was as good as anybody's. What that job was isn't important, but Harry and his partner Louis were the locals who had fucked up, making my outsider's presence necessary. Harry and Louis had not been friendly toward me. They had threatened me, in fact. They had beaten the hell out of me in my hotel room, when the job was over, for making them look bad.

I had never taken any sort of revenge out on them. I occasionally do take revenge, but at my convenience, and only when a score strikes me as worth settling. Harry and Louis had really just pushed me around a little, bloodied my nose, tried to earn back a little self-respect. So I didn't hold a grudge. Not a major grudge. Fuck it.

As to why Harry Something purchasing Tampax in the middle of the night at some backwoods convenience store was curious, well, Harry and Louis were gay. Like my old man used to say, queer as a three-dollar bill. Mob muscle who worked as a pair, and played as a pair.

And I don't mean to be critical. To each his own. I'd rather cut off my dick than insert it in any orifice of a repulsive fat slob like Harry Something. But, hey, that's just me.

Now while I'm as naturally curious as the next guy, I'm sure as hell not nosy, not even inquisitive, really. But when a faggot buys Tampax, you have to wonder why.

"Excuse me," Harry Something said, brushing by me.

He hadn't seen my face (had he?)—and he might not recognize me, in any case. Ten years and a beard and twenty pounds later, I wasn't as easy to peg as Harry was, who had changed goddamn little.

Harry, having stocked up on cookies and chips and Tampax, was now buying milk and packaged macaroni and cheese and provisions in general. He was shopping.

Stocking up.

And now I was starting to get a handle on what he might be up to....

I nodded to surly Cindy, who bid me goodbye by flickering her eyelids in casual contempt, and went out to my car, a steel-gray Jag I'd purchased recently. I wished I'd had the Lodge's four-wheel drive, or anything less conspicuous, but I didn't. I sat in the car, scooched down low; I did not turn on the engine. I just sat in the cold car in the cold night and waited.

Harry Something came out with two armloads of groceries—Tampax included, I presumed—and he put them in the front seat of a brown rental Ford Taurus. Louis was not waiting in the car for him.

Harry was alone.

Which further confirmed my suspicions....

I waited for him to pull out onto the road, hung back till he took the road's curve, then started up my Jag and glided out after him. He had turned left, toward Brainerd. That made sense, only I figured he wouldn't wind up there—he'd likely light out for the boonies somewhere.

I knew what Harry was up to, vaguely at least. He sure as shit wasn't here to ski—that lardass couldn't stand up on a pair of skis. And he wasn't here to go ice-fishing, either. A city boy like Harry Something had no business in a touristy area like this, in the off-season...

...unless Harry was hiding out, holing up somewhere.

This would be the perfect area for that.

Only Harry didn't use Tampax.

He turned off on a side road, into a heavily wooded area that wound back toward Sylvan Lake.

Good. That was very good.

I went on by. I drove a mile, turned into a farm-house gravel drive and headed back without lights. I slowed as I reached the mouth of the side road, and could see Harry's taillights wink off.

I knew the cabin at the end of that road. There was only one, and its owner only used it during the summer; Harry was either a renter, or a squatter.

I glided on by and went back home.

I left the Jag next to the deck and walked up the steps and into the A-frame. The nine millimeter Browning was in the nightstand drawer. The gun hadn't been shot in months—Christ, maybe over a year. But I cleaned and oiled it regularly, because you never know.

It would do nicely.

So would my black turtleneck, black jeans, black leather bomber jacket, and this black moonless night. I slipped a spare .38 revolver in the bomber jacket right side pocket, and clipped a hunting knife to my belt. The knife was razor sharp with a sword point; I sent for it out of the back of one of those dumb-ass mercenary magazines—which are worthless except for mail-ordering weapons.

I walked along the edge of the lake, my running shoes crunching the brittle ground, layered as it was with snow and ice and leaves. The only light came from a gentle scattering of stars, a handful of diamonds flung on black velvet; the frozen lake was a dark presence that you could sense but not really see, the surrounding trees even darker. The occasional cabin or cottage or house I passed was empty. I was one of only a handful of residents on this side of Sylvan Lake who were staying year-round.

But the lights were on in one cabin. Not many lights, but lights. And its chimney was trailing smoke.

The cabin was small, a traditional log cabin of the Abe Lincoln and syrup variety, only with a satellite dish. Probably two bedrooms, a living room, kitchenette and a can or two. Only one car—the brown rental Ford.

My footsteps were lighter now; I was staying on the balls of my feet and the crunching under them was faint. I approached with caution and gun in hand and peeked in a window on the right front side.

Harry Something was sitting on the couch, eating corn curls, giving himself an orange mustache in the process. His feet were up on a coffee table. More food and a sawed-off double-barreled shotgun were on the couch next to him. He wore a colorful Hawaiian shirt; he looked like Don Ho puked on him, actually.

In the nearby kitchenette, which was open onto the living room, Louis was fussing as he put the food away—a small, skinny, bald ferret of man, who wore jeans and a black shirt and a white tie. I couldn't tell whether he was trying for trendy or gangster, and frankly didn't give a shit.

Physically, all the two men had in common was pockmarks and a desire for the other's ugly body.

And neither one of them seemed to need a tampon, though a towelette would've come in handy for Harry Something. Jesus. Imagine having a Burberry topcoat like that and a Hawaiian shirt underneath; they can make gay marriage legit if they want to, but *that* should be fucking illegal.

I could hear them talking—muffled but audible through the window, the sound of the television, some old movie, underneath.

From the couch Harry said, "Chip me!"

From the kitchenette Louis said, "With *your* cholesterol? Isn't a bag of cheese curls *enough*?"

"Don't mama me!…I wanna Coke, too."

"I thought you were *off* caffeine!"

"Not when you expect me to sit up all fuckin' night."

Louis was in the living room now. "*I'm* the one *dealing* with her—what a spoiled little cunt *she* is!"

Harry laughed; the laugh was like Uncle Fester, too. "That's why daddy'll pay up, sweet cheeks!"

I peeked at them—Louis was delivering barbecue chips and Harry took them with a "Thank you," and they interrupted their bickering to exchange fond expressions. Then Harry worked at adding a new shade of orange to his junk-food mustache.

Me, I huddled back down beneath the window, wondering what I was doing here.

Boredom, for sure.

Curiosity, maybe.

I shrugged. Time to look in another window or two.

Because Harry and Louis clearly had a captive, and a female one at that. That's what they were doing in the boonies. That's why they were stocking up on supplies at a convenience store in the middle of night and nowhere. That's why there were in the market for Tampax.

And through a back window, I saw her.

She was on a single bed in the small rustic room, naked but for white panties—a wrist cuffed to a nearby bedpost, sitting on the edge of the bed, bending over in obvious discomfort, crying…a dark-haired, creamy-fleshed beauty in her early twenties, suffering menstrual cramps.

Obviously, Harry and Louis had nothing sexual in mind for this captive; the reason for her nudity was to help prevent her fleeing. The bed was heavy with blankets, and she'd clearly been keeping under the covers, but right now she was sitting and doubling over and crying. Right now was a bad period for her any way you sliced it.

Thing was, I recognized this young woman. Like Harry, I spent a lot of hours during cold nights like this with my eyes frozen to a TV screen. And that's where I'd seen her: on the tube.

Not an actress, no—an heiress. Jonah Green's daughter—"Daddy" was a Chicago media magnate whose name you'd recognize if I was using his real one, a guy who inherited money and wheeled-and-dealed his way into more, including one of the satellite super-stations I'd been wasting my eyes on lately. The Windy City's answer to Ted Turner, right down to sailboating and baseball teams and womanizing.

His daughter was a little wild—seen in the company of rock stars (she had a tattoo of a star—not Justin Timberlake, a five-pointed star—on her white left breast, which I could see from the window) and was a Betty Ford clinic drop-out. Nonetheless, she was said to be the apple of her daddy's eye, even if that apple was a tad wormy.

So Harry and Louis had put the snatch on the snatch; fair enough. Question was, was it their own idea, or something the Outfit put them up to?

I heard a door open, and peeked in carefully, just barely able to hear the muffled speech through the window.

Louis came in and tossed the box of Tampax in her lap.

The girl snarled, "You took long enough!"

"We're being nice—*you* be nice."

"Fuck you. Fuck you!…I need the bathroom."

A clearly disgusted Louis dug a handcuff key out of his pocket, and worked at undoing her wrist.

The girl, a spoiled brat even in the presence of kidnappers, said, "Hurry the fuck up, faggot! You want blood everywhere?"

He looked at her coldly. "Do you?"

That sobered her a little.

Maybe Daddy should've tried some of Louis's brand of psychology.

Then Louis walked her off somewhere as the girl clutched the Tampax box like treasure.

I dropped down from the window, hidden there in the dark in my dark clothes with a gun in my hand and my back to the log cabin, and I smiled.

When I'd come out into the night, armed like this, it hadn't been to effect a rescue. Whatever else they were, Harry and Louis were dangerous men, and I had to be ready to protect my ass. And if I was going to spend my sleepless night satisfying my curiosity and assuaging my boredom by poking into their business, I had to be ready to pay for my thrills.

So I sat in the cold and dark and decided, finally, that it just didn't matter who or what was behind it.

My options were to go home, and forget about it, and try (probably without any luck) to get some sleep; or to rescue this somewhat soiled damsel in distress.

And if I went home, they'd kill this girl.

What the hell. I had nothing better to do.

I went to the front door and knocked.

No answer.

Shit, I knew somebody was home, so I knocked again.

Then I got right against the door, putting my ear to the wood, so I could gauge their reaction within....

Harry was saying, "Who the fuck is *that*? Who could that be?"

Louis was calming him, saying, "Could be that security company the owner told us about—on patrol. Saw lights on."

TV sound stopped—muted.

Harry's voice again: "You want me to—"

"No! Hide the shottie...."

"Louis, no one knows we're *here*...."

"That's right—nothing to worry about."

Louis cracked open the door and peered out and said, "What is it?" and I shot him in the eye.

Three

The still night was cut by the harsh, shrill sound of a scream—not Louis, who hadn't had time for that, but the girl in the next room, scared shitless at hearing a gunshot, one would suppose.

I paid no attention to her and shouldered the door open—no night latch or anything—and stepped over Louis, kicked aside the .38 revolver he'd been hiding behind him when he answered the door, and moved into the claustrophobic living room, pointing the nine millimeter at Harry, whose orange-ringed mouth was frozen open and whose bag of barbecue potato chips dropped to the floor, much as Louis had.

"Don't, Harry," I said.

I could see in Harry's tiny dark eyes behind his thick black-rimmed glasses that he was thinking about the sawed-off shotgun under the pillow on the couch next to him.

"Who the fuck…?"

I moved slowly to the couch; behind me, an old colorized movie was playing on their captive's daddy's superstation. With my left hand, I plucked the shotgun from under the cushion next to Harry and tucked it under my arm.

"Hi, Harry," I said. "Been a while."

His orange-ringed mouth slowly began to work and his eyes began to blink and he said, "Quarry?"

That was the name he'd known me by.

His eyes showed white all around and he pointed at me. "You're that fucker *Quarry!*"

I dipped down to pluck the .38 from the floor. "Taking the girl your idea, or are you still working for the boys?"

His words came to him from some remote part of his brain, a response not unlike the kick from a doctor-applied mallet to a knee. "We…we retired, couple years ago. God."

He looked past me, wide-eyed, at the thing on the floor and pointed again, this time like a kid in the backseat who just spotted a Dairy Queen. But not as happy.

"You…you killed…Jesus Christ, you killed *Louis*…!"

I sat on the arm of the sofa and kept the gun on him, casually but on him. "Right. What were you going to put the girl's body in?"

"Huh?"

"She's obviously seen you. You were obviously going to kill her, once you got the money. So. What was the plan?"

Harry wiped off his orange barbecue ring with a hand. He was blinking, trying to think. "Got a roll of plastic in the closet. Gonna roll her up and dump her in one of them gravel pits they got around here."

"I see. Do that number with the plastic right now, with Louis, why don't you? Okay?"

Tears were rolling down Harry's chubby, stubbly pockmarked cheeks. I didn't know whether he was crying for Louis or himself or the pair of them, and I wasn't interested enough to ask.

"Okay," he said thickly, apparently resigned to his fate, his mouth slack but his eyes moving with thought.

I watched him roll his partner up in the sheet of plastic, using duct tape to secure the package; he sobbed as he did it, but he did it. He got blood on his Hawaiian shirt; it didn't particularly show, though.

"Good job, Harry. Now…I want you to clean up the mess. Go on. You'll find what you need in the kitchen."

Dutifully, Harry shuffled over to where the open kitchen met the little living room, got a pan of warm water and some rags, and dropped to his knees to clean up the brains and blood. He wasn't crying anymore. He moved slow but steady, a fat zombie in a colorful shirt.

"Stick the rags in the end of the plastic there, Harry, would you? Thank you."

Harry did that, then the big man lumbered to

his feet, hands half-heartedly in the air, and said, "Now me?"

"I might let you go, Harry. I got nothing against you."

His eyes jumped. "Not…not how I remember it."

I laughed. "You girls leaned on me once. You think I'd kill a person over something that trivial? What kind of asshole do you think I am, Harry?"

Harry had sense enough not to answer.

"Let's see how Daddy's little girl's doing," I said, and with the nine millimeter's nose kissing Harry's neck, I walked him to the door of the bedroom.

"Open it," I said.

He did.

We went in, Harry first.

The girl was under the covers, holding the blankets and sheets up around her in a combination of illogical modesty and legitimate fear.

Her expression melted into confusion mingled with the beginnings of hope, when she saw me.

"Everything's going to be all right, Miss Green," I told her. "I've already taken care of the skinny one." I nudged Harry with the gun in his neck. "You got a handcuff key?"

Harry swallowed and nodded.

"Uncuff her."

My gun trained on him from nearby, Harry was complying as she asked, "Did…did my Daddy send you?"

I held out my hand to Harry and he dropped the cuff key in my palm.

"Fatso and me are taking a moonlight stroll," I told her. "Meantime, you stay put. I'm going to get you back to your father."

Her confusion didn't leave, but she began to smile, wide, a kid Christmas morning, seeing her gifts. Her gift to me was dropping the blankets and sheets to her waist. The cute cupcake breasts had pierced nipples with rings, like beer cans waiting to be opened.

"Remember," I said, and waggled a teacherly finger. "Stay right there."

She swallowed and nodded and her eyes sparkled. Well, they did.

I walked my host out, pulling the bedroom door shut behind me.

"Where are her clothes, Harry?"

He nodded to a closet. Same one he'd gotten the plastic out of.

"Good," I said. "Now let's go for a walk. Just the three of us."

Harry frowned in confusion, glanced back toward the bedroom. "Girl's comin'?"

"No. Louis. Better give him a hand."

Now Harry got it.

He leaned down and hefted his partner in the plastic shroud and held the crinkly corpse in his arms like a B-movie monster carrying a starlet. The plastic was spattered with blood, but only on the inside; you could sort of see what was left of Louis's head trying to look out. Harry seemed like he was going to cry again.

I still had the sawed-off shotgun under my arm, so it was awkward, getting the front door open.

Cold came in, but I barely noticed. I don't think Harry much noticed, either.

"What…?" he asked. "Where…?"

"Out on the lake," I said, and nodded in that direction.

"…can I get my coat?"

"I don't think so. I think the cold will keep you on your toes, and anyway, suppose you have a gun in your pocket, and I have to kill you, and mess up that beautiful Burberry. Which would be a fucking shame, plus which I'd have to make two trips, carrying Louis, and your fat ass."

He swallowed, nodded, as if all that sounded reasonable enough. "Okay. I…there's a shovel I could get…?"

"We won't need it. Ground's too hard, anyway."

Harry looked at me, his eyes behind the glasses wary, glancing from me to his plastic-wrapped burden and back again.

I responded to the question his face was asking: "We're going to bury Louis at sea."

"Huh?"

Now I was noticing the cold. "Outside, Harry. My

nipples are getting hard, and not in a good way. Okay? Outside."

He moved past me, his plastic bundle over one shoulder—he might have been delivering a rug.

The chubby ex-gangster walked into the trees, heading toward the yawning white expanse of frozen water. I followed behind, nine millimeter in one hand, sawed-off in the other. Harry in his Hawaiian shirt was an oddly comic sight, but I was too busy to be amused.

As we wound through the pines, the snow got deeper, ankle deep in places. As his glasses got unfogged and made his trek easier, Harry made conversation.

"Was…was that you, Quarry? Back at that fucking convenience store?"

"That's right."

"And, what? You…you thought we'd come after you? This has nothing to do with you."

"Does now. And anyway, I got my question answered."

He risked a frown back at me. "What question?"

"What the Odd Couple needs with Tampax in the middle of the night….Keep moving."

Finally, at the snowy edge of the wooded shore, Harry came to a stop, and half turned, Louis turning too, Harry asking another question with his face: *What now?*

"Go on, Harry."

Harry frowned. "Go on? What the fuck, 'go on?'ž"

"Keep walking."

"*Where?*"

I gestured with the shotgun, toward the lake.

Harry followed the gesture, eyes tight, and it took a few seconds for him to absorb the meaning. Somehow, though, he couldn't turn his confusion and apprehension into words.

So I said, "When you sense the ice getting thin, give Louis a toss...let the lake have him. Then head back here, and we'll talk."

Harry looked at the lake, then at me; the lake, me.

His voice seemed even higher pitched than before, almost childish, his wide eyes buggy behind the lenses. "What...what if the ice gives, under me? I mean...it's gonna get thin, farther out I get...."

"We'll keep the stress to a minimum."

"*How?*"

"I'll stay put."

All the air went out of Harry, and if Louis had been one pound heavier, both men would have gone down in a pile in the snow, right there. But he stayed on his feet, even though the despair must have been heavier than Louis.

"Quarry...Quarry...will you just fuckin' kill me. Kill me here and be done."

I shrugged. "Thought you might like a sporting chance, Harry. Before you know it, you'll be out of range…maybe you can make it over to those trees, where I can't catch up with you."

He summoned a sneer from somewhere. "If the ice don't break first."

I shrugged again. "That's between you and the ice."

He sneered at me; but the sneer dissolved into this pitiful, lower-lip trembling thing that got only a single shake of the head out of me. That, and another nod toward the lake.

Cradling Louis like a groom carrying a bride across the threshold (which was fitting, as Louis had been the wife), Harry heaved a sigh, took a tentative step, and found the ice firm. He drew a deep breath, as if he were diving into water, not about to walk on the frozen variety, and then he was making his way with the mummy-like bundle out onto the lake, walking carefully, hesitantly, testing the ice with one baby step after another, always letting the tentative ground settle under him.

It took a long time—maybe two minutes. Harry would look at his feet, then off to the bank on the right and the thick darkness of trees, clearly considering that option. His breath was visible, small puffy clouds, and the heavy sound of it came back over the stillness of the lake, interrupted only by the call of a

loon. Or something—some damn bird too stupid to
fly the fuck south.

Subtle at first, the cracking seemed something I
was only imagining, in my anticipation; but Harry
had heard it, too, because he was poised out there as
frozen as the lake.

Actually, more frozen, because suddenly the ice
was snapping under his shoes, as if he were standing
on a window, and that window was breaking....

He didn't even have time to run. He was clutching
onto Louis, which might have been bittersweet, only
I think he was hoping he could use Louis like a big
piece of driftwood or something, but it didn't work
out that way.

Louis disappeared, sliding under like a turd down
the crapper, leaving Harry to flail, and try to hold
onto the bigger chunks of ice; he was screaming my
name and swearing, then the splashing was louder
than the screaming and then the screaming stopped
altogether and finally the splashing subsided.

And he was gone.

I studied the lake—soon you could barely see the
hole Harry had made—with the black starry sky my
only companion. Even the loon had nothing to say,
the frozen expanse and the surrounding blackness
of trees as quiet as, well, death. Suddenly this wintry
world seemed austerely beautiful to me, a study

in white and gray and gray-blue and black, but enjoying myself like that seemed vaguely creepy, so I headed back to the cabin, shotgun slung over my arm.

Back inside, I got the girl's clothes out of the closet—her cell phone was in a pocket—and went in and gave them to her, keeping the phone. A black hip-hop t-shirt and designer jeans and Reeboks.

"Did you kill those men?" she said, breathlessly, her eyes dark and glittering. She had her clothes in her lap.

"That's not important. Get dressed."

"You're wonderful. You're goddamn fucking wonderful."

"I know," I said. "Everybody says so. Get dressed."

She got dressed.

I watched her.

She was a beautiful piece of ass, no question, and even with those rings in them, the titties were cute as puppy dogs. The way she was looking at me made it clear she was grateful.

I said, "We need to call your father."

"What's your hurry? After a *reward*? There's all kinds of rewards...."

I held her cell phone out to her. "We should call him."

She shrugged and came at me and I found myself backed against the wall, as if she were holding a gun on me. Then her arms were around me and the pretty little mug was looking up at me devilishly.

She had to get up on tiptoes to do it, but she kissed me long and slow and her tongue knew things it shouldn't have at her age.

Then she drew away from me, her arms still around me. "What do you say, hero?"

"Kind of a bad time, isn't it?"

Her eyes flashed. "I think it's exciting."

"I mean...of the month."

That made her laugh. She raised an eyebrow. "Other ports in a storm...?"

"Maybe later," I said, and smiled.

She looked like AIDS-bait to me. I could be reckless, but not that reckless.

Disappointed, she took a step away and accepted the cell phone, and within seconds was saying, "Daddy?...I'm fine, I'm fine...yes!...Daddy, you know that *man* you sent...what?"

She frowned up at me in confusion. "He says...he says he didn't send anybody."

I gestured impatiently for the phone and she gave it to me.

"Good evening, sir. I have your daughter. As you can hear, she's just fine....Get together one hundred thousand dollars in unmarked, non-sequential tens, twenties and fifties, and wait for the next call."

I hung up.

She looked at me with wide eyes and wide-open mouth.

"Relax," I told her. "I'm not going to kill you—just turning a buck."

"You bastard! You *prick!*"

She spit in my face.

I wiped it off with a hand and gave her a look.

She started backing up, her eyes wild, and I got hold of her, carried the squirming creature back to her bed and dumped her there.

I thrust a stern finger in that cute face. "Look! I gotta get some sleep. Pipe down, or I'll duct-tape your little trap."

She behaved after that, though she cried and sniffled and tried to make me feel as sorry for her as she did for herself, which would have been impossible; on the other hand, some of it was genuine—she did have cramps. I cuffed her to the bedpost and she was able to recline. I even covered her up.

Then I went over and curled up on the other bed, nine millimeter in my waistband.

I'd taken some risks tonight.

I lived and worked on this lake, after all. But it was winter, and the bodies wouldn't turn up for a long time, if ever, and the Outfit had used this part of the world to dump its corpses since Capone was just a mean street kid. Very little chance any of this would come back at me. And killing Harry and Louis had, at least, killed my insomnia.

For the first time in a long time...

...I slept like a baby.

Four

The Log Cabin, true to its name, was a log cabin, a roadside gas station and latter-day diner a good hundred miles from Lake Sylvan, a minor intrusion of civilization into a world of snowy pines. At eleven A.M., breakfast was a memory and lunch the future, so the graveled parking lot was home to only a couple of cars and two trucks.

I was keeping watch through binoculars on the slope across the two-lane highway, sheltered and concealed by more of those snowy pines; the ground had only a dusting of snow but the air was brittle with cold. I'd left the ninja-black wardrobe home—in daylight, it would have only made me stand out against the winter whiteness—and was in work boots and jeans and a brown corduroy fleece-lined jacket that were comfortable enough. I'd been keeping tabs on this ransom drop for half an hour already, and it took that long for the girl to speak.

"He won't come himself, you know."

Julie Green was seated like an Indian, leaning back against a big nearby tree, looking utterly bored, an old brown leather jacket of mine loose over her shoulders, her nipples perked under the black hip-hop t-shirt that peeked out, her designer jeans brushed with snow, her handcuffed hands in her lap.

Basically, she looked like a surly high school student waiting outside the principal's office.

"Well, Daddy *should* come," I said, "if he has any use for you. Those were the terms."

She shrugged and smirked. Her teeth chattered now and then. "He doesn't have much use for me. Plus, don't ever forget—he's a lying untrustworthy shit."

I lifted the binoculars again. "Good to know."

A money-green Lexus was pulling in, taking one of half a dozen stalls next to the restaurant. I re-focused the binoculars and watched millions of dollars get out from behind the wheel.

Jonah Green was not exactly a typical patron of the Log Cabin. At least sixty, he had a commanding presence, even from a distance, six foot one and perhaps two-hundred-twenty pounds with only a slight paunch and a close-cropped, almost military haircut that minimized both the gray and the receding hairline. His face was square, including his jaw, and grooved with lessons learned and given.

From my perch I couldn't see his eyes, but they were searching the landscape and, for one unnerving moment, his gaze seemed to linger on me, even though he couldn't be seeing me, not without his own binoculars.

I lowered mine. "Your father."

"No shit!"

"He's early—a good hour."

"So are you."

I raised them. "I'm a lying untrustworthy shit."

"...Good to know."

From a pocket of his topcoat—dark gray and probably Saville Row, unbuttoned and providing a glimpse of a well-tailored gray suit over Italian loafers—he withdrew something. I couldn't tell for sure, but it seemed to be a cell phone.

He spoke into it, briefly.

The object was returned to the topcoat pocket, and Green stood there inhaling deeply and exhaling smoky breath until, within a minute, a second car pulled in, a nondescript number, a brown Taurus.

This gave me a momentary start, because the car was similar if not identical to the rental Harry Something had driven, an automobile I had yet to deal with (it would need disposal, probably in one of the gravel pits intended for Julie, before I came along).

But this turned out to be a coincidence—and how I hate those—when its driver got out, a brawny dip-shit in a brand-new green-and-black hunting jacket and matching flop-ear Elmer Fudd cap. In his early twenties, this ripe specimen had broad shoulders and close-set eyes in an oval face that seemed utterly blank from this distance. I had a hunch a closer look wouldn't fill that oval in much.

The two men began to speak, though Green did most of the talking, gesturing, giving orders. At the start of this one-sided exchange, Green's flunky took off the Fudd cap respectfully, revealing blond hair, cut even shorter than his boss's; he would nod when it seemed appropriate.

I centered on their faces, and I had a good three-quarter angle on Jonah Green, with a decent side view of his boy. Much of what I have done over the years involves surveillance, and while I never studied the art, I'd picked up lip-reading early on.

Green was saying, "Prick'll probably show early. Stay sharp."

"How will I recognize him?"

"Oh, I don't know—maybe because he has my *daughter* with him?"

The subordinate blushed. I'm not lying. He fucking blushed, and shook his head and said, "Right. Right! Sorry. That was dumb. Really dumb."

The millionaire just looked at him, for the longest time, then said, "Form the thought. Examine it. Decide if it's worth sharing. Understand this concept, De-something?"

Green didn't say "De-something," obviously; I just hadn't gotten the name—DeWitt maybe?

Whatever his handle, the Fudd-hatted fool nodded, his eyes lowered, ashamed. "Yes, sir."

Then his disgusted boss, with a dismissive gesture toward his subordinate's brown rental, headed inside the restaurant, and the doofus got in the Taurus and drove it over and parked in the graveled overflow lot, turning the engine off but not emerging.

Keeping watch.

I lowered the binoculars again. "Your daddy's not alone—young guy. Blond. Body builder."

"That would be DeWayne."

"DeWayne."

She shrugged, not giving a shit. "He was some kind of…I don't know, super soldier."

I looked at her. "Really."

She shrugged again. "Cleans things up for Daddy, these days."

"…Too young for Desert Storm."

"Iraq."

That made me smile, and she said, "What's so funny?"

"Nothing," I said.

An hour went by, during which the girl said she had to pee, twice, and I ignored it the first time and the second time said, "Hold it. You can use the restaurant's john."

"*When?*" Her teeth were chattering again. "How

much longer are you going to keep my daddy waiting like this?"

"Not much."

I'd spotted Green in a window, seated in a booth within the restaurant, and right now he and DeWayne were having a cell phone conversation, a little heated on Green's part. No lip-reading was possible, but I got the gist—*where the fuck was I?*

I put the binoculars in my left jacket pocket, and stuck my right hand in the other pocket for the nine millimeter which I then stuffed in my waistband, and said to her, "Time for Daddy and pissing," and she said, "Aren't I the lucky one," and I hauled her up off the snowy ground by the elbow.

"What's the plan?" she asked, as I led her through the woods.

But I didn't answer her till we'd crossed the highway, a good half-mile down from the Log Cabin, when we were in the wooded area, heading back around behind the restaurant.

"The plan," I said, "is you behave yourself and I don't kill your pretty ass."

"I didn't know you cared."

When we entered through the kitchen, the girl's handcuffed hands were still under my draped-over loaner jacket, and I had to give her credit, she didn't cause any trouble or indicate anything was wrong.

The short-order cook, an olive-skinned guy who

might have been Greek or Turkish or some shit, didn't understand English; but he got the drift of a ten-spot quick enough, and—when I gestured toward the dining area—let us pass without incident.

We stopped at the ladies' room ("Setters")—a single seater, but there was room enough in there for both of us.

"What are you—kinky?" she asked, as she undid her jeans.

"No," I said. "Careful."

She sat. "You *could* turn your back."

"Girls with nipple rings don't get to be shy and retiring."

"Fuck you," she said over the noise she was making.

"I already passed—remember?"

She smirked, wiped herself, stood, pulled up her drawers; her pussy was shaved, and I caught a glint of another ring down there—why was I not surprised?

But punkette or not, she took time to wash her hands, dainty little thing that she was. I gave her plenty of room, not caring to have her toss soapy water in my eyes.

As we emerged, a middle-aged woman in a kitty sweater was waiting and she gave us a look.

"You don't want to know," I advised her, and she seemed to agree, slipping inside the little ladies room. The gulf between shaved pussy and kitty sweaters is a wide one.

The folksy, hunting-themed restaurant had filled up some, farmers, truck drivers, assorted locals—half the booths taken, most of the stools at the counter, too.

Sticking out like a well-tailored sore thumb, Jonah Green—still in his Saville Row topcoat in his window booth—half-rose when he spotted us coming from behind the counter toward him. He glanced ever so slightly, frowningly, toward the window—out where DeWayne was sitting guard, not missing anything, remember?—and Julie and I slid in opposite him.

"Mr. Green," I said, with a nod.

He formed a tiny sneer large with contempt; his eyes, like his car, were money color. "And what shall I call you? Besides forty-two fucking minutes late."

"Quarry."

"What kind of name is that?"

"A false one." I glanced at Julie. "You seem overjoyed to see your daughter, alive and well."

Prompted, he leaned forward and sent his eyes to her. "Are you all right, Julie?"

"Fuck you," she said.

Her list of responses was limited, but got the job done.

Her father sighed and looked at me as if seeking support or sympathy or something the fuck he wasn't going to get.

He asked, "Do you have any children, Mr. Quarry?"

"Besides your daughter? No."

He shook his head. "I fly through the goddamn night in a goddamn private jet to deliver this goddamn money, and *this*…"

"Mr. Green," I interrupted tightly. "Some discretion, please?"

"…is the *thanks* I get. The appreciation." Another sigh, a world-weary shrug. "But that's the modern world, isn't it, Mr. Quarry? Values. They're nonexistent these days, aren't they?"

I shifted in the booth. "You really don't want to stall me, Mr. Green. Your daughter will tell you how little compunction I have about making people who annoy me go away."

He studied me for perhaps five seconds—it seemed longer; and he smiled a little, as he did, which would have been unnerving if I impressed easily.

"An intelligent man," Green said softly. "Possibly educated."

"Flattery is probably not the approach you want to take, Mr. Green."

"…How did you happen to, uh…intercept my daughter from those people?"

I shook my head. "That information is not included in the purchase price—shall we get on with business?"

His eyes tightened and he nodded. "Yes. Why don't we?…And let me assure you, sir, that's how I view this transaction—strictly business."

Julie said, "Jesus Christ—now I'm a transaction. Can I get some fucking apple pie or something?"

Her long-suffering parent closed his eyes.

"Charm school didn't take?" I asked him.

The millionaire flagged down a waitress, and said, "Apple pie for my daughter, please. And coffee. She likes it black."

The waitress, a redhead who'd been beautiful fifteen years ago, scribbled, then looked at me over her pad. "Anything for you, honey?"

"No. Thanks."

She disappeared.

Julie was sitting forward and grinning nastily at her old man. "Wow—I'm blown the fuck away!" Then she looked at me. "Son of a bitch knows how I like my *coffee!*" And back at him: "How old am I, Jonah? What's my *boyfriend's* name?"

Her father gave her an expression as blank as brick. "You don't *have* a boyfriend, not since I paid Martin Luther Van Dross to take a hike. He loved you a whole ten grand worth, angel. So, yes, I *know* you like it black."

"You bastard," she said, and her eyes were tearing. "You heartless fucking bastard...."

I said, "This is touching, and would make great reality TV; but if you two don't mind—business?"

Julie glared out the window.

Green shifted his weight, his eyes unblinking but

not exactly cold as they settled on me. "I just want you to know, Mr. Quarry, that there will be no efforts made against you. Not with the law, not privately— and a man with my resources could easily do that, either way. But you saved my daughter's life…and I value that. I do value that."

Julie's jaw tightened but her eyes didn't leave the window.

"Swell," I said. "I value money. Where is it?"

Green lifted an eyebrow, offered up a half-smile that was wholly conspiratorial. "If you'll reach under the table…I trust you prefer that I not reach under there myself…you will find a briefcase."

My left hand found it easily. I hauled the brown-leather attache up beside me, near the aisle, away from the girl.

I said, "I'd be annoyed if this contained pepper spray or dye or some such shit."

"I'm sure you would be," Green said, reasonably. "But you'll find it's all there—just as you asked.…" He lowered his voice to a whisper. "Small bills. Unmarked."

"Is this case locked?"

"No."

"Well, your daughter's handcuffs are," I said, a foot in the aisle. "I'm going to the men's room to count this. I'll be back with the cuff key."

Julie, eyes finally leaving the window, chimed in:

"Good. That way I won't have to stick my face in my pie....Mr. Quarry here *loves* it when I talk dirty, Daddy."

Green ignored her, saying to me, "You really trust me, trust *us*, to be here when you get back?"

All sarcasm and attitude gone, serious as a heart attack, Julie leaned forward and gave her father the following advice: "Don't *fuck* with this guy, Daddy...."

The magnate lost his cool momentarily: "Why— didn't *you*?"

Her upper lip peeled back over teeth as white as they were feral: "No...but not for lack of trying."

Green heaved his largest sigh yet, gathered his dignity and said to me, "You'll have to forgive our little family bickering, Mr. Quarry, but—"

"If this isn't money," I told him, hefting the brief-case, already half out of the booth, "I'll find you in hell."

Green summoned another half-smile but his eyes were narrow. "Isn't that a little melodramatic, coming from you, Mr. Quarry?"

"Yeah," I admitted. "But from what I see, melo-drama is what you people understand....If you'll excuse me."

I could feel the millionaire's eyes on my back as I headed to the men's room, passing the redheaded waitress bearing Julie's pie and coffee as I did.

And before I took the turn toward the restrooms, I could hear the handcuffed girl blurt, "Ah shit," behind me. Maybe she'd have to stick her face in that pie, after all.

The men's room ("Pointers") was another small single-stool affair, but I knew that. I was not a regular here by any means, having only stopped at the Log Cabin twice since coming to the area; but I remembered the window, and the briefcase and I went out it.

DeWayne was behind the wheel, keeping loyal if pointless watch when I slipped in on the passenger side, the briefcase handle in my left hand and the nine millimeter in my right.

The gun was low, in my lap, as I pointed it up at the oval, unformed face.

His eyes were light blue and wide as hell when he looked at me, and then down into the dark unfathomable eye of the automatic's snout.

"Fuck a duck," he said.

His voice was on the high side, about a second tenor; but at least he didn't squeak.

I asked him, "Are you going to make me kill you, DeWayne?"

His eyelashes, which were long and oddly feminine, fluttered. "No. Hell no!"

He put his hands up, shoulder high.

"Put those down," I told him.

He did.

He seemed a little hurt—here he'd been trying to cooperate and voluntarily raised his hands, and all he got for it was a sharp rebuke. It's a tough world, DeWayne.

I gestured with the nine. "Now put your weapon and your cell phone, pager, keys, anything in your pockets, on the seat here between us."

DeWayne carried that out—his gun was a glock—and he was about done when I asked, "What branch?"

He frowned, parsing that, then said, "Marines."

That got a dry chuckle out of me. "Semper fi, Mac."

This caused DeWayne to brighten with hope. "You, too…? Where'd you serve?"

"In a real war….Now get out and open the trunk."

He swallowed, nodded, and within seconds he was crawling up inside the Taurus trunk, a big ungainly fetus making a tight fit. The overflow lot was empty, except for us, and the windows on this end of the restaurant were vacant. So we were cool.

His expression was pitiful when he said, "Thanks."

"What for?"

"Not…not killing me."

"It's early yet," I said.

And slammed the trunk shut.

Super soldier.

Jonah Green's face was in his booth's window when I pulled out casually in DeWayne's rental vehicle. Julie Green's face was in the window, too. She was laughing her ass off.

"Goddamnit!" her father yelled.

Didn't take a seasoned lip-reader to make that out.

Five

And that should have been the end of it.

I'd left DeWayne in the trunk of his rental at the rest stop where my Jag waited. The kid's glock and belongings I left in the front seat—no call to take them and, anyway, I'm not a fucking thief.

I'd cleaned up after myself, disposing of Harry's brown Taurus in the gravel pit, and doing further clean-up at the cottage, and put the money in a safe deposit box at Brainerd.

Rationalization is a seductive bitch, and I'd pretty much convinced myself that if Harry and Louis turned into floaters on that lake after the thaw, their mob credentials would get the killings written off as Chicago fun and games.

Almost a month had passed when, on an afternoon so overcast that the northwoods were more blue and gray than green and brown, I was lounging in the hot tub in the barnwood-sided building that housed my personal off-season sauna and swimming pool. The world outside was cold as fuck, but my indoors universe was pleasantly muggy, the jet streams working on that chronic low back of mine like Spanish dancers minus the castanets.

I didn't even have trunks on. Since I was the sole winter resident of Sylvan Lodge, except on the two days a week José came around, I would just jog across the private lane to the pool building without even my jacket, and go in and strip down and swim a few laps, sauna a while and wind up in the Jacuzzi. I liked the free feeling, but in retrospect, bare-ass was vulnerable.

And vulnerable is not a condition I like to put myself in.

I was nursing a can of Diet Coke, the tub's jets feeling just fine, and the events of less than a month ago were nowhere in my mind. Even over the hot tub burble, I heard the sound of the glass doors opening—this was *not* one of José's days—and my hand drifted toward my folded towel, under which was the nine millimeter.

Bare-ass is one thing; unarmed something else again....

Jonah Green appeared to be alone.

I could see another Lexus parked out front—this one sky-blue—and no driver was apparent. The millionaire was in a jogging suit the color of his name with running shoes and no jacket or topcoat, despite the cold; and his face was red with the weather because of it.

My first instinct was, he wanted me to know (or anyway think) he was not armed.

Very tentatively, he stood there with a glass door slid open, halfway in, and—with a deference I didn't figure was usual coming from this man—asked, "May I come in?"

I just looked at him.

When he didn't get permission, he came in just the same, closing the door behind him, and was god-damn lucky he wasn't dead by the time he turned and said, "Don't get your balls in an uproar, Mr. Quarry— I'm alone."

Deference hadn't worked, so he'd gone straight to hard-nosed.

He was moving cautiously my way, saying, "And if you kill me, you won't know how I found you."

I said nothing.

He nodded, as if I'd actually answered, then came over and pulled up a metal deck chair and sat at the edge of the Jacuzzi, nearby but not getting in my space.

"Don't worry," he said, patting the steamy air. His expression was soft, the grooves in his face at ease; but the money-color eyes were hard. "I didn't waste my resources finding you to get...*even*, or some idi-otic bullshit."

I said nothing.

Sitting forward slightly in the chair, Green said, "Before you kill me—strangle me with that towel or whatever, I would—"

I showed him the nine millimeter from under the towel.

"There's an elegant expression," he said with admirable cool. "'Don't shit where you eat'....You live here, you manage this place, you have a *life*... why risk that with a death?...Hear me out."

I said nothing, but I lowered the gun a fraction.

He put his hands on his chest. "I really do appreciate what you did for me, and my daughter. I'm well aware that those mob fagellehs would've killed the little smartass."

I said, "Our business is over."

He shrugged, a tiny smile forming, pleased he'd finally drawn me out into at least speaking. "Our *old* business is over, Mr. Quarry—I really do admire your resourcefulness, your abilities. Take DeWayne, for example."

"No thanks."

He shrugged in an admission of his subordinate's imperfection. "DeWayne isn't brilliant, but he's dangerous. You handled him as if he were a helpless child."

"A couple thousand DeWaynes have died in Iraq."

The millionaire sighed, nodded, slumping in his metal chair. He shook his head. "And a goddamned shame."

I shrugged with one shoulder. "We spilled more than that."

Picking up on my attitude, and instantly getting over his sorrow for the lost lives in Iraq, Jonah Green said, "I'm sure you did. Which is why I won't make the mistake of sending a boy to do a man's work again....I've asked around about you, Mr. Quarry. By the way, is that a first name or a last name?"

"Probably."

That stopped him for a beat, then he moved on briskly, almost cheerfully. "At any rate, I did some asking around....I do business in all kinds of circles, you know."

"You talk in circles, too. What do you want, Mr. Green?"

He semi-ignored that question. "Seems there's a certain freelance assassin who dropped out of sight, a few years ago. He had a reputation as the best man in a tough game, sort of a killer's killer. He wasn't mob, although sometimes he did jobs for—"

"I'm impressed you found me. Trouble is, now I have to move."

I raised the gun.

Finally he got it, or maybe my raising the nine just let out the nervousness that had been inside him all along. His hands flew up, as if this were a stick-up.

He was half a second away from dead when he blurted, "I want you to do a job for me! Another job!"

My finger froze on the trigger.

This was a lot of money seated near me, begging me to let him give me some. I'm not a greedy man; but I'm not a monk, either.

I said, "I'm retired."

He knew he'd made a dent and something lively came into the green eyes. "That would've been just before the stock market went to shit, wouldn't it? How are your investments doing, Mr. Quarry? Did you get out before the dotcom bust?"

"I'm comfortable," I said, which was funny in a way, because I was naked in a hot tub, so of course I was comfortable. On the other hand, I was holding a nine millimeter, thinking about killing this prick; so that part wasn't so comfortable.

"So comfortable," he said, unintentionally mirroring my thoughts in an openly Faustian manner, "that you wouldn't come out of retirement for a quarter of a million dollars?"

Again I lowered the gun a hair. "...It's not a political job, is it?"

"No! No, no, no."

I sighed again, this time for my own benefit. "One last job is always a bad idea. Guys die trying to retire on one last job all the time."

"But you are not just *any* guy, are you, Mr. Quarry?" He smiled; he had the same white feral teeth as his daughter, only his might have been false. The teeth part. The feral was real.

"No," I admitted, "I'm not. What makes it worth a quarter mil?"

He answered with another question: "Do you have any reservations about taking out a woman?"

"I take women out all the time."

"Not the way *I* mean."

I smiled just a little. "Are you sure?"

We sat in my kitchen.

Jonah Green already knew the lay of my land, so there was no harm in taking him across the road to the A-frame cottage...no further harm, anyway. Plus, I was tired of negotiating with my dick hanging out. Water's a bad place to hold a serious conversation, at least your half of it; the other guy can always make his point by kicking something electrical in—I know, because I've been that guy.

So now we were both dressed. The Mr. Coffee was on, and we were exploring the job. The only step remaining was me deciding to do the thing or not—the money required no further discussion.

A captain of industry through and through, Jonah Green had a folder of information, including half a dozen photos. The woman in the photos—all candid, surveillance-type—was in her early thirties, attractive but not making the most of it, her hair up, with reading glasses on in some of the shots.

She did not look like a likely contract-murder

victim, but you never know. Karen Silkwood didn't look like much, either (no, I didn't do that one).

He was handing me across several information-crammed sheets. "Here's everything you need to know about the woman—work and home addresses, personal habits and friends, everything."

I glanced up at him. "Time frame?"

Green blinked. "Say again? I don't follow."

"You need her dead—I get that. *When* do you need her dead?"

He sat forward; for the first time the talk took on a truly conspiratorial feel. "In two months, her being alive is...a bad thing for me." He sighed, and something that might have been regret, real or feigned, came into his expression and his voice. "Understand, Mr. Quarry, she didn't do anything to deserve—"

I cut him off with a traffic-cop palm. "Mr. Green...you're a powerful guy. You've decided you need her dead. That means she's already dead."

His forehead and eyes tightened. "I...now I really don't follow...."

Tossing the pictures on the table, I said, "She's already dead—she just doesn't know it yet. My doing the job is...a detail."

That made the millionaire slightly ill at ease, and he said, maybe for his own peace of mind, "Well, it's strictly a matter of business—nothing personal. She's a nice woman, I'm sure—"

"Nice women," I interrupted, "don't make them-selves the targets of men like you, who aren't nice."

Blood drained from his face, but he said nothing. Hard to get indignant when the guy you're hiring to kill somebody points out that you're not Mr. Wonderful.

I gestured with the information sheets.

"This stuff is fine," I said. "But understand, Mr. Green, I have to watch her a while, anyway. A few days, at least."

He frowned, shaking his head, pointing to the info sheets. "But...I've got all her patterns recorded, already...library...apartment...."

"How old is the information? A P.I. gathered this. When?"

The frown deepened into irritation, as if I had questioned his professionalism. "I tell you, it's fresh!"

"*How* fresh?"

Now he sounded defensive, and did a Rodney Dangerfield tug of his jogging-suit collar. "A month, six weeks at the outside."

I shook my head. "I have to watch her a while. Patterns change. Shift." I sat forward. "Mr. Green, the elimination side is only part of the process—it starts with surveillance. Otherwise the cops find me. And if they find me, they find you."

In the old days, the guy hiring me wouldn't have

been sitting across from me; it would have been the Broker or someone like him.

Jonah Green let out a sigh worthy of a Christian martyr. "Fine." His eyebrows rose and he shook a finger. "But *two months*, and she's a problem, Mr. Quarry."

"I heard that the first time."

He tasted the inside of his mouth and didn't seem to like it much. "There's, uh…one other thing. It's a part of why your fee is so generous."

"Let's hear it."

"It's…well, it's got to be an accident."

I didn't like the sound of that. "Say again?"

He gestured with both hands, obviously finding it distasteful to have to discuss this. "You know…slip and fall in the tub, brakes go out, hell, *I* don't know… that's *your* department!"

I looked at him for a while.

He was getting uneasy by the time I said, "I don't usually do 'accidents.'ž"

Irritably, he said, "For a quarter mil, make an exception—you mind if I smoke?"

"Take it outside."

Dusk had settled on us as we stood on the deck, looking out on Sylvan Lake's still frozen expanse; you couldn't see Harry and Louis's hole at all from here.

The millionaire leaned on the deck rail, gazing out

at the stark, serene landscape, his plumes of breath alternating with exhales of tobacco smoke. I was standing there, arms folded, looking at my prospective employer, wondering if I should take the job or go out there and drop another one in that hole.

"Beautiful," Green said, shaking his head admiringly. "Beautiful goddamn country, up here. I can see why you like it."

"I'll be moving on soon," I said. "You could probably buy this cottage from the guy who owns the lodge."

Green flicked his gaze my way.

I continued: "Of course, if you do move in, for a summer home? Every time you look out at this lovely lake, you'll be looking at those numbnuts who grabbed your kid."

He wasn't studying the lake, anymore; his eyes were on me. "Why moving on?"

"You know where I live, Mr. Green." I shrugged and smiled. "Even if I *do* do this job, I'm out of here."

Eyes narrowed to slits, Green said, "You don't need to do that, Mr. Quarry. I swear to you I was discreet about finding you. I used a number of people, and no single investigator was—"

"Sure. Fine."

Green sighed. "*Will* you do the job?"

I nodded.

Relief flooded his features. "How do I make my payment?"

"I'll give you the offshore banking info. When $125K hits the account, I go to work. When I deliver, put the rest in."

Green frowned. "You trust me to do that?"

"Sure." I grinned at him. "I'm kinda my own collection agency."

He didn't allow himself to be frightened by that; instead he again stared out at the hauntingly beautiful lake.

For the first time, I heard a genuine melancholy in the mogul's voice. "She's...she's *already* dead."

I nodded. "It just hasn't made the obits yet.... Coffee?"

Six

The Homewood Library seemed modern to me, but only because of my age—it dated to the '70s and you walked into a big high-ceilinged area with wide steps leading up to a surrounding second floor that was like a landing that got out of hand.

The place was all cheerful oranges and greens and yellows, dotted with oppressively cheerful posters encouraging reading and featuring lots of Asian and black faces, though everybody I saw in there was white. What had once been open and spacious was now a little cluttered, with an area obviously intended for seating given over to portable bookcases of NEW RELEASES and AUDIOS, and various computer stations.

It didn't remind me much of the austere church-like libraries of my youth—hardwood floors and institutional green walls and endless shelves of anonymous dustjacket-less books overseen by cold-eyed old-maid librarians with their hair in gray buns and their bodies in gray dresses that a nun would've considered needlessly unflattering.

And Janet Wright didn't remind me of those old-maid librarians, either, though her white blouse and black skirt were a little stark, at that. Her dark blonde hair was pinned up (though not in a bun), attractive stray curls of it struggling free to give her heart-shaped face unbidden decorative touches. Her reading glasses were wireframe and merely serviceable, like the touches of lipstick and eyeliner that appeared to be her only makeup. She seemed to have a nice shape, too, though her wardrobe played it down.

But there was no getting away from that nice, creamy complexion and eyes so brown they almost looked black from a distance, and she had a very nice smile that she flashed generously at the grade-school kids—third-graders?—who were sitting on the floor in the Children's Section staring up adoringly at her, lost in the story she was reading...a book called *The Glass Doorknob*, something or other about a sock monkey.

I was impressed—not one of these kids was fidgeting or squirming or looking to need their Ritalin dosage, even if their laughter did seem unnecessarily shrill. Of course, eight kids who were spending their Friday after-school time at the library probably weren't the type to be fussy; plus, the six girls probably wanted to be Janet Wright when they grew up, and the two boys probably wanted to marry her when they did (although right now they had no idea why).

As she sat in the chair, her audience gathered

around like little Indians, it was obvious she related well to the tykes, stopping to ask them questions, involving them, really looking at them and even listening to their answers.

Already I understood what Jonah Green had meant about this woman not deserving what I was here to do to her. Nobody looking at her would have guessed a contract kill would be her fate. On the other hand, nobody looking at me would have guessed I was stalking my prey—in jeans, running shoes, brown sweater, lighter brown shirt-with-collar, I might have been a teacher or writer, the kind of rumpled jerk who browses endlessly at Borders and never buys a goddamn thing, then complains that book sales are down because the world has gone illiterate.

Right now I was fucking around in the War Section, flipping through books on Vietnam written by idiots who hadn't been there. And, by the way, if you ever have a question about where any specific subjects can be found in the stacks of the Homewood Library, from gardening to the Holocaust, I'm your guy.

She'd been easy enough to spot—from the handful of pictures Green had given me, plus when I came in she was sitting at the HELP DESK with her name on a nameplate in front of her. It didn't take Sherlock Holmes or Miss Marple to make her.

She also worked the front desk, during lunch hour, checking out books, pleasant, friendly, helpful to various library patrons, clearly good at what she did and happy doing it.

I kept browsing, "reading" magazines and books while I kept up my surveillance, lately keeping track of Janet Wright interacting with these laughing children. It was the kind of thing that would give you a warm feeling if you weren't here to kill her.

After the kids scampered off to their suppers, Janet returned to the help desk where she was doing paperwork when a narrow-faced, conventionally handsome guy approached her, a thirty-something would-be Yuppie with a tan, perfect hair, a pale yellow shirt with an alligator on it and jeans that were too new-looking.

I was nearby, pretty much directly behind my subject, going through old bound volumes of *Life* magazine from the '40s and '50s, stopping at the surprisingly frequent shots of starlets in bathing suits.

A conversation started up between my librarian and the Yuppie, for which lip-reading would not have been a necessary step—in fact, the obnoxious Yuppie made it hard not to overhear. Apparently this whole quiet-it's-a-library concept was foreign to him.

He flicked the HELP DESK sign and said, with a grin that told me he appreciated his own wit, "*I* could use some help."

The librarian I could barely make out, and her back was to me.

But I think she said, "Rick—please. Not here."

He leaned a palm against the edge of the desk and his smile was a white slash in the too-tanned face.

"Come on—you're not still *mad*...."

She said nothing, her head down. She was doing paperwork, or pretending to.

The smile disappeared and he leaned in, his expression approximating humility. "Baby. Come on. I didn't mean anything by it."

On her response, I heard her just fine: she wasn't talking any louder, but the words were crisp and clear.

"Next time," she said, looking right up at him, "I'll call nine-one-one. I swear I will."

He drew back; shrugged. "Hey. You pissed me off. Deal with it."

She slammed a book shut.

"I *am* dealing with it," she said.

"Baby..."

"You had no right—no right."

And now she looked back down at her work.

"It's over, Rick," she said. "Don't make me call security."

He leaned in again, got another smile going, though it bordered on a sneer. "Why—you want another scene?" He laughed and it sounded forced. "Sometimes I think you *like* scenes."

She said nothing. Did not look up at him.

He turned to go, but had only moved a step when he looked back and said, "Hey—pick you up. Usual time."

"No. No!"

"Meet you, then."

He shot her a goodbye with a gun of thumb-and-forefinger, and sauntered off, cocky as hell. She didn't bother to reply.

Pity—seems like nobody ever hires you to kill a prick like that.

Another librarian, a busty, almost plump woman also in her early thirties, moved in and pulled up a chair-on-wheels from somewhere and sat behind the desk with Janet. The second librarian had on a bright pink blouse and darker pink slacks; her hair was very blonde and big and sprayed, and her makeup was loud. Fuckable, though.

"Janet," she was saying, making no attempt to keep her voice down, "you have *got* to do something about that *creep!*"

Janet shrugged. "I told him it's over, Connie. I told him just now."

"Do you think he *heard* you? You think he ever really listens to *anything* you say? Listen to me, sweetie. He is going to *really* hurt you, next time."

Janet, who had swiveled on her own wheeled chair, to face her colleague, sighed and shook her head. "Maybe....maybe he's right. Maybe it was my fault."

"*Your* fault?"

She was shaking her head. "I shouldn't've made him mad. I mean, I knew about his temper. When you touch a hot stove and get burned, you can't blame the—"

Connie put her hand over Janet's mouth and leaned in closer.

"Talk like that," she said, "and *I'll* send you to the emergency room."

Then Connie withdrew her hand from Janet's mouth and cupped her friend's chin with that same hand and leaned in close. I had to lip-read now, but I got it. Probably I'd have got it just from the busty one's compassionate expression and the other's chagrined one.

"Do you hear what I'm saying, Janet?"

"I do. I do. I'm not seeing him anymore."

"And if he hurts you—the police?"

A laugh that wasn't a laugh. "What good would that do, in this town?"

Connie's features were stone. "They have to write it up. And you can see a lawyer if you need to. There are ways to deal with jerks like Rick."

She was right about that.

Connie said, "Word to the wise," and shook a

mildly scolding finger, got up, and moved away, guiding the wheeled chair back to wherever the hell she got it.

A few moments later, Janet left the help desk and I followed her, a half room of shelved books between us, me seeing her flickeringly as I moved along, strobe style. Or maybe I was just getting punchy spending all this time around so many books.

Finally she stopped at a water fountain.

Nervously, she put something in her mouth— a pill?

She bent at the fountain and, when she pressed the handle to create an arc of water, her sleeve rode up a little, and revealed part of a purple bruise.

I shook my head.

Rick might have been somehow important or connected in this town (as the busty librarian had indicated), but that didn't make him any less a brutal dunce. Takes a lot of awful people to make up this old world.

From another conversation Janet and Connie had, I got the drift that my target's work day was drawing to a close, so I gathered my jacket from a chair at a reading table and headed outside into the cold, clean—if thin—mountain air.

Homewood reminded me a little of Boulder, Colorado, minus the heavy tourism. Thirty thousand or so had the privilege of living in this idyllic little burg, where mountains edged a sky so blue, clouds should've paid rent for the privilege. I felt lucky to have a contract take me to such pleasant if dull surroundings; it helped make up for having to kill somebody as harmless as Janet Wright seemed to be.

Dusk was settling when Janet emerged from the library with her friend Connie and another librarian, whose name was Don, my surveillance had gathered. A nerd.

From my rental vehicle—a blue Taurus (was that all these fucking rental agencies had these days?)—I watched as the librarians paused to chat and then go their separate ways.

Janet's vehicle was parked on the street—I'd observed her going out and feeding the meter every two hours, during the six I spent in the library. She got into the little yellow Geo, mid-'90s vintage, started it up and pulled away, moving right across my line of vision.

Her rear bumper had stickers that I could have predicted—she was still advertising KERRY/EDWARDS 2004, among other lost leftist causes—and started my own car and took off after her, in slow pursuit.

I followed her, usually with a few cars between us, through sleepy Homewood, from the downtown and on through a quietly affluent residential section; it was the kind of place Norman Rockwell could have painted, though had he spent much more than an afternoon here, he might have hanged himself out of boredom.

Soon the town had disappeared, as had my cover traffic, and she was out into the countryside, making my job harder.

Already my point was proven about the staleness of my client's research: Janet Wright was not headed in the direction of her own apartment, the address for which was the first place I'd checked out getting to town. Nor was there anything in the written reports indicating that anything out this way was a regular stop of hers.

When Janet Wright turned down a lane into a deeply wooded area, I almost missed it; then I caught the tail of her Geo between the trees, and drove on. Pulled into a driveway half a mile later, turned around, and followed.

In five minutes, I caught sight of her pulling off the lane into a private drive. Cutting my speed to almost nothing, I waited until she was well out of view, then moved on by, and parked alongside the road, what there was of it. I walked back and slipped into the trees along the private drive; the snow on the ground was minimal, my shoes crunching on leaves and twigs underneath the dusting, and I was in no danger of earning my Inconspicuous Tracker Merit

Badge. But I didn't worry about that—I could see her getting out of her Geo, fiddling for her keys in her purse, clearly oblivious to my presence.

Still, my hand was on the nine millimeter in my jacket pocket. You never knew.

The Geo was parked in front of a secluded, expensive, sprawling home, not quite a mansion but oozing money, modern in the Frank Lloyd Wright manner, a story and a half with lots of wood and stone blending in nicely with the surrounding naturescape.

At the front door, she stooped on the stoop to pick up a newspaper, then gathered mail from the mailbox.

I was closer to the house now, and watched through a side window as she entered, mail and paper bundled in one arm, entering via a key in her other hand, pushing the door open—it was a little stubborn. A security tone kicked in, and a dog began to bark…from the sound of it, a small one, lapdog likely.

Which was good. A pinscher or a pit bull can ruin your day.

Janet went to a touchpad by the door and entered a code. I had an angle through the window that showed me her fingertips doing it, and I committed the numbers to memory, even if I did have to move my lips.

At a table near the door, already piled with rolled-up newspapers and stacked magazines and envelopes, the librarian stood and sorted through the mail, putting individual items into their respective piles. Throughout, two things were a constant: I watched; and the dog barked.

She spoke to one of us, in a loud firm voice: "Just a sec, Poochie! Gimme a sec."

Housesitting, most likely.

Through a kitchen window I watched as she unpenned the small dog—a little black-and-white rat terrier—who danced and yapped and danced and yapped for Janet. She knelt and petted it and it stood on its hind legs and lapped her face and whimpered orgiastically. About thirty seconds of good-girl-good-doggie talk followed. This I did not commit to memory.

I'd missed it, but while she was down there, Janet had attached a small leash to the dog, and when she and the doggie headed toward the back door, near the window I was peeking through, I damn near blew it.

But I got behind a tree in time, and then she was walking the terrier in the expansive, unfenced back yard, being careful not to walk in spots where the pooch had already made a deposit.

Over the next fifteen minutes, I kept watch as the

woman and dog returned inside, and the woman put water and food down for the dog, re-penned it, then went around the house, watering plants.

Housesitting, for sure.

She was in the dining room when she finished the watering, and that's where and when she began unbuttoning her blouse.

I kept watching as the blouse came open and a pinkish excuse for a bra was revealed; then the blouse and bra came off and nice breasts were revealed. Though she was in her thirties, no sag at all was apparent, full almost-C cups with half-dollar-size areolae and nipples that extended perhaps a half inch, soft.

She dropped the blouse and the bra to the floor, casually, and walked back into the kitchen, topless. There she stepped out of her skirt and revealed a half slip, which she also shed, letting me in on one of Victoria's best secrets: lacy-edged pink panties cut high on the hip. Then she stepped out of those, as graceful as a dancer but so much more natural, moving on, leaving the clothes behind, littering lingerie. Her ass didn't sag, either, her back beautifully dimpled above the firm roundness.

I paused for a moment. Shadowing this woman to fill a contract was one thing; but watching her disrobe seemed wrong, somehow.

Still, surveillance was surveillance....

Taking to the trees again, I scurried around the house, tripping on a root but not quite falling, and found my way to the rear of the place, where glass doors looked in on a swimming pool room, fairly elaborate, about two-thirds the size of the similar area back at Sylvan Lodge, and similar faux-rustic.

I positioned myself where I could see her as she entered—she was nude now, and wholly at ease, because how could she know some asshole was watching her, getting a hard-on?

But who could blame my dick for getting stiff? This was a nice-looking woman. No shaved pussy for my librarian, this was a full, old-fashioned bush, maybe trimmed back just a little, dark blonde and a nice contrast to her pale, creamy flesh. She had a classic shape, five foot five with a rib cage providing a nice display area for the perky rack, waist wasping in, hips flaring out. Her legs were a little heavy by today's standards, but fuck today's standards.

This was a woman.

A woman who walked to the deep end and dove in.

Which to witness, I don't mind telling you, was in its way thrilling.

So I watched her swim. I watched her swim for a long time, taking her relaxation at the end of her working day by stroking the water, smoothly graceful, and then on her back, a dreamily sensuous if unintentional performance, and why wouldn't it be?

She was nude, and she was beautiful.

And so I did my job, keeping her under surveillance, and my dick throbbed in my pants. Which is where I left it. I wasn't going to unzip and jerk off or anything.

Jesus.

What kind of guy do you think I am?

Seven

Pushing the southern outskirts of Homewood, Sneaky Pete's was one of those slightly upscale country-western bars where shitkickers were not welcome but young professionals were. In the low-slung brick building's barely lighted parking lot—asphalt not gravel—you'd be more likely to see a Navigator than a Ford F150. Once inside, the music was that painfully homogenized country pop of the Faith Hill and Brooks and Dunn variety; the only saving grace was line dancing having gone out of fashion.

This was just your typical middle-class/upper-middle-class meat market, and a guy in his fifties had to work to look inconspicuous among all these twenty- and thirty-somethings.

It helped that the place was packed—this was Friday night, and lively with laughter, clinking glasses, and the promise of hooking up. Even though I was not a smoker, the notion that a bar like this was A SMOKE-FREE ENVIRONMENT seemed wrong, even wacky. Would entire generations of Americans grow up going out Friday and Saturday nights, not coming home with their bodies and clothing reeking of smoke? Another communal experience lost....

I was not able to sit as near Janet and her friend Connie as I would have liked. They were in a booth to my back, with a cluster of tables between us. But I was facing a bar with a mirrored wall, and my lip-reading skills came in handy.

The conversation I am about to report I admit took some filling in with my imagination, when my vision was blocked by patrons or wait staff, including the bartender (or 'tendress—a good-looking brunette in her mid-twenties in the red-plaid shirt and jeans that all the help wore, though she had her top tied into a Daisy Duke's halter).

And I could actually hear some of Janet and Connie's discourse. The nature of the loud music and yelled conversation made it possible to hone in on them, and pick some of it up.

Janet, in her emerald silk blouse and new jeans, was probably the most conservatively dressed woman in the joint—her blowsy gal pal Connie, for instance, was in a low-cut red sweater, an angora number that would've put a big grin on Ed Wood's face, and jeans camel-toe tight.

They were drinking margaritas—on their second round.

And Connie was saying, more or less, "Honey! You should go after it—*really*."

And Janet shook her head and said, "But you're more qualified, Con. Plus, I can think of three people with more tenure than me!"

"*You're* the qualified one, Jan—*you* have the *degree.*"

A guy stopped alongside Connie, facing Janet; he was angled enough that it made him a tough read, but I got it: "*My* wife won't have to work."

Rick.

Hadn't recognized him at first—there were dozens of Ricks in Sneaky Pete's. But this was a specific Rick, Rick the prick, the abusive boyfriend who had dropped by the library this afternoon, in his ongoing campaign to make this young woman's life miserable.

Slender, taller than I remembered, he wore a brown leather jacket and black jeans, a glimpse of darker brown shirt beneath. A good-looking guy, as vapid sons of bitches go.

Connie said something I didn't catch, but Rick said, "Fuck you very much" to her, and shoved in beside Janet.

He was turning toward her, so I only got part of his face, but figuring out what he was saying wasn't tough—he wasn't exactly Noel Coward.

"Very funny," he said to her.

She didn't look at him, concentrating on her margarita, or pretending to. "What is?"

"Keeping me waiting."

"Is that what I did?"

"I waited my ass off at the Brew for you, for half a fuckin' hour."

Now she looked at him. Her expression was commendably withering. "We weren't meeting. We didn't have anything set up."

He shook his head, peeved. "So you make me go *lookin'* for you? Lotta bars in this town. That any way to act?"

Connie, staring daggers at their uninvited guest, said, "Do you *mind*? We were *talking*."

He leaned toward the big-hair blonde. "Probably *you* were talking....You mind giving us some privacy?"

"Let me see, let me give that a little thought—how about, I don't frickin' *think* so."

Rick's expression turned menacing. "*I* think so."

Connie looked at Janet.

Janet, reluctantly, nodded to her friend.

Disgusted with both of them, Connie got up and left. She hadn't gone two steps when a guy asked her to dance, and they went out onto the floor and bumped loins to Kenny Chesney.

Rick came around to the other side of the booth, to sit across and make eye contact with Janet, who wasn't cooperating.

Leaning halfway over, he said, "I wasn't kidding, you know. About marriage."

Janet's eyes widened and she began to shake her

head. "The last thing I want to do is marry you, Rick."

"That's not what you said, before."

"That was weeks, maybe months ago. That was when…when you were still being…nice."

"I'm always nice to you!"

She just looked at him.

He shrugged. "Well…I'll be nice in the future. How's that sound?"

"Insincere." Now she leaned forward, and worked hard at softening her expression. "Rick—we're over. You must know that. Can't you see? Let's just walk away friends."

Suddenly he was out of the booth and reaching for her, dragging her out of her seat. He said something I didn't quite catch, but along the lines of: "We're gonna talk this out, *now*."

Then he took her roughly by the arm and hauled her through the bar, toward the door. She was protesting, and I didn't have to read her lips to catch what she said—hell, everybody in the place caught what she said: *"Rick! Please! No…no…."*

Half the eyes in Sneaky Pete's were on the unhappy couple; the other half were making a point of not looking, ignoring what I gathered was a familiar scene around town.

The good-looking brunette bartender was bringing me my third beer. She looked toward the door, and said, "Pity. Hope he doesn't hurt that poor kid, again."

I said, "Isn't anybody going to do anything about it?"

She raised an eyebrow. "You see anybody doing anything about it?"

I threw a five-spot on the counter and said, "Drink that last one yourself."

"Anything you say, Daddy..."

When I was exiting onto the parking lot, half a dozen tobacco addicts were coming back in hurriedly, pitching their smokes sparking into the night. They apparently had no desire to be witnesses to what Rick might do to Janet.

Those two were the only ones in the lot, besides myself, and Rick had her cornered against a big blue Navigator, his hand against the metal, her face turned away from his, eyes shut tight.

"Two people," he shouted at her, "who love each other oughta be able to talk to each other! God! Fuck!"

He used his keys to click open the vehicle's door and shoved Janet in the front seat, rider's side. He was about to shut her in when I put a hand on his shoulder.

Rick whirled, and took a few seconds to size me up—I'm not small, but to him I must have looked no threat, just some ancient asshole sticking his nose in.

He brushed my hand off his shoulder. "Go away. Not your business, dude."

I punched him in the throat.

Rick went down on his knees, clutching his neck, trying to breathe, not having much success, gurgling, his face scarlet, his eyes popping.

From the nearby rider's seat of the SUV, door still open, Janet Wright was taking this in with huge eyes...though not as huge as Rick's.

"Excuse me," I told her, and I took Rick by the collar of his leather jacket and dragged him like the sack of garbage he was across the asphalt. Hauled him through some brush and into the surrounding trees. Deposited him in a small clearing.

Finally able to breathe again, Rick had not, however, found his way up off the ground.

Hurt in more ways than one, he managed to squeak, "You...you coulda *killed* me!"

"No," I said. "Next time I'll kill you."

"What the fuck...fuck business is it...of—"

I bitch-slapped the prick.

The sound surprised me—it was as loud in the night as a gunshot, and the woman in the SUV probably heard it, too. I hoped to hell she wasn't like some abused women, her next move running off and getting her poor abuser some help.

Rick was down on his knees, as if praying. If he really was praying, he was keeping it inside his head, because the "dude" wasn't saying anything—just whimpering.

I knelt before him and I locked my eyes onto his face, though his eyes tried to escape.

"Do you believe I'll kill you?" I asked him.

"Yeah…yeah…sure."

But I wasn't convinced he was convinced.

I took the nine millimeter from my jacket pocket.

He drew in a breath, eyes and nostrils flared.

"Open wide," I said.

"Fuck you!" he said.

The epithet gave me the opening I needed, and I inserted the nine's snout.

I asked him again: "Do you believe I'll kill you?"

Rick, all but deep-throating the barrel, nodded, his eyes white all around, something like "yes, yes" emerging from his throat.

"That's too bad," I said. "Because I really didn't want you to."

And I ripped the gun out of Rick's mouth.

Rick's hand clutched his face and blood streamed through his fingers in little red ribbons. As I'd intended, the weapon's gunsight had carved a notch in the roof of his mouth and maybe chipped a tooth.

He was crying now.

"Anything you'd care to say to me?" I asked.

He lowered his hand; his mouth was a bloody mess, his teeth smeared red; one was, in fact, broken.

Good.

When he spoke, it was through bubbling blood.

"I won't go near her," he said. "Won't ever go near her again."

I shrugged. "Don't decide all at once. Sleep on it."

I whacked him with the nine millimeter and he went to sleep even before he collapsed in a pile in the brush.

The nine's snout had a little blood on it, which I wiped off on the kid's newer-than-new jeans, giving them a little character, wondering if Rick would know, when he woke up, how very lucky he'd been.

I put the gun back in my jacket pocket.

When I came out of the brush and trees, the woman I was here to kill was coming toward me. She was moving steadily, though her expression betrayed an uncertainty about whether she should be afraid or not.

I came to a stop.

She did, too, and asked me, "Is…is he all right?"

"No," I said. "He's a sick fuck."

"Well…" She smiled just a little. "I know that, of course. But you didn't…."

"He'll be fine tomorrow. And I don't think he'll bother you again."

"His family….They're important."

I nodded. "Sent him to the best schools, I bet. But he got his most important lesson tonight….I don't care if his father is named Bush—he won't bother you again."

The brown eyes were wide with worry. "Why did you do that? You...you shouldn't have."

I sighed. "I know."

With no urgency, I took her by the arm and walked her toward the bar.

Her sideways look indicated worry had given way to curiosity. "What's your name?"

"Jack," I said. "Jack Ryan."

"Like in the Tom Clancy novels?"

"Yeah, only a little more heroic."

Her eyebrows lifted. "So I see...."

We were in front of Sneaky Pete's now.

"I'm taking off," I said. "You need a ride anywhere?"

"No...thanks. My friend'll take me home."

I frowned and gestured behind me, toward the trees. "Not *that* friend...."

"No! No. My friend Connie."

She was studying me now, and I felt ill at ease, suddenly. Her face told me what she was thinking—how St. George had just saved her from the dragon, but how strange and even frightening her savior was.

Then her eyes tightened and she spoke. "Were you at the library today?"

"Yes," I said. I gave her a little lame one-finger goodbye salute. "....Good night."

I moved hurriedly to my rental vehicle.

And I could feel her eyes on me, getting in the car and behind the wheel, and even with the window up, I could hear Rick's voice: "*Unnggh....oh...Jesus!*"

He had stumbled from the edge of the wooded area, his mouth bloody, looking like he'd fallen down a couple flights of stairs. He sat on the asphalt, on his knees, prayer-like again, shoulders hunkered over, crying.

I could see Janet thinking about it. She even started toward him, then thought better of it, and yelled, "You deserve it, you dick!"

And she went into the bar.

Starting up the car, I smiled, thinking, *Good for you.*

Then I caught my reflection in my rearview mirror and frowned.

I shoved my hand into the steering wheel, furious with myself, muttering, "Fuck you think you're doing...."

Soon I was pulling into the Homewood Motor Court, which had last been remodeled about five years after Bonnie and Clyde stayed there. Inside, sitting on the edge of my bed with the nine millimeter in one hand and a photo in the other.

I was staring at one of the surveillance shots of Janet Wright, a fairly close-up shot in which she looked not bad at all. I thought about a lot of things, including about how Jonah Green's fucking P.I.

reports didn't even mention this Rick character, but I couldn't work up a healthy sense of indignation, since I was the dipshit who had exposed himself to the target. Saved her from harm and worked up a conversation with her.

Nothing good could come from it—and if this thing went to hell, I'd deserve it. That's what you get for being nice.

I put the photo on the nightstand, image side down. The nine millimeter I shoved under the pillow next to me on the double bed—easier to get to than under your own pillow, plus more comfortable.

Naked, I got between the sheets, shut off the light, but I'd be a fucking liar if I said I went to sleep right away. For a long goddamn time I thought about this young woman, and about what a sweetheart she seemed to be, but that she was dead already, just didn't know it yet, and I shouldn't go all soft in the center or anything, just because she had nice knockers and frilly pink panties.

A long goddamn time.

Five minutes, anyway.

Eight

Janet Wright's apartment—judging by the living room, which was all I could see from my vantage point—indicated an interesting woman lived there: funky '30s deco antiques, a big bookcase of hardcovers, a few striking modern art prints on light green plaster walls. This was a second-floor apartment over a beauty shop, in downtown Homewood, in the last business block before residential kicked in.

She slept in till nine-thirty, and by ten was sitting in a blue terrycloth robe on a big comfy-looking chair with her feet in bunny slippers up on a matching footrest (matching the chair, not the bunny slippers), drinking a cup of what I presumed to be coffee, taking her time, watching television absently.

Finally she got up and went into the next room and quickly came back in a state-college sweatshirt and jeans and went out to run a few errands and have breakfast.

I shadowed her.

Nothing happened.

She returned.

So did I.

The rest of the morning into the early afternoon, hair pinned up, she vacuumed and dusted the living room. At times she disappeared, presumably to have lunch and do laundry somewhere, probably her kitchen area—the apartment seemed to be laid out box-car style, how many rooms I couldn't be sure. The double windows gave me a generous view, but only of the living room.

Judging by my similar apartment, directly across the way, hers would have three big rooms, one after the other, back to the alley. Like hers, my apartment indicated someone interesting lived there—the complicated kind of guy whose decor runs to a metal folding chair with a cushioned seat, a crate near the double window serving as a table (my nine millimeter resting there, and sometimes my binoculars) and a cooler on the bare floor, where already several Coke cans, a wadded-up napkin and a sandwich wrapper lurked.

Unlike Janet's building, this one hadn't been renovated yet, or anyway the upper floors hadn't—the lower floor had been half-heartedly redone but a computer store filling the space was out of business. Homewood had one of those funky downtowns getting gradually rehabilitated, and this empty apartment was, as I said, "similar" to hers…in its positioning and layout.

But there were differences. Her apartment, for

example, was not a hellhole unfit for the foodstamp crowd who'd not long ago been consigned here.

My surveillance roost stank of old food and new ratshit, but it was free, and it was safe—some company of Jonah Green's owned the building and had it earmarked for eventual Yuppification. I'd been provided a key to the back door and an assurance that no nightwatchmen would be checking.

The building across the way mirrored this one, had probably been designed by the same architect and built by the same outfit somewhere after the turn of the century—19th century, that is. Fuck, I was old, having to keep track of goddamn centuries....

Anyway, my target had double windows, too, and she kept the shades up and the sheer, decorative white window dressing blocked almost nothing. She didn't worry about privacy, because you couldn't see in from the street, and the apartment across the way was dead.

But, unlike my swimming-pool surveillance yesterday afternoon, this was no peep show. After the morning of vacuuming, she spent the afternoon sorting and folding laundry, again with the TV on, though I extrapolated that, as my view didn't show it. She also read and listened to music, a CD player nestled in among the hardcovers in the big bookcase. Her comfy chair was near the two windows with a phone stand between.

She had a couple calls, one from Connie setting up another evening out, which interrupted the vacuuming, and another while she was reading.

In both instances, through my binoculars, I saw her checking caller I.D. before picking up—possibly avoiding Rick, although I found it extremely unlikely he'd ever call her again.

Still, she answered the afternoon call warily, then brightened. "Well, Sis!…Sure.…No problem.…Well, that's great!.…Cool!…Play it by ear."

Well, that was scintillating.

A dull call in a dull day, but somehow the mundaneness of her existence was getting to me. You shadow some Outfit cocksucker while he's bouncing between guys he's extorting money from and strip clubs where he's getting free blow jobs, you don't exactly brush a tear away when you remove him from the world. You take out some asshole exec who is embezzling from his bosses to maintain his coke habit, you're over it before you reload. You rid the world of a criminal lawyer who is more crim than law, you feel pretty damn good about your line of work.

But what was a nice girl like her doing in a bad place like this?

I had a Coke habit, too, and half a dozen empty cans were littering my feet by nightfall. This old empty apartment did have a working toilet, which was a nice perk, but I'd overdone the caffeine.

When Janet emerged from a street-level door below, between storefronts, I felt damn near jumpy.

She had disappeared from the living room about an hour and a half before, and the door to the street wasn't within my range of vision, so her change of appearance was a surprise. Nice one.

She looked lovely, the dark blonde hair nicely bouncy, brushing the shoulders of her suede jacket which was a darker brown than her slacks but the same color as her high heels. Barely had she stepped onto the sidewalk than a sporty little red Mazda drew up with gal-pal Connie at the wheel.

Janet got in, they took off, and so did I.

I wasn't thrilled when they went back to Sneaky Pete's—one thing a guy in my trade doesn't like to become is a regular at a joint in a town where he's working. The brunette bartendress welcomed me back like old home week, even asked my name now that I was hanging out so often, and I told her Jack. She asked me a few questions as the evening wore on, and I told her jack.

Janet and Connie had chosen another booth, but the bar was a long one and the mirror behind it, too, so I had no problem setting up reflective watch. I nursed a beer, and did my best not to go over to the jukebox and shoot it—surely there was a limit to how much Toby Keith a reasonable person can endure.

Again Janet wore a silk blouse, a cream-color one,

with a strand of June Cleaver pearls. Her buddy Connie was fetchingly slutty (or did I already have my "beer goggles" on?) in a black-leather motorcycle jacket, red rhinestone-studded Marilyn t-shirt, jeans she wouldn't have to remove when she next went to the gynecologist, and colorful cowboy boots.

Janet seemed embarrassed as Connie leaned forward, eyes and teeth gleaming, saying, "Spill! What happened to Rick?"

"I told you last night I didn't want to talk about it...." Now Janet sat forward. "Why, what have you heard?"

Connie's grin was unkind. "He's telling his friends he fell down the stairs."

"So, he, uh, didn't...go to the police or anything?"

Connie's eyebrows hiked. "Oh, now you *have* to tell me!"

Janet shook her head, then froze in mid-shake, and said, "Excuse me, Con..."

"Why? What...?"

And something unnerving happened.

Janet's eyes caught mine in the mirror.

Quickly I looked away, and said something inane to the brunette bartender, who complied by saying something equally inane.

I heard Connie yelling, good-naturedly, "You are definitely *not* excused! Janet—you come back here and dish, or *else!*"

I felt the finger tap my shoulder.

I winced, then swung easily around on the bar stool and glanced at her as casually as I could.

"Oh hi," I said.

"Oh hi?" Her smile went up a little more on one side than the other, creating a nice dimpled effect. "I guess I owe you a drink."

"You don't. Really."

"I do. Really."

The stool next to me was vacant; it would be. She took it. We looked at each other in the mirror again, this time on purpose.

She said, "Why do I think you're checking up on me?"

"Why do you?"

For several long seconds she studied me in the mirror, then she said to my reflection, "Well...I imagined I saw you in a booth at Denny's this morning."

"Some imagination you have."

Her eyes were smiling, too. "*Wasn't* it you?"

"That was me. But I wasn't looking for you."

She raised one eyebrow. "You were just there for that delicious Grand Slam breakfast, right?...And now you're here, Guardian Angel, seeing if Rick's had the good sense to..."

"Take a hint?"

Her smile went up on both sides, this time, and

ushered in some laughter. Shaking her head, she said, "I really do owe you one....Have a drink with us."

I didn't want to join her and Connie, and give the other librarian a closer look at me. But I was cornered. Turning Janet down would have been suspicious. Or so I told myself.

Whatever the case, I was soon sitting on Janet's side of the booth as she and bubbly Connie chitchatted, both of them nicely at ease around me, Janet revealing a new self-confidence.

Connie licked some beer foam from her upper lip and, just the tiniest bit drunk, said, "That little prick Rick? He's been a bully since grade school. But he always gets away with it, 'cause his family has money."

"Fuck him," I said. "His family hasn't given me any money."

They both laughed at my naughty talk.

Making reluctant eye contact with Connie, I joined in on the chitchat. "You're from here?"

"Born and raised, and too dumb and untalented to get out." She smirked at Janet, good-naturedly. "What's *your* excuse?"

Janet shrugged and said, "Destiny. Which is to say, answering an ad."

Connie, suddenly quite serious, locked eyes with me. "This little girl's gonna be head librarian one of these days. Just you wait and see."

"Really," I said, and narrowed my eyes and nodded.

Amused, Janet said, "Don't pretend to be impressed—doesn't suit you....And, so, Jack—what is it *you* do?"

"I'm in sales and service," I said.

Janet, apparently the designated driver, was drinking a Diet Coke. "What kind of sales and service?"

"Veterinary medicine."

"That sounds...interesting."

I smiled a little. "No it doesn't."

Connie, frowning, asked, "Do you sell vets that stuff they use to put animals to sleep?"

"Afraid so," I said.

Connie made a face. "Dirty job but...."

"I'm sure," Janet says, "he sells plenty of things that make the animals feel better."

"I try," I said.

Janet and Connie exchanged looks. Connie's smile at her friend told me I'd passed the test—for at least one night. Saturday at Sneaky Pete's, the options were limited.

Janet gave Connie a glance that I didn't at first understand, until Connie straightened herself, her breasts distorting Marilyn Monroe's image but not in a bad way, and said, "You know...I see a guy over there who's just cute enough to interest me, and drunk enough to think likewise...."

She got up and out of the booth less graceful than a ballet dancer, but more fun to watch.

Janet gave me a sideways look. "Now you'll think that's how I spend my weekends."

"What is?"

"You know. Picking guys up."

I offered half a smile. "Have I been?"

Her hands were draped around the Coke glass like it was the Silver Chalice. "It's just…I never had anybody do anything so…*sweet* for me, before."

"Sweet like pound the piss out of your boyfriend?"

I expected a laugh, but what I got was: "Exactly…. I'm not really the type to, I don't know…hit the bars on a Saturday night."

"I know."

Her eyebrows tensed with curiosity. "You do?"

"Today was your day off, right?"

Mildly surprised, Janet said, "Right."

I shrugged. "You cleaned all morning, did laundry all afternoon, and then you listened to music or maybe read, a while. You fell asleep and were almost late to go out with your girlfriend."

Astonished, she said, "My God—are you psychic?"

"No." I toasted her with my beer glass. "I'm shadowing you."

That got a smile and a laugh out of her. The truth will do that.

She was shaking her head. "I'm just not good at this. The game. The ritual. The small talk's all so…"

"Small," I said.

"I guess....I've always been kind of shy, frankly. A loner."

"Me, I'm a people person."

Another smile. "Oh, yeah, I can see that," she said.

"You often…gravitate toward people like Rick?"

Her smile was gone and a smirk took its place. "Connie says it's low self-esteem. I say it's bait and switch…guys on their best behavior when they meet you, but who aren't really, you know…"

"What they seem?"

Suddenly she sat up, something obviously occurring to her. She checked her watch.

"Shit," she said.

"Was it something I said?"

"No! No, no, there's just....Look, there's something I have to do, something that slipped my mind, I should've done earlier."

"You need a lift somewhere? Your friend seems busy."

Connie was flirting with a guy over by the jukebox, which was having the good if rare sense to play a Patsy Cline song, "Crazy."

Janet was shaking her head, saying, "Well, you see, I'm sort of semi-housesitting…for some friends of mine? Anyway, I need to bring in their mail, and their dog's probably half-starved....Somehow after last night, with Rick, I just…spaced out on it, today."

"I see."

She gave me a look that had some pleading in it. "I don't want to bother Con. Would you mind…driving me out there?"

"Sure," I said, getting out of the booth, and helping her do so, too. "But you'll have to show me the way."

Nine

She was a tad over-dressed, in that silk blouse, for watering the plants, but the plants didn't seem to mind, and I certainly didn't.

I followed her around as dutifully as a dog—she'd already fed the real dog, and put it on a leash and walked it, and I'd kept her company on those chores, too—and we'd already worked through a lot of small talk about the library and her friend Connie and a little bit about Rick, who she actually sort of felt sorry for (I let her get away with that) (for now) and currently she was filling me in on this beautiful house itself, which was as wood and stone inside as out, including a hall fountain that was like water rushing over mountain rocks.

I asked when the place was built, and she said, "In the fifties some time, by my friend's father…my friend, Dave Winters—he owns the office furniture plant, that keeps Homewood going? This is his house now, his and Lisa's….I met Dave at college."

Following her to the next plant, I said, "I thought you weren't a local girl."

"I'm not," she said, taking care not to over-water. She was using a little red watering can from the kitchen. "Dave's on the library board—when my application came in, he recognized the name of course, and helped me get the job. His wife is great, too."

"Lisa," I said.

She frowned at me. "How do you know Lisa?"

"I don't. You mentioned her, before."

"Oh."

And on to the next plant.

"Where are the Winters?"

She flicked me a longing little glance. "Nassau. A little month-long getaway."

"Must be nice."

Sighing, she moved to a corner where a palm-tree-like number waited; from the size of it, this triffid could have walked to the kitchen to get its own goddamn water.

She was saying, "Hard not to envy Lisa and Dave— swimming and sunning and swimming and sunning and eating wonderful food and swimming and sunning some more."

"Wouldn't that suck," I said.

She finished her rounds and I followed her to the kitchen, where she replaced the watering can under the sink. Turning to me with a lilting smile, she asked, "I bet you like to swim. You're a swimmer, aren't you?"

I frowned with my forehead and smiled with my mouth. "What are you, psychic?"

"No." Her smile turned mischievous. "Maybe I've got *you* under surveillance...."

The swimming pool room seemed even larger when you were in there, an echoey cavernous dark-wood space with the lighted swimming pool a blue shimmering centerpiece.

Janet, in a light blue one-piece bathing suit, balanced at the tip of the diving board, bouncing a little, dark-blonde locks flouncing when I came in from the dressing room in a suit two sizes two small for me. Well, it made the package look bigger, anyway, even if it did cut off my circulation. Of course, cutting off the circulation would eventually not do the package any favors, either.

She didn't say anything just grinned and bounced and laughed and bounced and laughed and grinned.

"Glad you're having such a good time," I said.

"Sorry....Dave's not...not a big man."

"Just in business," I said, eyeing the vast chamber. I was standing at the edge of the pool like a guy on a building ledge contemplating suicide. I pointed casually toward her. "That Dave's wife's suit?"

"Yes. Lisa and me, we're about the same size."

"She has a nice figure."

"Lisa thanks you, I'm sure."

With this, she dove in, an admirable, even elegant dive.

Even so, she splashed me some, doing it; but I

didn't mind. The flecks of water were quite warm, really, even inviting.

I dove in.

The pool was as warm as a bath, lulling—actually, I prefer it a little crisper, but this was nice. Very nice.

For a while we swam, doing a few laps together, sometimes underwater or on our backs, and splashed and clowned around, the kind of capering kids get in trouble for from the lifeguard, only there was no lifeguard present. We laughed and teased and talked, enjoying the usual pleasing swimming-chamber hollow effect.

We were treading water, facing each other, when I said, "Nice perk, for semi-housesitting."

"Swimming's the best."

"Oh yeah," I agreed sincerely.

A little out of breath, face droplet-pearled, she could hardly have looked more lovely, even though the long hair was matted down with moisture, the makeup mostly gone from her heart-shaped face, an indicator of just what a striking woman this was.

Paddling there, blinking the big brown eyes, she said, "Nothing quite relaxes you like a nice swim. Really takes you somewhere else."

"Couldn't agree more."

Treading doggedly, maybe a little tired now and having to work at it some, she said, "I mean, I don't envy Dave and Lisa much, but to have this handy, right in your own house? To be able to—de-stress any time you like, and just feel…really *free*…"

"You know," I said, a tiny bit out of breath myself, "you shouldn't swim here by yourself. Dangerous."

She laughed, treading water, more and more an effort. "What? You think I'm gonna dive in and klunk my stupid head?"

I plunge her head under water, my hand gripping the top of her skull and shoving her down, and holding her there; she struggles but can't get any-where, arms and legs flailing with fading force.

Finally, she is limp, dead weight, and I release her, and let her float to the surface, arms spread, reaching for nothing, tendrils of hair spreading like seaweed.

"Hey!" she said, bobbing there. "Aren't you lis-tening? Where did *you* go?"

"Somewhere else," I admitted. "For a second."

"I was just saying, I can fix you something, if you like. Have you eaten?"

Soon we were in the Winters' kitchen, sitting on stools at the counter in our respective robes (hers blue and fitting nice, mine white and, again, two sizes too small, my shoulders straining the seams), eating microwave dinners and drinking Diet Cokes. Nearby, the penned-up dog, although fully fed not forty-five minutes ago, was whining pitifully, as if it hadn't had a meal since summer.

Janet, gnawing a leg of Swanson chicken, said, "Toss her a scrap, why don't you?"

I speared a bite of Salisbury steak. "What, and spoil the bitch?"

"You're evil."

I didn't feel like contradicting her.

We had cleaned up after ourselves, and were standing at the sink like an old married couple when I asked, "What do you have on under that robe?"

Her smile was pixie-ish. "Wouldn't you like to know?...What do you have under yours?"

I opened mine and showed her. It was a good thing I wasn't wearing David's tiny trunks.

"You can get arrested in some states for that," she said, but her eyes were big and pleased.

I opened the front of her robe and saw the creamy skin and lovely breasts and the wonderful Old School muff.

"That's illegal in most states," I said. "Pubic nakedness."

"That's *public* nakedness. And, anyway, this is private."

I slipped the robe off her shoulders and let it slip down her narrow-waisted, full-hipped frame to puddle on the floor at her bare feet.

"Yeah," I said. "Isn't it?"

In the Winters Family Rec Room, I took the time to get a fire going in the big rough-stone fireplace while Janet waited, naked underneath an Indian blanket. Then I joined her and we necked a while, romantically. When I finally kissed her breasts, the nipples were erect, damn near an inch long and hard, so hard. I kissed her neck, she kissed mine. I put my hand between her legs and the moistness there wanted attention. I buried my head down there and licked and sucked; then her head was in my lap and she licked and sucked. Things were getting serious.

"On top of me," she whispered, her face looking up at me half-lidded, mouth open in terrible, exquisite pain. "On top...."

For all the moistness, she was tight—a little hand might have been gripping me down there—and she shuddered and cried in pain and delight as I entered her and slid myself slowly in and out. I cupped the full firm globes of her ass and nuzzled her breasts as she moved her hips in ways she hadn't learned in the library, the inside of her sucking out the inside of me. The blanket had fallen away, and our flesh was reflecting the licking flames, one body with many limbs and so much skin, blushed orange, and after a while her eyes rolled up in her head so that barely anything but white showed as I plunged in and out of her with the blade of flesh.

We hadn't talked about protection—we were just naked and together and the lust ran away with us and

I'd been in her. And now my seed was in her, too. Some detached voice in my head said, *She's already dead, she doesn't need protection....*

Then we were on top of the blanket. The fire had dwindled to a nice comfort level, and we were wrapped up in a post-coital embrace, sleepy, at ease with each other, so much so that we could just laugh as we picked pubic hairs off our respective tongues. My efforts to cough one up off the back of my throat almost made her hysterical.

After while she had quieted down enough to ask, "Were you a soldier?"

"How did you know that? Surveillance?"

Her smile was sweet for a girl who'd just given me a royal fucking. She shook her head. "I just feel it, *know* it, somehow....My grandfather was in Korea. You remind me of him."

"Well, that's made my day."

She laughed and her face crinkled apologetically. "No, no, no, I didn't mean...*that*."

She studied me; touched my face with a finger. Examining me. Like I was an old tree, cut in half, whose rings you could count.

Finally, over the sound of a crackling fireplace, she asked, "Vietnam? Are you that old? You couldn't be that old."

"But I am."

"How is that possible?"

I shrugged. "I was a baby when I went in."

She nodded wisely. "But not when you came out."

"...I was stupid."

Her brow tensed. " 'Stupid,' how?"

I shook my head. "*Real* stupid. Married a girl on leave, in San Diego? When I got home, she was fucking this guy."

"Oh dear," she said, as if reacting to my harsh language, which in part maybe she was. Her fingertips came to her lips, a dainty gesture for a girl who'd had my cock in her mouth not long ago. "I'm so sorry....What did you do?"

I shrugged again. "I went over to talk to him. Just reason with him. He was working under his car."

Her brow tightened further. "What did you do?"

"Kicked the jack out."

She didn't draw away or anything. Didn't even blink. Just asked, "...You got in trouble?"

One more shrug. "I didn't do much time. But I was a kid, and didn't understand."

Nodding, Janet said, "You mean, how your wife could do that to you?"

"I mean, why killing people I didn't know, in some other country, people who didn't deserve it particularly, was cool. But kill one jackass back home who earned it, and I get shit."

Her look of compassion, of sympathy, was so sincere, I could barely stand it.

She said, "I'm so sorry....You don't have to talk about it."

Surprised, I said, "I almost never do."

I had opened up to her as I had my Vietnam pal Gary, who was the only other human about whom that could be said; even my late wife, the second one—the nice, stupid one—I'd never shared it with. *Why the fuck had I tonight?* Couldn't be the little head controlling me, because it was all tuckered out down there.

Or anyway I thought it was.

Because all of a sudden Janet was crawling up on top of me, kissing me on the chest and the neck and then on the face, and the view of her, all that pale flesh, those breasts hanging down so full and beautifully shaped and gently swaying with those long tips sticking out at me accusingly, well, it woke the little head up, all right.

This time, however, having climbed on top, she stayed there. She was ready to take a little control.

And I was ready for somebody to take it.

Ten

Having been up and dressed a while, I was in the kitchen, at the stove scrambling eggs (bacon already made), when she drifted in in the blue terrycloth robe, hair looking nicely tousled.

Sleepily sexy, she paused to lean in the doorway and sniff the cooking smells approvingly.

"Wow," she said. "You're a surprise."

"Coffee's ready," I said.

She made her way over to the counter where the Cuisinart coffee-maker dripped and helped herself to a cup.

The dog was penned up, and—despite the cooking smells—sleeping in its bed.

"What did you do?" she asked, nodding toward the dog, the mug of coffee in both hands, blowing at it a little. "Drug the mutt?"

"No. Just fed it. All it wanted."

She laughed and risked a sip.

"Been walked, too," I said. "But I draw the line at that pooper-scooper crap."

"Even so," she said, "you definitely pass the audition." She settled on a stool at the counter as I served her up eggs and bacon and toasted, buttered English muffins.

"Eggs are *good*," she said.

"Thanks," I said, serving myself, then joining her. "Everybody has to learn *something* from their mother."

We ate a while, then between bites she asked, "How long you been awake?"

I shrugged. "Two, three hours."

She blinked at me; her eyes were puffy—but on her, it looked good. "It's only seven-something now."

"Went for groceries. Had a swim."

She gave me a sideways look. "You really like to swim....Helps you think?"

"Helps me not to think."

We ate in silence for a while, and somehow it became a little awkward or maybe pregnant. Which served me right, not using a rubber last night....

Finally, she pushed her almost-cleaned plate away, and got up and got herself some more coffee and refilled my cup, saying, "I, uh...really don't do this kind of thing."

"Wait on men?"

She laughed a little. "No...you know." She sat next to me again, sipped the coffee, raised an eyebrow. "I mean, I hardly know you. I just don't usually..."

"Kiss on the first date?"

She smiled over the coffee cup's lip. "Kiss on the first date."

I pushed my plate away. Sipped coffee. Said, "I live alone, too."

Her brow tensed. "Sorry. I…I don't follow you."

"Sometimes you just…need something."

She thought about that, and nodded. It was a sort of admission.

"There really haven't been a lot of 'Ricks,' " she said. "Some. But mostly, the last eight, ten years… I've kept to myself."

"Safer that way," I said.

"You, too?"

"…It's the easiest way to get hurt."

"Also the most painful," she said quickly. "When I was younger, I went with older guys…?"

I hiked an eyebrow. "And things have changed?"

"Well, you're the first…'older guy'…in some time. A shrink once told me I have some kind of 'daddy' complex."

I shifted in my seat.

I shrugged. "Every little girl wants to fuck her daddy. And lots of daddies want to fuck their little girls. It only counts against you when you go through with it."

She thought about that, then said, "You…scare me a little."

I gave her half a smile. "Just a little?"

She studied me and something devilish got into her eyes. "You might not be so scary, naked."

"You've seen me naked."

She shook her head. "Oh no, I haven't...."

Soon we were seated on the edge of the pool in our borrowed swimsuits, the place muggy as hell, a virtual steamroom, and she was about to apply a straight razor to my well-lathered beard.

"Be gentle," I said.

"Don't worry," she said, and kept her word, starting to shave me gently, tenderly, sliding, gliding the blade, taking whiskers, leaving smooth flesh. Occasionally she would dip the razor in the pool, getting rid of whiskery lather.

It took a while, my beard not terribly long but full, and it felt good, being the object of such care and attention; but when the blade pressed against my throat, I caught her wrist, stopping her.

For all the heat, we froze, my eyes locked with hers, and I wasn't smiling as I stared at her—she seemed quietly amused, if a bit taken aback by the clutch of my hand.

"What's wrong, Jack?" She seemed wholly serious, but for a pixie gleam in the eyes. "Don't you trust me?"

Now I studied her, tried to look inside—*did she know why I was here?*—and her amusement faded to concern.

I said, "Little tender there. Let me."

"Sure."

She gave me the razor.

As I finished the shave, she sat next to me, slightly shaken, holding her arms to herself as if feeling a sudden chill.

We did not make love again. Janet had to work today—it was Sunday, but the Homewood Library was open from eleven till four—and she needed to go to her apartment to shower and change. I dropped her in front of the beauty shop she lived over, and—before she got out—she said, "I'll never forget last night, Jack."

"Good," I said, and managed to smile.

Her eyes stayed on me a beat too long before she got out of the car. I thought I detected something hurt in the expression, but wasn't sure.

Maybe I decided to take Sunday off. Maybe that was it. But that afternoon, as Janet no doubt did routine work at the library and maybe did her story-hour shtick with another third-grade audience, I wasn't around to see it.

I was in my motel room, feeling bare with my freshly shaved face, on my back on the bed, elbows winged out, staring at the ceiling, lights off, sun filtering in a little through closed drapes. Janet's picture on the nightstand, face down. Nine millimeter on the nightstand.

By late afternoon, with the library closing so early,

she'd be back at her apartment. And somehow I hauled my dead ass off that bed and made it to my surveillance roost across the way from her.

She beat me home. There she was, already, in a bathrobe again (not the blue borrowed one, but a similar green one of her own), sitting in that comfy chair, bunny-slippered tootsies on the footrest, reading a book (*Memoirs of a Geisha*), nibbling a sandwich, sipping at a Diet Coke.

But I was having trouble watching her.

Mostly I just sat there, staring at the blank wall in the rattrap vacant apartment, not even dipping into the cooler for my own sandwich and Coke, not fucking hungry at all. The nine millimeter and the binoculars were on the crate, looking like decorative items as opposed to anything practical a person might actually use.

I did at dusk, at a good distance, follow her Geo to Sneaky Pete's, which was open Sunday nights, where she and Connie met in the parking lot. I drove past, then pulled a U-turn and headed back.

Inside, the place wasn't very busy, the meat-market aspect given over to a modest family night, where pizza was served from a small kitchen that usually only offered up burgers and fries. The same country-pop was playing, but overlaid with the squeal of kiddies, and it occurred to me it might do the Sneaky Pete singles crowd of Friday and Saturday night some good, stopping by here Sunday, just to see what kind of trouble they might be getting themselves into.

Janet and Connie had a booth, both young women dressed not to the nines now, just sweatshirts and jeans; this was about dinner and dishing, Connie pumping Janet for what had happened between her and "that big scary handsome guy."

That was the only thing I picked up, from my position at the bar. I couldn't risk sitting any closer, and I was conspicuous as hell in this family crowd. Even the bartender, not my familiar brunette but a potbellied guy with a mustache, was giving me a hinky look. So unless I wanted to be spotted and invited over to sit with the girls, I had better split.

I split.

Back at the motel, the room was nicely dark, just a little neon sign blush finding its way through the curtains. I deposited the nine on the nightstand and flopped onto the bed, fully clothed, curled up on my side and tried to go to sleep.

But it soon became clear sleep wouldn't come, and before long I found myself seated on the edge of the bed, slumped, hands loosely interlaced.

What were my fucking options?

Piss and poor, with maybe a couple stops in between. This was what I got, allowing myself to be talked out of retirement for "one last job." Fuck!

There are reasons why you quit the killing business, and going soft is one of them, because then it's you getting killed, which is no way to run a business.

They were my Achilles' heel, women. I had no goddamn sense where they were concerned. And it wasn't the fucking, the fucking was great, but a woman—not just any woman, but a woman like, say, Janet—could touch something inside of me that I liked to think had died a long time ago. Something human that could only put a dipshit like me in a jam.

I sat there, brooding, mentally listing the mistakes I'd made, but the list was so long, I got bored—being seen by the target was one thing, eating her pussy was another. That kind of up-close-and-personal contact can lead a guy to making bad calls.

So I could walk away. You can always walk away.

And someone else would kill her, and Jonah Green would, understandably, be miffed with me, and likely send people to kill me, loose end that I would become, people like me but not old and gone-soft ones, and then I'd be dead, too…or at least up to my asshole in dead assholes.

That didn't sound like any fun.

I could go after the guy who hired me. I had full confidence that I could make Jonah Green's death happen; but Green was an important guy, connected enough in Outfit circles to find out about my past, and with the wherewithal to find me at Sylvan Lake in short order. I killed him, who could say what the fuck I'd unleash?

And I'd be dead, and Janet Wright would be dead, too.

That left only one alternative: go ahead and do the job I'd been hired for. There was that little matter of a quarter of a million dollars, the kind of money that meant I'd never have to put myself in a situation like this again.

And if I accepted that Janet Wright was really dead already, just didn't know it yet—a premise I had expressed to Jonah Wright at the outset, a concept I knew to be true when any party had been marked for elimination—perhaps the only humane thing to do under the circumstances was kill her myself.

I could figure out some way that would be quick and painless. If I left her to the devices of some amoral monster who killed people for money, Christ knew *what* shit she would be put through....

I had always taken great pride in my lack of sadism, that I had never taken any sick pleasure or joy out of turning life into death. Mine had been a profession, and like a doctor with a patient or a lawyer with a client, I represented a person with a problem, and I just made that problem go away. Nothing fun about it. Nothing mean about it, either.

Such were my thoughts, threading through my

brain and the motel-room darkness, and I don't honestly remember going to Janet's. In my mind, I'm in the motel room one second, sitting on the bed, trying to figure this shit out, and the next second, I'm at the top of the stairs out on the small landing, staring at her apartment door, with the nine millimeter in one hand and working the doorbell with the other.

She didn't answer.

Well, it was the middle of the night; or rather, really, really early Monday morning....

So I rang it again.

And again.

Finally I could hear her moving in there.

I checked the action on the nine.

The sound of the night latch unlatching prompted me to slip the nine back in my jacket pocket, and then her face, pale and severe without makeup, was visible in the cracked-open door.

She frowned just a little. "...Jack?"

"I have to see you."

She frowned more than just a little. "You know, even *Rick* used to call the day after. Even *Rick* never showed up at three in the morning, demanding—"

"Please?"

She sighed.

She let me in.

Wrapped up in the green robe, which was feminine but not particularly sexy, Janet seemed embarrassed by my intrusion, self-consciously straightening her hair.

"Sit down," she said, leading me into a living room that I'd never been in before, though was entirely familiar with. "Give me a minute...freshen up." She turned toward me, not mad at all, now. "You want coffee or something? Jesus, what time *is* it?"

I took her into my arms, firmly but not roughly, and asked, "What time does it have to be?"

And I kissed her.

The kiss was a little over the top, zero-to-sixty kind of thing, and it surprised her; but she got into it, soon enough.

I lowered her to the floor, and I drew open the robe and she was almost afraid, looking up at me, and her throat was red, her face white, her breasts full and staring at me.

Then my pants were around my ankles and I was fucking her. Her knees were up and she was saying, "Oh, oh, oh," really liking it; but halfway through I slowed it down and kissed her neck and breasts and ears and shoulders and face, and she was crying, and maybe I was crying, what the fuck are you going to do about it?

The finish was slow and gentle and, again, I don't remember going there, but we were in bed, Janet sleeping contentedly next to me, snuggling to me. Killing her in her sleep would have been so easy. Not the accident Green had requested, but painless and she would never know a thing.

But I wasn't about to kill her.

She was coming alive, this woman, she'd been sleepwalking through a coma of a life, and now she was alive, and killing her would have been a goddamn crime. I had a new agenda I was working on, but a wonderful tiredness had me suddenly, and then I was asleep, too.

The next thing I felt was a hand gently caressing my neck, and then I heard Janet, saying, "Hey, Samson—wake up a second."

My eyes somehow opened, and she was sitting on the edge of the bed, in a white blouse and dark skirt, smelling great, but ready for work, not for me.

I sat bolt upright, startling her a little, though she laughed.

"Hey! Hey, relax....I'm leaving for the library. Thought I'd better see if you have anywhere to be."

I tasted my mouth; it wasn't worth the effort. "No. No appointments....Can I just crash here?"

"Sure." She stood, smoothed herself, looking professional and adult, whereas I felt like a kid sleeping in instead of going to school. "I'll leave the extra key on the kitchen table, if you wanna go in or out."

"When'll you be home?"

"I get off at five, today. Don't *you* fix supper— I will!"

"Listen—Janet...."

She was poised at the door to the kitchen, and turned to me, eyebrows arched. "Yes?"

"Tonight....We have to talk."

Her mouth twitched with amusement. "Isn't that usually the *woman's* line?...Or maybe you just want to explain why a guy selling veterinary medicine carries a gun."

That sucker-punched me, and I glanced over at the chair where my corduroy jacket was draped and saw the nine mil's butt sticking up out of the pocket.

When I turned back to Janet, she'd gone.

I ran after her, bare-ass, but she was already out the kitchen door and on her way across the alley to the lot were she parked her Geo.

Over the next hour or so, I showered and made myself a little breakfast, and tried to get my thoughts together. How much did she know about me? When had she noticed the nine millimeter—just now? She sure didn't seem worked up about it....

All the days of surveillance, and being on top of her in more ways than one, I still had no idea why anyone on the planet, much less a mogul like Jonah fucking Green, would want this sexy little librarian wasted. The only thing she was guilty of was shitty taste in men.

By late morning, I was pacing in her living room, the nine stuffed in my waistband. I'd come to a decision—I would tell Janet some kind of story that stopped well short of the truth, but would be enough to motivate her; and I would grab her and haul her ass out of here, to safety somewhere.

And I would deal with Jonah Green, and everything that meant. Killing the guy who hired you is a non-starter in my business, but then I was ready to retire again, anyway, so what the fuck.

But why wait?

The sooner I got Janet out of Homewood, the better. I would go yank her out of that library, run her back here to pick up a few things, and we'd be on the road. That was the plan. That was the new plan....

And I was just about to go out the door and head down to the street, where my rental was parked, when somebody on the other side of that door began to work a key in it.

I took a step back, and the door swung rudely open, and standing framed there, key in hand, was a young woman who was not Janet, but an attractive enough example of the female sex, even though her ragged jeans and a jean jacket and a black hip-hop t-shirt didn't do much for me.

I knew this woman, this girl. And so do you—she was, after all, the kidnap victim who started it all.

Jonah Green's daughter—Julie.

Eleven

I grabbed the little bitch by the arm extending the key and yanked her into the living room and hurled her across the room. Her jean jacket came off in my hand, and I discarded it like a used tissue as she did a half spin and landed rudely on the couch, opposite, breasts bobbling under the black t-shirt. A little suitcase was out in the hall, and I grabbed it and tossed it inside the apartment, and slammed the door and turned to glare at her.

But she didn't scare easy, scrambling back off the cushions to get right in my face, holding the keys in her upraised fist like a blade. Eyes and nostrils flaring, white little feral teeth bared, she all but screamed: "What the fuck are *you* doing here?"

The petite dark-haired beauty had a little ring in her nose now; she was packing enough piercings to set off an airport metal detector.

As would my nine millimeter automatic, the snout of which I stuck under her defiant chin as I slapped the keys rattlingly from her fist.

"You first," I said.

That took some of the fearlessness out of her. Her eyelids were quivering and she swallowed, or tried to. "Get…get that fucking thing out of my throat, you prick."

I did, shoving her back onto the couch with my free hand. Looming over her, keeping the nine trained on her, I paced a little area near where she sat, her arms folded tight as she looked up at me, face blank but for a crinkly chin.

"Explain yourself," I said.

"Fuck you!…I'm visiting my sister."

I frowned down at her. "Where?"

"Here!" Her eyes widened and tightened. "Where the hell else? She *lives* here!"

My eyes narrowed and tightened. "In this apartment…?"

"No, in a dumpster out back." She unfolded her arms, leaning forward on the heels of her hands. "What the hell are you *doing* here, Quarry?"

I was still pointing the gun at her, but suddenly I felt way off my game. "What's your sister's name?"

"You're in her apartment and you don't know? Janet Fucking Wright!"

I squinted at her, hoping that would help; it didn't. I could see neither a resemblance in her face, nor any sense in this situation.

"Your name is *Green*," I said.

"Aren't you the observant son of a bitch?" She sighed impatiently. "Jan doesn't use Daddy's name— she fucking hates Daddy, which is the one thing we have in common....Wright's our mom's maiden name. *Late* mom..."

Suddenly her face whitened, as if she'd finally noticed an asshole was pointing a gun at her.

"Oh shit," she said, pointing a gun-like finger back at me, for nobody's benefit in particular. "Oh hell. Oh *no*...."

"What?"

She was shaking her head, almost frantically. "You're not 'him,' are you? You couldn't be *him*...." She rolled her eyes and laughed harshly. "Oh fuck *me*....Jack? You're *Jack*? Jack Ryan...?"

I lowered the nine a hair. "She told you about me?"

Still shaking her head, she said, "Oh Christ— *you're* her white knight? Kill me. Kill me now."

"It's an option," I said.

Not knowing how much trouble she was potentially in, Julie sneered up at me. "I answered your question, now you owe *me* a fucking answer—what the hell are you doing here, anyway?"

She had a point.

I put the gun in my waistband. I could see no reason not to level with her. More or less.

I sat next to her and said, "Your father hired me."

She gave me a frowning sideways look, not so much disapproving as curious. "What'd he hire you for? Oh fuck...tell me it wasn't to rough up that abusive boyfriend of hers! That prick Rick?"

I shook my head. "That was my bright idea."

She grunted a non-laugh. "Not that Daddy would do anything that thoughtful." Confusion colored her features. "Then *why*—"

"Your father hired me to watch your sister. He didn't say why."

Her eyes narrowed. "Just watch her—like a P.I. or something?"

"Or something."

A little half-hearted laugh made the cupcake breasts bounce; you could see the nipple rings outlined against the black t-shirt. "Well, I can't say it surprises me."

"Why not?"

"Don't you know?" She leaned toward me conspiratorially. "Sis is about to come into a good share of the family fortune."

I said nothing.

My expression must have been talkative, though, because a faintly amused Julie Green said, "Huh... You look *shocked*, Quarry...I didn't know you were the fuck shockable."

Normally I wasn't.

"I liked you better with the beard, by the way," she said. She got up and collected her jeans jacket and laid it over a chair, and picked up her little suitcase and put it next to the same chair.

"It was your sister's idea," I said. "She shaved me."

She glanced at me, smirky but not unfriendly. "I bet she did....You okay?"

"Peachy."

Over the years, in my business, I'd run into lots of things, many of them disgusting or creepy or downright evil. A father hiring a hitman to take out his own daughter had just rocketed to the top of my personal chart.

With a bullet.

Twelve

Julie Green and I sat in her sister's tiny kitchen where the girl had a turkey sandwich and chips and a Diet Coke; I just had a Diet Coke, my appetite dulled somehow. She filled me in, chapter and verse, on the Green family fortune and how it impacted Daddy and his daughters.

Seemed Green's media empire had started when he married money—that money belonging to the late mother of Janet and Julie.

"It's a trust fund deal," Julie was saying, nibbling at the white bread and white turkey meat. She could wear hip-hop clothes all she wanted—this kid was Caucasian. "Jan's gonna be thirty next month, and she'll get a pile."

"What about you?"

She grinned as she chewed. "Oh, I will, too, when I'm her age....I still got a few years of youthful abandon left."

I was squinting again, but this time things were coming into focus. "And if something bad happened to Janet—before the trust fund money came available to her—your father inherits...?"

"Yeah. Sure. Who else?"

One aspect remained fuzzy, however, so I asked, "But why would that matter to a mogul like Jonah Green? He's *loaded*...."

She snorted a laugh, and the nose ring jiggled. "He *was*, before his second wife's settlement...and before he invested in fucking Enron. He's riding on fumes, my clean-shaven friend. Hope you enjoyed your hundred K for rescuing me, 'cause the bastard made me give him an I.O.U. for it!"

I leaned back in the hard kitchen chair. Sipped my Coke and mulled this new information.

Julie sat forward. "Okay, what wheels are turning in that fucked-up skull of yours?...Quarry, are you trying figure out a way to make a buck again? Squeeze Daddy over Janet?"

I flicked her a little frown.

Her eyes went big and her smile was big, too. "Don't *tell* me...don't tell me you really *fell* for my dowdy ol' big sis...? The degenerate hardass and the maiden librarian ....Didn't I see that on *Lifetime*?"

"I'm going to help her," I said.

She didn't seem to be sure whether to be amused by that or not, and just asked, "Help her where *Daddy's* concerned? How the fuck?"

"Will you help me do it?"

She smirked. "Sure. Do *what*?"

"Will...you...help?"

She shrugged magnanimously. "Sure—why the

fuck not? My sister is the only relative on the planet that I give two shits about, and anything that gives Daddy a bad day is my idea of a good time."

"Swell." I rose. "I'm going to call her at the library."

"Okay." She watched me go to the kitchen's wall phone. "You want privacy?"

"No."

The library was on a short list of numbers posted by the phone (Rick's had a line through it; mine at the motel was added on) and I dialed.

"Homewood Public Library," Janet's voice said pleasantly. "Help Desk, this is Ms. Wright, how may I help you?"

"Like you did last night," I said, "is just fine."

Her voice warmed up. "Hi, Jack."

"Listen," I said lightly. "Your sister dropped by the apartment, and we're getting along famously."

"Oh! Completely forgot about Jules! I should've mentioned her, Jack, sorry...but she didn't say when exactly she was coming. She's kind of a...you know, free spirit."

I glanced over at Julie. She was standing next to the kitchen table, now, slipping out of the t-shirt. She tossed it on the table and stood there grinning at me, fists Superman-style on her hips, the nice little pierced-nippled breasts bare and perky and proud.

My dick twitched.

"Free spirit, huh?" I said to the girl's sister. "I

noticed....How about after work the three of us meet for a drink, grab a bite together?"

"Great! I'll go straight to Sneaky Pete's, unless you're sick of it."

"No, that's fine. See you there."

We exchanged 'byes, I hung up, and the little topless punkette was right there, right on me, wrapping her arms around me, pushing me to the wall, cornering me like she had at Harry and Louis's cabin.

"I'm not on the rag *now*," she said with a wicked smile and a single arched eyebrow. "You finally ready for that reward?"

I put my hands on her hips, held her away from me at arm's length, and took a long, leering look at her and she grinned, pleased with herself.

Then I pushed her away. "Get your shirt on before your nipple rings rust."

She backed off and appraised me, frowning; now I finally could see the resemblance between the sisters—the tips of Julie's breasts were long, too.

"Turning me down again, Quarry?"

"I seem to be."

I wasn't sure if that had been a test or if she was just a little cockhound.

Maybe the former, because after she slipped the black t-shirt on, she winked at me and said, "Okay. Okay. Maybe you really *do* like my big sis."

Thirteen

Monday night at Sneaky Pete's was slow, the singles crowd modest and the laughter and conversation lessened, which only made the country western schlock on the jukebox all the more noticeable. I did my best to control the situation by plowing quarters in and selecting the Patsy Cline, Hank Williams and Willie Nelson numbers, trying to hold the crap at bay.

I had thought Janet chose the bar because it had somehow become "our" place; but I soon realized she'd made the choice to accommodate her sister, who drank more than she ate. Our burgers hadn't even arrived yet, and Julie was already on her second Scotch rocks.

Janet was on my side of the booth, looking fondly at her sister and me and back again, working a little too hard to get a family vibe going.

"So," she asked, "you two already *know* each other? How is that possible?"

Julie shrugged, glugged Scotch, and said, "He got me out of a jam, a while back."

Janet cocked her head, eyes flicking from her sister to me to her sister. "What kind of jam, Jules?"

Julie shrugged again. "Some assholes kidnapped me."

At that Janet laughed. Then, studying the dark-haired, nose-pierced girl, asked, "You're…not kidding, are you?"

Julie shook her head. "No. Some assholes grabbed me to squeeze ransom money out of Daddy. Our, uh, mutual friend Jack, here, got me away from the bad guys. You, uh…probably don't want to hear the details. Wasn't strictly legal. Jack, she doesn't want to hear the details, does she?"

"No," I said.

Janet looked from Julie to me. Her expression tried for trusting and came off wary. "Jack…you don't…you don't work for my *father*, do you?"

"Yes," I said.

The wary expression turned withering, and her nostrils flared, and her teeth were bared when she said, "Let me out," and tried to rise and push by me.

But she was sitting on the inside of the booth and I wouldn't let her, gripping her wrist, making her eyes meet mine.

"Hear me out," I said.

"Why *should* I?"

"So you'll know what's going on, and can make an informed decision."

Her upper lip curled back. "Don't patronize me!"

Across the way Julie was chewing ice from her drink, faintly disgusted. "Oh, brother, Sis...."

"Hear me out," I said, "and I'll let you out."

Still half up, Janet drew in a deep breath, exhaled melodramatically, and settled back in the booth, getting as far away from me as she could, short of knocking a hole through the wall.

Janet folded her arms and looked straight ahead. "My father is a monster. Anybody who does his bidding—"

Julie laughed and said, "Does his *bidding*! Jesus, library lady, cut the guy a break."

The older sister—without looking at me—said, "All right. I'll give you one minute, Jack, and then you either let me out of this booth or I start screaming."

Julie craned her neck out of the booth. "Can I get another Scotch rocks, please? *Thank* you...."

I said to Janet, "Your father hired me to keep an eye on you."

She couldn't help herself; she had to look at me. "Why, in heaven's name?"

"He didn't say."

"Is that why...you...with *Rick*...?"

I was halfway turned in the booth, to face her, and I did my best to keep my words simple, my tone earnest. "I was just supposed to keep track of you. But when that asshole got physical, I—"

"Blew your cover?" she asked bitterly.

"Or," Julie said with a nasty little smile, "maybe climbed under yours, huh, Sis?"

"You be quiet," Janet said.

"You asked about the gun," I said. "This is why."

She was shaking her head, grappling with all this. "You're a, a what...bodyguard? Why would he do that? Why would *my* father hire someone to protect *me*? He doesn't care enough about me to—"

"I've come to that same opinion," I said. "Which is why I think you may be at risk."

Janet didn't seem to hear my last statement, asking, "What...what kind of work do you generally *do* for my father?"

I shrugged. "Troubleshooter."

"Well...that's certainly vague."

"Right."

"I...I really should hate you."

"Probably."

Her chin started quivering and her eyes were getting moist. "You...*goddamn* you. Goddamn *me*—I let you into my life."

I nodded. "I know the feeling—I let you into mine."

We looked at each other...

...and suddenly it was fine between us.

Or I was pretty sure it was, and held my hand out.

She gave me her hand and I squeezed it, and Julie, said, "I'm gonna need *way* more Scotch...."

Our food came soon, and neither Janet nor I did much more than nibble at it. Julie ate about half of hers, but was downing the booze like a pro.

"What did you mean," Janet said, pushing her plate away, "I'm at…risk?"

I pushed my plate away, too. "You're coming into a lot of money, soon, aren't you?"

"Yes.…"

Julie, chewing cheeseburger, said, "And if you flatline, sister dear, guess who gets the gold?"

Janet frowned and then it turned into a smile of disbelief. "Oh, come on…you can't think…our own *father*? Even he wouldn't…*would* he?"

"He would," I said. "It's…a problem."

Janet's eyebrows went up. "A problem?"

"And I know just what to do about it," Julie said. She grabbed the passing waitress and said, "Scotch rocks, double—my sissy sis'll no doubt want a margarita…and how about you, big boy?"

"Coke," I said.

"Give him a twist of line," Julie said, "and let him live dangerously…and keep 'em comin'."

When the waitress had departed, Janet leaned across the booth and took some of the stress out on her sister, saying bitchily, "That's *always* your solution, isn't it? Getting drunk!"

"Or stoned," Julie said, "or laid. But this? This I think calls for drunk."

That was when I noticed someone at the bar, his back to us, as he watched us in the mirror—a brawny big-shouldered guy in gray sweats in his twenties with a close-cropped blonde haircut.

"Excuse me, ladies," I said, and slipped out of the booth.

I sat on the stool next to the guy.

"Hello, DeWayne," I said.

Jonah Green's flunky, his sweatshirt labeled USMC, sipped his beer and said, "Don't talk to me. Are you crazy?"

"That's a matter of opinion. Why are you here, DeWayne? What are you up to?"

DeWayne didn't look at me. He whispered: "Mr. Green has me following that crazy cunt."

"Julie?"

He forgot to whisper this time, saying, "You see any other crazy cunt around here? Mr. Green was afraid she'd screw things up. With the...you know, job."

"*My* job, you mean," I said.

Now he looked at me.

The close-set sky-blue eyes in the oval Clutch Cargo-ish face stared at me unblinkingly; his upper lip approximated a sneer. This was apparently his menacing expression.

"Your *job*," he said nastily, "which apparently includes hangin' out in public with the intended? What are you doin', making contact with—"

I put my hand on his sleeve, and smiled pleasantly. "Leave, DeWayne. Go home. Right now."

"You can't—"

"Do you want to die, DeWayne?"

That stopped him. But then he managed, "You don't—"

"Leave, DeWayne. Or die. Those are the options. Choose."

DeWayne turned away and looked at himself in the mirror. He was bigger than me and younger and he didn't like taking this from a geezer like me—he was trembling, whether with rage or fear or some combo, I couldn't say.

But take it from me he did. He finished the beer, threw a crumpled five-spot on the bar, and headed out the door almost at a trot.

I joined the sisters at the booth.

"Who was that?" Janet asked.

I looked sharply at Julie and shook my head; she, of course, knew who DeWayne was, but she nodded back, almost imperceptibly, and I told her sister, "Nobody, really. Just somebody I thought I knew, but didn't."

"Well, that's funny…" Janet's eyes narrowed, watching where DeWayne had gone. "…I'm pretty sure he was at the library today, just hanging around."

I said nothing.

We spent several hours in the bar, and I asked Janet and Julie lots of questions about their father, about his business, his private and public life. I was fairly subtle about it, and both young women were drinking enough to make my information-gathering relatively inconspicuous. By the time the evening was over, I had plenty of information on Jonah Green and his whereabouts and his patterns.

When it was time to go, I drove Janet home in my rental Ford—she'd had way too many margaritas— while Julie drove her sister's Geo. Julie was pretty drunk, too, but she was used to it, and could navigate well enough. Still, I followed her, to make sure she stayed on the road.

No one tailed us, by the way—just as there'd been no sign of DeWayne in Sneaky Pete's parking lot. Maybe he'd had the sense to follow my advice and survive.

Julie parked the Geo in the lot behind the building and entered through the kitchen to meet us at the apartment's front door. I carried the plastered Janet in my arms like a bride over the threshold into the apartment. Julie, with a display of intense concentration, worked at getting the door night-latched, and made her way to the couch—this time I didn't have to throw her over there.

I carried Janet into the bedroom, left the lights off,

and settled her on top of the covers, taking off her shoes but otherwise letting her sleep there, fully clothed. Already she was snoring gently.

Then I returned to the living room and checked the door, finding it locked and successfully night-latched. I turned off the lights and only a little neon from the street pulsed in—I glanced at the double windows past Janet's comfy chair and footrest; across the way, the windows of my surveillance post were dark and anonymous.

Janet's sister was curled up on the couch, in a fetal position. The heat was on but cool air leeched in those double windows, so I went off and found a blanket and came back and covered Julie with it.

She stirred a little and looked up at me, blinking. "You...you really do love her, don't you, you big jerk?"

I said nothing.

"I thought so," she said, and smiled a little, and then it faded dramatically and she said, "Daddy... Daddy's got something bad planned for Jan, doesn't he?"

"You're on a roll," I said.

I sat on the edge of the couch. I felt fond of this kid, suddenly, and I didn't even want to fuck her. I was getting so goddamn soft.

"Were *you* supposed to do it?" she asked.

"Do what?"

"The bad thing to Janet for Daddy."

I nodded.

"And now...instead...you're going to stop it?"

I touched her lips with a finger. "Get some sleep. You know where the bathroom is? 'Cause you're gonna have to piss like a racehorse."

"I know where the bathroom is....Some night?"

I frowned at her. "What about 'some night?' "

She got herself more comfortable. "Some night, when you're sittin' all bored and shit...with only my mousy little sis to keep you company...?"

"Yeah?"

"Maybe it'll occur to you."

"What will?"

"That you wound up with the wrong sister."

I stared at her. She did her drunken best to stare back.

"Well," I said, "you are more like what I deserve."

In a goofily good-natured way, she said, "Fuck you," stuck her tongue out and smiled and I tucked her in some more and she was asleep.

My nine millimeter and I went out and prowled the back alley, including checking the parked cars in the lot beyond, where the Geo was. Then I came back in and locked up and returned to the bedroom.

Janet was still on top of the covers, fully dressed,

really sawing logs now, looking not at all glamorous, and incredibly beautiful.

I placed my nine millimeter on the bedstand beside me and stretched out next to the slumbering woman, and lay there in the dark, elbows winged, staring at the ceiling.

Fourteen

The explosion jolted me from deep asleep to fully awake—or the sound of it did, anyway, coming from outside the apartment, to the rear.

Still fully dressed from the night before, I sat up straight, as if from a nightmare; but I was waking *to* a nightmare, and knew it, as I noted the absence of Janet on the rumpled bed next to me.

I grabbed the nine millimeter off the nightstand and bolted toward the noise, which had shifted from full-scale world-rattling boom to lion's roar of fire punctuated by snapping of flames.

The kitchen opened onto a small unenclosed porch and a half-flight of stairs down to the alley, across which lay half a block of metered parking lot, from which the smoke and flames curled a question mark into an overcast morning sky.

Something had exploded in that lot, and it didn't have to be Janet's car, could have been someone else's or something else entirely, gas main maybe, only I knew in my tightened gut that it *did* have to be Janet's car....

I took the steps three at a time and sprinted across to where I could see the Geo, transformed into a twisted mass of steel abstraction decorated with lashing tongues of flame and billowing smoky hands that turned to black fists opening to gray fingers.

Gun ready but with nothing and no one to shoot at, I dropped to my knees as if to pray. But I was not in a prayerful mood—my eyes were ignoring the smoke and taking in various sad, sick sights, from burnt-edged scraps of Janet's brown suede coat to jagged sections of smoldering human flesh.

Not far from where I knelt, half a female arm lay, fingers twitching, just a little, not burnt at all, not even the stump, as if cut off rudely at the elbow and discarded, flung to the asphalt, which was dotted with the red rain of blood. A little ways away, a shoe-less foot had landed on its sole, like the person it belonged to had stepped away, leaving it behind.

Mostly, however, the lot was littered with charred chunks of meat, as if the explosion had been in a butcher's shop, not rigged here in this lot to blow sky-high when the key of the little Geo had been turned.

A sane man might have gone mad.

I went coldly sane, getting to my feet, ignoring the civilians starting to approach the fiery scene, a chorus of *Oh my Gods* and *Oh my Lords* making a frantic premature funeral out of the ungainly pyre. But I was in no mood for ceremony and just turned away and headed for my rental Ford, which wasn't in the lot, parked instead over on the next side street.

In a weird way, the carnage of it made it easier for me to snap into the necessary gear—this was no clean kill, out of my more recent life, but a flashback to Vietnam, where I'd seen any number of friends blown to kibble thanks to land mines and mortar shells. Where you learned to react by retreating inside yourself, but not inviting the emotions in.

So I was in combat mode when I went looking for him.

Homewood had only seven motels, three of them major chains (Holiday Inn, Comfort Inn, Econo Lodge) which was where normally I would have started; but I had a hunch he would be staying close to my digs, since he was obviously keeping an eye on me.

That's why I began where I was staying, at the Homewood Motor Court. I even parked in my own space by my own door, and on foot prowled the line of cabins, looking over the parked vehicles, studying license plates, peering in windows to take in anything showing in front and back seats.

Not many cars were in the spaces, as the motel catered to salesman and other mid-range business people, who were off with their cars pursuing their livelihoods. And when I made his ride, I was relieved to see it parked in the last space belonging to the last cabin at the far end, with no vehicles parked in the nearest four spaces.

That was good.

And the car hadn't been hard to make—on the passenger seat of a Jeep rental were fanned-out magazines, *Soldier of Fortune*, *Black Belt* and several body building rags.

Seeing those had made me smile. Not much of a smile I grant you, a bitter little slash; but a smile. The magazines not only said who this car belonged to, it indicated a guy reading on the job, bored by surveillance work. Usually reading indicates intelligence.

Not this time.

Through the crack of the window, between the wood frame and the drawn blinds, I could see him, hurriedly packing his duffel bag, which was emblazoned with a Marine Corps insignia. The sweats had been replaced by a short-sleeved pale yellow shirt and dark brown slacks and shades-of-brown running shoes. He might have been the president of the Young Republicans on a campus somewhere.

When I went to his door, the nine millimeter was in my left hand, in front of me, so that anyone passing by wouldn't see it.

Not that anyone was passing by. The Homewood Motor Court on this Monday morning was deader than the driver of the Geo. I knew housekeeping didn't come on for another hour. Plenty of time.

The day, I noticed, was crisp and almost cold, the threat of rain making the sky dark. Days like this were surprisingly common in Vietnam, even if muggy hot ones were the norm, in the jungle.

I knocked with my free hand.

The door opened, allowing the room's inhabitant a suspicious look over the night latch, and I was tempted to replay what I'd done to Louis, just shoot the prick in the eye and be done with it...

...but instead I shouldered through, popping the night latch, shoving the door shut behind me with my right hand, and pointing the nine at him with the other.

DeWayne, stunned by the intrusion, belatedly raised the glock he'd had sense enough to take with him answering the door, and with my free hand, I batted it out of his grasp, like a mean sibling slapping a rattle out of a baby's pink fingers.

The gun landed on the nearby bed and bounced off onto the carpeted floor with a clunk, out of view, and reach.

DeWayne's room was larger than mine, a businessman's mini-suite with a meeting area. The framed paintings were abstractions, as if gore had been spattered around in here already.

My reluctant host—a little taller than me, and about as heavy, but overly muscular in a steroid-ish way—just stood there agape, his stubbly blond gyrene haircut seeming to stand on end. His light blue eyes—disturbingly long-lashed pretty eyes, really, feminine in the midst of all that otherwise rugged-jaw masculinity—had the same startled expression they'd worn when I slipped in beside DeWayne in his car outside the Log Cabin, a few months ago.

Right before he thanked me for not killing him and I locked him in his trunk—remember?

I shoved my nine millimeter in my waistband. But that didn't seem to make DeWayne feel any better— in fact, he seemed unnerved, perhaps because I appeared so calm.

And I was in fact calm, entirely matter-of-fact and unemotional. Which he should have been thankful for. If I hadn't slipped into my battle zone, he'd have been dead now.

I asked, in a purely conversational tone, "What the fuck was that about back there, DeWayne?"

DeWayne blinked.

I raised my eyebrows. "The *car*, DeWayne? The one you rigged that blew up this morning? Oh, but maybe you didn't hang around to watch."

His mouth twitched, like it couldn't decide whether to smile or frown or scream.

"In which case," I continued affably, "you'll be pleased to know it did go off and blow Janet Wright's car to hell and gone—driver and all."

His expression tightened into defensiveness.

"Well, *somebody* had to do it! After you've been *farting* around for *days*!"

"...How long have you been watching me, DeWayne?"

He shook his head. "I told you—I followed Mr. Green's slutty little princess here. She wasn't supposed to be part of the mix, you know."

My hands were on my hips. "But, then, neither were you, DeWayne. Was *that* the plan? Let me do the job, then get rid of the loose end?"

"No! Hell, no! I told you—"

My eyes slitted. "I told *you*, last night. This is *my* job."

DeWayne risked getting in my face, just a little: "Which included *fucking* her, I suppose? Where is that in your job description, old man? You ain't exactly a stealth missile."

I drew in a breath, let it out. "Car bomb," I said.

"Huh?"

"Car bomb. Yeah. *That'll* play as an accident."

My remark took the boldness out of him, replacing it with chagrin. "Yeah, well...things were...out of control. I made a...a *pre-emptive* strike. But you don't need to worry."

My eyebrows went up again. "I don't?"

He smirked humorlessly. "No—you'll get your money."

"...Well, isn't that thoughtful. And then there's all the credit—I'll get that, too." Finally I frowned at him. "Jesus, DeWayne—I've been seen all over town with that woman!"

Now his eyebrows went up. "Is that *my* fault?"

"No," I admitted. "That's my fault. Blowing her up in her car, that would be yours."

He backed away, hands half-up, saying, "Listen, I'm sorry I stepped on your fuckin' toes...but I had orders to follow...and now I got a plane to catch."

Cautiously DeWayne returned to the duffel bag he was packing; his gun was over there on the floor, somewhere. Part of me wished he would go for it, please go for it, right now, *go for it....*

"I need to finish packing," he said, doing his best to sound casual, gesturing to the bag. "You got a problem with that?"

I shook my head. "Not at all—but why don't you pack after your shower?"

"My what?"

"When's your plane, DeWayne?"

Various vague gestures accompanied his reply: "Two hours from now, but I got to drive over to—"

"You got plenty of time for a quick shower."

He stared at me like I was a raving madman, even though I was not raving. "What the *fuck...?*"

Slowly but steadily, I removed the nine from my

waistband and pointed it at him. "Take your clothes off, DeWayne."

His eyes and nostrils flared, the short blond hair damn near bristling. "The *hell!*"

I gestured a little with the gun, not vaguely. "Go on and strip....I'm locking you in the bathroom so you don't follow me."

He shook his head, wild-eyed, blurting, "I'm not gonna fucking *follow* your ass!"

"That's right," I said. "Because I'm locking *your* ass in the can, and taking your clothes. That'll give me the lead I need, to get out of this podunk."

DeWayne sighed. Shook his head. Opened his palms placatingly. "*Please*, buddy. Come on, will ya? What the hell'd I ever do to—"

"Skivvies and all, DeWayne. All the way."

"...Christ." His eyes popped with alarm. "Oh, Christ, you *fell* for her!"

"*Now*, DeWayne...."

Frantic, pawing the air, he said, "Look, you can't blame me for this. It was Mr. *Green*. Once a guy like Mr. Green decides you're dead, you're fucking dead! *You* know that! She was a dead man walkin'—I was just the means to an end, and if it wasn't me, it coulda been any—"

"Spare me the horseshit, DeWayne, and strip the fuck down."

DeWayne slumped in defeat.

Moving in slow motion, he began unbuttoning the pale yellow shirt, then—and this was admirable, he didn't telegraph it all—swept a curving martial-arts kick around that popped the nine millimeter right out of my grasp.

The gun slid across the carpet and hid under a chest of drawers, as if wanting nothing to do with any of what was about to come.

Shaking my head and smiling, I said, "This isn't really necessary, DeWayne."

He went into a karate-school stance that I wish I could say looked hokey, but it didn't—he was a muscular young ex-Marine who clearly knew his shit, and it hadn't all come out of *Black Belt* magazine, either.

"That's *my* call, Pops!"

It was my turn to sigh.

"Go ahead, kid. Take your best shot."

And he did, kicking high and out, aiming at my head. If it had connected, I'd likely have been dead, my neck broken.

So I ducked it.

DeWayne reared back, confusion coloring his face, and paused for a moment.

"Couldn't we just skip this, son?"

Teeth bared, he tried again, rushing me with a flurry of blows, bladed hands here, fists there, and I ducked and slipped and dodged.

He followed me as I circled away, and when he high-kicked, I got out of the way, and his running-shod foot broke a mirror over the dresser, shards raining noisily. I circled back and he charged me and I stepped aside and he busted off the top half of a chair, making a stool out of it.

Finally he began to lose his cool, which isn't a part of any martial arts program I know of; but you couldn't blame the poor bastard—I was frustrating the hell out of him, avoiding his every blow, never raising my hands. I didn't even bother taunting him, ignoring anything he said to me ("Stand still, gramps!") and, with the mini-suite half demolished, he went for broke with a flying kick that I stepped aside for, and he crashed to the floor with a whump.

I just stood there, arms folded causually, not having broken a sweat, while he got to his feet, then bent over, exhausted, panting, pausing with his hands on his thighs.

"*Je*-sus," he said, trying hard to catch his breath, still hunkered over, "*Je*-sus...why don't you...you... *fuckin'*...fuckin' *do* something?"

I slammed a fist into the side of his head, connecting with his ear and temple, and the big guy went down, in a pile.

He wasn't out, but he was out of it, and when he finally looked back up at me, pitifully—his face red and fully sweat-beaded, his ear bleeding from the

side of his head where I'd hit him—the nine millimeter was back in my hand, its dark eye staring
him down.

"See, DeWayne? You do need a shower."

That made him slump some more, as if all the
remaining energy just drained out of him, but he was
still breathing hard. He sat there, kind of sideways,
his legs sprawled, like a cripple whose faith-healing
hadn't taken.

"Just," he said, and heaved a couple breaths, and
then tried again: "Just *do* it. Awright? Just…fucking…
kill me."

I shook my head and my expression was fairly
pleasant. "I'm not gonna kill you, kid. Strip."

Allowing himself the luxury of being reassured,
DeWayne somehow got to his feet—it was kind of
like watching one of those demolition-of-a-building
film clips played backward, a structure reassembling
itself—and once again, back to slow motion, he
began to unbutton his shirt.

No tricks.

No attacks.

No surprises.

All he did was perform the least interesting
striptease I have ever witnessed, discreetly turning
his back to me at the finish, his arms—muscular, decorated with various USMC tattoos—hanging as slack
as his muscular buttocks were taut.

He glanced back at me for his orders.

"The shitter," I told him.

And I marched the dejected DeWayne into the bathroom. The young soldier wasn't looking for an escape route, or at least I didn't think he was. He seemed relatively unafraid, probably figuring I'd have killed him by now, if that was the point.

Just inside the cramped bathroom, he again looked over his shoulder and said, "You mind a little friendly advice? Don't tangle asses with Mr. Green. I know you're not happy about how this went down. But just…go your own way."

"Semper fi, Mac," I said.

There was no tub, just a shower stall with the familiar pebbled glass.

He swallowed. "Now what?"

"Get in."

This seemed to alarm him, and his head swivelled on the muscular neck. "What the fuck for?"

Keeping it low-key, sticking the nine back in my waistband, I said, "I'm going to wedge something against the door, and lock you in. Buy me some time."

"I told you I wouldn't—"

"Right. Get in."

Compliantly, DeWayne opened the door and stepped in the stall, and stood there with a good-size dick hanging and an expression that was neither moronic nor intelligent—perfect makings for a Marine.

"And?" he asked.

"And," I said, "be careful, DeWayne. You'd be surprised how many accidents happen in the bathroom."

He squinted at me, not getting that, and I used both hands to slam his head into the shower stall wall, with all the force I could muster.

The sound of his skull cracking wasn't loud but it was distinct, and perhaps DeWayne even had time to hear it; either way, he was already dead, wide-eyed and frozen in time, as he slid slowly down the wall, leaving a bloody snail-smear behind him.

He sat there quietly, pretty blue eyes staring into eternity, his limbs like kindling, as I unwrapped a motel bar of soap and then flipped the thing to land near DeWayne's big dead feet. I'd been careful to bash his head into the wall on the side where my fist had hit him earlier, the only blow I'd delivered in our hand-to-hand exercise.

Then I turned on the shower, nice and hot (to make time of death a mystery), and let the steamy spray do its tapdance on the corpse.

I hadn't touched much in the room—the soap would be worn down by the needles of water—so I didn't have much cleaning up to do.

Not in Homewood I didn't.

Fifteen

The massive ornate granite gravestone was a family affair, reading on top:

> *MARY ANN GREEN*   *JONAH ALLEN GREEN*
>   *(1940–1985)*   *(1938–)*
> *Beloved Wife and Mother*

and below:

> *JANET ANN GREEN*   *JULIA SUSAN GREEN*
>   *(1975–2005)*   *(1985–)*
> *Cherished Daughter*

From my post behind some rich man's mausoleum, I couldn't see that lettering; but I'd been at the cemetery since last night, and had taken in the inscription by moonlight. I'd been by far the first to get here for Janet Green's farewell appearance.

Her casket, on the other hand, I could easily see from here, my position elevated enough to view the copper capsule, which had already been deposited in the ground, the metallic tubes of the lowering device still in place. I'd skipped the funeral, not really feeling wanted, and the graveside ceremony was long since over.

The morning was crisp and cold with moving clouds that sent phantom-like shadows gliding across the snow-brushed grounds of Oak Brook Memorial Cemetery. The mourners had drifted away, though a few lingered to pay their respects to the grieving father—Jonah Green, in his dark gray Saville Row topcoat, saying nothing, just nodding severe thanks with that square head with its square jaw, the short-cut bristly haircut giving him a vaguely military cast.

And now Green was a solitary figure at his daughter's graveside, standing with hands figleafed before him, head lowered, making a mournful picture that maybe, maybe not, had some real feeling in it.

Who knows—could be there was some humanity left in this son of a bitch. Could be he felt a pang about killing his oldest daughter to gain more of his late wife's money. He certainly seemed truly mournful as he bent to collect a handful of piled graveside dirt, then standing and tossing it in. Even from where I was tucked back watching, I could hear the soil shower the casket like hard, brief rain.

The final cars drew away, leaving only the Cadillac hearse and a second vehicle, a BMW. The mourners, other than Green himself, were gone. The only company remaining was keeping a respectful distance, but staying alert: half a dozen scattered security men in dark raincoats and sunglasses, peppered here and there on the periphery, keeping in touch via headsets.

Not that I'd give them high marks, since I'd easily kept out of their sight when they did their advance sweep of the cemetery, early this morning. Nor were they aware that the uniformed chauffeur assigned to drive the hearse was currently tossed in the back of the vehicle wrapped in more duct tape than a leaky drainpipe.

Which was why—when the liveried "chauffeur" in cap and sunglasses approached Jonah Green at the graveside—neither the millionaire nor any of his six security boys thought anything of it.

I stepped to Green's side and, head still lowered, he said, "Just a few more minutes, Roger—I'm...I'm not ready just yet."

"My final payment hasn't reached my off-shore account," I said, removing the sunglasses and tucking them in a breast pocket. "Why the delay?"

Green looked at me sharply with those money-color eyes, but he'd been to the rodeo a few times himself, so his surprise and alarm quickly faded to a weary bitter smile.

"Quarry. Nice of you to come."

My cap was in hand now, respectfully. "Wouldn't miss it."

He turned back to the grave, looked down into it.

"As for your payment, well…you didn't do the work, did you?"

"You interfered with the job. Or, anyway, that dope of yours did."

The square head swung toward me again, his forehead creased with a frown but his mouth a straight line. "Was that really necessary? What you did to DeWayne?"

"Not as necessary as you killing your daughter.… Nice turnout today."

He stared down into the grave again. "Not many of them knew Janet—they were kind to pay their respects."

"Where was her sister? Was Julie at the funeral? Didn't spot her at the graveside service."

He was maintaining an admirable cool; on the other hand, he knew we had that security crew of his, all around us. Still, he was well aware what I was capable of, and a certain tension, even nervousness, flicked in and around his eyes.

"I thought maybe *you* knew where Julie was," he said. His tone was surface cordial, underlying contemptuous. "Hell, I thought I might get another phone call from you, wanting more unmarked money."

"That hurts."

He lifted his shoulders and set them down again. "All I know is, Julie's dropped out of sight."

"Well, maybe she's afraid Daddy might be thinking of doubling up on the trust fund action."

Green glared at me. "I would *never* harm that girl."

"Sorry. How could I ever think such a thing?"

"I adore that child!"

"I was just thinking maybe it was a set-up all along—that maybe you engineered that snatch.... After all, you said yourself you had certain business connections, in those circles."

He sneered. "Don't be an ass."

"Makes sense—the wild child dies, Daddy inherits. But I came along and screwed it up for you. So Plan B was daughter number one."

He was shaking his head, looking out past the gravestone, at the world beyond; mostly all you could see of that world was more gravestones, some trees, and the gray tombstones of suburban Oak Brook's business buildings.

"You're wrong, Quarry—though why I should care what a creature like you thinks is beyond me."

"There I agree with you."

He swung toward me with his eyes slits, his face grooved grimly. "I was not responsible for that kidnapping—no. Julie has potential. She has fire. Spirit. She's just...going through a phase."

I nodded toward the hole in the ground. "So is your other daughter—it's called decomposition."

He leaned toward me, eyes furious, face otherwise blank; he'd been keeping his voice down, and his movements small, obviously not anxious to start a fracas between his boys and me, out here in front of God and everybody, with himself in the middle.

"What the hell do you want, Quarry? The rest of your money?"

"That would be a start."

He shook his head, quietly disgusted. "Well, I don't want a scene, here. Can you understand that? Can you have a little respect for the dead?"

"Did you really say that, or am I hallucinating?"

"Fuck you. Just go. Go, and I'll make your god-damn money happen."

I said nothing. Now I was the one looking down into that hole in the ground. "...You warned me that she didn't deserve it."

He winced. "What—Janet?...No, she was a nice enough young woman. Harmless. Silly, naive, in how she viewed the world, but...anyway. She was lost to me. Lost to me long ago."

"Oh?"

He had a distant expression now. For the first time I detected a genuine sense of loss in him, if edged with a bitter anger. "To her...to her I represented everything bad about this country."

I shrugged. "Kids."

He glared at me again. "She had a nothing life, Quarry—a librarian."

He said "librarian" the way another disappointed father might have said "shoplifter" or "prostitute."

He was saying, "I have a small empire to maintain—thousands of employees, with families, depending on me for their paychecks."

"Hey," I said. "You sacrificed a child. Worked for God."

He winced again. Sighed grandly. Said, "Go—just fucking go. Do that, cause no more trouble, and there'll be a nice bonus for you—not that you deserve shit."

"Oh," I said, "I deserve shit...but your daughter didn't. Mr. Green...Jonah? Okay I call you 'Jonah'? I feel a certain closeness to you."

"Are you insane?"

"Is that a rhetorical question? See, I always assumed the people I killed were marked for death, anyway, and I was a means to a predetermined end."

Green—studying me now, clearly wondering where this was going—said, "I gathered as much."

"People I put down probably did deserve it...or anyway put themselves in the gunsights, one way or another. By something they'd done."

"Of course."

"But Janet..." I smiled at him, only it didn't really

have much to do with smiling. "...she was a good person. A decent person. She didn't deserve to die."

He bit the words off acidly: "I *told* you that going *in*."

"Yeah. My bad." I shook my head, laughed a little. "You know, Mr. Green, in a long and varied career in the killing business, I've never encountered anyone quite like you—ready to kill your own daughter for another chunk of the family fortune."

The security guys had started getting suspicious, taking notice of this unlikely long conversation between chauffeur and boss. From the corners of my eyes, I saw them talking into their headsets; it was like being stalked by air traffic controllers.

"Walk away," Green said softly. "Your money will be doubled, and—since we've come to find each other so distasteful—we don't ever have to have contact again."

I raised a forefinger, gently, and nodded toward the names carved in granite. "One little thing—you're going to need to revise that headstone."

"Really?"

"That wasn't Janet in that car."

He took it like a slap. Time stuttered, and his mouth dropped open, his eyes flaring; but despite this obvious alarm, the millionaire went into immediate denial, saying, "Well, certainly it was Janet."

"No. She's alive and well and somewhere you can't find her."

"You *are* insane...."

"See, Jonah, your girls got a little tipsy, the night before," I said, "and next morning Julie put on one of her sister's coats...it was chilly...and went out to get the car, to bring it around to give her hungover sister a ride to work."

His face turned white, like the dead skin a blister leaves.

I went on: "I liked Julie. You're right—she did have fire. Particularly at the end, there."

"No," Green said, and he tried to smile, tried to shrug it off. "No, I don't believe you....This is some sick—"

"Hey, what's the difference, Dad? Trust fund money is trust fund money."

That was when he lost it, and rushed me, reaching out with curled fingers to try to strangle me, I guess. And he was a big man, bigger than me, and powerful, despite the years he had on me. I could hear the security guys, not bothering with headsets now, flat-out yelling, on the run.

But then I had Jonah Green locked in an embrace, my arms pinning his, and I was close enough to kiss the bastard.

I grinned into his fucking face and said, "That's not *all* you'll need to revise on that headstone...."

Then I shifted, holding him by one arm, and I let him sense the nose of the nine millimeter in his gut, just so he could know it was coming, and I fired twice. The sounds were muffled by his clothing and his body, and were like coughs, not even loud enough to echo.

Stepping back, releasing him from my embrace, I watched with pleasure as he stumbled back, open-mouthed, awkward and—arms windmilling—tripped over the metal tubing of the lowering device and tumbled backward into his daughter's grave, smacking the metal of the casket, hard.

Now *that* echoed.

The security guys had me surrounded and I wheeled, going from face to face, smiling easily, my gun in hand pointed skyward, my other hand up, too.

"No need, fellas!" I said. "You're off the payroll. Time to hit the unemployment lines...."

They began trading glances, considering my words—after all, they had just seen the prick they worked for gut-shot, twice, and presumably they'd been told I was dangerous, I was in fact why they were fucking here, so I was clearly a guy with a gun who, if confronted, would take some of them down.

But Jonah Green was a tough old bird, and badly wounded though he was, bleeding from the mouth, front of his clothing splotched with blood, he was nonetheless alive, and trying to crawl, claw his way up and out of the ground.

When his head popped up in that grave, his men jumped a little; and maybe I did, too.

"Shoot him!" Green cried, gargling blood a little as he did. He was holding onto a metal tube of the lowering device. "Cut him *down*!"

When the guns started appearing in the hands of the security men, I moved out, ducking back behind the massive Green family gravestone, firing the nine millimeter at the only guy in sunglasses, headset and raincoat on that side of the world.

The guy took it in the head, and fell backward, like a narcoleptic suddenly asleep, but leaving blood mist behind.

With the headstone as cover, I took out the two closest ones, and each did an individualistic death dance, though with much in common—spurting blood, tumbling to the snowy grass—while the surviving trio went scrambling for cover, behind other gravestones.

I used the rest of the clip exchanging gunfire with them, bullets careening and *whing*ing off the granite headstones, carving nicks and holes. But they were spread out just enough to make my task difficult.

Concentrating on one at a time, I took the nearest to me when he slipped his head out to take aim, my shot sending him back, sprawling against another gravestone, staring in surprise with both eyes and the new hole between them.

We all stayed put while shadows chased each other under the cold cloud-shifting sky. Wind riffled branches and stubborn leaves whispered and some of us were breathing hard, but not me. I felt fine, and was thinking what a tempting goal the Caddy hearse on the hillock made.

The keys to it were in my pocket, but the remaining security boys were between me and the vehicle. I needed to get closer.

Plus, I had to get a better angle on the other shooters, so I quickly reloaded and took a chance, breaking cover to sprint for a better position. I heard three shots but none of them came close to catching me, and I flopped behind another headstone, alive and well.

"Now," I heard one of them say, and peeked out and saw them both running for new positions, in opposite directions.

I could only choose one. He had almost made it to cover when my shot caught him in the side of the head and he went tumbling on now useless legs.

The other guy had found a new spot, a good one, behind a massive affair with a granite angel perched on top. He and I both had good cover now, and we traded shots and chipped pieces off our respective headstones and didn't get anywhere.

But I could hear him breathing—breathing hard—and, hell, I wasn't even winded. I was older by fifteen years easy, but I was a swimmer, remember; this guy must have been a smoker, and that can kill your ass.

So I had that advantage, if nothing else. Listening carefully, I could hear him doing a speed-reload, and I was grinning as I popped up, blasting away at his headstone, specifically at the decorative angel, emptying the clip.

The cupid-like statue flew apart, into fragments, bursting into the guy's face. He cried out as he reared back, and I took the opportunity to sprint for that hearse, shoving in a fresh clip as I did.

My opponent was too busy blinking away dust and chips, his face flecked with shards of granite, to get a good aim at my fleeing figure.

Still on the run, I took a look back and thought *what the hell* and aimed and fired.

He, too, took a bullet in the head and fell backward, haloed in blood, flung between stones, just as dead as anybody already underground.

I got into the hearse and started it up, then swung around onto the little gravel roadway, where the windshield gave me a view on a tableau that would have been memorable even without the scattered bodies of the security team…

…Jonah Green emerging from his daughter's grave, crawling up over those metal lowering tubes, the front of him shot up, but definitely still alive, and then he was on his feet, albeit weaving like a damn drunk.

He teetered at the edge of the grave, his back to it—unsteady yes, but standing, and the square face set with almost crazed determination.

To do what? I wondered. *Survive? Kill me?*

So I floored the fucking thing, found a lane between gravestones, and went charging across the grass, and he must have heard the engine's roar because he turned toward me, the determination shifting to terror, as the hearse bore down.

I clipped him good as I passed, garnering a truly satisfying crunch, and sent him toppling back into the grave, landing to make another metallic, echoing *thud*.

Slamming on the brakes, I hopped out, nine millimeter in my fist, and ran to the grave, where Green—down in there on top of his daughter's copper coffin, arms in crucifixion position—looked up at me with the money-color eyes wide open and staring.

But he didn't see me. He was very, very dead.

Which was a bit of a disappointment, because I would just as soon have shot him some more.

Time to go.

I was paused just long enough to dump the duct-taped mummy of the real hearse driver, and got back in a vehicle that looked little the worse for wear for having just run a guy down.

This time I didn't floor it, just cruised out of the cemetery in my chauffeur's uniform, my hands on the wheel of the hearse, passing assorted Oak Brook Memorial personnel coming out of hiding, scurrying along the periphery, now that the shooting was over.

Sixteen

Oak Brook Memorial was easing into spring, the snow gone, the grass greening, but this could just as easily have been November as late March. Once again cloud cover threw shadows on the cemetery, but this time they more or less stayed put, just lending a blue-gray cast to the tombstone-studded landscape.

The gravesite still looked fresh, the unusual procedure of the contents of a grave needing to be shifted one to the right making it look like two relatively recent burials had taken place.

A correction had also been made on the massive granite gravestone. Whether this was a fresh slab, or whether tombstone cutters have their own kind of Liquid Paper, I couldn't tell you.

At any rate, it now read:

MARY ANN GREEN	*JONAH ALLEN GREEN*
(1940–1985)	*(1938–2005)*
Beloved Wife and Mother	*Husband and Father*

and below:

JANET ANN GREEN   JULIA SUSAN GREEN
(1975–)   (1985–2005)
Cherished Daughter

A woman in a black wool coat, black slacks and red sweater knelt to place a floral wreath at one of the graves, taking care to position it just right. She lowered her head and, apparently, began to pray.

I let Janet finish the mumbo jumbo before I wandered down from my surveillance post behind that mausoleum on the hillock, and when she finally stood, I was at her side.

At first, she was startled—couldn't blame her: she hadn't seen me for several months, not since I'd shuffled her out of Homewood and onto a plane. But very soon her expression turned calm, almost serene.

"Your friend Gary," she said, "was very nice."

I nodded. "Florida makes a nice getaway in the winter."

She was looking at me the way a mother checks a kid getting over the measles. "He wouldn't tell me anything about you."

And once again, I was glad I hadn't killed my old Vietnam buddy, after getting drunk and spilling my guts to him, that time. Even a prick like me can use a friend now and again.

"His wife's nice, too," she said conversationally.

"Ruthie. Yeah. A peach."

"She doesn't know *anything* about you."

"Yeah, well, I'm an enigma wrapped up in a riddle."

She almost smiled. "What now?"

My eyes met hers, and it wasn't the easiest thing I ever did. "We can do it two ways. I can tell you everything…or nothing."

She thought about that.

Then Janet said, "If you tell me everything…" She gestured toward the gravestone. "…will I be next?"

"No. But you were supposed to be."

She frowned. "My father…?"

My eyes remained locked with hers. "Can you live with it?"

She sighed; looked away; shivered—it was still cold, after all—and folded her arms to herself, her hands in leather gloves. Her gaze lingered on the gravestone and then slowly shook her head.

"You mean, what Daddy did? Or what you've done?…What you might have done?"

"All that," I said.

Her eyes came to mine again. "Or do you mean… could I live with *you*?"

I said nothing.

Our eyes remained locked.

"Your call," I said, and I walked away, moving across the cloud-shadowed landscape, finding my way between tombstones, heading up that hill.

I could feel her eyes on me, but she did not call out.

So I was back where we began, in my A-frame, still managing Sylvan Lodge for Gary Petersen, and caught up in getting the place ready for the new season. Next week staff would be in, and I'd have to start dealing with being around people again.

Harry and Louis hadn't shown up yet. Perhaps they were tangled in something down at the bottom of the lake, and were doing me the favor of feeding fish and turning to skeletons. I still felt that if their bloated remains did decide to float to the surface, their mob background would keep any heat off an innocent civilian like me.

And it was a big lake. Sylvan Lodge was only one little notch on it.

Of course, staying on at Sylvan at all was itself a risk—Jonah Green had found me here, hadn't he? Come walking right into my world?

But Jonah was dead; he wouldn't be crawling up out of that grave again, not even on Judgement Day. And he had no doubt been discreet in his inquiries about me—he had to be, since he was a selfish sociopath plotting his own daughter's death, which generally calls for discretion.

Thing was, I was just too goddamn old to start over. And I liked it here. I liked the cabin, and Gary, and the (must I use this word?) lifestyle. In the unlikely event that assholes with guns came looking for me, they would find another asshole with a gun who would kill them.

A rationalization, sure; but I could live with it.

You will be relieved, I'm sure, to learn that my problem with insomnia was a thing of the past—I was sleeping long and deep with my only problem that low backache I had on waking, but walking over and swimming and using the Jacuzzi and doing a few stretches got rid of that.

Still, old habits die hard, and three nights before the Sylvan staff was about to arrive, a sound woke me—a clatter out there that was not fucking Santa Claus, and my waking thought was that somebody had broken in.

Funny how I can sleep so deep, but the littlest goddamn noise and I'm suddenly wide awake, alert as a butt-fucked sailor; I sat up in bed, the nine millimeter from the nightstand tight in my hand.

Call it paranoia, if you will. But when you make a career out of killing people, you tend to think the worst.

And something was definitely rattling around out in my kitchen.

I crept through the darkened cabin and saw a little light was on in there. Gun in hand, I slipped in and flipped the overhead light switch.

"Shit!" Janet said, wincing at the flood of illumination.

As usual, she was wearing one of my shirts, legs bare, her long dark blonde hair fetchingly tousled, and she was bending down, looking in the refrigerator. She straightened like an exclamation point. "Are you trying to scare me to death?"

I lowered the gun. "No."

She shut the refrigerator door and turned to me, her expression innocently apologetic now. "Did I wake you?"

I sat at the kitchen table and put the nine millimeter down in front of me, like it was a fork or a spoon. Rubbed my face with two hands.

"I sleep light," I said.

"So I've noticed." She stood next to me and touched my shoulder and smiled in that way that meant she wanted something. "There's not a damn thing in that fridge....Would you do me a favor?"

"Who do you want me to kill?"

She gave me a reproving look. One might say, a wifely look.

Then her expression softened and she asked, "Could you please make a convenience store run?"

I just looked at her. She had no notion of the significance of her request.

Janet gestured around the little kitchen, like a disaster survivor talking to a reporter about the damage. "We have cereal here, but no milk. I can make a little list....Would you mind, terribly? And, uh—this is embarrassing, but…"

And now the poor-pitiful-me look.

"…would you mind picking up some Tampax?"

I let out a long sigh, pushed out the chair, stood, and said, "No problem."

She touched my face and kissed my cheek. "You are *so* sweet…."

Maybe I was.

But I took the nine millimeter with me.

Author's Afterword

This is the sixth novel about the hitman who calls himself Quarry.

The first was mostly written around 1973 at the University of Iowa, where I was studying in the Writers Workshop; it was published by Berkley Books in 1975 as *The Broker*, though my preferred title was *Quarry* (and it's been reprinted as such). Three novels followed in quick succession, at the publisher's request, and that seemed to be it.

In the mid-'80s, the success of my Nathan Heller series inspired a couple of editors at a couple of houses to ask me to revive Quarry and my other early character, the retired thief Nolan. So I did a Quarry novel called *Primary Target* for Louis Wilder at Foul Play Press, and a Nolan called *Spree* for Michael Seidman at TOR. These were not intended as relaunchings of those series, but a revisitation by an author in midstream of the creations that had launched him.

Over the years, Quarry has built a certain cult following (I always caution enthusiastic readers to remember the Donald E. Westlake definition of a "cult" success: "Seven readers short of the author making a living") and, more recently, I've written an occasional short story about him. Not long ago, those stories and *Primary Target* were collected by Five Star as *Quarry's Greatest Hits*.

One of the stories, "A Matter of Principal," has taken on a kind of life of its own. Of any short story of mine, over my thirty-some-year career, it has been reprinted most often, and was even selected by Jeff Deaver as one of the best *noir* short stories of the 20th century. I have no idea why. I wrote it on assignment, one afternoon, with no plot outline—just working from something that had happened the night before when I made a midnight run to a convenience store and saw a burly guy buying tampons.

Perhaps half a dozen years ago, a young filmmaker in California, Jeffrey Goodman, discovered the short story and began getting after me to give him permission to make a film out of it. For a while I kind of shrugged this off, but eventually he wore me down—I liked the short films Jeffrey sent me by way of samples, and I liked his persistence, too.

Coincidentally, I'd begun working as an independent filmmaker myself here in my native Iowa. This I'd done out of frustration about having so many things optioned by Hollywood but seeing nothing made (this was before "Road to Perdition," obviously).

So I finally told Jeffrey "yes," on two conditions.

The first condition was that I would write the screenplay for the short film, which Jeffrey intended to be a showcase piece for the festival circuit. The second was that I would be the executive producer and would have input in post-production (I did not want to be on set, because I knew I would interfere). Jeffrey was as good as his word, and in particular my suggestions on editing the piece had a nice effect on the final cut.

Jeffrey's short film "A Matter of Principal" became quite successful in the festival world, winning several and an official selection of several others. A year later, I combined Jeffrey's film into an anthology of short films written (and otherwise directed) by me, entitled "Shades of Noir," and that did well in several festivals, also. That anthology film eventually expanded to include my documentary "Mike Hammer's Mickey Spillane," and this novel is officially a tie-in to the Neo-Noir DVD release of the feature-length version of "Shades of Noir."

But this book would not exist if Hard Case Crime

editor Charles Ardai hadn't been kind enough to contact me about contributing to his first slate of books—he specifically wanted to reprint my Nolan novel *Blood Money*, which was the direct sequel to another of my Iowa City college-era books, *Bait Money* (both were published in 1973 by the now long-defunct Curtis Books). I suggested the two novels be published as one longer book, *Two for the Money*, and Charles generously agreed to put it out in that form.

Then Charles asked me to do an original novel for Hard Case—specifically, a Quarry. My previous commitments made that tough, but—knowing that Charles had lured the master of paperback painters, Robert McGinnis, into doing a cover or two for Hard Case—I said, "Sure, I'll do an original book, Charles… *if* you get me McGinnis for the cover."

It was a typical flip, kidding-on-the-square remark of mine—after all, McGinnis is the artist behind the classic Sean Connery "James Bond" movie posters!— but I'll be damned if Charles didn't call me up and say, yes, he had lined "Bob McGinnis" up for the cover of the new Quarry.

Having Mr. McGinnis's brilliant work adorning a book of mine is one of the happiest events of my career—the Mickey Spillane/Gold Medal Books era during which Robert McGinnis first flourished had everything to do with the perditious road I chose to spend my life going down. I thank Charles, and Bob, for their kindness and generosity.

The book itself is an expansion of that much-anthologized short story, "A Matter of Principal," with a dab from another Quarry tale, "Guest Services." The reason behind this approach is two-fold. For various personal agendas, both Charles and I wanted to make this book a tie-in to the release of "Shades of Noir" on DVD. But, also, filmmaker Jeffrey Goodman had decided he wanted to make a feature-length film version of "A Matter of Principal."

So the combined result of Charles's request for a new Quarry novel, and Jeffrey's request for an expanded version of "A Matter of Principal," was this novel (and a screenplay version). Whether Jeffrey and I are fortunate enough to see this story brought in its entirety to the screen remains to be seen—well, I hope it will be seen; in any case, I feel fortunate that Jeffrey created a wonderful short film that led to this one last Quarry adventure.

Editor Ardai, by the way, is responsible for the title, *The Last Quarry*. (The title of the short story was just a silly pun on "principle," and has confused readers, editors and viewers of the short film ever since. Not every writer can lay claim to causing so much confusion with so casual a stroke of the word processor.) Thanks for that, too, Charles.

Is this the last Quarry?

Well, Quarry and I are whores at heart, so anything is possible. But should I ever write any more stories about this man—who ties with Nate Heller as my favorite among my characters—the action will in all likelihood pre-date this novel. This, in my mind, is indeed the last story about him. He is, after all, retired and in the care of a good woman.

The most perverse conclusion I can envision for Quarry, you see, is a happy ending.

Max Allan Collins
Muscatine, Iowa
September 2005

Sexy Suspense From an MWA Grandmaster!

The Girl With the
LONG GREEN HEART
by LAWRENCE BLOCK

SHE WAS EVERY MAN'S DREAM — AND ONE MAN'S NIGHTMARE

Johnny Hayden and Doug Rance had a scheme to take real estate entrepreneur Wallace Gunderman for all he was worth. But they needed a girl on the inside to make it work.

Enter Evelyn Stone: Gunderman's secretary, his lover—and his worst enemy. Gunderman promised to marry her, but never came through. Now she's ready to make him pay...

ACCLAIM FOR LAWRENCE BLOCK:

"The narrative is layered with detail, the action is handled with Block's distinctive clarity of style and the ending is a stunning tour de force."
— New York Times

"Block is awfully good, with an ear for dialogue, an eye for lowlife types and a gift for fast and effortless storytelling that bear comparison to Elmore Leonard."
— Los Angeles Times

"Wonderful."
— USA Today

"Lawrence Block is a master of entertainment."
— Washington Post Book World

**Available now at your favorite bookstore.
For more information, visit
www.HardCaseCrime.com**